The Addiction Counselor's
Desk Reference

The Addiction Counselor's
Desk Reference

Robert Holman Coombs
William A. Howatt

WILEY

John Wiley & Sons, Inc.

For
CARLA CRONKHITE VERA,
our esteemed associate at UCLA,
with appreciation for all you have contributed.

CONTENTS

PART II: CONCEPTUAL TOOLS

PART VI: PROFESSIONAL MANAGEMENT

PART VII: CAREER ENHANCEMENT RESOURCES

PREFACE

We prepared this book to provide addiction counselors—and others whose work involves them with addicted people—with useful, easily accessible, up-to-date information.

Since addicted clients challenge even the most highly skilled counselor, every available skill and resource helps. How does one help a client who does not think he needs help? Of the more than 19 million Americans who currently use illicit drugs (8.3% of the U.S. population 12 years of age or older) and the 54 million who are regular binge drinkers, *many think they do not need help* (Office of Applied Studies, 2003). According to the federal government's *Household Survey* (recently renamed the *National Survey on Drug Use and Health*), more than 94% of those with substance abuse disorders thought they did not need treatment. "A denial gap of over 94% is intolerable," noted John Walters, White House Director of National Drug Control Policy (http://www.hhs.gov/neews/2003pres/20030905.html, 2003, para 4).

The federal Office of Management and Budget estimates that drug abuse costs the United States more than $300 billion a year. Substance abuse devitalizes American industries, where an estimated $60 billion to $100 billion is lost each year in work productivity—absenteeism, drug-related accidents, medical claims, and theft. Other drug-related problems include family disintegration, health care costs, and drug-related crime. Because of the problem's enormity, a veritable army of personnel—some better trained than others—now make their living dealing, directly or indirectly, with addicted people. More than 115,000 drug counselors make up the combined membership of *only two* of several prominent drug-counseling organizations. Drug counselors work in private treatment facilities (both inpatient and outpatient), detoxification facilities, halfway houses, prisons and jails, the courts, schools, hospitals, churches, and governmental facilities.

A resource book describing programs and giving contact information can help counselors locate appropriate treatment centers for their addicted clients. The *Household Survey* found that of the 362,000 Americans who recognized they needed treatment for substance abuse, 266,000 had tried to find treatment for alcohol abuse, but were unable to do so, and another 88,000 had been unsuccessful in getting treatment for an addiction to other psychoactive drugs. "There is no other medical condition for which we would tolerate such huge numbers unable to obtain the treatment they need," said Tommy G.

Thompson, HHS Secretary during George W. Bush's first administration (http://www.hhs.gov/neews/2003pres/20030905.html, 2003, para 4). Could this problem be ameliorated if all counselors had easily accessible information to direct everyone who comes to them for help—men, women, adolescents, family members, older adults, people from diverse cultures, and gays and lesbians— to the most appropriate treatment center or support groups? With fingertip access to such basic information—heretofore scattered among hundreds of publications and Internet web sites—counselors can more quickly and efficiently help their clients.

Until fairly recently, an addiction was perceived as a problem of imbibing alcohol and other chemical substances. But advances in neuroscience show that other behaviors besides using psychoactive drugs affect the pleasure centers of the brain in the same way as psychoactive chemicals. Today's addiction counselors must be sophisticated about sex addiction; compulsive gambling, working, and buying; food and body-image addiction; and Internet addiction (Coombs, 2004). Counselors having access to practical descriptions and contact information about programs that address these overlapping problems will greatly improve their effectiveness (Carnes, Murray, & Charpentier, 2004).

To make addiction counseling even more difficult, some addicted clients have co-existing psychiatric disorders. According to federal statistics, more than 4 million adults concurrently have a substance use disorder *and* serious mental illness. In 2002, 8.3% of all adults (17.5 million people) had a serious mental illness. Adults who used illicit drugs are more than twice as likely to have serious mental illness as those who do not (Office of Applied Studies, 2003). Addiction counselors relatively unsophisticated about the variety and scope of these disorders can find a quick overview in this book of the American Psychiatric Association's latest edition of the *Diagnostic and Statistical Manual of Mental Disorders (DSM-IV-TR)*.

In each section of this book, we have tried to include everything that will be practical and useful to an addiction counselor, and screened out everything that is not.

This book is organized into eight parts, each covering key practical topics. Part I, "Abused Substances and Their Effects," describes the various drugs of abuse, their street and pharmaceutical names, medical uses, methods of administration, indices of misuse, health consequences, overdosing, withdrawal symptoms, and physical and psychological dependency. It includes the five federal schedules for psychoactive drugs, explains how the U.S. Drug Enforcement Administration (DEA) determines these standards, and discusses controlled substance analogues.

Part II, "Conceptual Tools," highlights the basic concepts that underlie addiction: the various ways addiction has been defined and the three C's that characterize all addictions: compulsive use, loss of control, and continued use despite adverse consequences. Classification schemes are reviewed, such as the treatment stages that addicts typically pass through, the various levels of drug use, and the stages of predictable behavioral change. Prevention principles (including relapse prevention) are also explored.

Part III, "Treatment Planning and Assessment Resources," reviews treatment planning, screening and assessment, diagnostic summaries, treatment, client placement criteria, writing a treatment plan, and the various levels of care. This section provides assessment tools for diagnosing alcohol and drug abuse, instruments for assessing other addictive disorders, mental health measurements, recovery assessments, and multiple measures resources. Also included is information on dual diagnosis (i.e., addicts with diagnosable psychiatric illness) from *DSM-IV-TR*.

Part IV, "Clinical Skills and Resources," reviews the approaches of key clinical theorists, describes basic counseling techniques and clinical microskills, and provides homework assignments and exercises designed to enhance a client's health and stress management capabilities.

Part V, "Treatment Resources," details the various recovery tools and provides directories of recovery programs. This section also identifies harm-reduction programs and support groups (twelve-step and twelve-step alternatives) that are available to assist women, adolescents, family members of addicts, dually diagnosed patients, HIV/AIDS patients, and gays and lesbians who suffer from an addictive disorder.

Part VI, "Professional Management," discusses clinical management skills and responsibilities such as record keeping (sample forms are provided). Practical information is given about managing challenging issues (e.g., clinical crises, difficult clients) and dealing with legal and ethical dilemmas.

Part VII, "Career Enhancement Resources," offers information to enhance the counselor's career: the basic knowledge, skills, and attitudes expected of an addiction counselor, characteristics of a good training program, an overview of certification and licensing, continuing education requirements, and contact information for continuing education providers. Also included are practical business decisions (such as setting and discussing fees and making referrals). Pointers for developing a personal wellness plan and obtaining malpractice insurance are also featured.

Part VIII, "Information Resources," describes and gives specific contact information about organizations that offer drug abuse and addiction counseling services. This section provides an overview of federal, state, educational, professional, and grassroots organizations that deal with addictions. It identifies and describes grant funding resources and publications in the addictions, and provides information about policy organizations whose views differ from these of the federal government.

The Glossary lists the most frequently used terms in drug abuse and addiction.

ACKNOWLEDGMENTS

We gratefully acknowledge Tracey Belmont, Senior Editor at John Wiley & Sons, for the opportunity to write this book. Involved in every stage of development, she provided encouragement and valuable ideas that significantly improved this volume.

Carla Cronkhite Vera, our esteemed UCLA assistant, provided expert assistance with every aspect of development. Not only did she carefully copyedit the entire manuscript, she did a lion's share of the research (and writing of initial drafts) of several sections: Drugs of Abuse (in Part I), Addiction Recovery Programs (in Part V), Educational Resources (in Part VII), and Malpractice Insurance (in Part VII). She helped plan book features, obtained permissions to reprint materials, and handled myriad additional details with characteristic efficiency and good cheer.

Trygve Cossette, a graduate student at the New School University in New York City, played an invaluable role in every developmental step of this book, from day one until completion. He conducted much of the Internet and library research—locating many useful web sites and published materials—wrote first drafts of several sections, and evaluated (several times) all other sections. His critical improvements were invaluable, as was his careful copyediting of the entire manuscript.

Carol Jean Coombs, MS, copyedited the entire manuscript and provided valuable advice and expertise for improving all sections.

Marie Gengler, a promising graduate student in social work at Fordham University, prepared the Psychoactive Drugs Chart (Table I.1) and researched the Educational Resources (Part VII).

Lisa Coolen, a student studying social work at Saint Thomas University, did much of the library research for the Assessment Resources section in Part III.

Ann Marie Ward, a Nova Scotia freelance writer, spent many hours developing the initial draft of the Glossary.

Krista Coombs, an undergraduate student in Accounting, gathered the information on Publishing Resources (in Part VIII).

Mike Choi, a UCLA graduate applying to medical school, spent innumerable hours improving several revisions of the Glossary, as well as researching and writing an early draft on the History of Drug Treatment (which, because of space limitations, was omitted).

Sandra Brimhall and Steven Brimhall, scholars and friends, developed both the author and subject indexes.

PART I

Abused Substances and Their Effects

Part I describes drugs that are frequently abused: opiates, depressants, stimulants, cannabis, hallucinogens, inhalants, steroids (anabolic-androgenic) and designer drugs. An easy-to-use reference table of these psychoactive drugs covers their common name, pharmaceutical name, street names, medical uses, methods of administration, indices of misuse, health consequences (both short- and long-term effects), overdosing, withdrawal symptoms, and physical and psychological dependency. The Control Schedules for Abused Drugs describes the five schedules that are controlled and monitored by the U.S. Drug Enforcement Administration (DEA).

ABUSED DRUGS

    Opiates
    Depressants
    Stimulants
    Cannabis
    Hallucinogens
    Inhalants
    Steroids (Anabolic-Androgenic)
    Designer Drugs

PSYCHOACTIVE DRUGS QUICK SCREEN TABLE

    Common Name
    Pharmaceutical Name
    Street Names
    Medical Uses
    Methods of Administration
    Indices of Misuse

ABUSED DRUGS[1]

OPIATES

Opiates (also called narcotics) include heroin, an illicit substance, and such prescription medications as morphine, Demerol, codeine, fentanyl, and OxyContin (used to treat severe pain). Once in the bloodstream, opiates can have a variety of negative side effects—labored breathing, nausea, vomiting, difficulty urinating, constipation, abdominal pain, dizziness, blood disorders, anxiety, mood changes, restlessness, and skin rashes.

HEROIN

A naturally occurring substance extracted from the seedpod of certain varieties of poppy plants, heroin was commercially marketed in 1898 as a new pain remedy. It was used medicinally until 1914 when, under the Harrison Narcotic Act, it was designated as a controlled substance. A highly addictive Schedule I drug, heroin is the most abused and rapidly acting opiate. (See "Controlled Schedules for Abused Drugs" later in Part I.)

---

[1] This section was adapted from www.whitehousedrugpolicy.gov and www.drugabuse.gov /DrugPages; National Institute on Drug Abuse (NIDA; May 1999a; #99-4342); Simoni-Wastila and Strickler (2004); NIDA (2000); U.S. Department of Health and Human Services, Substance Abuse and Mental Health Services Administration, Office of Applied Studies (2001).

Usually sniffed/snorted or smoked, heroin is also injected intravenously (IV). The greatest intensity and most rapid onset of euphoria (7 to 8 seconds) result from IV use; when smoked, peak effects are usually felt within 10 to 15 minutes.

After ingestion, heroin crosses the blood-brain barrier, converts to morphine, and rapidly binds to opioid receptors in the brain. Users feel a "rush," a surge of pleasurable sensations and euphoria varying in intensity depending on the quantity and mode of ingestion. This rush is usually accompanied by a warm flushing of the skin, dry mouth, and a heavy feeling in the user's limbs. Nausea, vomiting, and severe itching may follow as well as drowsiness for several hours.

Heroin abuse is associated with serious health conditions, including fatal overdose, collapsed veins, cardiac depression, and blood-borne infectious diseases from sharing needles (HIV/AIDS and hepatitis). Health and social consequences—HIV/AIDS, violence, tuberculosis, fetal effects, crime, and disruptions in family, workplace, and educational environments—have a devastating impact on society, costing billions of dollars each year.

Chronic heroin users may also develop infection of the heart lining and valves, abscesses, liver disease, and pulmonary complications, including pneumonia. Because heroin abusers do not know the actual strength of the drug or its true contents, they are at great risk of overdose (slow and shallow breathing, convulsions, coma) or death. Street heroin is often cut with substances, such as sugar, starch, powdered milk, strychnine, or other types of drugs. These additives may not dissolve when injected into a user's system and can clog blood vessels that lead to the lungs, liver, kidneys, or brain, infecting or killing patches of cells in these vital organs.

Addiction, the most detrimental long-term effect of chronic heroin use, involves compulsive, drug-seeking behaviors. As higher doses are used, neurochemical and molecular changes in the brain reinforce physical dependence.

Within a few hours after ingestion, withdrawal may occur, manifested by drug craving, restlessness, muscle and bone pain, and vomiting. Major withdrawal symptoms peak between 48 and 72 hours after the last dose and subside after about a week.

PRESCRIPTION OPIATES

The abuse potential of injected morphine is just as high as that of heroin. Another commonly used and abused agent, fentanyl, exists in two formulations: (1) an injectable form used with other agents during induction of anesthesia, and (2) a skin patch used as a sustained-release form to treat pain.

The higher potency prescription opioids such as morphine, fentanyl, and meperidine (Demerol) usually appear as prepared injection forms that have been diverted from legal medical use. They may be injected either intravenously or subcutaneously (skin popping). The lower potency prescription opioids (codeine, propoxyphene) usually come in pill form and are taken orally.

Soon after ingestion, opioids cross the blood-brain barrier to produce a rush, or feelings of euphoria. The intensity of these feelings depends on how much drug was used and mode of ingestion. After the initial effects wear off, users become sleepy.

Regardless of how ingested, opioid use can cause respiratory complications and death through respiratory or cardiac depression. Physical dependence on narcotics develops dramatically as soon as regular use begins, whether from appropriate clinical use or self-administration. Narcotic withdrawal symptoms include restlessness, irritability, nausea, diarrhea, sweating, and gooseflesh.

DEPRESSANTS

Depressants include alcohol and prescription drugs taken orally, such as barbiturates, methaqualone, tranquilizers, chloral hydrate, and glutethimide. Prescribed to help relieve anxiety, irritability, and tension, depressants are informally called "downers" because they calm users down. With regular use, they have a high potential for abuse and development of tolerance. They produce a state of intoxication similar to alcohol, and these effects are intensified when combined with alcohol. Although small amounts cause calmness and relaxed muscles, large amounts cause slurred speech, impaired judgment, and loss of motor coordination; doses that are even larger may cause decreased breathing rate, coma, and death.

ALCOHOL

Alcohol is produced by fermentation that occurs when yeast reacts with the sugar in grains, fruit, or vegetable juice. Products are wine, beer, and distilled drinks.

Some beverages have more alcohol content than others (beer has about 4.5% alcohol; table wines average from 11% to 14%; "fortified," or dessert, wines have 16% to 20%; distilled spirits range from 40% to 50%). However, in a normal portion, each drink (i.e., 12 ounces of beer, 5 ounces of wine, and 1½ ounces of distilled spirits) contains approximately the same amount of alcohol.

Because alcohol is a depressant, the more one drinks, the more depressed and adversely affected one's brain activity becomes. The cerebrum, the part of the brain that controls advanced functions such as recognition, vision, reasoning, and emotion, is slowed. At the lowest levels, alcohol impacts inhibitions, and affects judgment. As alcohol levels increase, vision, movement, and speech are impaired (at a blood alcohol level of 0.01% to 0.30%). Alcohol also affects the part of the brain that coordinates movement, causing problems with coordination, reflexes, and balance (at a blood alcohol level of 0.15% to 0.35%). The medulla, the part of the brain that controls basic survival functions such as breathing and heartbeat, is also affected, reducing the brain's ability to control respiration and heart rate. Death can result when blood alcohol levels reach 0.30.

When a person drinks an alcoholic beverage, about 20% is absorbed in the stomach and 80% in the small intestine. Alcohol absorption depends on:

• *The concentration of alcohol in the beverage:* The greater the concentration, the faster the absorption.

- *The type of drink:* Carbonated beverages tend to speed up the absorption of alcohol.
- *Whether the stomach is full or empty:* Food slows down alcohol absorption.

Alcohol leaves the body in three ways: (1) the kidneys eliminate 5% of alcohol in the urine, (2) the lungs exhale 5% of alcohol (detected by Breathalyzer and similar devices), and (3) the liver chemically breaks down the remaining 90% of alcohol into acetic acid.

The liver can oxidize only a certain amount of alcohol each minute; for example, the oxidation rate of alcohol in a person weighing 150 pounds is about 7 grams of alcohol per hour. This is equivalent to about ¾ of an ounce of distilled spirits, 2½ ounces of wine, or 7¾ to 8 ounces of beer per hour. If a person drank no more than ¾ of an ounce of whiskey or half a bottle of beer every hour, the alcohol would never accumulate in the body; the person would feel little of the effects and would not become intoxicated. Oxidation continues until all the alcohol has left the body. Since the body can remove only a small amount of alcohol at a time, those who choose to drink are advised to drink slowly.

Alcohol affects virtually every organ system in the body. Both acute and chronic intoxication have unique consequences on physiology and quality of life.

Alcohol increases the risk for injuries through the impairment of cognitive and psychomotor functioning. It decreases reaction time and impairs sensory processing, motor control, attention, and the use of seat-belt devices. Drunken driving accidents kill about 16,000 people per year, with many more than that number injured. Alcohol also increases the risk for injury or death from fire and suicide. It causes social and legal problems, interacts with medications, and creates birth defects as well as the long-term health problems listed here:

- *Liver disease:* Epidemiological data show that alcohol abuse is the leading cause of liver-related mortality in the United States.
- *Cardiovascular disease:* The deterioration of heart muscle (alcoholic cardiomyopathy) is one of the most serious consequences of chronic heavy drinking. Similarly, there is a well-documented association between heavy alcohol consumption and increased blood pressure, or hypertension.
- *Cancer:* Those who consume more than three drinks per day (21 drinks per week) have an almost tenfold higher risk of esophageal cancer than do those who drink less than one drink per day.

Physiological dependence on alcohol leads to alcoholism—a condition with the following symptoms:

- *Craving:* A strong need, or urge, to drink
- *Loss of control:* Not being able to stop drinking once drinking has begun
- *Tolerance:* The need to drink greater amounts of alcohol to get "high"
- *Physical dependence:* Withdrawal symptoms, such as nausea, sweating, shakiness, and anxiety after stopping drinking

Alcohol abuse and alcoholism cut across socioeconomic status, gender, race, and nationality. Nearly 14 million people in the United States—1 in every 13 adults—abuse alcohol or are alcohol dependent. In general, more men than women are alcohol dependent or have alcohol problems. Those who start drinking at age 14 or younger greatly increase their chances of having alcohol problems in their adult lives.

BARBITURATES/SEDATIVE-HYPNOTICS

Barbiturates, taken orally as pills or sometimes in liquid form or suppositories, include secobarbital (Seconal) and pentobarbital (Nembutal). Like alcohol, these chemicals affect the central nervous system (CNS) by slowing or decreasing neurological activity in the mind and body.

Short-term effects, lasting 15 hours after ingestion, include relief of tension and anxiety, sleepiness, feeling of intoxication, slurred speech, memory impairment, emotional instability, and inability to control simple bodily functions. Long-term effects are chronic tiredness, general lack of coordination, vision problems, dizziness, slowed reflexes and response time, sexual dysfunction, menstrual irregularities, and breathing disorders.

Barbiturates are prescribed for treatment of such disorders as sleeplessness, anxiety, tension, and epileptic seizures. These drugs also are used illegally for euphoria and relaxation.

Barbiturates in combination with other drugs can be dangerous, especially when used with other CNS depressants such as Demerol, heroin, morphine, and codeine. It is important to be aware that any combination of these is often lethal. Antihistamines, found in most allergy, cold, and sinus medicines, are another type of CNS depressant that can cause respiratory arrest when taken with barbiturates.

Since barbiturates produce both physical and psychological dependence, continued use may result in tolerance (i.e., one needs ever larger doses to achieve the desired effects). When regular users suddenly discontinue these drugs, withdrawal symptoms may include restlessness, insomnia, anxiety, or even convulsions and death. Psychologically dependent users feel they need the drugs to function. Procuring them then becomes an all-encompassing endeavor.

BENZODIAZEPINES SUCH AS DIAZEPAM (VALIUM) ABUSE

Antianxiety medications (also known as anxiolytics, tranquilizers, or sleeping pills) are benzodiazepines. They come in pills of various colors, in liquid form, or in suppositories. Typically prescribed for anxiety, acute stress reactions, and panic attacks, the more sedating benzodiazepines, such as triazolam (Halcion) and estazolam (ProSom), are prescribed for short-term treatment of sleep disorders.

During the first few days of taking a prescribed CNS depressant, a person usually feels sleepy and uncoordinated, but as the body becomes accustomed to the effects, these feelings disappear. A long-term user will develop tolerance for the drugs, and larger doses will be needed to achieve the same initial euphoric effects. Continued use can lead to physical dependence and, when reduced or stopped, withdrawal. Because all CNS depressants work by slowing the brain's activity, it can rebound and race out of control when these drugs are stopped, possibly leading to seizures and other harmful consequences.

Benzodiazepines work in the brain affecting emotional reactions, memory, control of consciousness, muscle tone, and coordination by enhancing the action of the neurotransmitter gamma-aminobutyric acid (GABA). This major inhibitory neurotransmitter slows or calms things down.

Neurotransmitters are chemicals that enable the brain cells to transmit impulses from one to another. Once released from brain cells by electrical signals, these neurotransmitters signal inhibition or excitation of neighboring brain cells.

The long-term effects of benzodiazepine usage include depression, aggression, subtle personality changes, fatigue, passivity, and symptoms of cognitive impairment. Memory function is markedly and measurably impaired, especially the ability to store acquired knowledge in long-term memory. Benzodiazepine usage may cause psychomotor impairment; users should not drive a car or other kind of motor vehicles such as boats or all-terrain vehicles. The elderly are particularly vulnerable to these psychomotor effects, and the risk of falls and fractures is pronounced in this population when under the influence of these drugs.

STIMULANTS

Stimulants, including cocaine, amphetamine, and methamphetamine, are central nervous system stimulants that produce euphoria, a feeling of super strength and absolute self-confidence. With cocaine (but not amphetamines), there is also an anesthetic effect (i.e., a dulling of pain). Stimulant users tend to become hyperactive (e.g., nervous, extremely talkative, and unable to stand still). Stimulants also tend to release the user's inhibition and affect their ability to perceive time and distance. They become easily confused and lose the ability to concentrate or to think clearly for any length of time. The effects of stimulants vary from 5 minutes to several hours, depending on which CNS stimulant is used.

COCAINE

A white powder that comes from the leaves of the South American coca plant, cocaine was first extracted from the leaf of the Erythroxylon coca bush in the mid-nineteenth century and used in tonics and elixirs. Two chemical forms are hydrochloride salt and *freebase*. The salt, or powdered form, dissolves in water and can be abused intravenously or intranasally. Freebase is smokable.

The major routes of cocaine administration are sniffing or snorting, injecting, and smoking (including freebase or crack). Snorting and sniffing involve inhaling cocaine powder through the nose where it is absorbed into the bloodstream through the nasal tissues. Injecting with a needle releases the drug directly into the bloodstream. Smoking involves inhaling cocaine vapor or smoke into the lungs where absorption into the bloodstream is as rapid as by injection.

Cocaine, a strong central nervous system stimulant, interferes with the re-absorption process of dopamine, a chemical messenger associated with pleasure and movement. Dopamine is released as part of the brain's reward system and produces the high that characterizes cocaine use. The duration of cocaine's immediate euphoric effects—hyperstimulation, reduced fatigue, and mental clarity—depend on the route of administration. The faster the absorption, the more intense the high. On the other hand, the faster the absorption, the shorter the duration of action. Whereas the high from snorting may last 15 to 30 minutes, the high from smoking may last 5 to 10 minutes. Increased use can reduce the period of stimulation. As a result of cocaine's actions in the brain, increased impulses activate the reward system. With continued use, the person is no longer able to feel the positive reinforcement or pleasure of natural rewards (food, water, sex) and relies on the drug to maintain rewarding feelings.

Crack is cocaine that has been processed from cocaine hydrochloride with ammonia or sodium bicarbonate (baking soda) and water, then heated to remove the hydrochloride. This produces a form of cocaine (freebase) that is smoked. Crack is highly addictive; it became popular in the mid-1980s because it provides an almost immediate high and is inexpensive to produce and buy.

Users of this strong central nervous system stimulant may also experience feelings of restlessness, irritability, and anxiety. Smoking crack delivers large quantities of the drug to the lungs, producing effects comparable to intravenous injection. These effects are felt almost immediately after smoking and are very intense, but do not last long.

Physical effects of cocaine use include constricted peripheral blood vessels, dilated pupils, and increased body temperature, heart rate, chest pain, respiratory failure, nausea, abdominal pain, strokes, seizures, headaches, malnutrition, and panic attacks.

Prolonged cocaine snorting can result in ulceration of the mucous membrane of the nose and can damage the nasal septum enough to cause it to collapse. Cocaine-related deaths are often a result of cardiac arrest or seizures followed by respiratory arrest. When cocaine and alcohol are consumed together, the liver combines them to manufacture a third substance, cocaethylene. This intensifies cocaine's euphoric effects, while increasing the risk of sudden death.

The injecting drug users are at risk for transmitting or acquiring HIV/AIDS if they share needles or other injection equipment.

Prolonged use of cocaine/crack can trigger paranoia and aggression. When addicted individuals stop using, depression ensues. This depression causes users to continue to use the drug to alleviate their depression despite harmful physical and social consequences.

AMPHETAMINES AND METHAMPHETAMINES

Amphetamines were first used in nasal decongestants and bronchial inhalers for the treatment of narcolepsy, obesity, and attention deficit disorder. Methamphetamine ("meth"), a derivative of amphetamine, is a powerful chemical stimulant that affects certain systems in the brain and the central nervous system far more than amphetamine. Made in illegal laboratories, methamphetamine has a high potential for abuse and dependence.

Methamphetamine is taken orally or intranasally (snorting the powder), by intravenous injection, and by smoking. Whereas oral ingestion takes about 20 minutes for the user to feel the effects, snorting affects the user in about 5 minutes.

Immediately after smoking or intravenous injection, the methamphetamine user experiences an intense sensation—a rush or flash—that lasts only a few minutes and is described as extremely pleasurable. Oral or intranasal use produces euphoria—a high, but not a rush. This intense high and rush results from the release of high levels of the neurotransmitter dopamine into the brain. This action stimulates cells that enhance mood, pleasurable feelings, and body movement with effects lasting up to 12 hours. Methamphetamine use also appears to have a neurotoxic effect, damaging brain cells that contain dopamine and serotonin, another neurotransmitter. Over time, methamphetamine appears to reduce levels of dopamine, which can result in symptoms similar to Parkinson's disease, a severe movement disorder.

Even small amounts of methamphetamine can lead to increased wakefulness/ insomnia, increased physical activity, decreased appetite, increased respiration, hyperthermia, respiratory problems, and euphoria. Other CNS effects are irritability, confusion, tremors, convulsions, anxiety, paranoia, and aggressiveness. Methamphetamine causes increased heart rate and blood pressure and can cause irreversible damage to blood vessels in the brain, producing strokes. Cardiovascular collapse and hypothermia can lead to death.

Chronic methamphetamine abuse can cause psychotic behavior that includes intense paranoia, visual and auditory hallucinations (some users have body sores from scratching at "crank bugs"—a common delusion that bugs are crawling under the skin), and out-of-control violent rage episodes. When tolerance develops, users begin to seek the desired effects by taking higher and more frequent doses, or changing the method of ingestion.

CANNABIS

Cannabis sativa is the hemp plant from which several drugs are produced including marijuana (pot, grass, joints, reefer, roaches, weed, Mary Jane), tetrahydrocannabinol, hashish, and hashish oil. All are smoked or taken orally.

MARIJUANA AND HASHISH

The most commonly used illicit drug in the United States today, marijuana is a mixture of the dried and shredded leaves, stems, seeds, and flowers of the hemp plant. Hashish is made from marijuana resin found in the tops of a flowering marijuana plant where the level of marijuana's main ingredient, tetrahydrocannabinol (THC), is most concentrated. Marijuana is much stronger and thereby more addictive today than it was 30 years ago when average THC levels were less than 1%. Today, THC levels range between 7 and 20%.

Although marijuana is used medically to relieve pain and suffering from such disabling conditions as multiple sclerosis, glaucoma, and the side effects of chemotherapy, it is also used illicitly in many ways. Some users brew it as tea or mix it with food. Others smoke blunts—cigars hollowed out and filled with the drug—or smoke it through a water pipe called a bong. The most common method is smoking loose marijuana rolled into a cigarette called a joint or nail.

Within minutes of inhaling marijuana, a user begins to feel pleasant sensations. THC triggers brain cells to release the chemical dopamine. Once dopamine starts flowing, a user feels the urge to continue smoking. Repeated use can lead to addiction.

THC finds brain cells, or neurons, called *cannabinoid receptors* and binds to them. When it attaches to a neuron, THC interferes with the normal communication between neurons. Certain parts of the brain have high concentrations of cannabinoid receptors: the hippocampus, the cerebellum (controls balance and coordination), the basal ganglia (controls movement), and the cerebral cortex.

When the hippocampus, which controls certain types of learning and memory, is disrupted, problems of recall can result. Interference with the hippocampus may also lead to lasting memory loss. Smoking marijuana may increase the risk of heart attack and lung cancer because it has some of the same cancer-causing substances found in tobacco. Marijuana smokers also tend to inhale more deeply and hold their breath longer than cigarette smokers, so more smoke enters the lungs. Other harmful effects include respiratory illness, compromised immune system, accidental injuries, cardiovascular disease, and cognitive impairment. In addition, contrary to popular belief, users become addicted to marijuana. Chronic marijuana smokers can experience withdrawal symptoms such as irritability, depressed mood, anxiety, panic attack, and craving. Depression, anxiety, and personality disturbances are all associated with chronic marijuana use.

HALLUCINOGENS

Hallucinogens, or psychedelics, are drugs that stimulate the brain and create distorted auditory and visual sensations, thinking, self-awareness, and emotions. Some hallucinogens come from natural plant sources, such as mescaline from the peyote cactus. Others such as lysergic acid diethylamide (LSD) are synthetic or manufactured. These drugs produce impaired judgment and psychological effects that often lead to dangerous decision making or accidents. For example, a user might think he can fly and jump out a window to prove it.

Lysergic Acid Diethylamide

In 1938, a Swiss chemist synthesized LSD as a circulatory and respiratory stimulant. Later it was used as a possible medicinal treatment for schizophrenia. In the early 1960s, the first group of recreational LSD users—Timothy Leary (a Harvard professor who regarded these substances as elixirs) and his ideological followers—formed a subculture, largely based in San Francisco, California, whose members came to be called "hippies."

An odorless and colorless substance with a slightly bitter taste, LSD is sold on the street in tablets or capsules to be taken orally, and in liquid form applied to blotter paper, sugar cubes, or gelatin squares. A Schedule I substance (a high potential for abuse), LSD has no medical use, even under supervision.

LSD effects are often unpredictable and depend on the amount taken, the surroundings in which it is used, and the user's personality, mood, and expectations. Some LSD users experience a feeling of despair; others report terrifying fears of losing control and going insane.

LSD is not considered an addictive drug; it does not produce compulsive drug-seeking behaviors. However, users may develop tolerance to the drug, meaning that they must consume progressively larger doses to continue experiencing the hallucinogenic effects that they seek. Within 30 to 90 minutes after ingestion, the user feels the first effects of the drug; they last for an extended period, typically clearing after about 12 hours.

LSD produces powerful visual hallucinations and delusions that cause acute panic reactions when the user cannot control them but wants to end the drug-induced state. Sensations may seem to "cross over," giving the user the feeling of hearing colors and seeing sounds. These changes can be frightening and can cause panic. While these panic reactions, more often than not, are resolved successfully over time, prolonged anxiety and psychotic reactions can result. These mental side effects cause psychotic crises and may add to already pronounced psychiatric problems.

Many LSD users experience flashbacks, recurrences of certain aspects of their experience, without having taken the drug again. A flashback comes on suddenly, often without warning, and may occur within a few days or more than a year after initial use. LSD's chemical action on the brain chemistry of users may cause relatively long-lasting psychoses, such as schizophrenia or severe depression.

Physical effects include dilated pupils, higher body temperature, increased heart rate and blood pressure, sweating, loss of appetite, sleeplessness, dry mouth, and tremors. Deaths related to LSD abuse have occurred as a result of panic reactions, hallucinations, delusions, and paranoia-induced experiences.

PSILOCYBIN, PEYOTE, AND MESCALINE

Psilocybin is a mushroom that is typically eaten or smoked. (For additional information on psilocybin mushrooms, see John Allen's list of 186 kinds at www.erowid.org/plants/mushrooms/mushrooms_info12.shtml.) Members of the Native American Church legally use peyote, a small cactus that is usually eaten in religious ceremonies. Mescaline is the active ingredient in peyote or other cacti.

Individuals use these hallucinogenic agents to alter their consciousness, and in some cases, to have a mystical or spiritual experience; for this reason, the term *entheogen* (meaning "god within") has been proposed for this class of drugs. Generally, lower doses produce alterations in emotion, thought, and sensation. The boundary between self and others begins to disappear and a connectedness with others and the universe may be experienced; users report feelings of elation, awe, and bliss. At higher doses, "normal" consciousness is lost, and hallucinations or visions are indistinguishable from reality.

The immediate and short-term risks associated with this hallucinogen use come from the powerful effect these agents have on consciousness. Instead of bliss and calm, a trip may produce panic attacks and paranoia. Because they are out of touch with reality, individuals who take high doses of hallucinogens are at increased risk for accidental injury. The potential for having a *bad trip* is unpredictable, although one's environment and mental set may be influential. Even those who have had several positive experiences using a hallucinogen can experience a bad trip, typically involving extreme anxiety and paranoia. Flashbacks, relatively rare phenomena in which a person who has used a hallucinogen reexperiences some of the same effects several weeks or months later, also occur. Prolonged psychotic reactions have been observed and may resemble schizophrenia, particularly (though not exclusively) in individuals with prior histories of psychiatric illness.

INHALANTS

The term *inhalant* refers to many household and commercial products that can intentionally be abused by sniffing or huffing (inhaling through the mouth). Volatile solvents, these substances are commonly found in commercial adhesives, lighter fluids, cleaning solutions, gasoline, nitrous oxide, and paint products. Easy accessibility, low cost, and ease of concealment make these substances some of the first substances abused by adolescents.

Inhalants are sniffed directly from rubber cement or correction fluid containers; sniffing fumes from plastic bags over the head, or sniffing cloth saturated with the solvent. The substance may also be inhaled directly from an aerosol can or out of alternative containers such as a balloon filled with nitrous oxide. Some volatile substances may release intoxicating vapors when heated.

Although different in composition, most inhalants slow the body's functions producing effects similar to anesthetics. Inhalant abuse causes intoxicating effects when taken into the lungs in sufficient quantities.

Sniffing highly concentrated amounts of the chemicals in solvents or aerosol sprays, especially fluorocarbons or butane-type gases, can cause heart failure. Additionally, high concentrations of inhalant ingestion can lead to the displacement of oxygen in the lungs and central nervous system resulting in suffocation.

Permanent effects of inhalant abuse include hearing loss, peripheral neuropathies or limb spasms, central nervous system or brain damage, and bone marrow damage. Additional serious side effects include liver and kidney damage.

STEROIDS (ANABOLIC-ANDROGENIC)

There are more than 100 different types of anabolic-androgenic steroids, synthetic substances related to male sex hormones (androgens). *Anabolic* refers to increased muscle building, and *androgenic* refers to increased masculine characteristics. *Steroids* refers to the class of drugs. These drugs are available legally only by prescription to treat conditions that occur when the body produces abnormally low amounts of testosterone, such as delayed puberty and some types of impotence. They are also used to treat body wasting in patients with AIDS and other diseases that result in loss of lean muscle mass. Abuse of anabolic steroids, however, can lead to serious health problems, some irreversible.

Used mostly by people seeking to enhance their athletic performance or improve their overall physical appearance, anabolic steroids are taken orally, injected intramuscularly, or rubbed on the skin as a gel or cream. These drugs are often used in varying patterns:

- *Cycling:* Taking multiple doses of steroids for a specific period of time (weeks or months), stopping for a period, and starting again.
- *Pyramiding:* Slowly escalating steroid use (increasing the number of drugs used at one time and/or the dose and frequency of one or more steroids), reaching a peak amount at midcycle, and gradually tapering the dose toward the end of the cycle.
- *Stacking:* Combining several different steroids to maximize their effectiveness while minimizing any negative effects. Users believe that by doing this, the different steroids will interact to produce a greater effect on muscle size than the effects of using each drug individually.

Health consequences, occurring in both males and females, include liver tumors and cancer, jaundice (yellowish pigmentation of skin, tissues, and body fluids), fluid retention, high blood pressure, heart attacks, increases in LDL (bad cholesterol), and decreases in HDL (good cholesterol).

Adverse side effects for men include shrinking of the testicles, reduced sperm count, infertility, baldness, acne, increased risk for prostate cancer, and the development of breasts. Women experience the growth of facial hair, male-pattern baldness, changes in or cessation of the menstrual cycle, enlargement of the clitoris, and a deepened voice. For adolescents, steroid use may prematurely stop the lengthening of bones, resulting in stunted growth and accelerated puberty changes.

People who inject steroids also run the risk of contracting or transmitting hepatitis or HIV/AIDS. When some steroid abusers stop taking the drug, they experience withdrawal symptoms that include fatigue, restlessness, and loss of appetite, insomnia, and reduced sex drive. Extreme mood swings also can occur, including manic-like symptoms leading to violence. Depression often is seen when the drugs are stopped and may contribute to dependence on anabolic steroids. If untreated, the depression can lead to suicide attempts. Users may also suffer from paranoid jealousy, extreme irritability, delusions, and impaired judgment stemming from feelings of invincibility.

DESIGNER DRUGS

Designer drugs are copies of controlled substances produced by bootleg chemists. Sometimes called *analogs,* they are compounds whose chemical structure closely resembles that of the drug they are designed to copy. In fact, the chemical structure of a designer drug may differ from that of the drug it copies by only a few atoms.

Designer drugs are generally manufactured in clandestine laboratories from readily available chemicals. These synthetic drugs can be twice as powerful as cocaine or heroin, yet they cost little to produce. Designer drugs are most commonly encountered at nightclubs and raves. The most commonly abused is Ecstasy or 3,4-methylendioxymethamphetamine.

3,4-Methylendioxymethamphetamine (MDMA)

A relatively simple chemical belonging to the amphetamine family of compounds, MDMA (Ecstasy) has properties of both stimulants and hallucinogens. While MDMA does not cause true hallucinations, many people have reported distorted time and perception while under the influence of this drug. Most users ingest MDMA orally, and its effects last approximately 4 to 6 hours. Tablets often contain not only MDMA but several other drugs, including methamphetamine, caffeine, dextromethorphan, ephedrine, and cocaine.

MDMA is typically produced in capsule or tablet form and taken orally, although some may use it by injection and snorting. Ecstasy and other club drugs can produce a range of unwanted effects, including hallucinations, paranoia, amnesia and, in some cases, death. When combined with alcohol, these drugs can be even more harmful. Also, there are great differences among individual reactions to these substances, and no one can predict how a user will react. Some people have been known to have extreme, even fatal, reactions the first time they use club drugs. Studies suggest club drugs found in party settings are often adulterated or impure and thus even more dangerous.

MDMA works in the brain by increasing the activity levels of at least three neurotransmitters: serotonin, dopamine, and norepinephrine. MDMA causes these neurotransmitters to be released from their storage sites in neurons resulting in increased brain activity. Serotonin is the neurotransmitter that plays an important role in regulation of mood, sleep, pain, emotion, appetite, and other behaviors. By releasing large amounts of serotonin and also interfering with its synthesis, MDMA significantly depletes this important neurotransmitter. For people who take MDMA at moderate to high doses, depletion of serotonin may be long-term. These persistent deficits in serotonin are likely responsible for many of the long-lasting behavioral effects that the user experiences and that are the chief concern about this drug.

MDMA is not a benign drug. Although users of club drugs often take them simply for energy to keep on dancing or partying, research shows these drugs can have long-lasting negative effects by damaging brain cells.

Because MDMA produces long-term deficits in serotonin function, and serotonin function has been implicated in the etiology of many psychiatric disorders including depression and anxiety, investigators have suspected that heavy MDMA users may experience more psychopathology than nonusers and score significantly higher on measures of obsessive traits, anxiety, paranoid thoughts, and disturbed sleep.

KETAMINE

An anesthetic drug, a small amount of ketamine can result in loss of attention span, learning ability, and memory. At higher doses, ketamine can cause delirium, amnesia, high blood pressure, depression, and severe breathing problems.

GAMMA HYDROXYBUTYRATE (GHB)

GHB may be made in homes using recipes with commonly available ingredients. At low doses, GHB can relax the user, but, as the dose increases, the sedative effects may result in sleep and eventual coma or death.

ROHYPNOL

Tasteless and odorless, it mixes easily in carbonated beverages. Rohypnol may cause amnesia. Other effects include low blood pressure, drowsiness, dizziness, confusion, and stomach upset. Because it is colorless, tasteless, and odorless, it is easy to slip into drinks. Sometimes referred to as a "date rape drug," it has been associated with sexual assaults.

Additional Resources

For more information on drugs of abuse and prescription drugs, see the two federal government web sites: (1) National Institute on Drug Abuse (n.d.). *Information on common drugs of abuse.* Available from www.drugabuse.gov /DrugPages; and (2) National Institute on Drug Abuse (2000). *Research report series—Prescription drugs: Abuse and addiction* Available from www.drugabuse.gov /ResearchReports/Prescription/prescription9.html.

CONTROL SCHEDULES FOR ABUSED DRUGS[2]

The U.S. Drug Enforcement Administration (DEA) regulates the distribution of psychoactive drugs—excluding alcohol—by placing them into categories ranging from Schedule I ("the most dangerous") through Schedule V ("the least dangerous"). (See Table I.1.) The placement of a (text continues on page 30)

---

[2] This section was adapted from the U.S. Drug Enforcement Administration (DEA) web site at www.usdoj.gov/dea and the Controlled Substances Act (CSA), Title II of the Comprehensive Drug Abuse Prevention and Control Act of 1970 found at www.usdoj.gov /dea/agency/csa.htm.

TABLE I.1 Psychoactive Drugs Quick Screen Chart

Opiates					
Common Name	Pharmaceutical Name	Street Names	Medical Uses	Methods of Administration	Indices of Misuse
Heroin	Diacetylmorphine	Brown sugar, dope, H, horse, junk, shag, skunk, smack, white horse	None	Injected, smoked, snorted	Scars (tracks) from injections, constricted pupils, loss of appetite, sniffles, watery eyes, cough, nausea, lethargy, drowsiness, nodding, syringes, bent spoons, needles, and other paraphernalia
Codeine	Empirin with Codeine, Fiorinal with Codeine, Robitussin A-C, Tylenol with Codeine	Captain Cody, Cody, schoolboy, doors and fours, loads, pancakes, syrup	Pain relief, antitussive	Injected, swallowed	Scars (tracks) from injections, constricted pupils, loss of appetite, sniffles, watery eyes, cough, nausea, lethargy, drowsiness, nodding, syringes, bent spoons, needles, and other paraphernalia
Fentanyl	Actiq, Duragesic, Sublimaze	Apache, China girl, China white, dance fever, friend, goodfella, jackpot, murger 8, TNT, Tango, Cash	Analgesic	Injected, smoked, snorted	Scars (tracks) from injections, constricted pupils, loss of appetite, sniffles, watery eyes, cough, nausea, lethargy, drowsiness, nodding, syringes, bent spoons, needles, and other paraphernalia
Methadone	Methadone	Dolopine, Amidone, methadose	Analgesic, addict maintenance	Oral, injected	Scars (tracks) from injections, constricted pupils, loss of appetite, sniffles, watery eyes, cough, nausea, lethargy, drowsiness, nodding, syringes, bent spoons, needles, and other paraphernalia

Opiates					
Short-Term Effects on Health	Long-Term Effects on Health	Overdosing	Withdrawal Symptoms	Physical Dependency	Psycholigical Dependency
State of warm gratification; dry mouth; pain relief; euphoria; sense of contentment, detachment, and freedom from distressing emotion; drowsiness; staggering gait; constricted pupils	Tolerance, nausea, confusion, constipation, sedation, respiratory depression and arrest, weight loss, reduction in sex hormone levels, frequent infections, unconsciousness, coma, hostility, paranoia, kidney and liver damage	Slow and shallow breathing, clammy skin, convulsions, coma, possible death due to suppression of breathing	Headaches, cramps, tremors, panic, chills, loss of appetite, irritability, yawning	High	Very high
State of warm gratification, dry mouth, relaxation with an immediate rush, pain relief, euphoria, drowsiness, sedation, respiratory depression, restlessness, nausea, constricted pupils	Tolerance, nausea, confusion, constipation, sedation, respiratory depression and arrest, weight loss, reduction in sex hormone levels, frequent infections, unconsciousness, coma, hostility, paranoia, kidney and liver damage	Slow and shallow breathing, clammy skin, convulsions, coma, possible death due to respiratory depression	Headaches, cramps, tremors, panic, chills, loss of appetite, irritability, yawning	High	Moderate
State of warm gratification, dry mouth, pain relief, euphoria, drowsiness	Tolerance, respiratory depression and arrest, nausea, confusion, constipation, sedation, unconsciousness, coma	Slow and shallow breathing, clammy skin, convulsions, coma, possible death due to respiratory depression	Chills, headaches, cramps, tremors, panic, loss of appetite, irritability, yawning	High	Moderate
State of warm gratification, dry mouth, pain relief, euphoria, drowsiness	Tolerance, respiratory depression and arrest, nausea, confusion, constipation, sedation, unconsciousness, coma	Slow and shallow breathing, clammy skin, convulsions, coma, possible death due to respiratory depression	Chills, headaches, cramps, tremors, panic, loss of appetite, irritability, yawning	High	Moderate

(continued)

TABLE I.1 *Continued*

Opiates					
Common Name	Pharmaceutical Name	Street Names	Medical Uses	Methods of Administration	Indices of Misuse
Morphine	Roxanol, Duramorph	M, Miss Emma, monkey, white stuff	Analgesic	Injected, swallowed, smoked	Scars (tracks) from injections, constricted pupils, loss of appetite, sniffles, watery eyes, cough, nausea, lethargy, drowsiness, nodding, syringes, bent spoons, needles, and other paraphernalia
Opium	Laudanum, paregoric, pantofen, parepectolin	Big O, black stuff, block, gum, hop, Dover's powder	Analgesic, antidiarrheal	Swallowed, smoked	Scars (tracks) from injections, constricted pupils, loss of appetite, sniffles, watery eyes, cough, nausea, lethargy, drowsiness, nodding, syringes, bent spoons, needles, and other paraphernalia
Depressants					
Alcohol	Ethyl alcohol, ethanol	Alcohol, booze, beer, wine, liquor, juice, brew, sauce, vino	Antidote for methanol poisoning	Oral	Confusion, disorientation, loss of motor nerve control, convulsions, shock, shallow respiration, involuntary defecation, drowsiness, respiratory depression
Barbiturates	Amobarbital, secobarbital, pentobarbital, phenobarbital, methaqualone, flurazepam, triazolam	Reds, red birds, yellows, yellow jackets, tooies, phennies, blue heaven, barbs	Prescription drugs for anesthetics, anticonvulsant, sedative, and hypnotic	Oral (swallowed), injected	Behavior similar to alcohol intoxication without alcohol odor on breath, dilated pupils, staggering, stumbling, lack of coordination, falling asleep while at work, difficulty concentrating

Opiates					
Short-Term Effects on Health	Long-Term Effects on Health	Overdosing	Withdrawal Symptoms	Physical Dependency	Psychological Dependence
State of warm gratification, dry mouth, pain relief, euphoria, drowsiness	Tolerance, respiratory depression and arrest, nausea, confusion, constipation, sedation, unconsciousness, coma	Slow and shallow breathing, clammy skin, convulsions, coma, possible death due to respiratory depression	Chills, headaches, cramps, tremors, panic, loss of appetite, irritability, yawning	High	Moderate
State of warm gratification, dry mouth, pain relief, euphoria, drowsiness	Tolerance, respiratory depression and arrest, nausea, confusion, constipation, sedation, unconsciousness, coma	Slow and shallow breathing, clammy skin, convulsions, coma, possible death due to respiratory depression	Chills, headaches, cramps, tremors, panic, loss of appetite, irritability, yawning	High	High
Depressants					
Initial relaxation, loss of inhibitions, slurred speech, disorientation, impaired coordination, staggering, slowed reactions and reflexes, attitude changes, poor judgment, increased risk taking, blackouts	Higher tolerance, suppression of sex hormone production (especially in males), gastritis, pancreatitis, cirrhosis of the liver, cancer of the gastrointestinal tract, heart disease, brain and nerve damage, Wernicke syndrome, Korsakoff syndrome, fetal alcohol syndrome	Shallow respiration, cold, clammy skin, dilated pupils, weak and rapid pulse, coma, possible death due to respiratory depression	Sweating, vomiting, anxiety, insomnia, altered perception, psychosis, fear, auditory hallucinations, convulsions, delirium tremens, possible death	High	Moderate
Tension, anxiety relief, calmness, depressed respirations, muscle relaxation, sleepiness when quiet or inability to sleep, inability to perform complex tasks, high feeling, slurred speech, staggering, unconsciousness	Depression; tolerance; unusual excitement; fever; abnormal sleep where the individual feels tired and irritable despite sleeping; liver damage; babies of abusers show dependence, withdrawal symptoms, behavioral problems, and birth defects	Shallow breathing, dilated pupils, clammy skin, weak and rapid pulse, coma, death from respiratory suppression	Loss of appetite, sleep disturbances, desire to use more of the drug, progressive restlessness, anxiety, delirium, convulsions, and possible death	High	Moderate

(continued)

TABLE 1.1 *Continued*

Depressants					
Common Name	Pharmaceutical Name	Street Names	Medical Uses	Methods of Administration	Indices of Misuse
Benzodi-azepines	Benzodiazepines	Activan, Dalnabe, Hal-cion, Librium, Valium, Xanax, Rohypnol,[a] roofies, can-dies, downers, sleeping pills, tranks, forget-me pill, Mexi-can Valium, R2, Roche, roofinol, rope, rophies	Prescription drugs for anesthetic, anti-convulsant, sedative, hypnotic, minor tran-quilizers, nerve medication	Oral(swal-lowed), injected	Drowsiness, con-fusion, impaired judgment, slurred speech, con-stricted pupils
Stimulants					
Cocaine	Cocaine hydrochloride	Blow, bump, C, candy, Charlie, coke, crack, flake, rock, snow, toot, girl	Local anes-thetic, vaso-constrictor	Injected, smoked, snorted	Excessive activity, talkativeness, irritability, argu-mentativeness, nervousness, increased blood pressure, dilated pupils, long peri-ods without sleep-ing or eating, euphoria
Ampheta-mines	Dextroampheta-mine, metham-phetamine, diethylpropion, phenteramine, methylphenidate, phenteramine	Biphetamine, Dexedrine, Methadrine, Tenuate, Ion-amin, Ritalin, Fastin,[a] bennies, black beauties, crosses, hearts, LA turn-around, speed, truck drivers, uppers, ice	Prescription drugs for medical con-ditions such as ADHD, obesity, and narcolepsy	Injected, swal-lowed, smoked, snorted	Excessive activity, talkativeness, irritability, argu-mentativeness, nervousness, increased blood pressure, dilated pupils, long peri-ods without sleep-ing or eating, euphoria

[a] These are registered trademarks and are not necessarily all the trademarks selling these drugs.

	Depressants				
Short-Term Effects on Health	Long-Term Effects on Health	Overdosing	Withdrawal Symptoms	Physical Dependency	Psychological Dependence
Reduced pain, less anxiety, relaxed muscles, reduced mental alertness, feeling of well-being, lowered inhibitions, slowed pulse, lowered blood pressure, skin rash, nausea, dizziness, memory loss (with Rohyonol)	Tolerance, increased aggression, visual and gastrointestinal disturbances, accumulation in body to increase effect, babies born with dependence and withdrawal symptoms	Shallow breathing, dilated pupils, clammy skin, weak and rapid pulse, coma, death from respiratory suppression	Tremors, cramps, sweating, vomiting, possible death	Low	Moderate to high
	Stimulants				
Feelings of exhilaration, energy, increased mental alertness, dilated pupils, increased heart rate and body temperature, increased blood pressure and metabolism, erratic and violent behavior, tremors, hallucinations, chest pain	Headaches, reduced appetite, weight loss, malnourishment, nausea, abdominal pain, prone to violence, kidney damage, liver damage, tissue damage (especially if snorted—nose damage), respiratory failure, rapid or irregular heart beat, chest pain, psychosis, heart failure, strokes, seizures, risk of AIDS, newborns experience withdrawal symptoms	Agitation, increase in body temperature, hallucinations, convulsions, possible death	Apathy, long periods of sleep, sleep disturbance, fatigue, disorientation, hunger, depression, violence	Low	High
Feelings of exhilaration, energy, increased alertness, aggressive, feeling of well-being, increased heart rate, rapid breathing, sweating, dizziness, loss of coordination, collapse, perspiration, dilated pupils, talkativeness, restlessness, increased metabolism and blood pressure, hallucinations	Tolerance, rapid or irregular heartbeat, loss of coordination, irritability, anxiousness, restlessness, delirium, tremors, panic, paranoia, violent behavior, impulsive behavior, aggressiveness, reduced appetite, weight loss, malnutrition, damage to blood vessels, risk of AIDS, heart failure, kidney damage, liver damage, lung problems, stroke, tissue damage, death from ruptured brain vessels	Agitation, increase in body temperature, convulsions, violence, severe paranoia, hallucinations, possible death	Sleep disturbance, fatigue, long but disturbed sleep, strong hunger, disorientation, irritability, depression, violence	Low	High

(continued)

TABLE I.1 *Continued*

Stimulants					
Common Name	Pharmaceutical Name	Street Names	Medical Uses	Methods of Administration	Indices of Misuse
Nicotine	Nicotine	Bidis, chew, cigars, cigarettes, smokeless tobacco, snuff, spit tobacco, Habitrol patch, Nicorette gum, Nicotrol spray, Prostep patch	Treatment for nicotine dependence	Smoked, snorted, taken in snuff and spit tobacco, transdermal	Smell of tobacco on clothes and body
Caffeine	Caffeine	Coffee, tea, soda	Treatment of hypertension when linked to severe headaches, found in many prescription and non-prescription pain relievers, cold remedies, and stimulant mixtures	Swallow	Elevated mood, insomnia, anxiety, psychomotor agitation

Stimulants					
Short-Term Effects on Health	Long-Term Effects on Health	Overdosing	Withdrawal Symptoms	Physical Dependency	Psycholigical Dependence
Increased heart rate, increased rate of breathing, decreased appetite, decreased skin temperature, rise in blood pressure, relaxation feeling, increased acid in stomach, reduced urine formation, stimulates then reduces brain and nervous system activity, loss of appetite, loss of physical endurance	Tolerance, 5.5 minutes taken from every life span for each cigarette, adverse pregnancy outcomes, narrowing and hardening of blood vessels throughout body, shortness of breath, chronic cough, respiratory infections, chronic bronchitis, emphysema, stomach ulcers, chronic lung disease, cardiovascular disease, stroke, predisposition to various cancers, risk of thrombosis in users of birth control pills	First acts like a stimulant, then depresses the CNS causing breathing paralysis, convulsions, and death	Cravings, difficulty concentrating, insomnia, depression, anger, irritability, frustration, restlessness, anxiety, constipation, weight gain	Moderate	Moderate
Increased alertness and sleeplessness, spontaneous tremors of hands, increased pulse rate, increased metabolism, increased body temperature, increased stomach acid, increased blood pressure, irregular heartbeat, decreased sleep, headache, nervousness, delirium	Dependence, insomnia, anxiety, depression, stomach ulcer, heart disease, bladder infection, cancer, birth defects	Restlessness, dizziness, nausea, headache, tense muscles, sleep disturbances, irregular heartbeats, delirium, drowsiness, ringing ears, diarrhea, vomiting, light flashes, difficulty breathing, convulsions	Irritability, restlessness, headache	Moderate	Moderate

(continued)

TABLE I.1 *Continued*

Cannabinoids					
Common Name	Pharmaceutical Name	Street Names	Medical Uses	Methods of Administration	Indices of Misuse
Cannabis	Hashish, marijuana, Tetrahydrocannibinol	Boom, chronic, gangster, hash, hash oil, hemp, blunt, dope, ganga, grass, herb, joint, Mary Jane, pot, reefer, sinsemilla, skunk, weed, THC, marinol	Pain relief, antiemetic	Oral (swallowed, smoked)	Animated behavior, loud talking, sleepiness, dilated pupils, bloodshot eyes, distortions in perception, hallucinations, distortions in depth and time perception, loss of coordination
Hallucinogen					
LSD	Lysergic acid diethylamide	Acid, blotter, boomers, cubes, microdot, green/red dragon, yellow sunshines	None	Swallowed, absorbed through tissue, sniffed, injected	Extreme changes in behavior and mood; sit in a trancelike state; look of fear; chills; irregular breathing; sweating; trembling hands; changes in sense of light, hearing, touch, smell, and time; increase in blood pressure, heart rate, and blood sugar

Cannabinoids					
Short-Term Effects on Health	Long-Term Effects on Health	Overdosing	Withdrawal Symptoms	Physical Dependency	Psycholigical Dependence
Euphoria; relaxation; calm; increased appetite; more vivid sense of taste, sight, smell, hearing, slow thinking; reflective; sleepy; slow reaction time; anxiety; depression; confusion; impaired balance and coordination; fragmentary thoughts; hallucinations	Tolerance, shortened attention span, frequent respiratory infections, decreased motivation, apathy, unrealistic thinking, impaired communication, impaired memory and learning, increased heart rate, anxiety, panic attacks, chronic bronchitis, lung cancer, reduction of sex hormone levels, birth defects, cancer, possible serious brain damage—amotivational syndrome	Insomnia, hyperactivity, decreased appetite	Irritability, aggressive behaviors, anxiety, insomnia, nausea, loss of appetite	Low	Moderate
Hallucinogen					
Rapid pulse, arousal, altered state of perception and feeling, brighter colors, fusion of senses, hallucinations, illusions, dizziness, extreme mood swings, fear or terror, increased body temperature, increased heart rate and blood pressure, loss of appetite, sleeplessness, numbness, weakness, tremors, nausea	Decreases motivation; increases depression and anxiety; violent behavior; chronic mental disorders; persisting perception disorder—spontaneous recurrences, flashbacks, of a prior LSD experience that may occur long after use	Longer more intense trip episodes, convulsions, coma, heart and lung failure, ruptured blood vessels in the brain, psychosis, coma, death	None	None	Low

(continued)

TABLE I.1 *Continued*

Hallucinogen					
Common Name	Pharmaceutical Name	Street Names	Medical Uses	Methods of Administration	Indices of Misuse
PCP	Phencyclidine	Angel dust, love boat, boat, hog	Veterinary anesthetic	Smoked, sniffed, swallowed (colorful capsules), injected	Extreme changes in behavior and mood, sit in a trance-like state; look of fear; chills; irregular breathing; sweating; trembling hands; changes in sense of light, hearing, touch, smell, and time; increase in blood pressure, heart rate, and blood sugar
Designer Drugs					
Ecstasy	MDMA (methyl-enedioxymetham-phetamine), DOB, DOM, MDA, MMDA	Adam, clarity, ecstasy, Eve, lover's speed, peace, STP, X, XTC	None	Swallowed, injected, smoked	Extreme changes in behavior and mood; changes in sense of light, hearing, touch, smell, and time; enhanced feelings of affection and emotion

Hallucinogen					
Short-Term Effects on Health	Long-Term Effects on Health	Overdosing	Withdrawal Symptoms	Physical Dependency	Psycholigical Dependence
Increased emotionality, state of pleasure, sense of separation, rapidly changing feelings, anxiety, distorted perception of time, aggressive paranoia, confused behaviors, hallucinations, illusions, dizziness, confusions, suspicion, loss of control, shallow breathing, profuse sweating, generalized numbness of hands and feet, vomiting, blurred vision, schizophrenic behaviors, mental confusion, blackouts	Flashbacks, depression, violent behavior, speech problems, severe psychological problems	Longer, more intense trip episodes, convulsions, coma, heart and lung failure, ruptured blood vessels in the brain, psychosis, coma, death	None	None	High
Designer Drugs					
Mild hallucinogenic effects; visual illusions; altered perception of one's own body; increased emotions; increased tactile sensitivity, empathic feelings; increased heart rate, blood pressure, and metabolism; feelings of exhilaration; energy; increased mental alertness; hyperthermia	Tolerance, flashbacks, rapid or irregular heartbeat, reduced appetite, impaired memory and learning, weight loss, heart failure, irreversible brain damage	Longer, more intense trip episodes that may resemble psychotic states, psychosis, coma, death	None	Unknown	Unknown

(continued)

TABLE I.1 *Continued*

Volatile Organics/Inhalants					
Common Name	Pharmaceutical Name	Street Names	Medical Uses	Methods of Administration	Indices of Misuse
Volatile substances or inhalants	Solvents (paint thinners, gasoline, acetone, ethyl acetate, chloroform, carbon tetrachloride, toluene, glues); gases (butane, propane, aerosol propellants, nitrous oxide); nitrites (isoamyl, isobutyl, cyclohexyl); fuel in glues, marking pens, gases, nail polish remover, lighter fluid, paint thinners, and cleaning agents	Laughing gas, poppers, snappers, whippets	None	Inhaled through nose or mouth	Poor motor coordination; impaired vision, memory, and thought; abusive behavior; light-headedness; slowed thought; headaches
Performance Enhancers					
Anabolic-androgenic steroids	Anadrol, Oxandrin, Durabolin, Depo-Testosterone, Nandrolene, Stanazolol, Equipoise	Roids, juice	Hormone replacement therapy	Injected, swallowed, applied to skin	Foul breath, severe acne, especially across the back

Volatile Organics/Inhalants					
Short-Term Effects on Health	Long-Term Effects on Health	Overdosing	Withdrawal Symptoms	Physical Dependency	Psycholigical Dependence
Light-headedness, euphoria, fantasy, recklessness, stimulation, loss of inhibition, visual and auditory hallucinations, headache, nausea, vomiting, slurred speech, loss of motor control, wheezing, decreased respiration and heart rate	Tolerance, feelings of weightlessness, fatigue, hostility, paranoia, unconsciousness, cramps, weight loss, loss of muscle control, slurred speech, drowsiness or loss of consciousness, excessive secretions from the nose and watery eyes, muscle weakness, depression, memory impairment, damage to cardiovascular and nervous systems, kidney damage, liver damage, increased blood levels can cause brain damage, sudden death	Death by suffocation, if an unconscious user is still breathing from plastic bag	Restlessness, anxiety, irritability, chills, headache, cramps, tremors	Moderate	Moderate
Performance Enhancers					
No intoxication effects, behavior changes, mood swings, change in sleeping patterns, weight and strength gains, anxiety and depression	Hypertension; blood clotting; cholesterol changes; liver cysts; cancer; hostility and aggression; rashes; severe acne; cataracts; liver damage; tendon damage; heart attacks; strokes; diabetes; hair loss; in adolescents: premature stoppage of growth; in males: prostate cancer, reduced sperm production, infertility, shrunken testicles, breast enlargement; in females: menstrual irregularities, development of beard and other masculine characteristics	High blood pressure, liver damage, evidence of liver cancer	Depressive reactions, fatigue, restlessness, anorexia, insomnia, decreased libido	None	High

(continued)

TABLE I.1 *Continued*

Over-the-Counter (OTC) Substances					
Common Name	Pharmaceutical Name	Street Names	Medical Uses	Methods of Administration	Indices of Misuse
Ephedrine	Ma huang, Chinese ephedra, ma huang extract, ephedra, Ephedra sinica, ephedra extract, ephedra herb powder, epitonin or ephedrine	Herbal Ecstasy, Primatene, Broncholate, Tedral, mahuange	Relieving bronchial asthma	Oral, injection, snorted	Similar to amphetamines

drug into any of these schedules is based on (1) the substance's medical use, (2) potential for abuse, and (3) its safety or dependence liability. The procedure for classification is found in Section 201 of the Controlled Substances Act (21 USC 811).

PRESCRIBING DRUGS

Schedule I drugs (e.g., heroin) are forbidden except for scientific research. By contrast, authorization is not required for dispensing Schedule V drugs (e.g., Lomotil).

Physicians must apply directly to the DEA for authorization to prescribe Schedules II, III, and IV medications. The DEA provides special prescription forms to doctors who are approved to dispense these drugs after an additional application process.

Drugs classified as Schedule II cannot be prescribed by telephone, and there are no refills. Schedule III and IV drugs both require a new prescription after 6 months or five refills. Schedule IV drugs, however, have less severe penalties for illegal possession than Schedule III drugs.

THE FIVE CONTROL SCHEDULES

Schedule I Drugs: Heroin, hallucinogens, marijuana, methaqualone (Quaalude) are considered as having high potential for abuse, with no legally recognized medical use.

Over-the-Counter (OTC) Substances					
Short-Term Effects on Health	Long-Term Effects on Health	Overdosing	Withdrawal Symptoms	Physical Dependency	Psycholigical Dependence
Heightened awareness; increased energy; increases heart rate and blood pressure; harm increased if mixed with a decongestant, caffeine, or any other stimulant	Hypertension, insomnia, arrhythmia, nervousness, tremor, headache, seizure, cerebrovascular event, myocardial infarction, kidney stones, dizziness, headache, restlessness, insomnia, memory loss, muscle injury, gastrointestinal distress, irregular heartbeat and heart palpitations, heart attack, stroke, seizures, psychosis, death	Sudden rise in blood pressure, heart attack, and stroke	Similar to amphetamines	Has addictive qualities, but as of yet the extent is unknown	Has addictive qualities, but as of yet the extent is unknown

Schedule II Drugs: Opium or morphine, codeine, synthetic opiates such as meperidine (Demerol), barbiturates such as secobarbital (Seconal), amphetamines, methylphenidate (Ritalin), and phenmetrazine (Preludin); PCP, cocaine, methadone, and methamphetamine have high potential for abuse but are currently accepted for medical use with severe restrictions. Abuse of these drugs may lead to severe psychological or physical dependence.

Schedule III Drugs: Paregoric, methyprylon (Noludar); anabolic steroids, codeine and hydrocodone with aspirin or Tylenol, and some barbiturates have an abuse potential less than Schedules I and II drugs and currently have an accepted medical use in the United States. Abuse of these drugs may lead to moderate or low physical dependence and/or high psychological dependence.

Schedule IV Drugs: Chloral hydrate (Noctec), ethchlorvynol (Placidyl), flurazepam (Dalmane), pentazocine (Talwin), chlordiazepoxide (Librium), propoxyphene (Darvon), and diethylpropion (Tenuate), Equanil, Valium and Xanax have low abuse potential compared with Schedule III drugs and currently have an accepted medical use in the United States. Abuse of these drugs may lead to limited physical dependence and/or psychological dependence.

Schedule V Drugs: Narcotic-atropine mixtures (Lomotil) and codeine mixtures (less than 200 mg) have a low potential for abuse relative to Schedule IV drugs and have a currently accepted medical use.

Note: A few states (e.g., Massachusetts) recognize Schedule VI drugs such as adhesives, glue, and medications (ibuprofen and penicillin) that have little or no addictive potential.

CONTROLLED SUBSTANCE ANALOGUES

A new class of drugs—controlled substance analogues (e.g., GHB)—created by the Anti-Drug Abuse Act of 1986, includes substances that are not controlled, but may be found in the illicit drug trade. Pharmacologically similar to Schedule I or II controlled substances, with no legitimate medical use, these substances are legally treated as though they were Schedule I substances.

GOVERNMENT DECISION MAKING

Decisions to add, delete, or change the schedule of a drug or other substance may be initiated by the Drug Enforcement Administration (DEA), the Department of Health and Human Services (DHHS), or by petition from any interested person, such as the manufacturer of a drug, a medical society or association, a pharmacy association, a public interest group concerned with drug abuse, a state, or a local government agency. When the DEA receives a petition, the agency begins its own investigation of the drug.

The DEA uses these indicators that a drug or other substance has potential for abuse:

- There is evidence that individuals are taking the drug in amounts sufficient to create a hazard to their health or to the safety of other individuals or to the community.
- There is significant diversion of the drug from legitimate drug channels.
- Individuals are taking the drug on their own initiative rather than on medical advice from a practitioner licensed by law to administer such drugs.
- The substance is a new drug related in its action to a drug already listed as having a potential for abuse and is likely have the same potential for abuse as such drugs.

Additional Resources

A quick user-friendly online resource to view the schedule drug tables of *Drugs of Abuse* set out by the U.S. government DEA. Available from www.mrs.umn.edu /~ratliffj/Drugs_Course/drug_schedules_table.htm.

Also see the Canadian Drug Classification protocols for determining legal and illegal drugs, *Drugs and drug policy in Canada: A brief review & commentary*, by Dr. Diane Riley (1998). Available from www.parl.gc.ca/37/1/parlbus /commbus/senate/com-e/ille-e/library-e/riley-e.pdf.

PART II
Conceptual Tools

Part II highlights the basic concepts that underlie addiction. We first review the historical and contemporary definitions of addiction. We then discuss the three Cs—compulsive use, loss of control, continued use despite adverse consequences—that characterize all addictions and explore the similarities between addictions to chemicals (i.e., alcohol and other drugs) and behaviors.

Classification schemes are reviewed, such as the *stages* that each addict typically passes through en route to recovery, the *levels* of drug use, and the six stages of predictable behavioral change.

Prevention types and principles are outlined, including both the traditional classification—primary, secondary, and tertiary prevention—and the Institute of Medicine's classification—universal, selective, and indicated prevention. Prevention and relapse models are also explored.

DEFINITIONS OF ADDICTION
  Moral Model
  Self-Medication Model
  Medical/Disease Model
  Spirituality Model
  Impulse-Control Disorder
  Reward Deficiency and Neurophysiological Adaption
  Genetic Model
  Biomedical Model
  Social Learning Model

Erroneous Thought Patterns
Biopsychosocial Model
Public Health Model

CHARACTERISTICS OF ADDICTION

Compulsive Use
Loss of Control
Continued Use Despite Adverse Consequences
Tolerance
Withdrawal

TYPES OF ADDICTIVE DISORDERS

The Brain and Psychoactive Drugs
The Brain and Addictive Behaviors
Addictive Interaction Disorder

DRUG-USE STAGES

Initiation
Escalation
Maintenance
Discontinuation and Relapse
Recovery

LEVELS OF DRUG USE

Type 1—Abstainers
Type 2—Social Users
Type 3—Drug Abusers
Type 4—Physically But Not Psychologically Dependent Users
Type 5—Physically and Psychologically Dependent Users

STAGES OF BEHAVIORAL CHANGE

Stage 1—Precontemplation
Stage 2—Contemplation
Stage 3—Preparation
Stage 4—Action
Stage 5—Maintenance and Relapse Prevention
Stage 6—Termination

PREVENTION TYPES AND PRINCIPLES

The Traditional Classification
The Institute of Medicine Classification
Prevention Principles
Relapse Prevention

DEFINITIONS OF ADDICTION

The term *addiction* (derived from the Latin root *addicere,* meaning "to adore or surrender oneself to a master") also applies to behaviors beyond drugs and alcohol such as sex, work, gambling, buying, eating, and the Internet. Although "there is no single definition of addiction and a universally accepted, comprehensive theory of addiction has yet to be developed" (Doweiko, 2002, p. 21), here are the best known models of addiction, some of which share similar characteristics.

MORAL MODEL

This model, dating to the 1850s, defines an addicted client as weak in character. It is based on the idea that individuals have free choice and are responsible for their behaviors. As an example of this model, Lemanski (2001) cites a religion-based program (Oxford Group Movement/Moral Re-Armament) whose mission is to develop among clients morals that are aligned with God. This approach has influenced public policy and the American judicial system.

Additional Resources

For more information on the moral model, see May, C. (1997). Habitual drunkards and the intervention of alcoholism: Susceptibility and culpability in nineteen century medicine. *Addiction Research, 5*(2), 169–188; and *A History of Alcoholism.* Available from www.hoboes.com/html/Politics/Prohibition/Notes/Alcoholism History.html.

SELF-MEDICATION MODEL

This view, originating in the 1960s among psychoanalysts, assumes that people self-medicate to cope with life problems. A person in emotional pain will self-medicate to find relief, and this can eventually lead to addiction. This self-medication hypothesis, Khantzian (1999) asserts, "should be considered in parallel with other approaches and not in competition with them" (p. 5).

Additional Resources

For more information, see Khantzian, E. J. (1997). The self-medication hypothesis of substance use disorders: A reconsideration and recent applications. *Harvard Review of Psychiatry, 4*, 231–244.

Also see Self-Medication Hypothesis' web site at http://self-med-hypothesis.tripod.com.

MEDICAL/DISEASE MODEL

First proposed in 1810 by Dr. Benjamin Rush (White, 2005), addiction was identified as a disease, rather than a mental disorder or moral failure. *Disease* is defined as a severely harmful, potentially fatal condition that manifests itself in an irreversible loss of control over use of psychoactive substances. Although the disease may go into remission, there is no known cure, and since the disease is progressive and often fatal, complete abstinence is the treatment goal.

In 1945, the American Medical Association formally accepted this definition of addiction. Since then, the disease definition has been officially adopted by such professional organizations as the World Health Organization, the American Psychiatric Association, the National Association of Social Workers, the American Public Health association, the National Council on Alcoholism, and the American Society for Addiction Medicine.

Additional Resources

For more information, see White, W. (2000). *Toward a new recovery movement: Historical reflections on recovery, treatment and advocacy.* Available from www.ncaddillinois.org/whitelong.htm.

Ron Raizen's Rains Report (www.roizen.com/ron/rr11.htm) provides a critical review of Jellinek's (1960) report.

SPIRITUALITY MODEL

This model assumes that addictive disorders stem from a lack of spirituality, that is, of being disconnected from a "Higher Power," the source of light, truth, love, and wellness. "Every addiction is, in the final analysis, a disease of the spirit," notes Doweiko (2002, p. 49). Alcoholics Anonymous and its many derivatives help participants recover by developing a viable relationship with this Higher Power.

Additional Resources

For more information, see Kannaday, P., *The spiritual model,* available from http://ihcf.homestead.com/files/The_Spiritual_Model2.htm.

To review *The Big Book* web site (where the text is online), see www.recovery .org/aa/bigbook/ww.

IMPULSE-CONTROL DISORDER

A relatively new definition of addiction, this view assumes that either neurobiological or genetic deficiencies make a person unable to control and regulate impulsive behavior(s). Under certain conditions, such individuals will put themselves at risk and find temporary relief with self-destructive behaviors such as kleptomania, pyromania, and/or drug abuse (Hollander, Buchalter, & DeCaria, 2000).

Additional Resources

For more information, see *Mental Health Matters Information on Impulse Control Disorders.* Available from www.mental-health-matters.com/articles/art_cat .php?catID=31.

REWARD DEFICIENCY AND NEUROPHYSIOLOGICAL ADAPTION

This model assumes that chemical imbalance is manifested as one or more behavioral disorders called the "reward deficiency syndrome" (Blum, Cull, Braverman, & Comings, 2000, para. 3). This disorder, and others like it, are linked by a common biological substrate, a "hard-wired system in the brain (consisting of cells and signaling molecules) that provides pleasure in the process of rewarding certain behaviors" (Blum et al., 2000, para. 3). He suggests that this reward deficiency syndrome may cause a predisposition, or vulnerability, to addiction that includes alcohol, cocaine, heroin, nicotine, sugar, pathological gambling, sex, and other behavior disorders.

Additional Resources

For more information, see Blum, K., & Payne, J. E. (1991). *Alcohol and the addictive brain: New hope for alcoholics from biogenetic research.* New York: Free Press.

GENETIC MODEL

Research over the past 20 years has identified a genetic predisposition in some individuals to alcohol, tobacco, and other substances of abuse (Doweiko, 2002). Epidemiological studies indicate that 40% to 60% of an individual's risk for an addiction to alcohol, opiates, or cocaine is genetic (Kendler, Karkowski, Neale, & Prescott, 2000; Tsuang, Bar, Harley, & Lyons, 2001). A growing number of genetic researchers now believe different classes of substances may be connected to unique genetic preference and may help account for the individual's drug of choice (Blum et al., 2000).

Additional Resources

For more information, see Nestler, E. J. (2002). *The genetic basis of addiction.* Available from www.psychiatrictimes.com/p020256.html.

BIOMEDICAL MODEL

The 1990s gave rise to another disease theory of addiction that draws from both the biological and behavioral sciences. "Using drugs repeatedly over time changes brain structure and function in fundamental and long-lasting ways that can persist long after the individual stops using them" (Leshner, 2001, para. 3). Once the addiction impacts the brain, the client is driven behaviorally to support the demands made by the brain to prevent becoming ill from withdrawal.

SOCIAL LEARNING MODEL

Social reinforcement causes individuals to model the drug use behaviors of their parents, older siblings, and peers. Social learning theorist Albert Bandura (1977, 1986) indicates four stages of social learning: (1) Attention—The individual makes a conscious cognitive choice to observe the desired behavior; (2) Memory—The individual recalls what he has observed from the modeling; (3) Imitation—The individual repeats the actions that she has observed; and (4) Motivation—The individual client must have some internal motivation for wanting to carry out the modeled behavior.

Additional Resources

For more information, see Bandura, A. (1986). *Social foundations of thought and action: A social cognitive theory.* Englewood Cliffs, NJ: Prentice Hall; and Bandura, A. (1977). *Social learning theory.* Englewood Cliffs, NJ: Prentice Hall. Available from http://catalogs.mhhe.com/mhhe/home.do.

For information on behavioral theory, see Behavioral & Learning Theory at www.aa2.org/philosophy/bahavioral.htm.

ERRONEOUS THOUGHT PATTERNS

This model assumes that illogical thinking underlies addiction. Ladouceur, Gaboury, Dumont, and Rochette (1988) explain that, to help addicted clients, counselors must challenge erroneous thinking, correct flawed thinking, and teach them how to reason correctly. For example, when a compulsive gambler thinks, "I have a system that will beat this slot machine; I just need to stick to it long enough," educate the person about the laws of probability and how they are stacked against the gambler. Teach the person that gamblers cannot "beat the odds," and that this flawed repetitive thought leads to addictive problems.

Additional Resources

For more information, see Toneatto, T., Blitz-Miller, T., Calderwood, K., Dragonetti, R., & Tsanos, A. (1997). Cognitive distortions in heavy gambling. *Journal of Gambling Studies, 13,* 253–266.

BIOPSYCHOSOCIAL MODEL

Developed in the 1980s, this view holds that addiction vulnerability is affected by the complex interaction between one's *physical status* (functioning of the body), *psychological state* (how one views and perceives the world), and *social dynamics* (how and with whom one interacts). Chiauzzi (1991) points out that looking at addictions through these three windows allows for more flexibility in determining root cause and treatment.

Additional Resources

For more information, see Kumpfer, K. L., Trunnell, E. P., & Whiteside, H. O. (1990). The biopsychosocial model: Application to the addictions field. In R. C. Engs, *Controversies in the addiction's field* (chap. 7). Available from www.indiana.edu/~engs/cbook/chap7.html.

PUBLIC HEALTH MODEL

The Institute of Medicine (1989) defines addiction from a public health perspective, identifying three etiologic factors: (1) *Agents*—the psychoactive drugs; (2) *Hosts*—individuals who differ in their genetic, physiological, behavioral, and sociocultural susceptibility to various forms of chemicals; and (3) *Environment*—the availability and accessibility of the agent (Coombs, 1997, pp. 176–177).

Additional Resources

For more information, see the Institute of Medicine. (1989). *Prevention and treatment of alcohol problems: Research opportunities* [Report of a study by the Committee of the IOM, Division of Mental Health and Behavioral Medicine]. Washington, DC: National Academy Press.

Also see *Addictions are an illness: A Public Health response to the war on drugs.* The American Public Health Association. Available from www.medicalcaresection.org/2000_bullet_2.html.

CHARACTERISTICS OF ADDICTION

Regardless of how an addiction is manifested—through chemical use (e.g., cocaine or alcohol) or behaviors (e.g., cybersex or compulsive gambling), addictions generally have three characteristics. Called the three Cs—Compulsive use, loss of Control, and Continued use despite adverse consequences. A client may not necessarily display all three, but will have a problem with at least one.

COMPULSIVE USE

According to Blume (2005), compulsive use has three elements: reinforcement, craving, and habit. *Reinforcement* occurs when the addictive substance or behavior is first engaged. Being rewarded with pleasure and/or relief from pain and stress reinforces the user. As he or she continues to ingest the substance or engage in the behavior, *tolerance* develops and it takes larger doses of the substance or behavior to obtain the sought-after pleasure or relief.

Craving means that the body and brain send intense signals that the drug or behavior is needed. Using drugs on an ongoing (i.e., without stopping) basis alters the chemical balance of the brain. *Withdrawal symptoms* are unpleasant physical symptoms (the opposite of the drug effects) and may kick in when the drug(s) or behaviors are withheld. Psychological cravings related to the experience of taking the drug or engaging in the behavior can also occur.

Habit, the third element in compulsive use, results from deeply ingrained patterns in the memory of the nervous system. Addictive behaviors often involve automatic responses.

LOSS OF CONTROL

Typically, addicts cannot predict or determine *how much* of the drug they will use or *when* they will use it. However, once they begin, they cannot stop. This may be due in part to impairment of the brain and memory. This same loss of control also applies to other addictive behaviors such as compulsive gambling or sex.

Research on alcohol addiction has shown that intoxication can cause "alcohol myopia," a condition that decreases judgment, decision making, and planning and negatively affects the perception and skills necessary to effectively evaluate one's environment (Steele & Josephs, 1990).

CONTINUED USE DESPITE ADVERSE CONSEQUENCES

Addictive behavior has negative consequences. Addicts may not be aware of these consequences although those persons associated with the users are. Addicts, if they are aware, may feel that the pleasurable or pain-relieving features of drug use outweigh the problems.

TOLERANCE

When a drug is used continually, the body adapts to—and begins to tolerate the drug's pharmacological effects. As a result, the user needs more and more of the substance or the behavior to achieve the intensity and duration of the initial experience. The continual user must also take more drugs to avoid the physical discomfort and psychological distress that accompany withdrawal.

Doweiko (2002) indicates two types of tolerance: (1) *metabolic tolerance* (also called *pharmacokinetic tolerance*) when the body increases its efficiency in breaking down chemicals for elimination and (2) *pharmacodynamic tolerance* (also called functional tolerance) when the central nervous system becomes less sensitive to the effects of the drug of choice.

Additional Resources

See the web site on tolerance at the University of Plymouth, Department of Psychology. Available from http://salmon.psy.plym.ac.uk/year3/DrugAbuse/drugtolerance.htm.

WITHDRAWAL

When drug use is stopped, the addict suffers unpleasant effects that are usually the opposite of those induced by the chemical. Because the body has adapted to the drug, withdrawal (unless carefully monitored and managed) not only is miserable, but may be life-threatening as well.

Withdrawal may create the *rebound effect:* "The characteristic of a drug to produce reverse effects when the effect of the drug has passed or the patient no longer responds to it" (MedicineNet.com).

Alcohol withdrawal without medical assistance can escalate to the point where the client may experience *delirium tremens,* a condition that can create seizures, disorientation, and even death (National Institute on Alcohol Abuse and Alcoholism, 1993).

TYPES OF ADDICTIVE DISORDERS

Today, neuroscientists view addiction as a brain disorder expressed in compulsive behaviors. According to Alan Leshner former director of the National Institute of Drug Abuse, "The majority of the biomedical community now consider addiction, in its essence, to be a brain disease, a condition caused by persistent changes in brain structure and function" (Leshner, 2001, p. 1). Just as ingesting chemicals (alcohol and other psychoactive drugs) activate the pleasure center of the brain, so do compulsive gambling, sex addiction, compulsive eating, compulsive spending, and extreme work.

THE BRAIN AND PSYCHOACTIVE DRUGS

The brain's normal circuits include a system—*the brain reward system*—that induces pleasurable feelings when stimulated. To regain these rewarding feelings, this circuit encourages a repeat of the behaviors that stimulate pleasurable feelings.

For more information on how the brain reward system operates, visit Bardo (1998), *Neuropharmacological Mechanisms of Drug Reward: Beyond Dopamine in the Nucleus Accumbens.* Available from www.biopsychiatry.com/reward.htm.

All addictive drugs disrupt normal neurotransmission in the brain. "Addictive drugs change the brain's communication system by interfering with synaptic transmission," state Friedman and Rusche (1999, p. 48). "Some drugs mimic certain neurotransmitters and convey false messages," note Friedman and Rusche (p. 40). "Other drugs block neurotransmitters and prevent real messages from getting through." Still other drugs have different kinds of effects that modify the flow of information among neurons. But *all addictive drugs interfere with the way neurons communicate.* "They change the way the brain works, and *that* changes how people perceive the world, how they feel about themselves and their world, and how they behave" (p. 48).

False messengers, the term Friedman and Rusche (1999), give to psychoactive drugs, mimic the actions of natural brain chemicals, the *real messengers,* some of which make people feel pleasure by activating their brain's reward system. With a speed and intensity that greatly exceeds normality, these extremely pleasurable feelings lead some to seek them at any risk. As this use continues, changes occur in the brain to perpetuate continued use until it becomes compulsive, beyond control, and problematic.

Drugs of abuse negatively impact regions of the brain by sending false messages, or by weakening or intensifying real messages. Drug users describe the intensified pleasure produced by drugs as being "high." In fact, drugs turn on the brain's reward system with a potency that natural rewards can rarely match. Because of this, "drugs actually teach people to use more drugs" (Friedman & Rusche, 1999, p. 2).

Psychoactive drugs masquerade as neurotransmitters and interact with receptors and other components of the brain's synapses. "As such they interfere with normal synaptic transmission by introducing false messages or by changing the strength of real ones" (Friedman & Rusche, 1999, p. 51).

Repeated drug use also results in *tolerance,* meaning that after continued use, one needs more and more of the drug (or addictive behavior) to feel the same pleasurable effects. Not surprisingly, as drug tolerance develops, users tend to escalate their use to achieve their desired state. This increases the risk for physical and perhaps psychological dependency.

"The long-term abuse of drugs causes profound changes in the brain," notes Friedman and Rusche. "The behavior of addicts is strongly influenced by the maladaptive learning that takes place as addiction develops. As a result, recovering from drug addiction does not mean returning to a condition like the one that existed before drug abuse began. Instead, addicts must grow into a new level of personal awareness, with new patterns of behavior. That is one reason why the treatment of addiction is so difficult" (Friedman & Rusche, 1999, p. 63).

THE BRAIN AND ADDICTIVE BEHAVIORS

Until recently, researchers and clinicians limited the term *addiction* to chemical (alcohol and other drugs) dependence. But neuroadaptation, the technical term for the biological processes of *tolerance* and *withdrawal,* also occur when substance-free individuals become addicted to pathological gambling, pornography, forms of sexual excess, eating excesses, overwork, compulsive buying, and other compulsive excesses (Coombs, 2004).

New studies of the brain's reward system, using PET brain scan technology, dramatically show that drugs of addiction and behaviors that stimulate pleasure and elation (e.g., compulsive gambling) affect brain functions (Coombs, 2004). The human brain processes *all* positive rewards similarly, whether the reward comes from a chemical or a behavior such as gambling, shopping, sex, or work. Hence, those who become addicted do not necessarily crave a specific drug per se, but the rush of dopamine these drugs produce.

Remarkably, the term addiction was not included in the latest diagnostic manual of the American Psychiatric Association—the *Diagnostic and Statistical Manual of Mental Disorders*, text revision (*DSM-IV-TR*, 2000). Instead, *DSM-IV-TR* lists three forms of *chemical* abuse:

1. *Substance abuse disorders:* A maladaptive use of chemical substances leading to clinically significant outcomes or distress (recurrent legal problems and/or failure to perform at work, school, home, or physically hazardous behaviors, such as driving when impaired)
2. *Substance dependency disorders:* Loss of control over how much a substance is used once begun, manifested by seven symptoms: tolerance; withdrawal; using more than was intended; unsuccessful efforts to control use; a great deal of time spent obtaining and using the substance; important life activities given up or reduced in order to use the substance; and continued use despite knowing that it causes problems
3. *Substance induced disorders:* Manifesting the same symptoms as depression and/or other mental health disorder, which symptoms, the direct result of using the substance, will cease shortly after discontinuing the substance

Compulsive gambling, an addictive disorder that affects the pleasure center of the brain the same way as alcohol and other psychoactive drugs, is listed in *DSM-IV-TR* as an "impulse control disorder" and groups it with pyromania (fire setting), kleptomania (impulsion to steal), intermittent explosive disorder (failure to control aggression) and trichotillomania (constant pulling out of one's hair; *DSM-IV-TR*, 2000).

Yet, research on the brain's reward system indicates that, as far as the brain is concerned, "a reward is a reward, regardless of whether it comes from a chemical or an experience" (Holden, 2001, p. 980; Shaffer & Albanese, 2005, p. 6). For this reason, ". . . more and more people have been thinking that, contrary to earlier views, there is a commonality between substance addictions and other compulsions" (Alan I. Leshner, cited by Holden, 2001, p. 980).

Contemporary research shows that the neurobiology of nonchemical addictions approximates that of addiction to alcohol and other drugs. Some chemicals or excessive experiences activate brain reward systems directly and dramatically, notes addictionologist William McCown (2005, pp. 459–481). Essentially,

TABLE II.1   Commonalities between Pharmacological Addictions
and Gambling

Symptoms or Behavior	Alcohol and Other Drugs	Compulsive Gambling
Cravings	Yes	Yes
Denial of problem's severity or existence	Yes	Yes
Disruption of families	Yes	Yes
Effects on specific neurotransmitters	Yes	Unknown
High relapse rate	Yes	Yes
Loss of control	Yes	Yes
Lying to support use or activity	Yes	Yes
Preoccupation with use or activity	Yes	Yes
Progressive disorder	Yes	Yes
Tolerance developed	Yes	Yes
Used as a means of escaping problems	Yes	Yes
Withdrawal symptoms common	Yes	

Source: Best Possible Odds: Contemporary Treatment Strategies for Gambling Disorders (p. 17), by W. McCown and L. Chamberlain, 2000, New York: Wiley.

substances and behaviors provide too much reward for an individual's neurobiology to handle. Ingestion of certain chemicals is accompanied by massive mood elevations and other affective changes. These may lead to a reduction in other activities previously considered rewarding. Similarly, the ability of excessive behaviors to activate brain reward mechanisms alters normal functioning. This also results in a potentially addictive state (McCown, 2005).

Some traditionalists may argue that nonchemical addictions are really obsessive-compulsive disorders (OCD). But, as McCown (2005) points out, "There are no rewards associated with OCD behaviors except for the overwhelming reduction in anxiety. By contrast, addictions are initially extremely pleasant experiences. OCD, which plagues people with intrusive, unwanted thoughts or obsessions, is inherently distasteful" (McCown, 2005, pp. 468–469).

When comparing the characteristics of alcohol and other psychoactive drugs with compulsive gambling, Chamberlain (2004, p. 133) notes little difference (see Table II.1).

Addictions occur in constellations (Carnes, Murray, & Charpentier, 2004). That is, people addicted to one substance are often addicted to other substances and behaviors, as they note in these summaries of research studies:

- "For the contemporary drug addict, multiple drug use and addiction that includes alcohol, is the rule. The monodrug user and addict is a vanishing species in American culture" (N. S. Miller & Gold, 1990, p. 597).
- "As many as 84% of cocaine addicts, 37% of cannabis addicts, 75% of amphetamine addicts, and 50% of opiate addicts were also alcoholic. Other studies have shown that 80% to 90% of cocaine addicts, 50% to 75% of opiate addicts, and 50% of benzodiazepine/sedative-hypnotic addicts were alcoholics" (N. S. Miller & Gold, 1993, p. 122).

- "... clinical studies suggest a high comorbidity between eating and alcohol use disorders ..." (Stewart, Angelopoulos, Baker, & Boland, 2000, p. 77).
- "... Lesieur and Blume (1993) noted that 47% to 52% of pathological gamblers also exhibit symptoms of abuse or dependency for alcohol or other drugs" (Winters, Bengston, Dorr, & Stinchfield, 1998, p. 186).
- "The alcoholic under the age of 30 is addicted to at least one other drug-most commonly cannabis, followed by cocaine, and then benzodiazepines" (Sweeting & Weinberg, 2000, p. 22).
- "Therapists working with individuals abusing alcohol, tobacco, and other drugs should be aware of the comorbidity of gambling in this population" (Sweeting & Weinberg, 2000, p. 46).
- "Similarly, in female alcoholics, comorbid eating disorder rates far exceed prevalence estimates for eating disorders in the general female population" (Stewart et al., 2000, p. 77).
- "The results of our co-twin control analyses indicated that early initiation of cannabis use was associated with significantly increased risks for other drug use and abuse/dependence and were consistent with early cannabis use having a causal role as a risk factor for other drug use and for any drug use or dependence" (Sweeting & Weinberg, 2000, p. 431).
- "... identification of multiple drug addiction is critical in the diagnosis and treatment of today's alcoholics and drug addicts. Unless contemporary treatment methods are adapted to fit changing patient characteristics, attempts at rehabilitation may be futile" (N. S. Miller & Gold, 1990, p. 596).

ADDICTIVE INTERACTION DISORDER

Coining the diagnostic label, "Addictive Interaction Disorder," Carnes et al. (2004) define 11 ways that types of addiction impact one another:

1. *Cross tolerance:* A simultaneous increase in addictive behavior in two or more addictions or a transfer of a high level of addictive activity to a new addiction with little or no developmental sequence;
2. *Withdrawal mediation:* One addiction moderates, provides relief from, or prevents physical withdrawal symptoms from another;
3. *Replacement:* One addiction replaces another with a majority of the emotional and behavioral features of the first;
4. *Alternating addiction cycles:* Addictions cycle back and forth in a patterned systemic way;
5. *Masking:* An addict uses one addiction to cover up for another, perhaps more problematic, addiction;
6. *Ritualizing:* Addictive rituals or behavior of one addiction serves as a ritual pattern to engage another addictive behavior;
7. *Intensification:* One addiction is used to accelerate, augment, or refine the effects of another addiction through simultaneous use;

8. *Numbing:* An addiction is used to medicate (soothe) shame or pain caused by another addiction or addictive bingeing;
9. *Disinhibiting:* One addiction is used frequently to chronically to lower inhibitions for other forms of addictive acting out;
10. *Combining:* Addictive behaviors are used to achieve certain effects that can only be achieved in combination; and
11. *Inhibiting:* One addiction is used to substitute or deter the use of another addiction that is thought to be more destructive or socially unacceptable.

Carnes et al. (2004) suggest that diagnostic codes should be reorganized to reflect this reality.

Additional Resources

For a review of the most current research and thinking on various addictive disorders, see Coombs, R. H. (Ed.). (2004). *Handbook on addictive disorders: A practical guide to diagnosis and treatment.* Hoboken, NJ: Wiley.

For additional information on the Dopamine Reward System, see *The brain's drug reward system* (1996, September/October). National Institute on Drug Abuse Notes. *Addictions: Neurological/Biochemical aspects.* Available from www.aizan.net /families/npsy_substance_abuse.htm.

Also see *The brain & the actions of cocaine, opiates, and marijuana* at www.udel .edu/skeen/BB/Hpages/Reward%20&%20Addiction2/actions.html.

DRUG-USE STAGES

Drug use can be viewed as a series of developmental stages. Although conceived differently by various experts (Kandel, 2002; Wallen, 1993), we propose these stages: initiation, escalation, maintenance, discontinuation (sometimes including relapse), and recovery (Coombs, Fry, & Lewis, 1976). Although most clients evolve sequentially from one stage to another, others do not. Some relapse many times, whereas others bypass relapse altogether.

INITIATION

Drug experimentation typically begins during adolescence, in social contexts during middle or high school. Usually offered by acquaintances as gestures of friendship, teens rarely try drugs alone. Alcohol, the first psychoactive drug for most initiates, is often provided in homes by parents, family, or friends as a social gesture.

ESCALATION

When recalling the course of their addiction, chemically dependent clients typically view their drug initiation, not as a single point in time, but a period when they used drugs occasionally. During escalation, a time of increasing preoccupation with psychoactive substances and more frequent socializing with other users, intoxication is thought of as normal and fun—a healthy form of recreation. In this stage, the variety of substances used increases and users typically feel little or no concern about how these drugs might impair their health or future.

MAINTENANCE

Full addiction can occur at any age, and when it does, all other life activities become secondary to obtaining and using drugs. The social fabric of life unravels when using becomes a daily devotion, an obsession.

At the escalation stage, most friends also use drugs, but functional ties are maintained with nonusers; a survival consciousness has not yet developed. In contrast, drug using is no longer just "a lot of fun"; at this stage, it is a necessity.

During the initiation and escalation stages, users take drugs primarily for the social and psychological rewards they offer—that is, to feel euphoric. But, as these highs become more and more difficult to achieve, the quest becomes just to feel normal, to manage personal feelings with various chemicals. As this quest becomes more difficult, life turns into a struggle for survival. For nonaddicted people, survival connotes food, shelter, and clothing; but for the addict, survival means obtaining drugs first—a constant preoccupation—then everything else.

Early in their addictions, most clients manage their drug effects successfully, mixing this with that to achieve the desired mental and psychological effect—to be "happily stoned." But as it becomes more and more difficult to achieve these desired feelings despite their best efforts, physical and psychological health deteriorates, supportive social networks breakdown, and economic resources dwindle.

DISCONTINUATION AND RELAPSE

How long or why a person stops using mood-altering chemicals varies. Some stop abruptly due to drug overdoses, death, illness, or family pressure. Others stop temporarily because of incarceration or forced participation in a court-mandated treatment program. The downward spiral of loss and adversity—"hitting bottom"—motivates some to seek help, or another person may help them see that drugs are not the *solution* for their problems (the typical misperception), but the *problem*. Despite strong denial, bitter experiences bring them face-to-face with their increasingly desperate circumstances.

Some people break free of addictions on their own. "Several surveys by the Institute for Health and Aging (University of California) show that drinking problems with blackouts almost always disappear before middle age, without medical assistance, as do most teenage drug addictions" (Peele, 1989, p. 66). Over two-thirds of those who abuse alcohol quit on their own, with no help. Many addicts, however, require considerable assistance from caring others.

RECOVERY

Recovery, the cessation of all psychoactive substances, occurs when addicted clients acknowledge that the mood-altering substance is not their support, as they had supposed, but the cause of their increasing problems. Though betrayed by their chemical elixir, they grieve the loss of their drug lifestyle. Gradually, one small step at a time, they replace this presumed "best friend" with more healthy activities and networks at home, school, work, church/synagogue/mosque, and in recreational settings.

Regaining physical health is much easier than recovering lost emotional growth because, to develop emotionally, they must return to the time when they first began using drugs to cope with life's problems and begin solving problems. Though middle-aged, emotionally they may be adolescents—the point at which they first started using mood-altering substances and stopped struggling with emotional problems. Even worse, their emotional skills have likely atrophied.

Fortunately, struggling with life's problems without relying on psychoactive chemicals to block out uncomfortable feelings—"clawing oneself back to mental health"—brings accelerated emotional growth. This transition, though initially terrifying, can be exhilarating.

Recovering addicts go through three fairly predictable stages during their recoveries, each with its own challenges and difficulties.

EARLY STAGE RECOVERY

Spanning the first 6 months of sobriety, the risk of relapse is highest during this time. Not only is mental clarity impaired, so is physical health. Clients are beginning to develop new (nonchemical) ways of dealing with daily stressors at work and in personal relationships by building sober support networks, such as those offered by Alcoholics Anonymous or other support groups. In this phase, they also must experience the accompanying mood swings and depression that can derail treatment.

MIDDLE STAGE RECOVERY

During this time, usually the second 6 months of sobriety, individuals grapple with the physical, social, and psychological adjustments of sobriety. Among other profound emotions, they typically go through a grieving process, mourning for the loss of a best friend and the good times that they "enjoyed" while using drugs. At this stage, individuals begin to reestablish their ability to feel and to deal with their emotions without using drugs.

LATE STAGE RECOVERY

In this stage of recovery, beginning after roughly a year of sobriety, individuals begin to gain confidence in their new support systems and the psychosocial and spiritual tools they have learned in treatment and recovery groups. A time of increasing stability and comfort with their new life, individuals continue to advance in forming healthy support networks and activities (or reestablishing old ones, such as with family members) to replace drug-related ones.

Additional Resources

Coombs, R. H., Fry, L. J., & Lewis, P. G. (Eds). (1976). *Socialization in drug abuse.* Cambridge, MA: Schenkman. This edited book contains classical articles about the preconditions for using drugs, developmental stages in drug careers, and the implications for society.

Coombs, R. H., & Coombs, K. (1988). Development stages in drug use: Changing family involvements. In R. H. Coombs (Ed.), *The family context of adolescent drug use.* New York: Haworth Press. Elaborates on the five developmental stages of drug involvement—initiation, escalation, maintenance, discontinuation, and renewal—and the family circumstances that typically exist at each stage.

Coombs, R. H. (1997). *Drug-impaired professionals* (chap. 5). Cambridge, MA: Harvard University Press. "Developmental Stages" discusses the developmental stages experienced by addicted professionals.

Kandel, D. B. (Ed.). (2002). *Stages and pathways of drug involvement: Examining the gateway hypothesis.* Boston: Cambridge University Press. See chapter 4 (by Kandel & Yamaguchi) for the stages of drug involvement in the U.S. population.

LEVELS OF DRUG USE

At any particular time, individuals may fit any one of these levels of drug involvement: (1) abstainers, (2) social users, (3) drug abusers, (4) addicts who are physically dependent (but not psychologically dependent), and (5) addicts who are both physically and psychological dependent.

These categories are *ideal types* (useful for classification); people rarely fit neatly into a single category. A person categorized as an abstainer may, on rare occasions, drink alcohol. Many individuals shift during their lifetime from one category to another. In addition, psychological dependence varies by degree.

Note that these are *not drug stages*, but drug-related *conditions*; individuals do not necessarily move predictably from one condition to another; a person may swing from one extreme to another. For example, a person who experiments with crack cocaine for the first time can go from being an abstainer to full psychological dependence, while an addicted individual (Type 5) may stop using completely.

TYPE 1—ABSTAINERS

Roughly one-third of all Americans totally abstain from using psychoactive substances. Some consciously choose abstinence as a way of life for religious (e.g., Mormons and Seventh-day Adventists) or other reasons. Still others abstain after devastating experiences from a drinking and drugging lifestyle (e.g., participants in Alcoholics Anonymous and other Twelve-Step support groups).

Additional Resources

See the detailed report, "Who Are the Abstainers?" at the International Center for Alcohol Policy (ICAP Report 8, June 2000). Available from www.icap.org/pdf /report8.pdf.

TYPE 2—SOCIAL USERS

Constituting the majority of people, social users limit their intake of alcohol and other psychoactive drugs to social gatherings where using substances is peripheral, rather than the main purpose or attraction. Alcohol and other mood-altering substances are seen simply as ways to enhance the pleasure of the gathering while accomplishing other social goals.

Although those at Stage 5 (i.e., people that are psychologically as well as physically dependent on substances) often regard themselves as social drinkers/ users, they cannot, like social users, ingest their drug-of-choice intermittently, go long periods without it, or quit at any time. By contrast, social users may enjoy social events that offer psychoactive substances as part of the fare but are not preoccupied with drugs or getting high. Although clients may use alcohol or even marijuana regularly, they are in control of their consumption and experience few, if any, significant adverse consequences at home, work, in social settings or with law enforcement personnel.

There is still considerable debate whether people can experiment with certain mind-altering drugs (e.g., marijuana, methamphetamine, crack, or heroin) without escalating into misuse (Type 3) or dependency (Types 4 and 5). With some drugs, like alcohol, most people seem to be able to continue indefinitely as social users (Type 2); research shows only about 20% appear to develop a more dependent relationship. However, a larger percentage of marijuana users (as many as 25%) escalate into dependency if they regularly use over an extended time.

Nearly 85% of those who use cocaine, heroin, and methamphetamine over the long term become dependent.

Additional Resources

For a detailed report about social networks, drug abuse, and HIV transmission, see NIDA Research Monograph (No. 151; printed in 1995), *Social networks, drug abuse, and HIV transmission*. Available from www.drugabuse.gov /pdf/monographs/download151.html.

TYPE 3—DRUG ABUSERS

Like social users (Type 2), *drug abusers* use psychoactive drugs typically in social settings, but unlike them, their consumption is heavier, and intoxication is usually the purpose of their get-togethers. Unlike addicts (Types 4 and 5), their use is sporadic, usually on weekends. Partying—"getting plastered," or "smashed" with others who enjoy such activities is socially rewarding and a sign of acceptance. In some circles, especially among college students, it is considered "cool" to binge (i.e., consume more than five servings of beer or five glasses of wine at a single setting).

Depending on the drug, tolerance starts to develop—meaning it takes more to produce the desired euphoric effect. Drug abusers may increase their frequency, duration, and intensity of use and move to the next level of addiction.

Aside from social rewards, people have the following motivators to misuse psychoactive drugs:

- A coping strategy to avoid unwanted feelings
- A way to change mood or personality (e.g., be more up and bubbly)
- A way to escape unwanted obligations at home, work, or school (e.g., intoxication and hangovers provide an excuse to avoid undesirable responsibilities)
- A way to enhance social standing with other drug-using peers, to be "cool," hip, avant-garde
- Annoyance at being confronted about the use of alcohol and/or other drugs
- A way to enhance performance (e.g., using stimulants to prepare for exams by studying later into the night, using downers to play mellow music on one's instrument, or to feel relaxed in stressful situations)

Additional Resources

For more information, visit Gulf Coast Recovery. Available from www.drug -information.us/drug-abuse.htm.

TYPE 4—PHYSICALLY BUT NOT PSYCHOLOGICALLY DEPENDENT USERS

Clients inadvertently addicted to drugs prescribed by their doctor or dentist illustrate this type. Although such individuals may eventually come to despise these prescribed drugs—the opposite of psychological dependence—their bodies have gradually developed a tolerance to these substances (i.e., they have developed a physical dependence). Therefore, they must endure the sometimes painful experience of detoxifying, 3 to 5 days for relatively short-acting drugs (e.g., alcohol, heroin, and cocaine) but 2 weeks or longer for long-acting drugs (e.g., benzodiazepines like Valium or Zanax, or methadone).

Withdrawal symptoms may include insomnia, anxiety, tremors, and increased heart, pulse, respiratory rates, and body temperature. Withdrawal from *opiates* (e.g., heroin or prescription painkillers) includes pain, coughing, runny nose, and diarrhea. Withdrawal from *stimulants* (e.g., amphetamines, cocaine, and prescription diet drugs) involves depression, sleepiness, and increased appetite. These symptoms are sometimes preceded by marked agitation, hallucinations, and explosive violence. Central nervous symptom hyperexcitability persists long after the removal of the drug.

Situational addicts, such as some Vietnam veterans, offer another example of Type 4 addicts. Although numerous enlisted men became addicted to narcotics while serving in Southeast Asia, many stopped without aid on their return to the United States. They returned to normal living by reconnecting with schools, families, churches, and other social support structures that provided the psychological nourishment psychoactive drugs only simulate. After detoxifying, a large percentage walked away from drugs, or used them only intermittently for recreation. Surprisingly, full recovery did not require abstinence. Although nearly half of Vietnam veterans who became addicted tried narcotics again after their return, only 6% became readdicted.

Additional Resources

For additional information, see Robins, L. N. (1993). Vietnam veterans' rapid recovery from heroin addiction: A fluke or normal expectation? *Addiction, 88*(8), 1041–1054; and visit Goode, E. (1999). *Drugs in American society* (5th ed., chap. 1). New York: McGraw-Hill. Available from www.umsl.edu/~rkeel/180/addict.html.

TYPE 5—PHYSICALLY AND
PSYCHOLOGICALLY DEPENDENT USERS

Unlike Vietnam veterans, individuals in this condition cannot simply walk away from their addictions and resume a normal life. They depend on psychoactive drugs to cope with life. When the reward-pain ratio shifts and unpleasant and disruptive events accelerate, rather than discontinuing the drugs as Type 4 users do, they increase the dosage, switch to other drugs, or try to titrate various substances. Instead of blaming drugs for their spiraling decline, they regard them as the solution and often mourn their loss just as one mourns the death of a loved one.

Predictably, however, this best friend always betrays the user, who spends more and more time and effort trying to simply feel normal and survive. Even as users' lives deteriorate, they continue to medicate their feelings. In short, they are psychologically as well as physically hooked.

Research suggests the Type 5 addict who quits can seldom be a "social user" (Type 2) again. The AA expression captures this reality: "One cannot go back to being a cucumber after being pickled." Although Type 5 users may try to stop and may even succeed, the vast majority cannot sustain their abstinence without the support of others.

A period of sobriety, no matter how long, confers no protection from a relapse. Once begun, Type 5 addicts cannot restrain themselves. Unlike Types 2, 3, and 4 users, the Type 5 addict has a permanent, chronic chemical dependence—both physically and psychologically. Untreated, it eventually becomes debilitating and often fatal.

Additional Resources

Much of this section was adapted from Coombs, R. H. (1997). *Drug-impaired professionals: How physicians, dentists, pharmacists, nurses, attorneys, and airline pilots get into and out of addiction* (pp. 39–40). Boston: Harvard University Press.

For further information, visit the Family Practice Notebook found at www.fpnotebook.com/PSY26.htm.

STAGES OF BEHAVIORAL CHANGE

Behavioral change rests primarily with the motivation of the client, not the counselor. Since clients come in with varying degrees of motivation, the counselor should match this motivation with an effective treatment plan. This matching process is critical for achieving positive client change (Howatt, 2000).

The Trans-Theoretical Model—also called the Stages of Change Model (Prochaska, DiClemente, & Norcross, 1992) is a standard for determining a client's motivation for treatment. The six stages of change are (1) Precontemplation, (2) Contemplation, (3) Preparation, (4) Action, (5) Maintenance and Relapse Prevention, and (6) Termination. Success is defined as both a behavioral change and any movement toward change, such as a shift from one stage of change (readiness) to another. A powerful and effective strategy for assessing client motivation, this model helps the counselor match clients' treatment protocol with their level of motivation (Bishop, 2001).

STAGE 1—PRECONTEMPLATION

Clients do not perceive their actions as being problematic. DiClemente (1991) says clients are in this stage of change because of "the Four Rs"—reluctance, rebellion, resignation, and rationalization:

1. *Reluctant* precontemplators, through inertia or lack of knowledge, do not want to consider change. The real or potential impact of the problem is not yet apparent to them.
2. *Rebellious* precontemplators have a heavy investment in their behavior and in making their own decisions. They are resistant to being told what to do.
3. *Resigned* precontemplators have given up concerning the possibility of change and seem overwhelmed by the problem. Many have made numerous attempts to quit or control their addictions.
4. *Rationalizing* precontemplators have all the answers; they have plenty of reasons why their behavior is not a problem, or why a particular behavior is a problem for others but not for them.

The love and support of family and friends can help clients recognize the need to be concerned about self-defeating behaviors. A structured intervention led by an addiction counselor may facilitate this recognition. During treatment, professionals can use motivational interviewing to promote awareness.

STAGE 2—CONTEMPLATION

Clients become aware of the risks of present behavior(s), but still struggle with ambivalence. They may realize there is a problem, but feel that they can handle it. With the counselor's help; clients at this stage often make a risk-reward analysis. They consider the pros and cons of their behavior, together with the pros and cons of change. They may also review prior attempts to stop the problem behavior and evaluate the factors that contributed to past failures.

The addiction counselor continues to use motivational interviewing to overcome indecision (see Rossengren & Wagner, 2001, pp. 17–33). Reading or watching a movie on related topics may help clients rationally assess personal risk of continued behaviors. Listing the negatives and positives of current behavior can assist in raising consciousness.

STAGE 3—PREPARATION

Clients agree there is a problem but are not yet 100% committed to the recovery process. Although not fully motivated, ambivalence is no longer an insurmountable barrier to change. It is important that clients not stay in this stage for more than 30 days since they can slip back to Stage 2 (or even 1) again, and the process must begin anew. Most clients at this stage, however, appear ready and committed to action.

The addiction counselor's goal is to move clients toward the action stage as fast as possible, without irritatingly pushing them. Momentum in moving toward action can be achieved by having clients talk about their potential plans. Help clients develop a firm, detailed action plan.

STAGE 4—ACTION

Clients are now motivated to improve their lives by following a clearly defined action plan with goals leading to desired outcomes. A client who implements a good action plan begins to experience success, making adjustments along the way. Addiction-related losses begin to be restored, together with hope, self-confidence, and determination to not return to the problem behavior and/or substance. If clients have not done so already, they may enter an outpatient treatment program.

A manageable treatment plan with clear goals is essential. A recovery contract with specified goals and rewards for achieving milestones may be developed to systematically help the client stay motivated.

STAGE 5—MAINTENANCE AND RELAPSE PREVENTION

Clients in this stage have taken action and are now learning the necessary skills to avoid relapse. The longer the client stays on course, the less chance of relapse. Being free of the addictive disorder for 5 years significantly reduces the chance of relapse.

Ensure that the treatment plan is always being appropriately revised and updated with new core skills to support the client's ongoing treatment plan. Relapse often occurs when clients stop paying attention to the details that have kept them free from their particular problem behaviors.

STAGE 6—TERMINATION

Client have developed the core skills needed to move past their addiction and have developed new life habits. Subsequently, they are encouraged to proceed to other life goals.

Education and learning are important for the lifelong development of any person. It is recommended that addiction counselors assist clients to move forward by developing healthy activities in place of their former addiction. Planning ways to improve the overall quality of one's life is important.

Additional Resources

For additional background on this model, see Miller, W. R., & Tonigan, J. S. (1996). Assessing drinkers' motivation for change: The stages of change readiness and treatment eagerness scale (SOCRATES). *Psychology of Addictive Behaviors, 10*(2), 81–89; Prochaska, J. O. (2003). Enhancing motivation to change. In A. W. Graham, T. K. Schultz, M. F. Mayo-Smith, R. K. Ries, & B. B. Wilford (Eds.), *Principles of addiction medicine* (3rd ed.). Chevy Chase, MD: American Society of Addiction Medicine; and Prochaska, J. O., Redding, C. A., & Evers, K. E. (1997). The transtheoretical model and stages of change. In K. Glanz, F. M. Lewis, and B. K. Rimer (Eds.), *Health behavior and health education: Theory, research, and practice* (2nd ed.). San Francisco: Jossey-Bass.

PREVENTION TYPES AND PRINCIPLES

Two prevention models are currently used: (1) the traditional classification employed for decades by public health workers and (2) a more recent classification proposed by the Institute of Medicine.

THE TRADITIONAL CLASSIFICATION

This historical classification includes (1) primary prevention, (2) secondary prevention, and (3) tertiary prevention (Pransky, 1991).

PRIMARY PREVENTION

Implemented *before* a person begins using drugs, the intent is to prevent drug use completely, or at least delay consumption. Examples of primary prevention include educational seminars, reading materials, school instruction, marketing information, community awareness programs, help lines, changes in the laws and regulations to make drugs less easily available, and instruction in coping and life skills.

SECONDARY PREVENTION

Implemented *after* a person has *experimented* with drugs, the objective is to discourage escalation into more frequent or habitual use. Examples of secondary prevention include strengthening families, helping parents become aware of the signs and symptoms of substance abuse, medical staff intervention at first signs of drug use, harm reduction programs, and public education to increase awareness about caring for a drug-using person.

TERTIARY PREVENTION

Implemented *after* drug use has become a *problem*, the goal is to help the addicted person recover, or minimally, to reduce the harm resulting from drug use and to keep the addiction from worsening. Examples of tertiary prevention include educating the public about the long-term consequences of alcohol and drug addiction, home care programs for individuals who can no longer care for themselves because of damages incurred with heavy use, and educating addicted people about safe needle exchange techniques.

Additional Resources

See more on prevention by visiting the web site of the Division on Prevention, Public Health Service Office of Public Health and Science. Available from http://phs.os.dhhs.gov/ophs. See also Coombs, R. H. & Ziedonis, D. (Eds.). (1995).

Handbook on drug abuse prevention: A comprehensive strategy to prevent the abuse of alcohol and other drugs. Needham Heights, MA: Allyn & Bacon.

An outstanding prevention resource is provided at http://p2001.health.org /Ms03/PAM1SLID2.htm.

Also see the www.DrugsAlcohol.info web site for useful information on drug prevention, levels of prevention, and a list of references: www.drugsprevention.net /drugs/printpage.asp?d=G3.

THE INSTITUTE OF MEDICINE CLASSIFICATION

The Institute of Medicine (1989) proposed a new model of prevention types. Based on Gordon's (1987) operational classification of disease prevention, this new model has three parts—prevention, treatment, and maintenance. It subdivides the prevention category into three types: universal, selective, and indicated.

UNIVERSAL PREVENTION

Focusing on large populations (e.g., national, local community, school, or neighborhoods), these efforts seek to prevent or delay illicit drug use. An example is creating a prevention program for all students at a given school or school district.

SELECTIVE PREVENTION

The focus is on specific populations known to be at great risk for substance abuse, such as targeting children of drug users or poor school achievers.

INDICATED PREVENTION

These interventions are directed at those who have already experimented with drugs or who exhibit other risk-related behaviors. Examples include such well-documented programs as Project STAR and Adolescent Alcohol Prevention Trial. Other examples can be reviewed at National Institute on Drug Abuse, Prevention Research (n.d.). Available from www.nida.nih.gov/DrugPages/Prevention.html.

Additional Resources

For more information on the Institute of Medicine go to www.iom.edu.

See a detailed list of indicated prevention programs. Available from www.unf .edu/dept/fie/sdfs/program_inventory/list.html.

PREVENTION PRINCIPLES

Prevention programs typically focus on three elements: (1) The *person* (e.g., prior drug use, skills, physiological reactions, and perceptions), (2) the *situation* (e.g., peer influence, family influence, opportunity, and social norms), and (3) the *environment* (e.g., access, media impact, schools, and community policies, and financial factors). The last two—situation and environment—have proven the most effective target areas for designing addiction prevention programs (McCrady & Epstein, 1999).

Categories of risk factors include the following:

- *Community:* Access to drugs and firearms, community laws, and norms favorable toward drug use, crime, media portrayals of violence, transition and mobility, low neighborhood attachment and community disorganization, and extreme economic deprivation
- *Family:* Family history of problem behaviors, family management problems, family conflict, favorable parental attitude, and involvement in problem behaviors
- *School:* Early and persistent antisocial behavior, academic failure beginning in late elementary school, and lack of commitment to school
- *Individual/peer:* Alienation and rebelliousness, friends who engage in the problem behavior; favorable attitude toward the problem behavior; early initiation of the problem behavior and constitutional factors (Hogan Gabrielsen, Luna, & Grothaus, 2003, pp. 16–17)

Some headway is being made in understanding what constitutes effective prevention message presentation and content. A meta-analysis of 120 school-based preventive interventions for 5th- through 12th-grade students indicated that interactive programs change drug knowledge, attitudes, and behaviors, whereas noninteractive programs change only knowledge.

Prevention research has addressed how to encourage program participation, why programs are more or less effective, and how prevention interventions can have positive and negative effects (Gorski, 1989). For optimal success, program planners and implementers should include:

- Flexibility scheduling
- Reduction of initial time commitments; active involvement of both parents and peers
- Multiple positive rewards aligned to the target population, such as: free food coupons, refreshments, and child care (Spoth, Redmond, & Shin, 1998)

The multidisciplinary prevention research program (NIMH Prevention Research at www.drugabuse.gov/DrugPages/Prevention.html) of the National Institute on Drug Abuse (NIDA) released a set of prevention principles that enumerate what has been learned through 20 years of research. Here are a few examples:

- Prevention programs should *target all forms of drug use,* including tobacco, alcohol, marijuana, and inhalants.
- Prevention programs should *include skills to resist drugs when offered, strengthen personal commitments against drug use,* and *increase social competency.*
- Prevention programs should *include an instruction component for parents (or other caregivers) that reinforces what the children are learning,* such as facts about drugs and their harmful effects.

Additional Resources

For additional research findings about the impact of prevention, visit the NIDA web site, www.nida.nih.gov/DrugPages/Prevention.html, where you will learn facts such as, "For every $1 spent on drug use prevention, communities can save $4 to $5 in costs for drug abuse treatment and counseling."

See the Prevention web site of the Office of National Drug Control Policy (2004). Available from www.whitehousedrugpolicy.gov/prevent.

For a review of the current research on prevention programs and their effectiveness, see the web site of the *Research supporting alternatives to current drug prevention education for young people.* Available from www.drugpolicy.org/library /skager_drug_ed2003.cfm.

RELAPSE PREVENTION

Recovery, typically defined as abstinence from mood-altering substances, plus a full return to biopsychosocial functioning, involves six stages (Gorski & Kelley, 2002):

1. Abstaining from alcohol and other drugs
2. Separating from people, places, and things that promote the use of alcohol or drugs, and establishing a social network that supports recovery
3. Stopping self-defeating behaviors that prevent awareness of painful feelings and irrational thoughts
4. Learning how to manage feelings and emotions responsibly without resorting to compulsive behavior or the use of alcohol or drugs
5. Learning to change addictive thinking patterns that create painful feelings and self-defeating behaviors
6. Identifying and changing the mistaken core beliefs about oneself, others, and the world that promote irrational thinking

Relapse, the return to a familiar dysfunctional lifestyle, typically involves renewed dependence on chemical use, physical or emotional collapse, or suicide (Doweiko, 2002). The relapsing individual usually experiences progressively increasing distress leading to physical or emotional collapse.

Relapse management helps prevent a "slip" (one incident) from becoming a full-blown relapse (Curry & McBride, 1994). As many as half of those in recovery relapse within the first 3 months after becoming abstinent (Hunt, Barnett, & Branch, 1971).

Relapse episodes are usually preceded by observable warning signs. These include:

- Being in the presence of drugs or alcohol, drug or alcohol users, or places where chemicals are used or bought
- Painful feelings (sadness, loneliness, guilt, fear, anxiety, and especially anger)

- Positive feelings, a cause for celebration
- Boredom
- Getting high on any drug
- Physical pain
- Listening to drinking/drugging "war stories" and dwelling on getting high
- Suddenly having a lot of cash
- Using prescription drugs that produce a high even if used properly
- Complacency, believing there is no longer cause to worry (Support System Homes, www.drug-rehabilitation.com/relapse_signs.htm).

Relapse prevention involves helping recovering clients recognize warning signs of relapse (Annis & Davis, 1989). Clients are at greater risk when symptoms intensify and they do not have a prevention plan (Gorski & Kelley, 2002).

Additional Resources

For a wealth of information on Relapse Prevention, visit the web site at Narcotics and Alcohol Services for Addiction Recovery/Network International-Coalition. Available from www.nasarecovery.com/relapsepreventionkit.html.

Two popular relapse prevention models used today are (1) Marlatt and Gordon's Relapse Prevention Model (RP) and (2) Gorski's Center for Applied Sciences (CENAPS) Model.

MARLATT AND GORDON'S RELAPSE PREVENTION MODEL

Based on the observation that relapse is the most frequent outcome of any treatment for substance abuse, Alan Marlatt and Judith Gordon developed this relapse model rooted in social learning theory and cognitive psychology. Marlatt's earlier research asked (1978) clients to describe the situation(s) that precipitated their relapse. Marlatt and Gordon (1980) classified these high-risk situations into categories; the three named most frequently accounted for nearly three-fourths of the relapses: (1) negative emotional states, (2) social pressure, and (3) interpersonal conflict.

The RP model helps clients (1) anticipate and identify high-risk situations, (2) develop skills to effectively deal with those situations, and (3) confidently expect that using these skills will result in a positive outcome (Marlatt, 1983). The RP approach also helps clients minimize damage by reacting quickly and effectively, reframing it as a slip, an unfortunate but isolated incident rather than a confirmation of a deep inability to recover (Marlatt & George, 1984).

Additional Resources

For an outstanding overview and explanation of the RP model, see Marlatt, G. A., & Gordon, J. R. (Eds.). (1985). *Relapse prevention: A self-control strategy for the maintenance of behavior change.* New York: Guilford Press.

For a clear and concise review of *Relapse prevention therapy: A cognitive-behavioral approach* written by G. A. Parks & Marlatt, G. (2000), go to the National

Psychologist web site. Available from http://nationalpsychologist.com/articles/art_v9n5_3.htm.

GORSKI'S CENAPS RELAPSE MODEL

The Gorski relapse prevention model, grounded in cognitive-behavioral psychology, involves these six stages of recovery:

1. *Transition:* The individual recognizes problems but tries to surmount them by controlling his or her substance use.
2. *Stabilization:* The individual decides to refrain from substance use completely and recuperates over an extended length of time (6 to 18 months).
3. *Early recovery:* The individual becomes comfortable with being abstinent.
4. *Middle recovery:* The individual repairs past damage caused by his or her substance use and develops a balanced lifestyle.
5. *Late recovery:* The individual overcomes barriers to healthy living that stem from childhood experiences.
6. *Maintenance:* The individual recognizes a need for continued growth and for balanced living (Correctional Service of Canada, Relapse Techniques, n.d., para. 7).

This approach, deriving from Gorski's clinical work as a chemical dependency counselor, assumes that recovery will be punctuated by setbacks—"getting stuck on the road to recovery" (Gorski, 1989, p. 5). A restatement of the traditional 12-step (AA) program, aided by structured written exercises, this approach has a strong spiritual component (Correctional Service of Canada, Relapse Techniques, n.d., para. 10).

Additional Resources

To learn more about this relapse prevention model see Gorski, T., & Miller, M. (1982). *Counseling for relapse prevention.* Independence, MO: Independence Press.

For detailed information about Gorski's model and training visit his web site at www.cenaps.com.

PART III
Treatment Planning and Assessment Resources

Part III describes the resources available for treatment planning and diagnostic assessment. The first section, *Treatment Planning,* covers competencies and goals, screening and assessment, diagnostic summaries, treatment, client placement criteria, writing a treatment plan (includes a sample), and the levels of care.

The next section, *Assessment Resources,* provides an overview of basic resources available to diagnose a client. These include assessment of alcohol and other psychoactive drugs, instruments for other addictive disorders, mental health measurements, recovery assessments, and multiple measures resources.

The final section, *Dual Diagnosis,* covers psychiatric illness combined with addiction. It provides a brief description of the American Psychiatric Association's *Diagnostic and Statistical Manual of Mental Disorders* (*DSM-IV-TR*) and details the psychiatric diagnostic categories.

TREATMENT PLANNING

    Competencies and Goals
    Screening and Assessment
    Diagnostic Summary
    Treatment
    Client Placement Criteria
    Writing a Treatment Plan
    Sample Treatment Plan
    Levels of Care

ASSESSMENT RESOURCES

Alcohol Assessment Instruments
Other Drug Assessments
Nonchemical Addictions
Mental Health (Dual Diagnosis) Assessments
Recovery Potential Assessments
Multiple Measures Resources

DUAL DIAGNOSES: PSYCHIATRIC ILLNESS WITH ADDICTION

The *Diagnostic and Statistical Manual* (*DSM-IV-TR*)
Psychiatric Diagnostic Categories

TREATMENT PLANNING

A treatment plan involves a counselor and client developing a program that will outline the measurable, time sensitive, incremental steps toward achieving mutually agreed-on goals.

COMPETENCIES AND GOALS

The National Curriculum Committee of the Addiction Technology Transfer Centers (ATTC, 1998) suggests counselors be competent in the following areas:

- Explain assessment findings to the client and significant others involved in potential treatment.
- Provide the client and significant others with clarification and further information on potential treatment options as needed.
- Obtain and interpret all relevant assessment information.
- Examine treatment implications in collaboration with the client and significant others.
- Confirm the readiness of the client and significant others to participate in treatment.
- Prioritize the client's treatment needs in the order they will be addressed.
- Formulate mutually agreed on and measurable treatment outcome statements for each need.
- Identify appropriate strategies to achieve each outcome.
- Coordinate treatment activities with community resources.

- Develop with the client a mutually acceptable plan of action and method for monitoring and evaluating progress.
- Inform client of confidentiality rights and program procedures that safeguard them, as well as the exceptions imposed by regulations.
- Reassess the treatment plan at regular intervals and/or when indicated by changing circumstances.

SCREENING AND ASSESSMENT

In its publication, *Addiction Counseling Competencies: The Knowledge, Skills, and Attitudes of Professional Practice,* the ATTC's National Curriculum Committee (1998, pp. 29–34) outlined these components of thorough client screening:

- Establish rapport, including management of crisis situations and determination of the need for additional professional assistance.
- Gather data systematically from the client and other available collateral sources using screening instruments and other methods that are sensitive to age, developmental level, culture, and gender. At a minimum, data should include current and historic substance use; health, mental health, and substance-related treatment history; mental status; and current social, environmental, and/or economic constraints.
- Screen for psychoactive substance toxicity, intoxication, and withdrawal symptoms; aggression or danger to others; potential for self-inflicted harm or suicide; and coexisting mental health problems.
- Assist clients in identifying the impact of substance use on their current life problems and the effects of continued use.
- Determine clients' readiness for treatment and change as well as the needs of others involved in the current situation.
- Review the treatment options that are appropriate for clients' needs, characteristics, goals, and financial resources.
- Apply accepted criteria for diagnosis of substance use disorders in making treatment recommendations.
- Construct with clients and appropriate others an initial action plan based on clients' needs, preferences, and available resources.
- Based on initial action plan, take specific steps to initiate an admission or referral to ensure follow-through.

Completing a comprehensive assessment with the client's full understanding is essential. This must be a collaborative process—not one developed by the counselor and then given to the client; the counselor recognizes the client's rights and need to understand the assessment results. Counselors should welcome client ideas about how to transform the assessed problems into positive outcome goals (Lewis, 2005).

Counselor and client then work together to set treatment priorities. Potential high priorities may include:

Intake Summary Confidential

CLIENT'S NAME:

DATE SEEN FOR INTAKE:

IF MINOR, PARENT'S NAME:

LEGAL CUSTODY: **PHYSICAL CUSTODY:**

THERAPIST'S NAME: **FILE NUMBER:**

SUPERVISOR'S NAME:

I.   IDENTIFICATION AND BEHAVIORAL OBSERVATIONS:

II.   PRESENTING PROBLEM AND HISTORY OF PRESENTING PROBLEM:

III.   SOCIAL AND FAMILY HISTORY:

IV.   MENTAL HEALTH HISTORY OF CLIENT AND FAMILY:

V.   MEDICAL HISTORY OF CLIENT AND FAMILY:

VI.   MENTAL STATUS EXAMINATION:

VII.   DIAGNOSTIC IMPRESSION—DSM-IV:

Axis I: _____

Axis II: _____

Axis III: _____

Axis IV: _____

Axis V GAF: _____

FIGURE III.1   Condensed Intake Interview Template. *Source:* From *Treating Drug Problems,* by Arthur W. Blume, 2005, New York: Wiley. Reprinted with permission.

- Resolving legal problems
- Attaining financial stability
- Attaining positive and stable family relationships
- Setting and meeting career goals
- Improving social skills
- Improving life management skills (e.g., relaxation, stress management, problem solving and decision making, recognizing and dealing with emotions)
- Enhancing physical health and fitness
- Adapting more effectively to work or school
- Developing social-support systems
- Increasing involvement in recreation and other social pursuits
- Dealing with psychological issues such as depression or anxiety (Lewis, 2005)

Arthur W. Blume (2005) provides the condensed template of an Intake Summary Form in Figure III.1.

DIAGNOSTIC SUMMARY

Many states as well as the Joint Commission for the Accreditation of Healthcare Organizations (JCAHO) require that addiction treatment and mental health programs complete a Diagnostic Summary prior to developing a comprehensive treatment plan. The Diagnostic Summary organizes all the available assessment information into an integrated interpretation of the client's current status including personal history, strengths, and challenges. When properly written, the Diagnostic Summary should help secondary clinicians understand the client's needs and treatment strategy.

The Diagnostic Summary might include, but is not limited to the following areas: the client's mental status (possible mental disorders), risk assessments, treatment history, reasons for treatment, physical health and nutritional status, substance use history, obstacles to recovery, work history, intimate relations and sexuality, beliefs and values, financial and educational history, military experience, legal problems, hobbies, personal assets and liability, special issues, and readiness to learn.

The industry standard for clinical diagnosis is the *Diagnostic and Statistical Manual of Mental Disorders* (*DSM-IV-TR*, 2000), published by the American Psychiatric Association. According to the *DSM-IV-TR*, severity of the client's condition can be determined by the following distinctions:

- *Mild:* Few, if any, symptoms in excess of those required to make the diagnosis, and the symptoms result in no more than mild impairment in occupational functioning or in usual social activities or relationships with others
- *Moderate:* Symptoms or functional impairment between "mild" and "severe"
- *Severe:* Many symptoms in excess of those required to make the diagnosis, and the symptoms markedly interfere with occupational functioning or with usual social activities or relationships with others

- *Early full remission:* For at least 1 month but less than 12 months, no diagnostic criteria have been met
- *Early partial remission:* For at least 1 month but less than 12 months, some, but not all, diagnostic criteria have been met
- *Sustained full remission:* No diagnostic criteria met for a year or more
- *Sustained partial remission:* Full criteria for dependence not met for 1-plus years, but one or more criteria are met
- *On agonist therapy:* Using a prescribed medication, like Antabuse, to avoid substance use
- *In a controlled environment:* For instance, a jail or hospital (American Psychiatric Association, 2000, pp. 196–197)

TREATMENT

Treatment is, according to the ATTC "a collaborative process through which the counselor and client develop desired treatment outcomes and identify the strategies for achieving them. At a minimum, the treatment plan identifies the abused substance(s) and related disorders, client motivation, and issues related to treatment progress, including relationships with family and significant others, employment, education, spirituality, health concerns, and legal needs" (1998, p. 39).

Once goals are set, the most promising counseling methods are specified. Here are the counseling methods most frequently used with addicted clients:

- Behavioral self-control training—teaching clients the techniques they need to monitor and change their own behaviors
- Contingency management—identifying and manipulating environmental contingencies that reward or punish the substance use behaviors
- Relaxation, assertion, and social skills training
- Couple and family therapy
- Career counseling
- Cognitive restructuring—helping clients alter their appraisals of self and environment
- Assistance with problem solving and decision making
- Aversive conditioning—coupling substance use with a real or imagined unpleasant experience
- Stress management training
- Group counseling
- Lifestyle and recreational planning
- Provision of information about the effects of psychoactive drugs and referral to such self-help organizations as Alcoholics Anonymous and Narcotics Anonymous (Lewis, Dana, & Blevins, 2002, p. 11)

CLIENT PLACEMENT CRITERIA

The American Society of Addiction Medicine's handbook (1991) *Patient Placement Criteria for the Treatment of Psychoactive Substance Use Disorders* (www.asam.org) indicates that all clients should be constantly assessed on the following dimensions:

- Acute intoxication and/or withdrawal complications
  - What risk is associated with the client's current level of intoxication?
  - Is there significant risk of severe withdrawal symptoms, based on the client's previous withdrawal history, amount, frequency, and recency of discontinuation of chemical use?
  - Is the client currently in withdrawal? To measure withdrawal, use the Clinical Institute Withdrawal Assessment of Alcohol Scale (CIWA).
  - Does the client have the support necessary to assist in ambulatory detoxification, if medically safe?
- Biomedical conditions and complications
  - Are there current physical illnesses, other than withdrawal, that may need to be addressed, or that may complicate treatment?
  - Are there chronic conditions that may affect treatment?
- Emotional/psychological/behavioral conditions and complications
  - Are there current psychiatric illnesses or psychological, emotional, or behavioral problems that need treatment or may complicate treatment?
  - Are there chronic psychiatric problems that affect treatment?
- Treatment acceptance/resistance
  - Is the client objecting to treatment?
  - Does the client feel coerced into coming to treatment?
  - Does the client appear to be complying with treatment only to avoid a negative consequence, or does he appear to be self-motivated?
- Relapse/continued use potential
  - Is the client in immediate danger of continued use?
  - Does the client have any recognition of, understanding of, or skills with which he or she can cope with addiction problems to prevent continued use?
  - What problems will potentially continue to distress the client if not successfully engaged in treatment at this time?
  - How aware is the client of relapse triggers, ways to cope with cravings, and skills to control impulses to use?
- Recovery/living environment
  - Do any dangerous family members, significant others, living situations, or school/work situations pose a threat to treatment success?
  - Does the client have supportive friendships, financial resources, educational or vocational resources that can increase the likelihood of treatment success?
  - Are there legal, vocational, social service agencies, or criminal justice mandates that may enhance the client's motivation for treatment?

WRITING A TREATMENT PLAN

Counselors employed in addiction treatment settings will likely have an official treatment plan form used in their specific organization. In general, these forms include:

- Demographic information about the client
- Diagnosis (*DSM-IV-TR*)
- Brief history
- Case formulation
- Short-term and long-term goals including interventions, time frame, measurement and follow-up methods

Perkinson and Jongsma (2001) suggest the following treatment plan elements:

- *Problem summary:* Write a short version of the diagnostic summary, a snapshot of the treatment trajectory. This executive summary defines the goals and tools to be used in the process.
- *Primary, secondary, and tertiary problem list:* Throughout the accumulation of assessment information, both counselor and client list present problems and update regularly;
- *Selection of primary, secondary, and tertiary goals:* Prioritize the problem list to target the most important issues to deal with first;
- *Objectives:* Identify specific, time-sensitive, and measurable steps to be taken to achieve each goal; identify target dates for achieving each objective and specify the types and frequencies of services to be utilized in achieving each objective;
- *Therapeutic interventions:* List the therapeutic tools, matched with client needs, to achieve treatment goals. [See Section III F, Addiction Recovery Tools]. It is important, of course, to track and monitor progress by keeping written records [see III K, Record Keeping Forms].

SAMPLE TREATMENT PLAN

Judith Lewis (2005, p. 376) offers this example of treatment plan goals:

- *Desired outcome:* Attain abstinence from alcohol.
  - Monitor alcohol use and cravings for alcohol.
  - Identify situations that are usually associated with drinking (e.g., at home alone at night).
  - Identify ways to avoid or cope with these high-risk situations.
  - Participate in training sessions to learn the skills for successful coping.
  - Practice new ways of thinking about self and environment.
  - Learn relaxation techniques to cope with anxiety and insomnia.
- *Desired outcome:* Increase social contacts.
  - Attend an Alcoholics Anonymous meeting and identify a potential sponsor.
  - Participate in social skills training sessions.
  - Identify and follow through on at least one evening activity, in addition to Alcoholics Anonymous (AA), that involves social contact with other people.
- *Desired outcome:* Reconcile with spouse.
  - Contract for a period of abstinence.

- Participate in couple communication training.
- Invite spouse to open AA meeting.
- Invite spouse to social evening activity.
- *Desired outcome:* Initiate career planning.
  - Improve work habits in current position.
  - Participate in career assessment at local community college.
  - Analyze the pros and cons of career change.
  - Generate ideas for long-term career goals.
  - Avoid immediate change.

Arthur W. Blume (2005) offers a condensed template for treatment planning (Figure III.2 on page 72) and also a sample planner (Figure III.3 on page 73) for structuring a client's time.

LEVELS OF CARE

The American Society of Addiction (www.health.org/govpubs/bkd157/10l.aspx pp. 19) indicates six levels of care that every addicted client fits into at one time or another.

LEVEL 0.5: EARLY INTERVENTIONS

An organized service delivered in a wide variety of settings, early intervention is designed to explore and address problems or risk factors related to substance use so the individual recognizes the harmful consequences of inappropriate substance use. These clients do not meet the diagnostic criteria of either chemical abuse or chemical dependency, but have significant problems with substances.

The remaining treatment levels include clients who meet the criteria for psychoactive substance abuse or dependency.

LEVEL 1: OUTPATIENT TREATMENT

Outpatient treatment takes place in a nonresidential facility or office. The client comes in for individual counseling or group therapy sessions, usually for fewer than 9 hours per week.

LEVEL II: INTENSIVE OUTPATIENT/PARTIAL HOSPITALIZATION

- *Level II.1: Intensive outpatient treatment:* This program is a structured day or evening program with 9 or more hours of programming per week. These programs can refer clients for their medical, psychological, or pharmacological needs.
- *Level II.5: Partial hospitalization:* Partial hospitalization generally includes 20 or more hours of intense participation per week. These programs have ready access to psychiatric, medical, and laboratory services.

A Condensed Template for a Treatment Plan

MASTER TREATMENT PLAN:

TARGETED PROBLEMS:	GOALS:	PLAN:

Treatment Review Date:	Targeted Problems:	Progress and Changes in Plan:

SIGNATURE OF CLIENT: _____   **DATE:** _____

SIGNATURE OF THERAPIST: _____   **DATE:** _____

FIGURE III.2   A Condensed Template for a Treatment Plan. *Source:* From *Treating Drug Problems*, by Arthur W. Blume, 2005, New York: Wiley. Reprinted with permission.

A Sample Planner for Structuring a Client's Times

Day of the week: _____:

Hour of the day:	Activity planned	How will you get to this activity	Why is this activity important to you?
6 am			
7 am			
8 am			
9 am			
10 am			
11 am			
12 pm			
1 pm			
2 pm			
3 pm			
4 pm			
5 pm			
6 pm			
7 pm			
8 pm			
9 pm			
10 pm			

Activities I can do if I get stressed or bored that will help me feel better:

FIGURE III.3   A Sample Planner for Structuring a Client's Times. *Source:* From *Treating Drug Problems,* by Arthur W. Blume, 2005, New York: Wiley. Reprinted with permission.

Level III: Residential/Inpatient Services

- *Level III.1: Clinically managed, low-intensity residential services.* This is a halfway house.
- *Level III.3: Clinically managed, medium-intensity residential services.* This is an extended care program oriented around long-term management.
- *Level III.5: Clinically managed, high-intensity residential services.* This is a therapeutic community designed to maintain recovery.
- *Level III.7: Medically monitored intensive in-client treatment.* This is a residential facility that provides 24-hour, daily structured treatment. This program is monitored by a physician and can manage the psychiatric, physical, and pharmacological needs of clients.

Level IV: Medically Managed Intensive Inpatient Treatment

This facility, a 24-hour program, has the resources of a hospital with physicians providing daily medical management.

Additional Resources

The ASAM levels are also discussed in "Definitions of Substance Abuse and Mental Health Services" (Appendix C). Available from www.treatment.org/taps /tap22/appc.htm.

A wealth of information about treatment planning is provided in the *Addiction counseling competencies: The knowledge, skills, and attitudes of professional practice* (pp. 39–45), by the ATTC National Curriculum Committee (1998).

For an excellent overview of treatment planning, see Lewis, J. A. (2005). Assessment, diagnosis and treatment planning. In R. H. Coombs (Ed.), *Addiction counseling review: Preparing for comprehensive, certification and licensing exams.* Mahwah, NJ: Erlbaum; Seligman, L. (1996). *Diagnosis and treatment planning in counseling.* New York: Plenum Press; Seligman, L. (1998). *Selecting effective treatments.* San Francisco: Jossey-Bass; Sperry, L. (2003). *Handbook of diagnosis and treatment of the* DSM-IV-TR *personality disorders* (rev. ed.). New York: Brunner/Routlege; and Center for Substance Abuse Treatment. (2000). "Changing the Conversation: Improving Substance Abuse Treatment." In *The National Treatment Plan Initiative* (Vol. I). Rockville, MD: U.S. Department of Health and Human Services.

Perkinson, R. R., & Jongsma, A. E. (2001). *The addiction treatment planner* (2nd ed.). New York: Wiley; provides an excellent resource for treatment planning in meeting the requirements of HMOs, managed care companies, third-party payers, and state and federal review agencies.

Thera*Scribe*®'s Version 4.0. (New York: Wiley) is an outstanding computer program for developing treatment plans with high efficacy. It is detailed and meets all the preceding requirements of HMOs. Available from www.wiley.com/legacy /products/subject/psychology/therascribe.

For information on the Joint Commission for the Accreditation of Healthcare Organizations see JCAHO, see www.jcaho.org.

ASSESSMENT RESOURCES

We use the words *test, measures,* and *assessments* interchangeably when describing assessment tests. For each test, we provide a brief overview and additional source material. Reliability and validity, the determinants of clinical efficacy, are also discussed. For a test to be considered *reliable,* it should reach a statistical value— called a *consistency reliability coefficient*—of .70 or above (Domino, 2000, p. 45).

Validity (i.e., a test measures what it purports to measure) has no statistical standard. Instead, it is classified in three categories:

1. *Construct validity:* The degree to which the test measures the hypothetical trait it purports to measure;
2. *Content validity:* The degree that the test adequately samples the field for information, knowledge, or skill that it purports to measure; and
3. *Criterion validity:* The correlation between the predictor(s) and the criterion.

The following assessments, a cross section of the most commonly used, are organized into six categories and alphabetized within each: (1) Alcohol Assessment, (2) Other Drug Assessment, (3) Nonchemical Addictions, (4) Mental Health (Dual Diagnosis) Assessment, (5) Recovery Potential Assessment, and (6) Multiple Measures Resources.

ALCOHOL ASSESSMENT INSTRUMENTS

ADOLESCENT ALCOHOL INVOLVEMENT SCALE (AAIS)

A 14-item scale developed by Filstead and Mayer (1984), the AAIS assesses adolescents with drinking problems by measuring the impact of alcohol use and psychosocial consequences in three domains: psychological functioning, social relations, and family living. Filstead and Mayer report the AAIS as having a reliability consistency ranging from .55 in a clinical sample to .76 in a general sample. For additional information, go to: www.qolid.org/public/list. (This URL provides an alphabetical list of 1,000 instruments.)

Adolescent Drinking Index (ADI)

Authored by Adele Harrell and Philip Wirtz, the ADI measures the severity of drinking problems of adolescents in four domains: loss of control of drinking, social indicators of drinking problems, psychological indicators, and physical problems related to drinking. Identifying adolescents who need to be referred for further alcohol assessment, this instrument contains two subscales—one measuring self-medicating problem drinking and the other aggressive, rebellious drinking behavior. Harrell and Wirtz (1989) report internal consistency reliability coefficients above .80. For further information, go to: www.parinc.com /product.cfm?ProductID=143.

Alcadd Test Revised (AT)

A paper-and-pencil tool developed by Morse Manson, AT assesses probability that the subject is an alcoholic. Easily administered in approximately 10 minutes, it has high reliability and validity ratings. Training is required to score and administer this test. See www.wpspublish.com/PDF/catalog2002wps /072_wps02.pdf.

Alcohol Abstinence Self-Efficacy Scale (AASES)

Developed by Carlo DiClemente, the AASES assesses an individual's efficacy (individual's ability to achieve desired outcomes and goals) in abstaining from consuming alcohol in 20 situations. This measure can be used to evaluate Alcoholics Anonymous program participation. DiClemente and Carbonari (1994) report that the consistency reliability coefficients ranges between 82 and 92. See www.umbc.edu/psych/habits/SelfEf.html.

Alcohol Clinical Index (ACI)

Developed by Harvey A. Skinner, the ACI is used mostly by physicians, nurses, and other health professionals to identify alcohol problems and assist in clinical decisions. It consists of four parts, each using separate forms: (1) clinical signs (17 items) that a physician or nurse elicits; (2) medical history (13 items) completed by the patient; (3) alcohol questionnaire (10 items) that includes a history of drinking during a typical 4-week period in the past 6 months, as well as the CAGE screening items; and (4) early indicators and risk factors (14 items). Skinner, Holt, Sheu, and Israel (1986) report accepted internal validity for detecting alcohol addictions. For further information, go to www.camh.net.

Alcohol Dependence Scale (ADS)

A widely used clinical tool, the ADS is a short, self-administered screening tool created by Harvey A. Skinner. Measuring the severity of alcohol dependence, it contains 25 multiple-choice questions focusing on alcohol dependence withdrawal symptoms, obsessive/compulsive drinking, tolerance, and drink-seeking behavior. Training is required to administer this 5-minute test. Skinner (1984) reports good reliability coefficients ranging from 85 to 92. See www.camh.net.

ALCOHOL EFFECTS QUESTIONNAIRE (AEQ)

A 40-item, self-administered tool developed by Damaris J. Rohsenow, the AEQ assesses undesirable effects of alcohol and personal beliefs. The questionnaire takes approximately 10 to 20 minutes to complete. Brown (1980) reports consistency reliability coefficients to be strong at .93. See National Institute on Alcohol Abuse and Alcoholism at www.niaaa.nih.gov/publications/instable.htm. (This URL contains many current tests used for assessing alcohol use.)

ADOLESCENT EXPECTANCY QUESTIONNAIRE (AEQ-A)

Developed by Mark Goldman, Sandy Brown, and Bruce Christiansen, the AEQ-A is a 90-item, self-administered report, derived from the Adult Alcohol Expectancy Questionnaire and interviews conducted with adolescents. It measures seven expectancy factors: global positive changes, changes in social behavior, cognitive and motor abilities, sexual enhancement, cognitive and motor impairment, increased arousal, and relaxation and tension reduction. The instrument takes approximately 30 minutes to complete. Minimal training is needed to administer this test. Validity and consistency reliability coefficients have been found at .82 (Brown, 1980). See www.niaaa.nih.gov/publications/acq_a.htm.

ALCOHOL USE DISORDERS IDENTIFICATION TEST (AUDIT)

Developed by the World Health Organization, the AUDIT is a brief, self-reporting questionnaire used to identify people at risk of developing alcohol problems. Focusing on the preliminary signs of harmful drinking and mild dependence, it consists of questions relating to frequency and quantity of alcohol consumption, drinking behavior, and alcohol-related problems. Babor, de la Fuente, and Saunders (1982) purport validity to be acceptable; consistency reliability coefficients at .82 to .89 range. Training is required to administer this test. See www.prodigy.nhs.uk/clinicalguidance/releasedguidance/webBrowser/pils/plaudit.htm.

ALCOHOL USE INVENTORY (AUI)

A reliable, self-report inventory developed by John Horn, Kenneth W. Wanberg, and F. Mark Foster, the AUI identifies patterns of behavior, attitudes, and symptoms associated with the use and abuse of alcohol. Targeted for those

16 years and older who have a minimum sixth-grade reading level, it assesses alcohol-related problems, and differentiates drinking styles. Training is required to administer this test. Completion time is 35 to 60 minutes. See www.pearsonassessments.com/assessments/tests/aui.htm.

CAGE Questionnaire

A four-item, self-report screening test developed by John Ewing, the CAGE is widely used in clinical settings and is easily administered. The questions focus on lifetime drinking patterns and two "yes" responses indicate possible hazardous drinking. C—Have you ever tried to *Cut down* your use of chemicals? A—Has anyone ever *Annoyed* you by criticizing your drinking? G—Have you ever felt *Guilty* about your behavior when drinking? E—*Eye opener:* Have you ever used alcohol in the morning to reduce the effects of a hangover? Ewing (1984) reports the CAGE is an effective tool for predicting at-risk drinking. See www.niaaa.nih.gov/publications/cage.htm.

Drinking Refusal Self-Efficacy Questionnaire (DRSEQ)

Developed by Ross Young and P. Tian, the DRSEQ is a 314-item, self-administered tool that measures drinking-related self-efficacy in three areas: social pressure, opportunistic drinking, and emotional relief. The test takes approximately 30 minutes to complete, and no training is required for administration. This test shows internal consistency and clinical efficiency (Young & Knight, 1989). See http://chipts.ucla.edu/assessment /topic.html and http://chipts.ucla.edu/assessment/Assessment_Instruments /Assessment_files_new/assess_rse.htm.

Drinking Related Locus of Control Scale (DRIE)

Created by Juliann Rotter, the DRIE is a 25-item self-report questionnaire that assesses an individual's perceptions of control over alcohol. It determines whether a person believes that he has an internal or external locus of control over important life events. No training is required to administer this test, which takes approximately 10 minutes to complete. DRIE has reliability and validity (Donovan & O'Leary, 1978). See www.niaaa.nih.gov /publications/drie.htm.

Drinking Restraint Scale (DRS)

A seven-item, self-administered report created by Southwick and Steele, the DRS provides information to identify social drinkers at risk for the development of alcohol problems. It takes about 10 minutes to complete and requires minimal training. Southwick and Steele (1987) report DRS validity and reliability coefficients of .82 to .96. See http://gwbweb.wustl.edu/Users/cac/ae5.htm.

DIAGNOSTIC AND STATISTICAL MANUAL OF MENTAL DISORDERS, TEXT REVISION (DSM-IV-TR)

The *DSM-IV-TR* provides diagnostic guidelines for mental disorders. The clinician compares the signs and symptoms the client is experiencing with the mental disorders criteria list set out in the manual for each mental disorder. Refer to the *DSM-IV-TR* or visit www.psychologynet.org/dsm.html.

FAST SCREENING

Developed by Ray Hodgson, the FAST is an alternative, shorter version of AUDIT used in hospitals and clinics to detect harmful drinking patterns and mild dependence. Consisting of only four questions, it measures the frequency of risky alcohol consumption. FAST identifies 930 of every 1,000 people misusing alcohol, which is congruent with the AUDIT (Hodgson, Alwyn, John, Thom, & Smith, 2002). Brief training is required. See www.ncbi.nlm.nih.gov/entrez/query.fcgi ?cmd=Retrieve&db=PubMed&list_uids=11825859&dopt=Abstract.

F-SMAST/M-SMAST

F-SMAST and the *M-SMAST* are both 26-item brief questionnaires, developed by Kenneth Sher from the Adapted Short Michigan Alcoholism Screening Test (ASMAST). They assess an individual's father's (F-MAST) or mother's (M-MAST) lifetime alcohol abuse. Although adults and adolescents are the target populations, these measures can also be used to identify children of alcoholics. A pencil-and-paper test, it takes about 15 minutes to complete and training is suggested. The test has shown internal consistency of .85 for assessing parental history of alcoholism. Sher and Descutner (1986) report that it also has clinical efficacy. See www.niaaa.nih.gov/publications/asmast.htm.

INVENTORY OF DRINKING SITUATIONS (IDS)

A 100-item, self-report questionnaire developed by Allan Marlatt, the IDS is designed to assess drinking situations in eight categories: unpleasant emotions, physical discomfort, pleasant emotions, personal control, urges and temptation, conflict, social pressure, and pleasant times with others. A tool that may serve as the focus for designing an individual treatment plan, it requires about 20 minutes to complete. No training is required, and it may be scored by hand or by computer. Annis (1982) reports consistency reliability coefficients of .87 to .96. See www.camh.net.

MAST-G (Geriatric Version)

A 24-item questionnaire, The MAST-G was modified by Fredric Blow from the Michigan Alcohol Screening Test (MAST) and is the most widely used questionnaire for older adults. Taking about 10 minutes to complete, it might be supplemented with additional assessments regarding the frequency and quantity of alcohol use (i.e., CAGE). Available from www.agingincanada.ca.

Semi-Structured Assessment for the Genetics of Alcoholism (SSAGA-II)

Developed by Victor Hesselbrock, the SSAGA-II contains 45 multipart items to assess substance abuse/dependence, anorexia, bulimia, depression, mania, antisocial personality disorder, obsession-compulsive disorders, and other disorders. Although it assesses demographic information, medical history, and suicide attempts, its emphasis is on substance use and correlated diagnoses. The assessment takes about one hour to complete, and training is required to administer it. Bucholz et al. (1994) report consistency reliability coefficients of 70 to 90. For more information, visit www.niaaa.nih.gov/publications /arh26-3/208-213.htm.

Situational Confidence Questionnaire (SCQ)

Developed by Helen Annis, the SCQ is a 39-item, self-reporting questionnaire administered to assess self-efficacy for alcohol related situations. Clients are asked to imagine themselves in a variety of situations and indicate their confidence to resist the urge to drink in each situation. This test is self-administered and requires approximately 15 minutes to complete. Minimal training is required. For additional information, go to www.camh.net.

Michigan Alcohol Screening Test (MAST)

An assessment instrument developed by Melvin Selzer (1971), the MAST consists of 24 "yes" or "no" items regarding the client's drinking habits. No training is required for this test, as it is self-scoring. There are several variations of the MAST, including the brief MAST and short MAST. Zung (1980) is supportive of MAST validity and suggests a consistency reliability coefficient of .84 to .97. See www.silcom.com/~sbadp/treatment/mast.htm.

Yale-Brown Obsessive Compulsive Scale (YBOCS)

A 10-item scale developed by Modell, Glaser, Mountz, Cyr, and Schmaltz (1992), the YBOCS measures obsession and compulsivity related to heavy drinking. It is useful in detecting the presence of alcohol abuse and dependence and may be used to differentiate between subgroups of heavy drinkers with and without obsessive-compulsive drinking characteristics. It may also be used to characterize the similarities between alcohol abuse and dependence. Taking about 10 minutes to complete, no training is required and computerized scoring is available. See www.brainphysics.com/ocd/ybocs.html.

OTHER DRUG ASSESSMENTS

ADDICTION SEVERITY INDEX (ASI)

Developed by Thomas McLellan, the ASI examines seven potential areas of concern for substance-abusing patients: medical, employment, family and social relationships, drug and alcohol use, legal, and psychological status. It explores approximately 200 questions during the interview, which takes one hour to complete. Training is required to administer. ASI's consistency reliability coefficients range between 83 and 89 (McLellan & Luborsky, 1985). See www.uwm.edu/Dept/CABHR/MATE/addictionseverityguide.htm.

ADOLESCENT DRUG ABUSE DIAGNOSIS (ADAD)

A 150-item interview created by McLellan, Luborsky, Woody, and O'Brien, the ADAD examines eight areas of an adolescent's life: drug and alcohol use, medical status, legal status, family background and problems, social/employment, social activities and peer relations, and psychological status. A 10-point scale is used to rate the client's need for treatment. The ADAD reviews specific areas of drug involvement, including: polydrug use, withdrawal symptoms, use in school, and attempts at abstinence. It takes about 25 minutes to complete and requires minimal training. Reliability and validity are reported by A. S. Friedman and Utada (1989). See www.testsymptomsathome.com/DSO01screening_assessment_instruments .asp. These two URLs also provide several other tests for screening adolescents: www.4troubledteens.com/teen-issues.html and www.drugstrategies.org/teens /screening.html.

ADOLESCENT DRUG INVOLVEMENT SCALE (ADIS)

Developed by Moberg and Hahn (1991), the ADIS is a 12-item, self-administered questionnaire that assesses levels of adolescent drug use, excluding alcohol. The ADIS measures drug use frequency, reasons for use, social context, effects of use, and self-appraisal of drug use. The questionnaire takes approximately 5 minutes to complete and has not been validated as a clinical measure. See www.testsymptomsathome.com/DSO01_screening_assessment_instruments.asp.

ADOLESCENT PROBLEM SEVERITY INDEX (APSI)

Metzger and colleagues (Metzger, Kushner, & McLellan, 1991) designed the APSI to assist juvenile probation officers in identifying, documenting, and responding to drug and alcohol abuse, and problems in other important areas of life functioning. Containing 85 items and taking about 45 minutes to complete, it assesses legal problems, family relationships, medical issues, and high-risk sexual behavior. Training is required. See http://www.drugstrategies.com /teens/screening.html.

American Drug and Alcohol Survey (ADAS)

A paper-pencil questionnaire developed by Fred Beauvais, Ruth Edward, and Eugene Oetting, the ADAS asks students about their experiences with a variety of drugs, including alcohol and tobacco. The survey examines attitudes about substance use, perception of the harmfulness of drugs, intention to use, peer influences, and problems related to drug use. The test takes approximately 30 minutes to complete. Results can be used to assess community needs, evaluate prevention programs, and identify trends. No training is required, and it can be computer scored. See www.rmbsi.com.

Drug and Alcohol Problem Quick Screen (DAPQS)

A 30-item questionnaire created by Schwartz, the DAPQS is used for rapid in-office testing of adolescent substance use disorders and behavior patterns. The test takes about 15 minutes to complete. Validity and reliability outcomes are not available. See http://gwbweb.wustl.edu/users/cac/ac13.htm.

Chemical Dependency Assessment Profile (CDAP)

A self-assessment questionnaire designed by Thomas Harrell, the CDAP consists of 232 items that evaluate drug use, alcohol use, and polydrug abuse of adults and adolescents who have chemical dependence problems. It explores chemical use history, patterns of use, use beliefs and expectations, use symptoms, self-concept, and interpersonal relations. It requires roughly 45 minutes to complete this test. CDAP validity and consistency reliability coefficients of .77 to .96 are reported (T. H. Harrell & Honaker, 1991). See www.niaaa.nih.gov/publications/cdap.htm.

Drugs, Alcohol, and Gambling Screen (DAGS)

A 45-question test developed by William Howatt to assess potential drug, alcohol, and gambling risk, asking 15 Likert-type questions for each. DAGS score indicates potential risk of dependence on the following scale: mild, moderate, medium, and serious. See Howatt, W. A. (2000). *The human services counseling toolbox*. Belmont, CA: Brooks/Cole.

Drug Abuse Screening Tool (DAST)

A 20-item test developed by Harvey Skinner to assess potential drug concerns, the DAST measures the use of psychoactive substances other than alcohol during the past 12 months. Scoring indicates no concern, low concern, moderate concern, substantial concern, and severe concern. No training is required to administer. Contact Dr. Skinner at the Addiction Research Foundation, 33 Russell St., Toronto, ON M5S 2S1, or visit: www.csc-scc.gc.ca/text/rsrch/reports/r11/r11e_e.shtml.

Drug Use Screening Inventory (DUSI)

A 159-item questionnaire developed by Tarter to assess drug-related problems among adults or adolescents, this self-administered test assesses 10 areas: substance abuse, psychiatric disorder, behavior problems, school adjustment, health status, work adjustment, peer relations, social competency, family adjustment, and leisure/recreation. Its purpose is to assess current status, identify areas in need of change, or follow outcome after a treatment intervention. Taking about 20 minutes to complete, no training is required. Validity and consistency reliability (.91) have been reported by Tarter and Laird (1992). See www.pitt.edu/~cedarspr/dusir.html.

Substance Abuse Problem Checklist

Developed by Jerome F. X. Carroll, this extensive 300-item self-administered checklist covers motivation for treatment, health, personality, social relationships, job-related problems, leisure time, religious or spiritual problems, and legal problems. For more information, contact Dr. Carroll at Jfxc4318@aol.com.

Substance Abuse Subtle Screening Inventory-3 (SASSI-3)

A nationally recognized, reliable psychological assessment screening tool designed by Glen Miller, the SASSI assesses individuals for substance abuse disorder, including chemical dependence of alcohol and/or other substances. It provides separate scoring for males and females. Training is required to perform this assessment, and literature is supportive of SASSI validity and a consistency reliability coefficient (89 to 97). Contact the SASSI Institute at (800) 726-0526, or visit www.sassi.com/sassi/index.shtml.

Substance Use Disorders Diagnostic Schedule (SUDDS)

A 99-item diagnostic test developed by Harrison and Hoffmann, the SUDDS is especially useful for chemical abuse/dependency and other dual-diagnosis populations. This test takes approximately 45 minutes to complete and is administered by a trained chemical dependency professional. It is computer scored and the results prove to be adequately reliable for clinical use. Davis, Hoffmann, Morse, and Luehr (1992) are supportive of SUDDS validity and suggest a consistency reliability coefficient of 71 to 86. For additional information, see www.niaaa.nih.gov/publications/sudds-text.htm.

Teen-Addiction Severity Index (T-ASI)

A 133-item interview designed by Yifrah Kaminer, the T-ASI is a reliable and valued evaluator of adolescent substance abuse. The T-ASI rates six domains: psychoactive substance abuse, school or employment status, family functioning, peer and social relationships, legal status, and psychiatric status. The test takes approximately 30 minutes to complete and is administered by a trained mental health professional. Kaminer and Bukstein (1991) report a consistency reliability coefficients value of .78. See www.niaaa.nih.gov/publications/t_asi.htm.

NONCHEMICAL ADDICTIONS

Gambling Attitudes Scale (GAS)

A 59-item instrument developed by Jeffrey Kassinove (2000), the GAS measures attitudes toward gambling. It can be used to predict which people may be more likely to engage in gambling behaviors. The results of the GAS may be used to develop prevention and education programs. The four subscales of this instrument measure casino gambling, horse race gambling, lottery gambling, and general gambling. See www.hms.harvard.edu/doa/index.htm For additional information on gambling measures, also see www.grp.vic.gov.au/domino/web_notes/grp/grpreports.nsf/pages/vgsReviewExistingInstruments.

Global Appraisal of Individual Needs (GAIN)

A self-reporting instrument created by Michael Dennis, the GAIN implements a biopsychosocial model of assessment of substance use, physical health risk, mental and emotional health, and interpersonal relationships. The test takes approximately 50 minutes to complete, and scoring is obtained by adding the corresponding responses together. A valid test, no training is required. Dennis and Rourke (1993) report consistency reliability coefficients of .80. See www.chestnut.org/LI/gain/GAINSUM1299.pdf.

Internet Addiction Test

This 20-item, self-reporting questionnaire, designed by Kimberly Young, assesses whether an individual has an Internet addiction. Taking about 10 minutes to complete, it is easily scored and no training is required. See Young's book *Caught in the Net* and also these web sites: www.netaddiction.com and www.gospelcom.net/kregel/Hooked_Net/addiction.

Online Cognition Scale (OCS)

A 36-item, multidimensional instrument used to assess problematic Internet use, the OCS measures thoughts related to the Internet and scores the answers on a scale from 1 to 7 (strongly agree to strongly disagree). The OCS explores four areas of problematic Internet use: impulsive use, lonely/depressed use, distraction, and social comfort use. To obtain a scoring guide for this measure, one must contact the author at davisr@yorku.ca. Also see www .internetaddiction.ca/scale.htm.

SEXUAL ADDICTION SCREENING TEST (SAST)

A 25-item questionnaire developed by Patrick Carnes (1991), the SAST assesses sexual compulsion by discriminating between addictive and nonaddictive behavior. The test takes approximately 10 minutes to complete and no training is required. See www.sexhelp.com/sast.cfm.

SOUTH OAKS GAMBLING SCREEN (SOGS)

A 26-item questionnaire developed by Henry Lesieur and Sheila Blume to assess possible gambling problems, the SOGS scores indicate the extent to which subjects are at risk: no problem, some problem, or probable pathological gambler. Battersby, Thomas, Tolchard, and Esterman (2002) report consistency reliability coefficients of 86 to 94. See www.gov.ns.ca/heal/gambling/IsThereAProblem /SouthOaks/ and www.addictionrecov.org/southoak.htm.

EATING ATTITUDES TEST (EAT-26)

A 26-item questionnaire developed by David Garner, the EAT-26 is widely used for assessing the possibility of eating disorders. A score with 20 positive responses suggests cause for concern and recommends a consultation with a physician. Taking roughly 10 minutes to complete, it requires no training. Garner, Olmsted, Bohr, and Garfinkel (1982) report high internal consistency of .97. See http://river-centre.org/pretest.html.

WORK ADDICTION RISK TEST (WART)

A 25-item screening measure by Bryan Robinson to differentiate individuals who work to succeed from those who work to excess, this self-administered tool is scored on a rating system of one (never true), two (sometimes true), three (often true), or four (always true). Individuals are asked to put the number that best describes their work habits in the blank beside each statement. High summated scores suggest workaholic behavior. See Robinson's book, *A Guidebook for Workaholics, Their Partners and Children, and the Clinicians Who Treat Them* (1989) and visit www.theway.uk.com/types/work.htm.

MENTAL HEALTH (DUAL DIAGNOSIS) ASSESSMENTS

ADULT SUICIDAL IDEATION QUESTIONNAIRE (ASIQ)

A 25-item, self-reporting questionnaire created by William Reynolds, the ASIQ screens college students and adults in general for suicidal ideation. Used during intake interviews or during treatment, this test alerts professionals of a possible suicide risk. The test takes approximately 10 minutes to complete and training is required. Reynolds (1990) reports a consistency reliability coefficient of .95. See www.sigmaassessmentsystems.com/asiq.htm.

BECK HOPELESSNESS SCALE (BHS)

A 20-item scale developed by Aaron Beck, the BHS is used to measure three major aspects of hopelessness: feelings about the future, loss of motivation, and expectancies. A high BHS score alerts counselors to unstated or denied suicidal intentions. Taking about 15 minutes to complete, training is required. A. T. Beck and Steer (1989) report consistency reliability coefficients ranges of .82 to .93. See www.cps.nova.edu/~cpphelp/BHS.html.

BECK DEPRESSION INVENTORY (BDI)

A self-administered 21-item instrument developed by Aaron T. Beck, the BDI measures symptoms of depression. It takes approximately 10 minutes to complete and clients usually require a sixth-grade reading level to accurately respond. The BDI has different forms, including a shorter version with 13 questions, computerized forms, and a BDI-II. A. T. Beck and Steer (1997) explains that the BDI is reliable in distinguishing between depressed and nondepressed people and yields a consistency range of 73 to 95. Scores determine normal ups and downs, mild to moderate depression, moderate to severe depression, and severe depression. See www.cps.nova.edu/~cpphelp/BDI.html. To learn more about Beck's other inventories for assessing Anxiety and Suicide, see the Beck Institute web site at www.beckinstitute.org.

CHILDREN'S DEPRESSION SCALE (CDS)

Created by M. Lang, the CDS measures depression and depressive symptoms in children and adolescents between the ages of 9 and 16. The CDS may also be used with younger or learning-disabled children. It consists of 66 questions divided into 48 depressive and 18 positive items including social problems, self-esteem, preoccupation with sickness and death, and pleasure and enjoyment. Kazdin (1987) report consistency reliability coefficients with a range of 82 to 97. See www.criminology.unimelb.edu.au/victims/resources/assessment/affect /cds.html.

DETAILED ASSESSMENT OF POSTTRAUMATIC STRESS (DAPS)

A 104-item clinical measure designed by John Briere, the DAPS assesses trauma exposure and posttraumatic stress in individuals who have a history of exposure to one or more potentially traumatic events. The DAPS assesses both current and lifetime history of *DSM-IV-TR* trauma experiences and symptoms, including substance use, avoidance, hyperarousal, and suicidality. The test takes approximately 30 minutes to complete, and training is required. The DAPS scales have a higher internal consistency than many other measures of PTSD. See www.parinc.com/product.cfm?ProductID=528.

Millon Clinical Multiaxial Inventory-II (MCMI-II)

A 175-item self-reporting instrument created by Theodore Millon, the MCMI-II assesses personality disorders and clinical syndromes in adults undergoing psychological and psychiatric assessments. Used in clinical and counseling sessions, this test consists of 175 true/false questions and takes approximately 25 minutes to complete. An eighth-grade reading level is required. Results are based on a national sample of 1,292 male and female clients who have *DSM-III-R* diagnoses. This assessment is specifically designed to assess both Axis I and Axis II disorders. Domino (2000) documents good reliability and validity. See www.cps.nova.edu/~cpphelp/MCMI-2.html. Also note that Psychological Publications, Inc. 2002 Catalog provides a URL listing of other personality tests and tools www.tjta.com/cat03B.html.

Minnesota Multiphasic Personality Inventory-Adolescent (MMPI-A)

James Butcher and Carolyn Williams developed the MMPI-A to identify personal, social, and behavioral problems among adolescents. Common problems identified are family issues, chemical dependency, and eating disorders. Administered by school, clinical, and counseling psychologists, the MMPI-A aids in diagnosis and treatment planning specifically for youth, ages 14 to 18. A sixth-grade reading level is required for completion, and the test takes approximately one hour. Literature is supportive of MMPI-A validity, and the test yields an estimated consistency reliability coefficient of .90 (C. L. Williams, 1992). See www.pearsonassessments.com/assessments/tests/mmpia.htm.

Minnesota Multiphasic Personality Inventory-2 (MMPI-2)

Authored by Starke Hathaway and Charnley McKinley, the MMPI-2 is one of the most used personality assessments. Developed in 1943 and revised in 1989, it assesses chemical dependency; physical and psychological health; political and social attitudes; educational, occupational, family, and marital factors; and neurotic and psychotic behaviors. The MMPI-2 also includes the Addiction Admission Scale (AAS) with built-in lie detecting that increases the reliability and validity of the test. Domino (2000) reports that because of the complexity of the MMPI-2, it is difficult to assess reliability and validity, though the research generally supports the MMPI-2. See www.pearsonassessments.com.

MULTIDIMENSIONAL ANXIETY QUESTIONNAIRE (MAQ)

A 40-item multidimensional self-report measure for assessing a wide range of anxiety symptoms, the MAQ targets adults aged 18 to 89 years. It provides a global assessment of anxiety symptoms in four areas: physiological-panic, social phobia, worry-fears, and negative affective domains of anxiety. Useful in clinical and college settings, the test takes about 20 minutes to complete and minimal training is required. See http://cstl-cla.semo.edu/snell/books/student/chap17.htm.

NOVACO ANGER INVENTORY-SHORT FORM

This form, adapted and first put into Tony Kidman's book *Tactics for Change,* contains 25 of the original 90 questions. For each question, clients are asked to rate their degree of anger on a scale of 1 to 4, with results indicating that anger is remarkably low, more peaceful than the average person, average amount of anger, more irritable than the average person, and anger is out of control. Self-administered or given by a counselor, Mills, Kroner, and Forth (1998) report validity and reliability coefficients of 78 to 91. See Novaco, R. W. (1975). *Anger control: The development of an experimental treatment.* Lexington, KY: Lexington. Also available from www.gu.edu.au/school/psy/testlibrary/tlcat_m-r.html.

OBSESSIVE-COMPULSIVE INVENTORY (OCI)

A self-administered inventory developed by Foa, Kozak, Salkovskis, Coles, and Amir (1998), the OCI distinguishes between individuals who have obsessive-compulsive disorder and other anxiety disorders. It examines seven areas: washing, checking, doubting, ordering, obsessing, hoarding, and mental neutralizing. Each item is scored on a Likert Scale of 0 to 4 for frequency, occurrence, and distress. No technical expertise is required to administer this test. Foa et al. (1998) report validity and a consistency reliability coefficients range of .86 to .95. See www.criminology.unimelb.edu.au/victims/resources/assessment/affect/oci.html.

PSYCHIATRIC RESEARCH INTERVENTION FOR SUBSTANCE AND MENTAL DISORDERS (PRISM)

A clinician-administered interview developed by Deborah Hasin, the PRISM measures *DSM-IV* diagnoses of alcohol, drug, and psychiatric disorders. It provides information about experiences with drugs and alcohol and is useful in studying the effects of comorbidity on alcohol and drug treatment. It takes one to three hours to complete. Results have shown it to be reliable. See www.niaaa.nih.gov/publications/prism-text.htm.

Psychopathy Checklist (PCL-R)

A measure of psychopathic personality disorder developed by Robert Hare (1998) explains that PCL-R predicts violent behavior. Consisting of 20 items, each of which reflects a different characteristic of psychopathic behavior, this test assesses an individual's *lifetime* functioning, not solely the person's present state. Reportedly the single best predictor of violent behavior currently available, it takes about two hours to complete and should be done by a trained interviewer. See www.hare.org/pclr and www.hare.org/pclr/index.html.

Trauma Symptom Inventory (TSI)

Created by John Briere, the TSI is used to assess posttraumatic stress and other traumatic events, such as: rape, major accidents, natural disasters, early childhood trauma, spouse abuse, and combat trauma. The TSI is scored on a four-point scale about the frequency of occurrence over the previous 6 months. Self-administered, it is intended for those with at least a fifth-grade reading level. Briere's (1995) reports a high validity for the TSI. See www.parinc.com /product.cfm?ProductID=149 and http://aac.ncat.edu/newsnotes/y01spr.html.

RECOVERY POTENTIAL ASSESSMENTS

Alcoholics Anonymous 20 Questions

A self-administered test developed by AA, these questions give insight into the possibility of an alcohol addiction and help guide people in exploring the 12-step program. See http://home.vicnet.net.au/~csoaasa/20Questions.html.

Alcohol Timeline Followback (TLFB)

Developed by Linda Sobell and Mark Sobell, the TLFB estimates daily alcohol consumption by having clients use a calendar to record estimates of their daily drinking (and other drugs) over a specified period ranging from 30 to 360 days. A feedback tool to motivate clients to change, this instrument is self-administered in pencil-paper format and is scored by the interviewer or computer. Sobell, Maisto, Sobell, and Cooper (1979) report a high reliability among alcohol users. See www.camh.net/publications/clinical_tools_assessments.html.

AWARE Questionnaire (Advance WARning of RELapse-Revised)

A self-administered test designed by Terrance Gorski, the AWARE measures the warning signs of relapse. Higher scores indicate a higher number of warning signs being reported by the client. It takes about 20 minutes to complete. W. R. Miller, Westerberg, Harris, and Tonigan (1996) report validity and reliability scores. See www.tgorski.com/relapse/AWARE_Relapse_Questionaire.pdf and http://casaa .unm.edu/inst/forms/Aware.pdf.

Structured Addictions Assessment Interview for Selecting Treatment (ASIST)

A self-reporting inventory developed at the Addiction Research Foundation in 1984 (www.camh.net), the ASIST examines dependence on alcohol and drugs, psychopathology, authoritarianism, intelligence quotient, and organicity. See www.csc-scc.gcca/text/rsrch/reports/r75/r75e_e.shtml#_Toc437159319.

Beck Codependence Assessment Scale (BCAS)

A 35-item, self-report scale created by William Beck, the BCAS measures codependence or enabling behaviors toward a dysfunctional significant other. The client identifies a set of diagnostic behaviors and cognitions that are typical of codependents. Taking about 10 minutes to complete, it is a summated score. Beck (1991) reports an internal consistency of .86. See the Alcohol and Substance Abuse Measurement Instrument Collection at www.utexas.edu/research/cswr/nida /Instrument%20Listing.htm.

Brown-Peterson Recovery Progress Inventory (BPRPI)

A 53-item self-administered inventory developed by H. P. Brown and Peterson (1991), BPRPI measures an individual's current level of functioning in a 12-step recovery program. Taking about 20 minutes to complete, it is scored by hand. See www.niaaa.nih.gov/publications/bprpi.htm.

Circumstances, Motivation, and Readiness Scales (CMR SCALES)

A 180-item self-report inventory developed by De Leon, Melnick, Kressel, and Jainchill (1994), the CMR use Likert scales to indicate external pressure to enter treatment, external pressure to leave treatment, motivation to change, and readiness for treatment. The test takes approximately minutes to complete, and no training is required. See www.niaaa.nih.gov/publications/cmrs-text.htm.

Clinical Institute Withdrawal Assessment (CIWA)

An eight-item assessment tool developed by the American Medical Association, the CIWA measures the severity of alcohol withdrawal symptoms. It takes about 5 minutes to complete, and no training is required. Validity and reliability (.89) have been reported (Stuppaeck et al., 1994). See www.niaaa.nih.gov/publications /ciwa.htm and www.oqp.med.va.gov/cpg/SUD/SUD_CPG/ModuleA/app/A _App4.htm.

COMPREHENSIVE DRINKER PROFILE (CDP)

A structured interview designed by Miller and Marlatt (1984), the CDP contains 88 gender specific questions that explore substance consumption, life problems, medical history, motivations for change, and self-efficacy. Recommended for use in treatment planning. A shorter version is available. Training is usually required to score this test. See www.niaaa.nih.gov/publications/cdp-text.htm.

COMPUTERIZED LIFESTYLE ASSESSMENT (CLA)

A 350-item instrument to assess lifestyle strengths as well as health-risk behaviors, the CLA examines a wide range of lifestyle activities and assesses the individual's interest or readiness for change. It includes components of the Alcohol Dependence Scale (ADS), CAGE screening items, and Drug Abuse Screening Test (DAST). Taking about one hour to complete, it is scored by computer. No training is required. Bungy, Pols, Mortimer, Frank, and Skinner (1989) report its validity. See www.niaaa.nih.gov/publications/cla-text.htm.

COPING RESPONSES INVENTORY (CRI)

Developed by Rudolf Moos, the CRI assesses present coping skills in dealing with stress. It includes eight scales: *Approach Coping Styles* (Logical Analysis, Positive Reappraisal, Seeking Guidance and Support, and Problem Solving) and *Avoidant Coping Styles* (Cognitive Avoidance, Acceptance or Resignation, Seeking Alternative Rewards, and Emotional Discharge). See www .parinc.com/product.cfm?ProductID=138 and www.parinc.com/relatedfiles /LISRES_CRI_bib.pdf.

DRINKING SELF-MONITORING LOG (DSML)

A pencil and paper, self-administered tool created by Mark Sobell, the DSML is a personal journal that clients use to record their drinking patterns. Entries are made on a daily or drink-by-drink basis. In its simplest version, it collects information on the total number of drinks consumed each day and the type and time the beverage was consumed. Certain logs may also ask clients to indicate where the drinking occurred (i.e., at home, bar) and their emotional state at the time of drinking. See www.niaaa.nih.gov/publications/dsml.htm.

FOLLOW-UP DRINKER PROFILE (FDP)

An 88-item instrument, the FDP is one of a "family" of structured interviews that also includes the *Comprehensive Drinker Profile*, and the *Brief Drinker Profile*. All assess client status during intake and follow-up sessions. Measures include motivation, drinking history, demographic information, and self-efficacy. It requires about 30 minutes to complete. See www.niaaa.nih.gov/publications/fdp.htm.

Individual Assessment Profile (IAP)

A clinical assessment tool developed by Flynn, Hubbard, and Luckey (1995) for treatment planning purposes, the IAP explores demographic background, reason for admission, living arrangements, smoking, alcohol and drug use, illegal activities, sources of support, and medical and mental health. Clients rate their concern and opinion of need on a 4-point scale in each specific area. The interviewer then rates each area as to need for treatment. See www.scottishexecutive.gov.uk /library5/health/dtap-27.asp.

Life Satisfaction Scale (LSS)

A 34-item self-report designed by E. Diener, the LSS measures an individual's life satisfaction as a whole, a global measure not limited to health or finances. Using Likert-type scoring, it takes about 10 minutes to complete. Pavot, Diener, Colvin, and Sandvik (1991) report validity and reliability. See www.sci-queri .research.med.va.gov/swls.htm.

Recovery Attitude and Treatment Evaluator Questionnaire (RAATE)

Developed by New Standards, Inc. the RAATE assists in determining the appropriate level of care by measuring five areas: resistance to treatment, resistance to continuing care, severity of medical problems, severity of psychological problems, and social/environmental support. Training is required to score this test that takes approximately one hour to complete. M. B. Smith, Hoffmann, and Nederhoed (1992) report validity and reliability (75 to 87). See www.niaaa.nih.gov /publications/raate.htm.

Stages of Change Readiness and Treatment Eagerness Scale (SOCRATES)

Developed by W. R. Miller and Tonigan (1996), this instrument assesses a client's current state of change: taking steps, recognition, and ambivalence. It takes approximately 10 minutes to complete. For more information, see: www .niaaa.nih.gov/publications/socrates.htm.

Steps Questionnaire

A 42-item, self-administered instrument developed by Francis Gilbert, it measures an individual's attitudes and beliefs related to the first three of the 12 Steps in AA: a client's beliefs about powerlessness and unmanageability, the use of a Higher Power as a critical component in the recovery process, and the individual's willingness to turn over his or her life to a Higher Power to achieve sobriety. Taking approximately 20 minutes to complete, it requires no training. See www.niaaa.nih.gov/publications/steps-text.htm.

READINESS TO CHANGE QUESTIONNAIRE (RTCQ)

A 12-question measure developed by Heather, Gold, and Rollnick (1991), it assesses a client's readiness for change. Based on Prochaska and DiClemente's stages-of-change model, individuals are assigned to precontemplation, contemplation, or action stage of change. The RTCQ may be especially helpful for harmful drinkers who are not seeking treatment. No training is required to administer this measure. Heather, Rollnick, and Bell (1993) report consistency reliability coefficients of .93. See www.niaaa.nih.gov/publications/rtcq.htm.

MULTIPLE MEASURES RESOURCES

Measures for Clinical Practice: A Source Book Volumes 1 and 2, are outstanding resources for developing treatment plans. Both volumes contain specific measures that cover a wide range of issues that may arise in clinical practice. Check the table of contents for assessment tools pertinent to such problems as addiction, health, love, relationships, phobias, stress, anger, self-esteem, and sexuality. See Corcoran, K. and J. Fischer. (1994). *Measures for clinical practice: A sourcebook* (2nd ed., Vol. 1). New York: Free Press; and Corcoran, K. and J. Fischer. (2000). *Measures for clinical practice: A sourcebook* (3rd ed., Vol. 2). New York: Free Press. Available from http://chipts.ucla.edu/assessment/othersites.html.

To read more about these measures or to access the numerous assessment resources not selected, visit these online sources:

- Buros Institute of Mental Measurements, found at www.unl.edu/buros.
- Tests and Measures in the Social Sciences: Tests available in compilation volumes http://libraries.uta.edu/helen/Test&meas/testmainframe .htm#Collections.
- Psychological Tests and Measures:
  www.library.ewu.edu/help/LocatingInformation/PsychologicalTests.html.

These sites provide information on literally thousands of measures and assessments. They are invaluable resources for addiction professionals interested in finding information on a particular test (measure and assessments).

DUAL DIAGNOSES: PSYCHIATRIC ILLNESS WITH ADDICTION

According to the National Institute of Mental Health (www.nimh.nih.gov), a diagnosable mental disorder afflicts about one in five adults, many of whom suffer from more than one disorder at a time. Clients with drug problems frequently have an underlying psychiatric disorder (Ziedonis & D'Avanzo, 1998).

A national study—The NIMH Epidemiological Catchment Area (ECA) Study—found that substance abuse disorders are very common among psychiatric patients, with 20% having a current problem and 29% a lifetime substance use disorder. The most typical psychiatric disorders associated with substance abuse disorders are depression, anxiety, schizophrenia, and antisocial personality. Of those who commit suicide, 90% have a diagnosable mental disorder, generally a substance abuse or a depressive disorder. See the Dual Diagnosis web site at www.nyu.edu/odae/dualdiagnosis.html.

THE *DIAGNOSTIC AND STATISTICAL MANUAL (DSM-IV-TR)*

The *DSM* first appeared in 1952 with the second edition in 1968, the third in 1978, a revision in 1987, and a fourth edition, *DSM-IV*, in 1994. The current edition, *DSM-IV*, text revision (*DSM-IV-TR*) was published in 2000.

In the first two editions (*DSM-I* and *DSM-II*), only one axis was used for a diagnosis. Beginning with *DSM-III*, however, a five-axis scheme was developed to account for biological, psychological, and social functioning as well as overall adaptability to life's stressors:

Axis I: For specifying any disorders, as well as other conditions that may be a focus of clinical attention

Axis II: For specifying *personality disorders* and/or *mental retardation*

Axis III: Specifies any *general medical conditions* that are relevant to understanding or managing the individual's mental disorder

Axis IV: For reporting *psychosocial and environmental problems* that could affect the diagnosis, treatment, or prognosis of Axes I or II

Axis V: For specifying the individual's *overall level of functioning*

PSYCHIATRIC DIAGNOSTIC CATEGORIES[1]

More than 200 psychiatric diagnoses are categorized in the American Psychiatric Association's diagnostic manual, *Diagnostic and Statistical Manual of Mental Disorders,* fourth edition, text revision (*DSM-IV-TR*). The *DSM-IV-TR* (American Psychiatric Association, 2000) includes 17 broad categories of mental disorders with multiple diagnoses included in each category. The following is a summary of the major categories.

---

[1] The following overview of the *DSM-IV-TR* is adapted from "Psychopathology," by L. Sperry, M. P. Duffy, R. M. Tureen, and S. E. Gillig, in *Family Therapy Review: Preparing for Comprehensive and Licensing Exams,* R. H. Coombs (Ed.), 2005, Mahwah, NJ: Erlbaum.

Psychotic Thought Disorders

Schizophrenia

A psychotic disorder involving significant dysfunctions in a person's thought processes, speech patterns, behavior, mood, affect, motivation, and social and occupational functioning, symptoms may include delusions (cognitive distortions such as false beliefs and misinterpretations of experience that can be bizarre or highly unlikely) and hallucinations (perceptual distortions that are usually auditory in nature). Other symptoms may include disorganized speech, restriction and flattened affect, deterioration in self-care, and reduced ability to set and implement goal-directed behavior.

Schizophrenia's subtypes include:

- *Paranoid type:* Delusions and/or auditory hallucinations organized around a central persecutory and/or grandiose theme;
- *Disorganized type:* Disturbances in speech, affect, behavioral organization, goal-directedness, and self-care;
- *Catatonic type:* Significant disturbances in motor behavior ranging from immobility and rigidity to agitation and restlessness and echolalia;
- *Undifferentiated type:* Meets the criteria for schizophrenia but not the criteria for preceding subtypes; and
- *Residual type:* Meets the criteria for schizophrenia but lacks current psychotic symptoms yet has some negative symptoms.

Delusional Disorders

In this disorder, a nonbizarre delusion is present but without auditory or visual hallucinations, bizarre delusions, and disorganized speech, affect, and behavior. Subtypes include:

- *Erotomanic type:* Belief that a celebrity or well-known person is in love with you
- *Grandiose type:* Belief that you possess a superior talent or gift
- *Jealous type:* Belief that your spouse or lover is unfaithful and you gather evidence from normal events like finding a hair on your lover's coat
- *Persecutory type:* Belief that others are out to get you
- *Somatic type:* Belief that there is something wrong with your appearance or a part of your body

Mood Disorders

Major Depression

This is characterized by either a depressed mood or loss of interest and pleasure in daily life and the presence of four other symptoms from this list that appear regularly (daily or near daily) for at least 2 weeks:

- Significant weight loss or gain
- Persistent sleep disturbances, in particular, awakening in the middle of the night and having difficulty returning to sleep and/or early morning awakening

- Increased agitation or restlessness or decreased movement and motor activity that is noticeable to others; chronic fatigue
- Inappropriate feelings of worthlessness, guilt, and self-doubt
- Difficulties concentrating and making decisions
- Frequent thoughts of death and/or suicide with or without the formulation of a plan

Dysthymic Disorder

The client is chronically depressed for at least 2 years, without meeting the criteria for Major Depression, and manifests at least two of these symptoms:

- Disturbances of appetite and eating
- Sleep difficulties
- Chronic fatigue
- Difficulties in concentration and decision making
- Feelings of hopelessness or worthlessness
- Chronic self-doubt or self-reproach

Bipolar Disorder

This is the presence of either a manic episode or hypomania. A *manic episode* is a period of expansive or irritable mood, lasting at least 1 week with three or more of the following symptoms: grandiosity; excessive energy, and diminished need for sleep; talking more and faster than usual; racing thoughts and flight of ideas; distractibility; increase in goal-directed behavior; and high-risk activities such as overspending or bad judgment in business or sex. *Hypomania* is a distinct period of at least 4 days of expansive or irritable mood during which the client feels exceptionally well or cheerful and, when accompanied by cycles of depression, can signify a less severe form of bipolar disorder.

Anxiety, Dissociate, and Somatoform Disorders

Not as severe or disabling as psychotic disorders, clients with these disorders are able to maintain overall functioning and not lose contact with external reality.

Generalized Anxiety Disorder

Involves excessive worry about many things for at least 6 months and, despite effort, an inability to control the anxiety. Three or more other symptoms must also be present: restlessness, tiring easily, difficulties concentrating, irritability, muscle tension, or sleep problems.

Panic Disorders and Agoraphobia

A *panic attack* is a sudden onset of physiological symptoms such as sweating, trembling, racing heart, chest pain, shortness of breath, rapid breathing, dizziness, chills or hot flashes, numbness or tingling and perhaps a fear of dying, losing control, a sense of dread, or a fear of going crazy. *Agoraphobia* is the learned avoidance of events or activities that may trigger a panic attack (e.g., being in crowds).

Posttraumatic Stress Disorder (PTSD)

PTSD is characterized by recalling, dreaming about, or reexperiencing a traumatic event (e.g., rape, combat, a natural disaster), and responding emotionally and physically with unwanted thoughts and feelings of fear, shock, and helplessness and wanting to avoid thinking or talking about the event. An overactive startle response and hypervigilance are typical. Symptoms must be present for at least 1 month.

Dissociative Disorders

The result of a high level of suggestibility in which some (Dissociative Amnesia) cannot remember their names or past traumas, or abruptly leave their homes and cannot remember who they are (Dissociative Fugue). Previously called Multiple Personality Disorder, Dissociative Identity Disorder is characterized by the emergence of more than one personality and is associated with child sexual abuse. Depersonalization Disorder is the experience of detachment from one's self.

Somatoform Disorders

This is a physical symptom that cannot be fully explained with a medical problem. Some fear they have a serious disease because they misinterpret bodily symptoms, and/or overutilize medical services (e.g., frequent visits to doctors, lab tests). Examples include hypochondrias and pain disorder.

DISORDERS OF CHILDHOOD AND ADOLESCENCE

Attention Deficit Disorder (ADD)

An ongoing pattern of inattention and/or hyperactivity/impulsivity (ADHD), with symptoms manifested before age seven and in two settings (e.g., school and home). *Inattention* symptoms include (1) making careless mistakes, (2) not paying attention, (3) not listening, (4) not following instructions, (5) being poorly organized, (6) avoiding tasks that require concentration, (7) losing things, (8) being easily distracted, or (9) being forgetful in daily activities.

Hyperactivity-impulsivity symptoms include (1) fighting, (2) leaving one's seat in the classroom, (3) running about and climbing excessively, (4) having difficulty playing quietly, (5) talking excessively, (6) blurting out answers, (7) having difficulty awaiting one's turn, and (8) interrupting or intruding on others.

Autism and Asperger's Disorder

Autism and Asperger's Disorder are childhood disorders usually diagnosed before age three and marked by striking and enduring impairment in interpersonal and social interactions. Autism symptoms include *social interaction* deficits (e.g., impairment in such nonverbal behavior as eye contact, facial expression, posture, and gesture, or meaningful peer relationships, sharing with others, and lack of reciprocity), *communication* deficits (e.g., absence or delay of language development, odd and repetitive use of language in those with speech, and lack of imaginative and imitative play), and *repetitive, stereotyped movements and interests* (e.g., intense preoccupation with one thing, rituals, repetitive body movements like rocking, banging, or clapping, and preoccupation with parts of objects).

Asperger's Disorder differs from Autism in that the child uses language, probably in an eccentric way, but misses social cues from others. There is no clinically significant delay in language acquisition and less repetitive motor behaviors.

EATING DISORDERS

Anorexia Nervosa and Bulimia Nervosa are in this category. *Anorexia,* is the refusal to maintain body weight at a minimally normal level necessary for health and growth combined with an overwhelming fear of weight gain and a significant misperception about one's weight and shape. The Binge-Eating/Purging Type is a history of vomiting or inappropriate use of laxatives, diuretics, or enemas in the current episode. *Bulimia,* recurrent binge eating of inordinate amounts of food with a sense of loss of control and preoccupation with weight and shape, includes self-induced vomiting and the misuse of laxatives, enemas, diuretics, exercise, and fasting. The Nonpurging Type involves excessive exercise or fasting.

PERSONALITY DISORDERS

Inflexible and maladaptive pattern of inner experience and behavior that deviates markedly from expectations of the individual's culture, these disorders are manifest in at least two of the following areas: cognitions, affectivity, interpersonal functioning, or impulse control, and lead to clinically significant distress or impairment. While not usually diagnosed until the individual is an adult, the presence of a personality disorder may be recognizable by adolescence, and these disorders continue throughout most or all of adult life.

Personality Disorders, coded on Axis II of a *DSM-IV-TR* multiaxial diagnosis in three clusters, include:

- *Cluster A,* including Paranoid, Schizoid, and Schizotypal Personality Disorders, are characterized by odd or eccentric behaviors.
- *Cluster B,* including Antisocial, Borderline, Histrionic, and Narcissistic Personality Disorders, are characterized by dramatic, emotional, or erratic behaviors.
- *Cluster C,* including Avoidant, Dependent, and Obsessive-Compulsive Personality Disorders, are characterized by anxiety and fearfulness.

The two most common personality disorders seen in clinical practice are Borderline Personality Disorder and Narcissistic Personality Disorder.

Borderline Personality Disorder

A pervasive pattern of unstable self-identity, interpersonal relationships, and moods marked by (1) persistent disturbance of identity (e.g., uncertainty about career, values, and even sexual orientation); and (2) intense, unstable interpersonal relations and concerns about real or imagined abandonment, which give rise to a nearly constant state of emotionality that others perceive to be inappropriate (e.g., appearing jealous, suicidal, angry, or fearful). Mood instability and impulsivity are routine and often unpredictable.

Narcissistic Personality Disorder

This is a pervasive pattern of grandiosity, lack of empathy, and hypersensitivity to others' evaluations and self-criticism. Despite outward success, self-esteem tends to be fragile and there is a need for constant admiration. Despite fantasies of beauty, brilliance, and success, genuine pleasure is rarely acceptable since these feelings of grandiosity may lead to exaggerated feelings of failure.

COGNITIVE DISORDERS

Previously called Organic Mental Syndromes, these disorders are brain dysfunctions manifested in cognitive deficits.

Delirium

A disturbance in consciousness whereby one has difficulty maintaining attention and is easily distracted, delirium includes deficits in perception (e.g., hallucinations or illusions), memory (e.g., disorientation), or language dysfunction. Causes can include trauma (e.g., head injury), medication, substance use (e.g., intoxication or withdrawal), general medical condition, or a combination of these.

Dementia

Impairment of both short-term and long-term memory, dementia takes many forms, including Dementia of the Alzheimer's Type (DAT) where the deterioration of cognitive deficits develop slowly and progressively. Dementia may include visual hallucinations and delirium, and has at least one of these brain impairments:

- *Agnosia:* Inability to recognize and name objects
- *Apraxia:* Loss of a purposeful, voluntary motor skill; *aphasia*—inability to understand or produce language
- *Anomia:* Inability to speak or produce normal speech sounds

SUBSTANCE-INDUCED DISORDERS[2]

Secondary mental disorders brought on by substance abuse and substance dependence include:

---

[2] The following section was adapted from "Psychopathology," by L. Field and L. Seligman, in *Addiction Counseling Review: Preparing for Comprehensive, Certification and Licensing Exams* R. H Coombs (Ed.), 2005, Mahwah, NJ: Erlbaum.

- Substance intoxication
- Substance withdrawal
- Substance-induced delirium
- Substance-induced persisting dementia
- Substance-induced persisting amnestic disorder
- Substance-induced psychotic disorder
- Substance-induced mood disorder
- Substance-induced anxiety disorder
- Substance-induced sexual dysfunction
- Substance-induced sleep disorder
- Hallucinogen persisting perception disorder (flashbacks)

Depression, anxiety, and problems with sleep and sexual functioning, typical of clients who use drugs, often worsen when clients are stressed by trying to halt their drug habits.

These guidelines, proposed by Field and Seligman (2005) can help ascertain whether symptoms reflect an induced or preexisting condition or disorder:

- Obtain a detailed history. Conduct a thorough intake interview with the client and, if possible, family members and close friends, to determine whether the emotional symptoms preceded or followed the onset of the substance use disorder.
- Wait at least a month after the client has stopped using substances to make a judgment. Until then, withdrawal symptoms, cravings for the once-gratifying substance, and the challenge of adjusting to life without substances will cloud the picture.
- Consider the possibility that alcohol and other psychoactive drugs were used to self-medicate the emotional malady (Field & Seligman, 2005).

Additional Resources

Review the *DSM-IV-TR* criteria for the previously mentioned mental health issues at www.psychologynet.org/dsm.html (web site for Psychological Services, which provides the *DSM-IV-TR*).

For a detailed review of this topic, see Kranzler, H. R., & Rounsaville, B. J. (Eds.). (1998). *Dual diagnosis and treatment.* New York: Marcel Dekker; Dzieglielewski, S. (2002). *DSM-IV-TR in action.* Hoboken, NJ: Wiley; Othmer, E., & Othmer, S. (2002). *The clinical interview using DSM-IV-TR. Vol. 1: Fundamentals.* Washington, DC: American Psychiatric Press; Ries, R. K. (1994). *Assessment and treatment of patients with coexisting mental illness and alcohol and other drug abuse* (Treatment Improvement Protocol #9; DHHS Publication No. SMA 95-3061). Rockville, MD: Center for Substance Abuse Treatment; and Spitzer, R., Gibbon, M., Skodol, A., Williams, J. B. W., & First, M. B. (2001). *DSM-IV-TR Casebook: A learning companion to the Diagnostic and Statistical Manual of Mental Disorders* (4th ed., text rev.). Washington, DC: American Psychiatric Press.

PART IV
Clinical Skills and Resources

Part IV gives an overview of clinical skills and resources. After reviewing the clinical approaches of key clinical theorists, it describes basic counseling techniques and clinical microskills. Client homework assignments and exercises to enhance client health and stress management are also included.

CLINICAL MODELS
    Sigmund Freud's Psychoanalytic Therapy
    Carl G. Jung's Analytic Psychoanalysis
    Alfred Adler's Individual Psychology
    Carl Rogers's Person-Centered Therapy
    Fritz Perls's Gestalt Therapy
    Irvin Yalom's Existential Psychotherapy
    Viktor Frankl's Logotherapy
    Albert Ellis's Rational-Emotive Behavior Therapy
    William Glasser's Choice Theory and Reality Therapy
    Aaron Beck's Cognitive Behavioral Therapy
    Eric Berne's Transactional Analysis
    Other Behavioral Approaches

COUNSELING TECHNIQUES

CLINICAL MICROSKILLS

CLIENT HOMEWORK EXERCISES

CLIENT HEALTH AND STRESS MANAGEMENT
    Nutritional Counseling
    Exercise Counseling
    Affect-Regulation Coping Skills Counseling
    Stress-Management Training

Shaffer Coping Models
Common Styles of Negative Self-Talk
Rewriting Old Beliefs
Rewriting Irrational Beliefs

CLINICAL MODELS

This section provides a brief overview of key clinical models available to the addiction counselor.

SIGMUND FREUD'S PSYCHOANALYTIC THERAPY

Psychoanalytic Therapy (also called psychodynamic and psychoanalysis) is based on the assumption that behavior results from the conflict between the conscious and unconscious minds, and biological and social forces (H. S. Friedman & Schustack, 2003).

Every personality has three parts: *id*, the source of psychic energy that drives the instincts for survival and pleasure; *superego*, the conscience that promotes personal ideals and acts as moral judge of right and wrong; and the *ego*, the executive part that mediates between id and the superego, between inner strivings and reality, and tries to maintain mastery over the id's drives (Corsini & Wedding, 2001). Freud (1961) postulated that all human motivation derives from a biological drive to obtain pleasure and avoid pain—a dynamic he called "the pleasure principle" (Freud, 1958). According to Freud, a client's adult pathology can be traced to early sexual development, particularly a lack of sexual gratification during one of five psychosexual developmental stages that Freud labels *oral, anal, phallic, latency,* and *genital.*

THERAPEUTIC APPROACH

The client comes into the therapist's office, reclines comfortably on a couch, and free associates (there is no predetermined agenda) about thoughts that come spontaneously to mind. The counselor helps the client uncover unconscious dynamics by going with the flow of these unplanned expressions.

The therapist helps the client understand how unconscious ego states and defense mechanisms can negatively impact personal development. Although the following ego defense mechanisms may help a client manage unwanted emotions, they can also impede emotional growth: *Repression* (pushing a memory out of conscious memory), *Regression* (returning to an earlier stage of development), and *Reaction Formation* (reacting in the opposite way to an unacceptable impulse) (Corey, 2000).

Additional Resources

Dr. C. George Boeree provides a user-friendly introduction to the core work of Freud at www.ship.edu/~cgboeree/freud.html.

CARL G. JUNG'S ANALYTIC PSYCHOANALYSIS

Fascinated with the importance of spiritual development for an individual's mental health, Jung also assumed that people can find their place in the world by understanding their unconscious mind. He believed that each person has a personal unconscious made up of repressed events, wishes, feelings, and conflicts and also shares a "collective unconscious"—memories of their ancestral and racial heritage. These latter memories are organized around images called *archetypes* (Howatt, 2000).

THERAPEUTIC APPROACH

The unconscious mind, once explored, opens the door for healing mental illness (Jung, 1954a). Dream Analysis, Jung's method for communicating with the unconscious mind, reveals archetypes that the therapist interprets for the client (Jung, 1954b).

Although addiction counselors may not be trained in Dream Analysis (which takes years), they can use two counseling applications—personality and spirituality. Exploring personality traits such as introversion and extroversion assists clients in understanding how they interact with others. Jung's seminal work on extroversion and introversion led to the development of the Myers-Briggs Type Indicator (Howatt, 2005). Clients may complete this scale and use the results to develop awareness and determine core competencies needed to support their recovery.

As the history of Alcoholics Anonymous shows, addressing and strengthening spirituality in daily living can be vital in helping clients recover from their addictive disorders and develop healthier personalities.

Additional Resources

See the Jung web site at www.cgjungpage.org.

ALFRED ADLER'S INDIVIDUAL PSYCHOLOGY

Adler taught that each client pursues fictional goals in an unhealthy quest for superiority. Unrealistic goals may be overwhelming and lead to discouragement and such self-destructive behaviors as crime, addiction, and psychosis (Adler, 1929, 1958).

THERAPEUTIC APPROACH

The first step—assessment—is to learn about the client's family of origin, birth order, early recollections, dreams, and current life tasks. Next is helping the client develop insight about the cost of trying to fulfill unrealistic goals. With these insights, the client makes new, healthier goals. To move the client away from feelings of discouragement and inferiority, the therapist helps the client make a realistic action plan and develop the necessary skills to achieve his new goals (Howatt, 2005). Other Adlerian techniques, such as the Magic Wand and Confrontation, can also be used (see "Counseling Techniques" later in Part IV).

Additional Resources

See the web site of the International Association of Individual Psychology at www.iaiponline.org.

CARL ROGERS'S PERSON-CENTERED THERAPY

Rogers's client-centered philosophy assumes that each person is, by nature, good, worthy, and valuable (1951). This person-centered therapy trusts that clients have within themselves resources to improve their life situation. If this inner potential and ability emerges, the client needs only support, not direction.

THERAPEUTIC APPROACH

This nondirective and nonconfrontational counseling method assumes clients possess innate ability to evaluate and wisely choose their behaviors. The effective counselor adheres to what Rogers (1959) calls three core conditions of counseling: (1) *empathy*—responding to the client with intense interest, valuing the client's perception of the world and the meaning they attach to it; (2) *congruence*—being honest and consistent in behavior and thought; and (3) *warm regard*—showing nonjudgmental, accepting, positive regard for the client through word and deed. These three core conditions may appear simple, but their mastery takes a strong commitment of time and effort by the counselor.

Additional Resources

Visit the Center of Studies of the Persona at www.centerfortheperson.org/organizations.html.

FRITZ PERLS'S GESTALT THERAPY

Awareness, the principal goal of Gestalt Therapy (Perls, 1969), comes by focusing on clients' present situations and current behaviors, how they perceive their behaviors and how they interpret their experiences (Corey, 2000). The therapist observes only the client's behavior and does not attempt to determine the causes of the behavior.

THERAPEUTIC APPROACH

Awareness, the therapist's principal tool, is achieved by exploring current behaviors, feelings, and thoughts. The therapist assigns homework and assists the client in creating life experiments that demonstrate and reinforce how maladaptive behaviors have a negative impact on health and wellness. Experiments may include role-play to stress dysfunctional interaction patterns and to experiment with healthier ways (Perls, 1969, 1973).

Getting to the core of personality, Perls states, is much the same as peeling off the layers of an onion. These are the five layers of awareness (metaphoric onion): (1) *phony*—responding to others in an inauthentic and stereotypical manner; (2) *phobic*—avoiding the pain of realistic self-examination and taking responsibility for one's own actions; (3) *impasse*—stalling in the present level of maturity; (4) *implosive*—starting to get in touch with true self by questioning defense mechanisms; (5) *explosive*—a great release of energy when one finally lets go of all phony roles and pretenses (Howatt, 2000).

Because impasse in therapy is caused by the client's defense mechanisms (e.g., introjections—accepting others' beliefs without testing them), the therapist designs experiments to teach the client about these layers of awareness and how defense mechanisms underlie faulty perceptions of reality.

Additional Resources

For more information about Gestalt Therapy, see www.gestaltri.com.

IRVIN YALOM'S EXISTENTIAL PSYCHOTHERAPY

Existential means pertaining to existence. Working with the conscious rather than the unconscious mind, existential counseling seeks to ask and answer fundamental questions about being a human being (e.g., finding meaning in life) and the struggles inherent in this existence.

Yalom (1981) postulates that many psychological problems are directly rooted in one of four ultimate concerns: *death* (there is no escape), *freedom* (each client is free to define his or her own world), *isolation* (there is a gulf between self and others and self and the world), and *meaninglessness* (how one defines the meaning of life and its purpose).

THERAPEUTIC APPROACH

The therapist assists the client in exploring each of the four ultimate concerns and provides examples of how addressing them can improve life. As active participants, therapists share their personal views and ask questions related to the client's internal struggle. For related strategies such as *helper self-disclosure* and *paraphrasing*, see Counseling Techniques and Clinical Microskills, later in Part IV.

Additional Resources

To learn more, visit the web site at www.yalom.com.

VIKTOR FRANKL'S LOGOTHERAPY

Viktor Frankl, observing how he and his fellow prisoners coped with extraordinarily stressful circumstances in Nazi concentration camps, concluded that circumstances and events in the outer world (things outside the inner self) do not matter as much as the ultimate freedom of people to determine the meaning of their situation. In his classic book *Man's Search for Meaning*, Frankl (1963) explains that, although brutal guards may have inflicted suffering and pain on his body, they could not control his mind. Logotherapy, the idea that clients have the ability and responsibility to make their own choices regardless of their environment, assumes that a client always has a choice; and no-choice is still a choice.

THERAPEUTIC APPROACH

The therapist teaches clients how to avoid the victim role by mentally separating from their external environment and taking responsibility for their own lives. Two of Frankl's techniques are *dereflection* (turning clients' attention from their problematic situation to the creative ways they are coping or could cope) and *paradoxical intentions* (encouraging an exaggerated form of the undesired behavior).

Additional Resources

To learn more, visit the web site at http://logotherapy.univie.ac.at.

ALBERT ELLIS'S RATIONAL-EMOTIVE BEHAVIOR THERAPY

Ellis postulates that most, if not all, of a client's emotional problems result from irrational thinking, and moreover, everyone can learn how to think effectively (Ellis, 1962). Directive and didactic, this cognitive-behavioral approach works with clients at a conscious level, teaching new insights and skills in the therapist's office to be practiced at home. Ellis's Rational-Emotive Behavior Therapy (REBT) shares a common thread with Glaser's Reality Therapy and Beck's Cognitive Behavioral Therapy, all of which use problem-solving and learning by employing new behavioral skills (discussed in the paragraphs that follow).

THERAPEUTIC APPROACH

REBT addresses the client's irrational thinking with an ABC model: (1) **Activating Event**—an external event that upsets the client; (2) **Belief**—client's irrational belief about A; and (3) **Consequences**—what clients do and feel in response to their irrational belief about the activating event (Ellis, 1994).

Next the counselor focuses on the DEF part of the ABC model: (4) **Disputing**—the counselor challenges the client's irrational thinking and conclusions about A and B. Using techniques such as REBT homework sheets, the counselor teaches the client to recognize irrational thinking and to think realistically; (5) **Effect**—cognitive change in the client, rational thinking; and (6) **Feeling**—instead of anxiety or depression, client's feelings are appropriate to the situation.

Additional Resources

To learn more about the works, training, and publications of Ellis, visit www.rebt.org.

WILLIAM GLASSER'S CHOICE THEORY AND REALITY THERAPY

Choice Theory assumes that individuals choose most of their behavior and that it is internally motivated by the need to meet one or more of the following basic needs: love and belonging (the most important), power, fun, freedom, and survival. All behavior is total, meaning that clients' actions will affect their thinking, which in turn will control feelings and physiology. Using a car as a metaphor, Glasser (1998) teaches that what the front wheels (behavior and thinking) do, the rear wheels (feeling and physiology) will follow. For example, a depressed, lethargic client who is sitting around the house can change his or her emotional state by doing something different.

THERAPEUTIC APPROACH

Based on choice theory, reality therapy seeks to help clients build their love and belonging relationships. Glasser (1998) names *Seven Caring Habits:* supporting, encouraging, listening, accepting, trusting, respecting, and negotiating differences. He also identifies *Seven Deadly Habits:* criticizing, blaming, complaining, nagging, threatening, punishing, and bribing or rewarding to control.

Promoting the concept of an internal locus of control (self-responsibility), reality therapy offers a frame of reference to help clients see why they do what they do and how changing any element (e.g., spending time around the house) will change other aspects of the whole (e.g., feeling depressed and having low physical energy). Therapists ask strategic questions—What do you have now that meets your needs? What do you want? What are you doing to get what you want? Is what you are doing working? Reality therapy helps clients learn to meet their own needs.

Additional Resources

To learn about Glasser's work, training, and writing, visit www.wglasser.com.

AARON BECK'S COGNITIVE BEHAVIORAL THERAPY

Based on the premise that most of a client's negative thinking derives from automatic faulty thinking, Beck (1976) suggests that the client's present difficulties (e.g., depression) result from thinking errors and negative thinking. The therapist's goal is to help the client become aware of negative thought patterns and change them. Beck authored four popular clinical scales: Beck Depression, Beck Anxiety, Beck Hopelessness, and Beck Suicide (see Part III).

THERAPEUTIC APPROACH

The therapist first reduces the client's present level of anxiety by using empathy and reframing, then uncovers and monitors the client's faulty processing and negative schema. Using Socratic dialogue (thoughtful questioning of client), the client is taught how to think more accurately and effectively. After this, therapist and client design a behavioral experiment to test the client's beliefs and assumptions. Finally, behavioral strategies are implemented (e.g., journaling) to reinforce the new skills designed to prevent further faulty processing. Cognitive Behavioral Therapy (CBT) works best, Beck (1970) explains, with clients who have acceptable reality levels (no delusions).

Additional Resources

To learn more, visit the Beck Institute at www.beckinstitute.org.

ERIC BERNE'S TRANSACTIONAL ANALYSIS

Berne taught that everyone interacts from three ego states—each with its own feelings, thoughts, and ways of behaving—that make up the human personality: Parent, Adult, and Child (Berne, 1972).

THERAPEUTIC APPROACH

Helping clients develop a healthy life script—"I'm OK–You're OK "—is the clinical objective (Berne, 1961). All clients have the potential to make change and have a part in them that is acceptable to others. The actual work of Transactional Analysis (TA) revolves around four constructs: (1) exploration of transactions—what people say and do to and with each other; (2) games and cons—the games people play to get what they want; (3) scripts—how feedback from early transactions in childhood affect adulthood; (4) structures—the analysis of the different ego states a client communicates from in different transactions. "Strokes" (i.e., positive feedback) is one of the biggest motivators for behavior (Berne, 1961).

Additional Resources

To learn more, visit the International Transactional Analysis Institute at www.itaa-net.org.

OTHER BEHAVIORAL APPROACHES

Several other key behavioral approaches are available, such as Pavlov's classical conditioning, Skinner's operant conditioning, and Bandura's social learning theory. Although each stands alone as an independent therapeutic model, they all emphasize the environment's impact on behavior. Pavlov (1960) taught that behavior is the result of conditioned reflexes whereas B. F. Skinner (1971) states that behavior is the result of rewards (positive or negative). Bandura (1977) emphasizes that a person can learn by simply observing the environment.

THERAPEUTIC APPROACH

The counselor designs activities in five stages to help the client modify unwanted behaviors: (1) study the client's present behaviors; (2) define the primary problems; (3) determine client's goals; (4) select interventions and make an action plan; (5) start action plan, monitor, and follow up (Wilson, 2001).

Additional Resources

To learn more about Behavioral Therapy visit the Association for the Advancement of Behavioral Therapy, a comprehensive source of the current thinking and advancements in behavioral therapy at www.aabt.org. See also, James, R. K., & Gilliland, B. E. (1998). *Theories and strategies in counseling and psychocounseling* (4th ed.). New York: Allyn & Bacon, for detailed reviews of the most commonly used counseling theories applicable to addiction counseling.

Howatt, W. A. (2000). *The human services counseling toolbox*. Pacific Grove, CA. Brooks/Cole, contains information on theory, techniques, and strategies for working with persons with addictive disorders; it was developed with students learning to be addiction counselors. See also, Corsini, R. J., & Wedding, D. (Eds.). (2001). *Current psychotherapist* (6th ed.). Belmont, CA: Brooks/Cole (a detailed book on counseling theory).

COUNSELING TECHNIQUES

This section provides an overview of counseling techniques that may be useful with addicted clients. Arranged in alphabetical order, each technique is identified with a clinical model, as described in the preceding section.

We classify these techniques on a three-point scale: (1) *directive,* (2) *moderately directive,* and (3) *nondirective.* At one end of the scale, *directive techniques* openly confront and challenge the client to take specific action (e.g., complete home-work). At the opposite end, *nondirective techniques,* the counselor empathically supports the client. When using *moderately directive techniques,* the counselor focuses both on giving support *and* assisting the client in taking action (e.g., active scheduling):

- *Acting as if (individual psychology—directive):* In a role-play situation, clients act out the way they would like to be in various life scenarios and explore alternatives. The underlying premise is that with practice these behaviors feel more natural (G. Corey, 2000).
- *Active listening (person-centered—nondirective):* The counselor uses a cluster of skills to increase accurate understanding about what is being said. Good listening requires that the counselor interact with the client, offering affirming comments about what has been said, rephrasing the client's comments to encourage further commentary, and other appropriate expressions (see "Clinical Microskills" later in this part; Egan, 1994).
- *Activity scheduling (behavior therapy—moderately directive):* The counselor works with the client to initiate activities that move the client from inactivity to a more productive and vital state. Aside from these activities, scheduling—itemizing choices and strategies—may immediately impact the client positively (Corsini & Wedding, 2001).
- *Analogies or images to illustrate problems (REBT—moderately directive):* Analogies or images are used to see a problem from a different viewpoint (G. Corey, 2000).
- *Assertion training (behavior therapy—moderately directive):* Assertiveness, the ability to express one's needs and thoughts confidently without being either passive (hiding or muting) or aggressive (forcing and badgering), is useful for clients who cannot express anger or frustration, who have difficulty saying no, who allow others to take advantage of them, who have difficulty expressing affection, or who feel they do not have the right to express thoughts and feelings. This training is a collection of techniques—behavior rehearsal, exposure, modeling, and reinforcement (Meichenbaum, 1977). Elaboration of each is listed separately.
- *Attending and listening (individual psychology—nondirective):* The counselor learns the core of a client's thoughts and feelings by being psychologically involved, engaging the client with eye contact, and paying close attention to both verbal and nonverbal communication (Howatt, 2005).
- *Behavior modeling (behavior therapy—moderately directive):* Also called *vicarious learning* (developed by Bandura), the client learns by first observing the counselor (or someone else) perform a specific action, then imitates the modeled behavior (Corsini & Wedding, 2001).
- *Bibliotherapy (behavior therapy—moderately directive):* Reading assignments stimulate discussion, convey new values and attitudes, help reframe the problem, and provide possible solutions (G. Corey, 2000).

- *Brainstorming (individual psychology—moderately directive):* This is an uncritical discussion of *all* responses to open-ended, thought-provoking questions and problems, each designed to stimulate a list of ideas pertinent to various choices and options (Egan, 1994).
- *Catching oneself (individual psychology—directive):* This technique is useful with clients who catastrophize, are perfectionists, have eating disorders, and demonstrate obsessive-compulsive behavior. It raises awareness of self-destructive behavior or irrational thought without self-condemnation. Clients learn to anticipate events and change their behavior patterns (G. Corey, 2000).
- *Challenging (choice theory—directive):* This is an invitation to recognize thoughts and/or behavior that is self-defeating, harmful to others (or both), and to change that behavior (Howatt, 2000).
- *Cognitive modeling (behavior therapy—moderately directive):* The counselor performs tasks while engaging in self-encouragement to demonstrate how clients may talk themselves successfully through a task (Howatt, 2005).
- *Cognitive restructuring (behavior therapy—nondirective):* The counselor teaches clients to identify and evaluate their thoughts and to replace negative ones with more realistic and appropriate thoughts (James & Gilliland, 2001).
- *Congruence (person-centered therapy—nondirective):* The counselor is honest and consistent in word and behavior (G. Corey, 2000).
- *Contingency contracts (behavior therapy—directive):* The client and counselor develop a contract together designating behavior to be performed or changed. Rewards are based on the achievement of stated goals, the conditions under which they will be received, and the specific time frames for completion (Howatt, 2000).
- *Continuum line (REBT—directive):* Clients rate their feelings about their addiction on a scale of 1 to 100 with 1 being the worst (they hate it) and 100 being the best (they love it). This provides an understanding of where the client is in the treatment process and generates middle-ground options for clients manifesting black or white thinking (Howatt, 1995).
- *Contracting for change (transactional analysis—directive):* Clients work with the counselor to develop a contract that specifically states what they plan to change in order to reach self-designated goals. The counselor is a witness and a facilitator (Howatt, 2000).
- *Counter-conditioning (behavior therapy—moderately directive):* Also known as reciprocal inhibition (Wolpe, 1982), the client practices being able to calmly respond to a stressful situation. The client learns to lower anxiety levels by breathing deeply, stretching, and relaxing shoulder and neck muscles.
- *Decatastrophize (cognitive—directive):* Using "what if" questions, clients discover that their problems may have grown out of proportion in their mind. This reduces anxiety so that positive collaboration and cooperation can take place between client and counselor (Howatt, 2000).
- *Description (existential—nondirective):* Clients vividly describe to the counselor what they are feeling or experiencing, thus facilitating a better understanding between them (Howatt, 1995).

- *Disputing perfectionism (REBT—nondirective):* The counselor shows clients (who thinks they must always be good at everything) that perfectionism is self-defeating (Corsini & Wedding, 2001).
- *Diversion (cognitive—directive):* The counselor distracts a sad or anxious client's attention away from the present concern, breaking an emotionally laden thought pattern, so that the client can return to the appropriate treatment track (G. Corey, 2000).
- *Empathy (person-centered therapy—nondirective):* The counselor sees and feels the client's world as though immersed in that world. By assuming the internal frame of reference of the other, the counselor understands the client's private pain (James & Gilliland, 2001).
- *Encouragement (individual psychology—directive):* The counselor praises clients' strengths and progress, recognizing, labeling, and accepting their positive qualities. This increases clients' self-confidence, counters discouragement, and helps them set realistic goals (G. Corey, 2000).
- *Exaggeration (Gestalt—directive):* The counselor asks the client to exaggerate a certain thought, emotion, or body movement that has just been expressed, allowing the client to become more aware of hidden feelings and defense mechanisms (Howatt, 2000).
- *Extinction (behavior therapy—moderately directive):* Undesirable behaviors are discouraged and eventually eliminated by removing rewards that stimulate the behavior (Corsini & Wedding, 2001).
- *Feedback (behavior therapy—moderately directive):* Praise, encouragement, and specific constructive suggestions for modifying errors help clients learn new behaviors (James & Gilliland, 2001).
- *Fruit basket technique (REBT—directive):* The counselor shows a fruit basket with good and bad fruit to demonstrate that although the client may have some flaws and done some bad things, the client also has virtues and is basically a good person (Howatt, 2000).
- *Goal setting (interpersonal—directive):* Brainstorming specific objectives and strategies and then arranging emerging plans in the best sequence for a positive outcome mobilizes the client to appropriate action (Corsini & Wedding, 2001).
- *Graduated exposure (behavior therapy—directive):* Step-by-step exposure to real-life situations enables clients to practice skills or preferred behavior in anxiety-provoking situations (Howatt, 2000).
- *Graduated task assignment (behavior therapy—directive):* Clients learn to reduce anxiety while developing new skills by taking an assigned task (often given as homework) that begins simply and then gradually becomes more difficult and complex (Howatt, 1995).
- *Helper self-disclosure (individual psychology—moderately directive):* The counselor appropriately shares selected and focused experiences, behaviors, and feelings with clients. This builds the client-counselor relationship and encourages the client to disclose hidden feelings and thoughts (Howatt, 2005a).
- *Humor and jolting language (sarcasm; REBT—moderately directive):* Appropriate humor by the counselor can relax clients and encourage them to open up.

Sarcasm may help clients identify their irrational beliefs and laugh at their behavior (Howatt, 2000).

- *Imagery (cognitive—directive):* Metaphors and/or visual pictures developed by counselor and client may help clients develop insight about their thinking and provide the counselor with a clearer impression of clients' automatic thoughts (G. Corey, 2000).
- *Immediacy (individual psychology—directive):* Addressing what is going on in the present counseling session may help the client see that what is occurring is a sample of everyday life (G. Corey, 2000).
- *Language exercises (Gestalt—directive):* An examination of speech patterns that helps clients increase self-awareness and personal responsibility by acknowledging their thoughts, feelings, and actions (Howatt, 1995).
- *Magic wand (individual psychology—directive):* Clients pretend they have a magic wand and can wish for anything to allow them to look beyond present circumstances and define their real wants in life (Howatt, 2000).
- *Offering options (individual psychology—directive):* The counselor offers clients a choice among several options (Corsini & Wedding, 2001).
- *Paradoxical intention (reality therapy—moderately directive):* Clients are instructed to consciously exaggerate debilitating thoughts and behaviors, creating an awareness of how out of proportion their response is to the situation. Also called prescribing the symptoms and antisuggestion (Wubbolding, 1988).
- *Paradoxical intervention (logo therapy—directive):* The counselor places clients in a double bind to cut through their resistance by asking them to exaggerate or even perfect a problematic behavior (G. Corey, 2000).
- *Paradoxical technique (REBT—directive):* Clients are asked to perform the presenting irrational behavior at a certain time every day, thus removing the gratification received from performing the irrational behavior (Howatt, 2000).
- *Playing the projection (Gestalt—directive):* Clients pretend to be the recipient of the statements that they make about others. These statements, often projections of attributes that clients possess, bring awareness of inner conflicts (G. Corey, 2000).
- *Push-button technique (individual psychology—directive):* Clients close their eyes and alternately picture a pleasant and an unpleasant experience while paying attention to the feelings accompanying each experience. This teaches clients that they can create whatever feelings they wish by relying on their thoughts (Corsini & Wedding, 2001).
- *Reframing (cognitive—directive):* Reframing provides a different interpretation of a particular situation, allowing a client to understand an original complaint from different angles (G. Corey, 2000).
- *Reinforcement (behavior therapy—directive):* A pleasant stimulus increases a desired behavior (James & Gilliland, 2001).
- *REBT self-help form (REBT—directive):* The client completes this form and the counselor uses it to determine the nature and extent of a client's faulty beliefs. (These REBT forms can be obtained from the Institute for Rational Emotive Therapy, 45 East 65th Street, New York, 10021, 212-535-0822; Howatt, 2005.)

- *Role play (behavior therapy—moderately directive):* Playing different roles enhances clients' ability to interact effectively with others in differing situations. Clients begin by acting out a designated situation and then develop their own scenario. They then keep track of difficult situations that occur outside therapy. One of these situations is chosen for role-playing, with either coaching or modeling by the counselor. After each role-play, feedback is given pertaining to the client's strengths and weaknesses (Corsini & Wedding, 2001).
- *Self-monitoring (cognitive—directive):* Clients monitor and record their thoughts just prior to, or during, problem behavior. During counseling sessions, the client discloses these thoughts, providing clues to the behavior and its treatment (James & Gilliland, 2001).
- *Sharing hunches (Gestalt—directive):* The counselor or group members share feelings and perceptions of other members in a tentative manner or in the form of an intuition or hunch. This provides clients with insight into how others see them (should only be done with clients' permission; G. Corey, 2000).
- *Spitting in the client's soup (individual psychology—directive):* When counselors determine that clients are getting a reward from maladaptive behavior, they may spoil the reward for clients by making them aware of the nature and consequences of this behavior (Howatt, 2000).
- *Staying with the feeling (Gestalt—directive):* When clients experience unpleasant feelings, the counselor encourages them to stay with these feelings. By experiencing and confronting negative emotions, courage develops, as does growth through experiencing pain (G. Corey, 2000).
- *Systematic desensitization (behavior therapy—directive):* Clients imagine various scenes so they gradually overcome fearful responses to anxiety-producing events. Clients are first helped to relax physically, then asked to imagine a low-anxiety item from a prepared list and maintain focus on that item while remaining calm until no more anxiety is felt. The counselor then has the client move on to imagine a more stressful scene, repeating the procedure step by step until the client can respond to the worst item on the list with calmness instead of fear (James & Gilliland, 2001).
- *Teaching the ABC model (REBT—directive):* This teaching tool is based on the idea that irrational beliefs are the core of an individual's problems: *A*—activating event; *B*—belief about that event; *C*—the consequence(s) of the belief. It teaches clients that their belief about an event, and not the event itself, leads to the subsequent feelings or behaviors (Corsini & Wedding, 2001).
- *Two-chair technique (Gestalt—moderately directive):* Chairs, set up across from each other, allow clients to dialogue with themselves and play all the roles. Clients change chairs when they change roles (Howatt, 2000).

Additional Resources

Gilliland, B. E., & James, R. K. (1998). *Theories and strategies in counseling and psychocounseling* (4th ed.). New York: Allyn & Bacon, is a well-written and detailed review of the most commonly used counseling theories useful in addiction counseling.

Howatt, W. A. (2000). *The human services counseling toolbox*. Pacific Grove, CA: Brooks/Cole, is a reference tool containing information on theory, techniques, and strategies for working with persons with addictive disorders. This book was developed with students who were learning how to become addiction counselors.

Corsini, R. J., & Wedding, D. (Eds.). (2001). *Current psychotherapist* (6th ed). Belmont, CA: Brooks/Cole; one of the most complete and detailed books on counseling theory in print today.

Sommers-Flanagan, J., & Sommers-Flanagan, R. (2004). *Counseling and psychotherapy theories in context and practice: Skills, strategies, and techniques*. Hoboken, NJ: Wiley.

CLINICAL MICROSKILLS

The following microskills work well with clients (Howatt, 2002):

- *Active listening:* Be actively engaged, totally focused, and show empathy for the client.
- *Body gestures:* Be mindful of your and your client's body language and remember that kinetics (body language) can influence up to 80% of all communication.
- *Chronemics:* Be accurate regarding time, locations, and recall.
- *Clarification statements:* State what you think the client is saying to determine if you are tracking the conversation properly.
- *Conflict avoidance:* While it is not necessary to always agree with a client, avoid debate.
- *Congruence:* Stay in tune with your intentions and motivations as you talk. Is your body language in sync with your verbal message?
- *Consequence questions:* Ask clients about the likely consequences of their actions. Are they aware of the cost of their choices?
- *Contextual listening:* Listen for content and details, and how the events impact the client, cognitively and emotionally.
- *Emotional filter:* Be aware of your own emotions when a client is talking and do not let clients override your rationality.
- *Empathy:* Be genuinely concerned about clients, their feelings, problems, and well-being.
- *Encouraging gestures:* Supportive statements by the counselor encourage the client to continue exploring a stressful topic.
- *Eye contact:* Maintain direct eye contact when it is comfortable and safe for a client, but be aware that clients from some cultures may initially regard direct eye contact as confrontational and threatening.

- *Favorite phrases:* Note the client's favorite words and expressions and use them when appropriate.
- *Frame of reference:* Ascertain clients' point of view—and "internal mental filters"—that shape their perceptions of events.
- *Gender and cultural differences:* Seek to understand and respect individual differences. If you don't know, ask.
- *Generalizing:* Help clients address specific issues and problems instead of masking them with general statements.
- *"I" language:* Help clients take responsibility for their feelings. It might be useful for the client to say, "When I say/hear/experience, I feel . . ."
- *Inferences:* Evaluate clients by their actions, not by their words.
- *Innocent probes:* Use expressions such as "Hmmm," "I understand," "yes," and so on, to keep the conversation going and to demonstrate that you are listening and engaged.
- *Justifying question:* Ask questions in a nonjudgmental manner if you need to point out inconsistencies in what is being said. This shows you are listening and tracking the conversation.
- *Mirroring:* Use similar body language—hand gestures, body position, and movement—as clients to make them feel more relaxed and comfortable.
- *Nonattention:* Ignore attacking or offensive comments and behaviors by looking away; do not reinforce the inappropriate behavior.
- *Nonthreatening communication:* Be aware of the inherent power of your position. Assist clients; don't try to control them.
- *Observe proximities:* Since the typical client prefers to communicate at a range of 4 to 6 feet, arrange the two counseling chairs at a 45-degree angle to each other, so that client and counselor each have an open field and free space in front. Since space preferences vary, ask if you're not sure.
- *Open-ended questions:* Ask questions that encourage clients to explore and elaborate, not just reply with a yes or no.
- *Overcoming deflection:* Help clients address the issues instead of shying away from painful subjects (by changing the topic, generalizing, asking questions, or extensive joking).
- *Positive assets statement:* Frankly and honestly point out clients' positive qualities.
- *Positive regard:* Maintain consistent nonjudgmental caring no matter what actions clients choose.
- *Reality congruence:* Note if clients' views of their situation are consistent with reality. Do clients say one thing but their voice and body posture suggest something else?
- *Reflecting:* Repeating key concepts presented by clients encourages disclosure of further information.
- *Reframing:* Provide clients with another, more optimistic way to look at a problem.
- *Selective attention:* Ask a question to get the client back on task with focus on the present situation and needs.
- *Shadowing:* Repeat what the client said, using the client's own words.

- *Summarizing:* Review what the client has said to ensure that you have properly heard and understood the client's story.
- *Silence:* Be calm and patient and allow spaces, when appropriate, to reflect.
- *Validating:* Make a clear statement that you understand the situation and acknowledge the client's views.
- *Voice tone:* Match the client's speech in terms of speed, volume, tone, timbre, and pitch when appropriate.
- *Values invasion:* Go with the client's personal values as to what is important and meaningful, do not impose your own.
- *Vocabulary:* Speak at the client's level and be aware of regionalisms and colloquialisms.
- *Warm regard:* Genuinely show nonjudgmental, accepting, positive regard for the client through thought and deed.

Additional Resources

Howatt, W. A. (2002). *Discipline of communication.* Kentville, Nova Scotia, Canada: A Way with Words. This, user-friendly tool, helps addiction counselors improve communication skills.

Find an excellent resource for to obtain additional information about microskill training at the web site of Microtraining and Multicultural Development: www.emicrotraining.com/microskills.html.

CLIENT HOMEWORK EXERCISES

Client homework assignments, designed by the counselor *and* client, allow clients to practice new behaviors. Once completed, they are then discussed in the next counseling session, and may continue long-term after formal counseling ends.

Regular homework assignments promote positive change in a short time (Finley & Lenz, 2003) and facilitate counseling sessions (Cormier & Cormier, 1998; Hay & Kinnier, 1998).

Clients rarely, if ever, master new skills by merely hearing or reading about them or watching others (Scott, Kern, & Coombs, 2001). Clients grow by *trying* new skills, making mistakes, identifying those mistakes, and trying again. Scott et al. (p. 201) recommend the following homework guidelines:

- Ask clients to practice a specific skill outside sessions and assess whether they think it will be helpful to do so.
- Ask clients why it is difficult to complete this task; failure to complete homework may have a variety of meanings.

- Leave enough time in each session to explain the homework assignment for the next session, and then review the process in detail at the beginning of each session thereafter.
- Follow-up will improve compliance and help assess the effectiveness of each task.
- Ask clients to elaborate what they have learned from the homework assignment.
- For clients who are not fully compliant with homework exercises, use shaping techniques to gradually achieve greater levels of compliance.

Blume (2005) offers the sample form shown in Figure IV.1 to help clients track their feelings, thoughts, situations, and events that precede drug use.

Weekly Drug Use Diary

Date and time you started using:	What kind of drug(s)? (list time you used each type)	What happened right before you used? (the situation, your thoughts and your feelings)?
Day 1		
Day 2		
Day 3		
Day 4		
Day 5		
Day 6		
Day 7		

Other notes about drug use this week (other observations you made):

_____

_____

FIGURE IV.1   Sample Self-Monitoring Form. *Source:* From *Treating Drug Problems,* by Arthur W. Blume, 2005, New York: Wiley. Reprinted with permission.

The following examples of client-oriented homework are reprinted with permission from Howatt's *Journal 45: A 45 Day Program to Create a New Beginning and Journal 51: Defining and Achieving New Goals* (Kentville, Nova Scotia, Canada: A Way with Words).

These samples of homework exercises are greatly influenced by the works of Glasser and Ellis:

- Box IV.1: Daily Affirmations Selection List
- Box IV.2: Overcoming Personal Frustrations
- Box IV.3: "What Do You Really Want?"
- Box IV.4: Disputing the Irrational Belief
- Box IV.5: Bibliotherapy: The Power of Reading
- Box IV.6: Personal Change Technique
- Box IV.7: Four Steps to Happiness
- Box IV.8: Life Planning (5 days)
- Box IV.9: Personal Reflection

Box IV.1   Daily Affirmations Selection List

Ellis (1980) teaches us that the key is to have "unconditional self-acceptance." To help accomplish this, each day choose one of the following affirmations as your own. This will help you "hard-wire" positive statements into your neurological system and increase positive thinking and self-acceptance. Remember, it takes daily practice and focus:

- I have equal worth and value to that of every other human being.
- I am entitled to my emotions and views, and I have a right to express them.
- I can love myself and others.
- I can succeed and find fulfillment in my work life.
- I can accept myself even when I am in conflict with others.
- I can make decisions about my relationships that are good for me.
- I am a bright and brilliant person.
- I am a kind, beautiful, and accepting person.
- I do not have to be perfect.
- I am strong enough to ask for help when I need it.

Box IV.2   Overcoming Personal Frustrations

The following four steps have been adapted from Albert Ellis (1999). They will help you recognize and be clear about what is stressful to you (who, what, where, and when). Answering these questions will help you resolve many of your frustrations. Pick one frustrating event for this exercise.

Step 1—Who or what is frustrating to you?

Step 2—What were your thoughts early on in the frustration (what was going through your mind as you started to feel stressful)?

Step 3—How did your body feel (heart racing, sweating, tense)?

Step 4—What was your emotional state at the time? Rate from 1 to 20.

Many times we become angry with those with whom we are close. This is because we have higher expectations, and share many emotions and experiences with these people. On the other side, the advantage to having great expectations is that we also have much more to gain by getting through our frustrations to improve the relationship.

Adapted from *Journal 45: A 45-Day Program to Create a New Beginning* (p. 94), by W. A. Howatt, 2001, Kentville, Nova Scotia, Canada: A Way with Words.

Box IV.3   "What Do You Really Want?"

Dr. Glasser (1998) teaches that each of us has unique individual wants. As you develop and explore personal change, ensure you are focusing on what you really want and what steps you can take to obtain these wants.

In the spaces below, answer the questions for each want.

1. **Desired State**—What do you really want in your life now?

1	
2	
3	

2. **Present State**—What are you presently doing to get what you really want?

1	
2	
3	

3. **What resources** do you presently have to get what you really want?

1	
2	
3	

4. **Interference**—What do you need to stop doing to get what you really want?

1	
2	
3	

Source: From *Journal 45: A 45-Day Program to Create a New Beginning* (p. 38), by W. A. Howatt, 2001, Kentville, Nova Scotia, Canada: A Way with Words.

Box IV.4   Disputing the Irrational Belief

The purpose of this exercise is to start building and practicing new positive self-statements to overcome old beliefs that led to our frustration. Below, create statements that are healthier and dispute the old beliefs.

Irrational Belief	Rational Belief
I should be perfect	I would prefer to do well, but if I do make a mistake, I am a fallible human being, and that's okay.
1	
2	
3	
4	
5	

Albert Ellis's Rational Emotive Behavioral Therapy (1999) suggests that irrational beliefs, in time, can be changed. After correcting an irrational belief, audiotape the new belief, and play it back over and over again until it becomes ingrained in your thoughts and feelings. This exercise can have a great impact on your personal success and personal growth. Ellis makes it clear that when making new statements, be very forceful, doing it with conviction. Paraphrased from *Journal 45: A 45-Day Program to Create a New Beginning* (p. 45), by W. A. Howatt, 2001, Kentville, Nova Scotia, Canada: A Way with Words.

Box IV.5 Bibliotherapy, The Power of Reading

You can learn much from the wisdom and personal growth of others who share their experiences and insights in books. For this assignment, find a self-help book, and each day read a minimum of XXX pages. Start with one of these books, taken from our shelves, and then develop your own list.

- Brian D. Biro, Beyond Success: *The 15 Secrets of a Winning Life*
- David D. Burns, *The Feeling Good Handbook*
- Stephen Covey, *7 Habits of Highly Effective People*
- Dale Carnegie, *How to Win Friends and Influence People*
- Robert D. Enright, *Forgiveness Is a Choice: A Step-by-Step Process for Resolving Anger and Restoring Hope*
- David Goleman, *Emotional Intelligence*
- David G. Myers, *The Pursuit of Happiness: Discovering the Pathway to Fulfillment, Well-being, and Enduring Personal Joy*
- M. Scott Peck, *A Road Less Travelled*
- Anthony Robbins, *Awaken the Giant Within*
- Ann Kaiser Stearns, *Living through Personal Crisis*
- Harold H. Bloomfield, *Making Peace with Yourself: Turning Your Weaknesses into Strengths*

Adapted from *Journal 45: A 45-Day Program to Create a New Beginning* (p. 98), by W. A. Howatt, 2001, Kentville, Nova Scotia, Canada: A Way with Words.

Box IV.6   Personal Change Techniques

This exercise provides a way to change your internal state and your behavior. Read the five steps first, then sit down, and *swish* to a new, more desired internal state.

Step 1—Identify the behavior you want to change or add, then imagine the behavior in your mind's eye.

Step 2—Create a new picture of what you want, as if you made the desired change, and see yourself doing it.

Step 3—Pretend you are looking at a large movie screen, and make a big, bright picture of the unwanted behavior you want to change (e.g., not reading books). Now, in front of the unwanted picture on the screen, put the desired picture (reading books), and then shrink it down to the size of a postage stamp, in the bottom left-hand corner of your screen. Be ready to take that small picture, and in less than a millisecond, have it blow up in size and brightness, and literally burst through the picture of the unwanted behavior, so you no longer can see that one. All you can see is the new picture, with all its excitement and rewards.

Step 4—Okay, so are you ready to go? On a count of three, take the small picture, and enlarge it, so you can see only the new picture. Ready—1-2-3—*SWISH IT!*

Step 5—Now clear the picture, and start all over again from Step 1, repeating this pattern until the picture of the unwanted behavior disappears, to the point that you can no longer find it.

Reprinted by permission from *Journal 45: A 45-Day Program to Create a New Beginning* (p. 104), by W. A. Howatt, 2001, Kentville, Nova Scotia, Canada: A Way with Words.

Box IV.7   Four Steps to Happiness

Step 1—Identify the upsetting situation: Describe the event or problems that are upsetting you. Who or what are you feeling unhappy about?

Step 2—Record your negative feelings: How do you feel about the upsetting situation? Use words like sad, angry, anxious, guilty, frustrated, hopeless. Rate each negative feeling on a scale from 1 (for the least) to 100 (for the most). (e.g., guilty—90)

Step 3—Creating new thinking: Focus on the negative thoughts that are associated with these feelings. What are you saying to yourself about the problem? Write these thoughts in the Automatic Thoughts column, and record between 0 (not at all) and 100 (completely) how much you believe each one. After you identify the distortions in these thoughts, substitute rational responses in the right-hand column, and record between 0 (not at all) and 100 (completely) how much you believe each one. Make sure that your rational responses are convincing, valid statements that assist you to get rid of your automatic thoughts.

Step 4—New Feeling: Once you have made a new rational statement, reevaluate your original, automatic thought, between 0 and 100. Once your beliefs in these thoughts are greatly reduced, notice how much better you are now feeling!

Feelings	Automatic Thoughts	Distortion	Rational Valid Statement
e.g., sad	*e.g., I never have any fun!* 90	*e.g., never*	*e.g., I would like to have more fun in my life.* 95
1.			
2.			
3.			

Adapted from *Feeling Good: The New Mood Therapy* [triple column technique], by D. D. Burns, 1999, New York: Avon.

Box IV.8   Life Planning (5 Days)

Spread the activity of creating a life plan over the next five days. As you grow, adjust your statements and make continual revisions. Complete the following steps, one per day, for a total personal life plan.

1. **Personal Inventory:** Break down all your relationships and responsibilities. This gives you picture of how complex your life is, and the value of organization and direction. Take your time, and be very specific and thorough. Notice the number of your relationships and responsibilities. The purpose is to help you focus on the importance of your life plan.

2. **Objective of the Life Plan:** In the space below, create the objectives of your Life Plan. For example, "promote personal health and well being so that I am better able to help myself, family, etc. to achieve personal happiness and balance.

Personal Inventory

_____

_____

_____

_____

_____

_____

My Life Plan Purpose

Name _____

_____

_____

_____

_____

3. **Exploring Individual Pictures:** In this section, ask yourself:

a) What do I *want* from my life? This will help clarify the desired outcome. Remember, Glasser (1998) teaches that we all have individual pictures to meet our five basic needs: fun, freedom, power, love, and survival.

_____

_____

_____

_____

b) What do you need from your life now?

_____

_____

_____

_____

c) When other people look at me, what kind of person would I like them to see?

_____

_____

_____

_____

The purpose of this exercise is to help you separate wants from needs. We all have thousands of wants; however, we have only five needs. Exploring individual pictures helps ensure a clear image of what we want and need, and how we want to be perceived. The final judgment is yours!

(Continued)

```
┌─────────────────────────────────────────────────────────────┐
│                                                             │
│  Unconditional Self-Acceptance Personal Ethics Statement    │
│ ─────────────────────────────────────────────────────────── │
│  In the end, I want to believe I lived my life:             │
│                                                             │
│  _____        │
│                                                             │
│  _____        │
│                                                             │
│  _____        │
│                                                             │
│  _____        │
│                                                             │
│  _____        │
│                                                             │
│  _____        │
│                                                             │
└─────────────────────────────────────────────────────────────┘
```

4. **Ultimate Objective:** Today, put some thought into what your ultimate objective is, what you really want to live like, and what direction you want to go. On Day 49, you will write out your Personal Life Plan.

Today's other task is to develop your Supporting Objectives: the action you are going to take so you will be able to achieve your Life Plan outcomes.

Life Plan Purpose Statement: Should be only a couple of powerful, well-thought-out summary sentences.

_____

_____

_____

Complete the following Brainstorm action statements to support your purpose statement: I will do _____ to help my ultimate objective into reality. (e.g., I will follow my daily fitness plan, and record it in my daily journal.)

_____

_____

_____

5. **Write Your Life Plan**

MY LIFE PLAN

Name: _____

Date: _____

Purpose Statement:

_____

_____

_____

Action Statements:

1. _____
2. _____
3. _____
4. _____
5. _____
6. _____
7. _____
8. _____

Signature: _____   Date: _____

Review your life plan at four weeks, eight weeks, three months, and six months, and update it each year. A life plan is always free flowing and changing. Its purpose is like the autopilot in a plane. It is to help keep you on course to your desired destiny.

Photocopy your life plan, and put a copy where you can view it daily.

Reprinted by permission from *Journal 45: A 45-Day Program to Create a New Beginning* (pp. 142–150), by W. A. Howatt, 2001, Kentville, Nova Scotia, Canada: A Way with Words.

Box IV.9   Personal Reflection

What have you done over the past 50 days, and what have those activities done for you? In no particular format, write yourself a letter about your success. Few of us provide ourselves with positive affirmation of our accomplishments. This is intended to provide you with evidence of what you have learned todate. This is only the beginning of many more exciting beginnings!

Dear Me,

_____

_____

_____

_____

_____

_____

_____

_____

Reprinted by permission from *Journal 45: A 45-Day Program to Create a New Beginning* (p. 110), by W. A. Howatt, 2001, Kentville, Nova Scotia, Canada: A Way with Words.

CLIENT HEALTH AND STRESS MANAGEMENT

Replacing negative behaviors (e.g., poor nutrition, sleep deprivation, limited exercise, and social isolation) with positive ones (e.g., healthy diet, regular exercise, and healthy social involvements) is essential in all treatment programs. Assisting addicted clients in developing a healthy lifestyle goes a long way in controlling their impulses to take psychoactive drugs. An insomniac might consider one of these alternatives to taking sleeping aids:

- *Biochemical alternatives:* An herbal sleep remedy such as melatonin, warm milk, acupuncture, avoiding caffeine drinks in the evenings
- *Behavioral alternatives:* Exercise, biofeedback, a hot bath, progressive relaxation exercise
- *Feeling alternatives:* Reflecting on pleasant memories, experiencing a good movie or book, reviewing a list of activities coming up such as vacations or holidays, meditating, using self-hypnosis, making affirmations, counting sheep, praying
- *Social environment alternatives:* Lying in a quiet room, turning off the TV, darkening the room (Scott et al., 2001, p. 196)

NUTRITIONAL COUNSELING

Since alcoholics and other addicts are chronically malnourished, nutritional counseling is a priority (Beasley, 2001). Clients with addiction disorders often eat poorly, limiting their supply of essential nutrients, which negatively affects their energy and their body's ability to maintain vital health. Alcohol is exceeded only by fat in calories per gram. As a result, while drinking, clients experience a sense of fullness despite having eaten very little or nothing. These "empty calories" inevitably lead to malnutrition (Reider, 2000).

Alcohol and other drugs prevent the proper absorption of vital nutrients and inhibit the body's natural ability to expel toxins. They also prevent proper processing of the essential amino acids (tyrosine and tryptophan) responsible for the production of norepinephrine, dopamine, and serotonin, brain neurotransmitters essential for emotional stability, mental clarity, and a general state of well-being. Decreased levels of these neurotransmitters adversely affect mood and behavior.

Educate clients in proper nutrition. When their diet is healthy, not only will they feel better, they will rebuild damaged tissues and organs and regain appropriate neurophysical functioning (www.diet-secrets.com). A general guideline for nutritional counseling includes developing an action plan that monitors weight, eating habits, overall food content and, since *dehydration* is common, an adequate intake of fluids. Water is the best beverage, both during and between meals (Alcohol and Nutrition, Alcohol Alert From NIAAA, n.d.).

Additional Resources

See Joseph D. Beasley's chapter, "Nutritional counseling: How to get the big high," in Coombs (2001).

For more information on proper nutrition during recovery, access natural impact.com for over 30 useful URL links on this at www.mens-health-links.com /sexual_health_resources/alcohol_nutrition.html.

Also visit Nutritional Information www.nutrition.org; www.nal.usda.gov/fnic and see the American Diabetes Foundation's powerful web site for more information on healthy eating: www.diabetes.org/main/health/nutrition/default.jsp.

To learn more about sugar's damaging impact, visit www.healthywealthyand-wiseshow.com/sugar.htm. And to learn more about caffeine, see "Frequently Asked Questions about Caffeine" at http://coffeefaq.com/caffaq.html.

To learn about "The natural high—Neurotransmitter restoration formula" designed specifically for recovering addicts, contact AddictionEnd Institute at 416 McDonald Avenue, Bellport, NY 11713, (800) 201-1141; www.addictionend.com.

EXERCISE COUNSELING

Before starting a moderate exercise program, clients should check with a physician. Most exercise programs appropriate for recovering addicts combine strength training with aerobics to increase metabolic rate, burn calories, and build muscle (Phillips, 1999). The National Standard recommends exercise at least four times a week for a minimum of 50 minutes. This should vary according to the client's age and fitness level. Among other benefits, exercise lowers blood pressure and increases the levels of mood-elevating neuro-chemicals—such as endorphins, that enhance one's mental and physical well-being.

Additional Resources

To find out more on how to develop a personalized fitness training program, visit www.workoutsforyou.com.

AFFECT-REGULATION COPING SKILLS COUNSELING

Most addicts use psychoactive drugs because they like the way it makes them feel (Scott et al., 2001). Psychoactive substances allow them to self-regulate their emotions and energy level. From their perspective, taking drugs is a purposeful, rational, and pleasurable activity.

The counselor's goal is to show recovering addicts that they can feel good and enjoy life in far less self-destructive ways. Teaching appropriate coping skills enhances a stable recovery, which becomes possible when the new way of living becomes more emotionally rewarding than the old, chemically dependent one.

The client needs to build emotional stamina—"emotional muscle"—to cope with the entire spectrum of life's problems without resorting to psychoactive drugs (Scott et al., 2001). Just as physical endurance comes through aerobic exercise, emotional stamina develops by struggling through emotional difficulties. When mood-altering drugs are used to suppress negative feelings or bypass stressful circumstances, emotional development not only stops, it atrophies.

In each clinical session, the counselor works on replacing the client's unhealthy emotional associations with healthy behaviors and thoughts. By adopting a coaching role, the counselor respectfully teaches the principles that underlie each skill, always avoiding shaming, blaming, or creating guilt.

Design each session to help clients:

- Become aware of how they feel at any given moment
- Understand that only by exposing themselves to their uncomfortable feelings will they progress
- Learn how feelings are manifested in their body and mind
- Realize what their thoughts are when such feelings occur
- Notice how their bodies respond
- See how they act when they feel that way (Scott et al., 2001)

Reinforce progress with praise and compliments. Acknowledge and emphasize the courage it takes to face fears head on. Encourage hope and confidence in learning new coping skills.

The concept of "emotional intelligence" may be helpful. This involves several core skills such as self-esteem, self-regulation, and empathy. Daniel Goleman (1995, 1998, 2003) coined this term in his book, *Emotional Intelligence,* suggesting that in predicting success, brain power (as measured by standard IQ and achievement tests) matters less than the qualities of mind.

Emotional intelligence is characterized by five domains (Mayer & Salovey, 1997):

1. *Knowing one's emotions:* Self-awareness, recognizing a feeling as it happens, is the keystone of emotional intelligence. Clients with greater certainty about their feelings have a surer sense of how they really feel about personal decisions.
2. *Managing emotions:* Clients who are poor in this area are constantly battling distress feelings. Those who excel at this, however, soothe themselves, shake off anxiety, gloom, or irritability, and quickly bounce back from a setback or upset.
3. *Motivating self:* Emotional self-control involves the ability to delay gratification and stifle impulsiveness. Clients with this skill tend to be more productive and effective.

4. *Recognizing emotions in others:* Emotional self-awareness is a fundamental "people skill" supported by empathy. Clients who are empathic are more tuned to the subtle social signals that indicate what others need or want.
5. *Handling relationships:* Managing emotional interactions with others increases social opportunities and decreases personal social problems.

Additional Resources

To learn more about emotional intelligence (EQ), visit the web site at http://eqi.org.

See also Salovey, P., Mayer, J. D., & Caruso, D. (2001). "The positive psychology of emotional intelligence," in C. R. Snyder and S. J. Lopez (Eds.), *The handbook of positive psychology.* New York: Oxford University Press. This book provides an excellent overview of how EQ can be used to assist a client develop positive emotions.

STRESS-MANAGEMENT TRAINING

Effective stress-management skills help reduce slips and relapse. To review research documents that are the scientific basis for these clinical observations, see Steven Stocker's "Studies Link Stress and Drug Addiction" at www.nida.nih.gov/NIDA_Notes/NNVol14N1/Stress.html.

A client's familiar style of thinking of what to do when stressed may include, Open a cold beer or pour a stiff drink. Had a hard day? Roll up a joint. Feel beat? Lay out a couple of lines. These solutions never remove the original stress. At best, they provide temporary relief, and often lead to more stress (e.g., money issues, legal issues) for the client.

Shaffer (1982) suggest the following stress-management techniques:

The 12 Steps to Wellness[1]

Step 1: Acknowledge that you are a wimp in the face of worseness. By admitting your obsessive, chemical and spiritual abdication of responsibility to the siren song of abusive self-ruination and slovenly destructive near-term gratification of an inappropriate nature, you take the FIRST STEP to liberation by wellness. Namely, you conclude that you are a pox on the Earth, a slime-bag of a human being, but that you need not and will not stay that way.

Step 2: Decide that you need to GAIN POSITIVE support and LOSE NEGATIVE support in getting started. Ask for the former from wellness seekers and dump your low level worseness "friends." Plant yourself in a healthful garden environment while weeding your social garden.

---

[1] *Source:* Donald Ardell is publisher of the Ardell Wellness Report. Copies can be obtained by writing to Ardell Wellness Report, 9901 Lake Georgia Dr., Orlando, FL 32817. (Reprinted from Schafer, W., 1992, pp. 31–32.)

Step 3: Choose yourself as guru or sovereign master for the course of your life. Make a commitment to independence and self-sufficiency tied to friendships, professional guidance, and a belief in a benevolent spirit or force that wants you to live joyfully and well.

Step 4: Conduct a searching inventory of where you are. Assess liabilities and strengths, with an emphasis on the latter. Look at extremes of past self-abuse. For instance, consider old patterns of blaming, denial, worry, anger, self-pity, and dead-end relationships and grim associations that reinforce "worseness." Make a conscious decision that these kinds of patterns are no longer acceptable.

Step 5: Write out, analyze, and discuss your old profile. By disclosing who you used to be as well as what you are becoming with special wellness-oriented friends and colleagues, you put the past in the past, where it belongs.

Step 6: Create a personal plan for wellness. Since the lack of wellness planning got you into a worseness frump in the first place, a written wellness plan is a sure way to lock in that lifetime slow-fix to self-actualization.

Step 7: Pursue realistic, worthy goals in a systematic way. Consider what you want from life and why that seems important.

Step 8: Identify very special people crucial for your wellness quest—and include them in your support network. Avoid isolation; wellness is challenging under any circumstances. Only die-hards could sustain wellness on uninhabited land.

Step 9: Explain your commitment to a wellness lifestyle to anyone who was a willing or other participant in your worseness past. Make amends, if necessary, in order to secure a tranquil spirit—and eliminate your guilt. Take a few disclosure chances.

Step 10: Reassess along the way. A wellness lifestyle is never finished as long as life remains; adjustments, variations, and fine-tuning are always appropriate—if you think so.

Step 11: Add a dash of imagery, meditation, or any other form of self-dialogue, if doing so helps you find inner peace. There are many ways and diverse paths to deepening your spiritual reservoir and finding balance and serenity.

Step 12: Reach out and assist others. Becoming involved, sharing insights about personal rewards and satisfactions are services to those who need support. The joy of living is potentially too great to keep to yourself. Offer to share it—without being a bore or a bothersome proselytizer.

SHAFFER COPING MODELS[2]

". . . let us now examine a range of options when dealing with stressful situations and your reactions to them, keeping in mind that this is a complex, dynamic, interactional process."

[2] From *Stress Management for Wellness* (2nd ed., pp. 227–231), by W. Schafer, 1992, Fort Worth, TX: Harcourt Brace Jovanovich College Publishers. Reprinted with permission.

Assuming an event is perceived to be important and sufficiently taxing of your resources to need a response, what are your adaptive options? Consider the following model.

OPTION 1: ALTER THE STRESSOR

Is the stressor controllable, changeable, or influenceable? Can I take action by myself? Is group action possible and desirable? What are likely gains and costs—for myself and others? This action might include the following:

- Seeking to change a specific situation
- Changing a physical stressor
- Pacing myself and my stressors better
- Spacing my life changes better
- Increasing challenges in my life (if the problem is boredom)
- Organizing time better
- Asking someone to alter her behavior

OPTION 2: ADAPT TO THE STRESSOR

Is it best to accept the stressor, finding ways to prevent or lower my distress? These might include:

- Manage self-talk.
  - Alter my irrational beliefs.
  - Control my situational self-talk.
  - Take it less seriously.
  - Turn the "threat" into an opportunity.
  - See this person or event as temporarily bearable.
  - Be okay no matter what.
- Control physical stress response.
  - Breathing methods
  - Muscle relaxation methods
  - Mental methods
- Manage actions.
  - Use effective listening.
  - Be assertive.
  - Be self-disclosing.
  - Use an appropriate communication style.
  - Take action that will get all involved in what we want.
- Maintain health buffers.
  - Exercise
  - Nutrition
  - Sleep

- Utilize available coping resources.
  - Social support
  - Money
  - Community or campus services
  - My beliefs or faith
- Avoid maladaptive reactions to distress.
  - Alcohol or drug abuse.
  - Smoking
  - Overeating
  - Dumping on or abusing others
  - Escapism
  - Spending sprees
  - Blaming others

OPTION 3: AVOID THE STRESSOR

Is it best for me to avoid or withdraw from this stressor? What would be the gains and costs? Have all other options been exhausted?

COMMON STYLES OF NEGATIVE SELF-TALK

Self-talk is an ever-present part of life. You continually appraise or assess stressors as to their nature and likely effects on your experience. In short, you think about them. As noted, the content of this thinking affects the emotional, physical, and behavioral responses that follow.

Life is challenging, hard, sometimes downright difficult. Yet people's thinking often makes events worse than they truly need be. Several common styles of negative self-talk can be identified through which individuals sometimes make themselves miserable—or miserable to be around:

- *Negativizing:* Filtering out positive aspects of a situation, while focusing only on negatives
- *Awfulizing:* Turning a difficult or unsatisfactory situation into something awful, terrible, and intolerable
- *Catastrophizing:* Expecting that the worse almost certainly will happen
- *Overgeneralizing:* Generalizing from a single event or piece of information to all or most such things
- *Miminizing:* Diminishing the value or importance of something to less than it actually is
- *Blaming:* Attributing responsibility for events, especially negative ones, to someone else, even when such responsibility rightfully belongs to self
- *Perfectionism:* Setting impossible standards toward self, others, or both in many situations
- *Musterbation:* Demanding that events must turn out as I want them to—otherwise, it inevitably will be very upsetting to me

- *Personalizing:* Believing that others' behavior or feelings are entirely caused by self
- *Judging human worth:* Evaluating total worth of self or others on the basis of traits or behavior
- *Control fallacy:* The belief that happiness depends on cajoling or coercing others to do what I think they should
- *Polarized thinking:* Things are black and white, right or wrong, good or bad. There is no middle ground
- *Being right:* I am continually on trial to prove that my opinions and actions are correct. Being wrong is unthinkable. Therefore, I must go to any length to demonstrate my rightness
- *Fallacy of fairness:* Feeling resentful because the world does not conform to my sense of what is fair
- *Shoulding:* Constant imposition of shoulds and should haves on self, others or both
- *Magnifying:* Making more of an event than it actually is.

REWRITING OLD BELIEFS[3]

The following are 20 common unreasonable or irrational beliefs that often lead to negative situational self-talk. Read them and then do the exercise, "Rewriting Irrational Beliefs."

Irrational Beliefs

- Other people and outside events upset me.
- I am think-skinned by genetic nature—I was born that way.
- I cannot control my thoughts and feelings.
- I cannot change. I am too old, too set in my ways, beyond hope.
- It is imperative that I be accepted by others, especially by those who are important to me.
- Most people are bad and wicked and cannot be trusted.
- If things do not go my way, it will be awful, terrible, or catastrophic.
- The only way to improve my stress is to shape up others around me who do such dumb things.
- It is easier to avoid responsibilities and difficulties than to face them.
- My early childhood experiences determine my emotions and behavior, and there is little I can do about it.
- I deserve to be upset or depressed over my shortcomings.
- I am fully justified in being aggravated over others' shortcomings, deficiencies, and blunders.
- I should be thoroughly competent, adequate, and achieving in all respects.
- The world should always be fair, justice should always triumph, and I am fully justified in feeling angry when these do not occur.
- I feel like I should do perfectly in nearly anything I attempt.

---

[3] From *Stress Management for Wellness* (2nd ed., pp. 235–237), by W. Schafer, 1992, Fort Worth, TX: Harcourt Brace Jovanovich College Publishers. Reprinted with permission.

- There usually is one solution to a problem. It is pretty intolerable when this solution is not found or followed.
- I have a clear idea how other people should be and what they should do most of the time.
- Others should treat me kindly and considerately at all times.
- I have a right to expect a relatively pain-free and trouble-free life.
- When people around me are upset, it is usually because of something I have said or done.

REWRITING IRRATIONAL BELIEFS

- Circle the irrational beliefs you recognize as more present in yourself than you would like.
- List those you would like to change in a separate list, leaving several lines between each one.
- Below each one, write a more rational or reasonable version, keeping in mind the three criteria of rational beliefs: factual, moderate, helpful.
- After rewriting each one, ask: What concrete difference would it make in my life to act on these new reasonable beliefs?

Additional Resources

To find an excellent online resource for life management tips, see the Willamette Learning Enhancement Resources at www.willamette.edu/cla/ler/managinglife.htm.

Mind Tools has a section on stress management that will assist clients learn how to cope with stress. For a host of effective stress management tips go to www.mindtools.com.

The National Institute on Drug Abuse has a useful report on the connection between stress and addictions: www.nida.nih.gov/StressAlert/StressAlert.html.

PART V
Treatment Resources

Part V details treatment resources for helping addicted clients. Addiction recovery tools are first described followed by a range of recovery programs and treatment directories for locating them. Support groups, both 12-step and 12-step alternatives, are identified for assisting women, adolescents, family members, dually diagnosed patients, HIV/AIDS patients, and gays and lesbians.

The final section describes harm-reduction programs of differing types.

ADDICTION RECOVERY TOOLS

> Motivational Tools
> Medical and Pharmaceutical Tools
> Cognitive-Behavioral Tools
> Psychosocial Tools
> Holistic Tools

ADDICTION RECOVERY PROGRAMS

> Residential and Outpatient Treatment Programs
> Support Groups
> Recovery Programs for Selected Populations

HARM REDUCTION PROGRAMS

> Characteristics of Harm Reduction Programs
> Harm Reduction Goals
> Harm Reduction Techniques
> Other Harm Reduction Techniques

ADDICTION RECOVERY TOOLS

This section reviews some of the most time-tested therapeutic modalities—tools—to help clients recover from their addictions. Though not an exhaustive list, these include *motivational tools, medical-pharmaceutical tools, cognitive-behavioral tools, psychosocial tools,* and *holistic tools.* Most treatment programs use a variety of these therapeutic tools.

MOTIVATIONAL TOOLS

These therapeutic modalities aim to motivate clients to overcome their reluctance to change out of their addictive behaviors.

MOTIVATIONAL INTERVENTION

A small group of family members and friends of the client who are concerned about their loved one meet in a surprise confrontation to express their concern about his or her addiction and urge treatment. Under the leadership of an intervention specialist, participants plan what they will say and arrange for admission to a treatment program. Prior to the meeting, the client's bags are packed, airline reservations are made, and a designated driver to the airport is appointed. Ideally, hearts are touched, the client agrees to set off for therapy, and all wave good-bye as they leave for the treatment center.

This type of intervention includes five steps (Storti, 1995, 2001, pp. 4–14; Storti & Keller, 1988):

1. *The inquiry:* A concerned associate of the addicted person contacts the intervention specialist and provides basic information.
2. *The assessment:* Key group members assist the specialist in tailoring the intervention to the specific patient's needs.
3. *The preparation:* All group members learn their assignments and collect their thoughts.
4. *The intervention:* Each person, in turn, expresses love, concerns, and hopes to the patient with the guidance of the therapist.
5. *The follow-up* (or case management): This takes place after the client enters and leaves the treatment program.

Even when a client does not agree to treatment, group participants typically find the intervention to be therapeutic. However, Storti and Keller (1988) advise that an intervention should not be carried out if certain conditions are present:

(1) a strong tendency toward violence or vindictiveness (especially involving a spouse or children); (2) a lack of sufficient documentation of the problem; or (3) a psychiatric disorder requiring treatment in its own right. Otherwise, motivational interventions are effective in bringing clients suffering from addictions into treatment, and also give them a foundation of support on which to rebuild their lives.

Additional Resources

Intervention Center—Family intervention for addictions at www.intervention .com.

MOTIVATIONAL INTERVIEWING

Addicted clients are often ambivalent about changing a behavior that provides some benefits to them, even though it may be inconsistent with their basic values, beliefs, and goals.

Clients may defend themselves against the counselor's unwanted advice and judgment because committing to, making, and maintaining changes in long-standing behavior is difficult. Motivational Interviewing (MI) addresses this challenge (Rosengren & Wagner, 2001). It is a nondirective modality designed to help clients resolve ambivalence about their behavior without confrontation.

Miller and Rollnick report, "MI does not use confrontation or aggression of any kind," and "MI helps clients become aware of the discrepancy between where they are and where they want to be," (Project Match Research Group, 1997, p. 8). To be effective, the client must first want help.

Additional Resources

To learn more about MI's several applications and strategies for implementation, see Miller, W. R., & Rollnick, S. (Eds.). (1991). *Motivational interviewing: Preparing people to change addictive behavior.* New York: Guilford Press. Also visit the Motivational Interviewing web site at www.motivationalinterview.org.

MEDICAL AND PHARMACEUTICAL TOOLS

These medical model tools typically involve collaboration with physicians and pharmacists who prescribe and dispense medication and disease-oriented treatment ideology.

DETOXIFICATION

Detoxification (detox), the first step in treating chemical addiction, is the removal of all harmful substances from the addicted client's system. When physical dependence is present, medical interventions are used to counter the uncomfortable and, in some cases, high-risk symptoms of withdrawal. These tools include medications to treat symptoms, to rebuild the patient's damaged system, and to combat cravings (D. E. Smith & Seymour, 2001). Some addictions can be treated using a substitution and tapering process, such as phenobarbital for sedative-hypnotic detoxification or methadone for opioid detox. Methadone is also sometimes used for maintenance purposes until a patient is better prepared for detoxification (see "Harm Reduction Programs" later in Part V).

Detoxification can only be done under the supervision of a physician. Not until the drug is fully eliminated can the brain return to its preaddiction potential. "When there is physical dependence, medical interventions may be needed to counter withdrawal symptoms and make full detoxification possible. The tools of detoxification include a pharmacopoeia of medications that work to ease withdrawal symptoms and help the patient's system regain a healthy balance," (D. E. Smith & Seymour, 2001, p. 63).

Additional Resources

For further information on detoxification services see Morse, G. R. (1999). *Detoxification: A guide for medically assisted withdrawal from chemical addiction.* London: Mark Allen Publishing. For a detailed description of the Detoxification Services Definitions that explains the levels of care for Substance Abuse and Mental Health Services visit www.treatment.org/taps/tap22/TAP22TOC.htm.

MEDICATIONS

In addition to minimizing withdrawal symptoms during detoxification, medications are used to treat co-occurring psychiatric disorders—some 25% to 75% of all clients have a current or past comorbid psychiatric disorder (Ziedonis & Krejci, 2001).

Addiction recovery medications are effectively used in three ways:

1. *Symptomatic treatment:* Using a drug whose pharmacological action is unrelated to the abused drug but whose effects ameliorate emotional or physical symptoms related to the use of the abused drug (e.g., to ease discomfort when detoxifying).
2. *Agonist substitution:* Treatment with a medication that has pharmacological actions similar to that of the abused drug (e.g., nicotine chewing gum for tobacco dependence).
3. *Antagonist treatment:* Utilizing pharmaceuticals to inhibit or block the chemical effects of the abused drugs (Coombs, 1997).

Antagonist medications commonly prescribed to facilitate addiction recovery include Antabuse for alcoholism, which creates an unpleasant physical response to drinking; naltrexone (Revia) and nalmefene, which block the opiate receptors for heroin/opioid and alcohol dependence; and agonists methadone, levo-alpha acetyl methadol (LAAM), and buprenorphine for addiction to heroin and other opiates, which reduce cravings and block euphoria (Ziedonis & Krejci, 2001).

Additional Resources

For a detailed review of pharmacotherapies, see Barber, W. S., & O'Brien, C. P. (1999). Pharmacotherapies. In B. S. McCrady and E. E. Epstein (Eds.), *Addictions: A comprehensive guidebook*. New York: Oxford University Press.

DISEASE ORIENTATION

In the past, drug dependency was viewed as a sin committed only by people with weak moral character. In 1956, the American Medical Association (AMA) published a statement saying, "Alcoholism must be regarded as within the purview of medical practice" (N. S. Miller, 2001, p. 104). The Council on Mental Health, the AMA's Committee on Alcoholism, promoted the idea that alcoholism is an illness that requires the participation and attention of physicians. This realization is based on the pioneering work of Jellinek (1960) who observed that alcoholics are more likely to have alcoholic family members. In these studies, environmental influences cannot be separated from the genetic influences, because alcoholic parents raise alcoholics.

Defining addiction as a disease relieves addicts of the overwhelming shame and responsibility for having caused the addiction and its devastating consequences. At the same time, it empowers the client to take corrective action. Refuting the discouraging idea that addiction is a moral failure allows clients to focus on getting better by accepting the hard truth: Abstinence is their solution. Just as lung cancer patients are expected to stop smoking and diabetics to avoid sugar, addicts must altogether avoid ingesting alcohol and other psychoactive drugs as part of their recovery.

Additional Resources

For further information, see Jellinek, E. M. (1960). *The disease concept of alcoholism*. New Haven, CT: College and University Press; and Miller, N. S. (1991). Drug and alcohol addiction as a disease. In N. S. Miller (Ed.), *Comprehensive handbook of drug and alcohol addiction*. New York: Marcel Dekker.

DRUG TESTING

Promoting accountability, determining compliance, and measuring success, drug testing is most often used in three settings: among employees whose contracts require them to remain drug-free, in criminal justice applications such as DUI or probationary screenings, and in clinical treatment programs (Coombs & West, 1991; Mieczkowski, 2001).

Two kinds of tests are commonly used: (1) immediate outcome drug tests (e.g., home drug testing kits that test marijuana, cocaine, amphetamines, morphine/opiates, PCP, alcohol, and nicotine) that provide immediate results and are economical and easy to use, and (2) confirmation tests sent to a lab to determine test accuracy and reliability. To minimize errors such as contamination, clerical error, improper execution, or cross-reactivity, select a sophisticated laboratory with a proven track record.

Additional Resources

For detailed information, see Mieczkowski, T. (1990). The accuracy of self-reported drug use: An evaluation and analysis of new data. In R. Weisheit (Ed.), *Drugs, crime, and the criminal justice system.* Cincinnati, OH: Anderson. To learn more about these tests visit www.drugdetect.com/index.shtml.

COGNITIVE-BEHAVIORAL TOOLS

Active, directive, time-limited, and structured, these therapeutic modalities assume that clients' behaviors are largely determined by the ways in which they think.

CONTINGENCY MANAGEMENT

Based in the theoretical underpinning of Skinner's operant conditioning, Contingency Management (CM) enforces desired behaviors that strengthen recovery. *Positive reinforcement* means delivering a reward. *Negative reinforcement,* not to be confused with punishment or a negative outcome, means removing an undesirable restriction or situation. *Positive punishment* means delivering an undesirable consequence, whereas *negative punishment* means removing a desirable one.

In CM, reinforcements are generally considered more effective than punishments. CM gives the recovery more firepower by competing with the rewards of the addict's drug or behavioral habit. This is especially important for the many users who resent authority figures and regulations (Coombs, 2001).

In designing CM plans, first determine the desired target outcome and criteria for success (e.g., weekly urine test). Incentive programs can use voucher systems where clients can earn points and then select a reward purchased or provided through the treatment practitioner. The list of incentives should be long enough to please a variety of clients, and its focus should be recreational (e.g., going to a movie). Although CM can be used with goals such as attendance at therapy sessions, Budney, Sigmon, and Higgins (2001) encourage treatment professionals to use this strategy first and foremost to reward clients for staying free from addictive behaviors.

Additional Resources

Higgins, S. T., Wong, C. J., Badger, G. J., Ogden, D., & Dantona, R. L. (2000). Contingent reinforcement increases cocaine abstinence during outpatient treatment and 1 year of follow up. *Journal of Consulting and Clinical Psychology, 68,* 64–72.

CUE EXPOSURE

Recognizing drug use as a habit, with addicts responding to accustomed cues and contexts by ingesting their substance of choice, Cue Exposure (CE) treatment trains clients to stop responding habitually to their traditional triggers. Called "extinction," it is the unconditioning of conditioned triggers and responses (e.g., local bars linked with drinking) by repeatedly exposing a client, in a controlled environment, to these potential triggers. Repeated exposures erase reaction to the cue (Coombs, 2001).

When administering cues, the counselor will need to track clients' responses, usually by asking them to self-report cravings, negative mood, and physiological responses on a scale of 1 to 10 (Conklin & Tiffany, 2001). Treatment for a particular cue is ended when a client no longer responds to the cue though an occasional review to ensure continued extinction is helpful. Properly administered, cue exposure treatment can strengthen the client's resistance to relapse.

Additional Resources

Bouton, M. E. (2000). A learning-theory perspective on lapse, relapse, and the maintenance of behavior change. *Health Psychology, 19,* 57–63.

AFFECT-REGULATION COPING SKILLS TRAINING

Coping skills training acknowledges that addicts generally use addictive substances or behaviors to regulate their own moods; they self-medicate to avoid uncomfortable feelings (Scott et al., 2001). This technique focuses on helping clients learn positive coping skills for addressing challenges and the unpleasant emotions they invoke.

The objective of coping skills training is to enhance and develop clients' internal locus of control. When clients achieve this control, they will possess the requisite skills to take charge of the emotions that influence positive behavioral choices. Clients learn that they can alter their unwanted moods and increase their self-confidence more by taking constructive actions than by using psychoactive drugs (Kern & Lenon, 1994).

Clinicians use the following five-step model: (1) Assessment; (2) Establishing commitment (to stay clean and away from unwanted emotions); (3) Identifying feelings (to learn how to identify emotions); (4) Homework (e.g., daily journaling); and (5) Setting goals that meet client needs and measuring progress (Scott et al., 2001).

Additional Resources

For a detailed review of this recovery tool, see Scott, R. L., Kern, M. F., & Coombs, R. H. (2001). In R. H. Coombs (Ed.), *Addiction recovery tools.* Thousand Oaks, CA: Sage.

RECOVERY CONTRACTS

Behavioral contracts reinforce positive behaviors and monitor supportive recovery. Talbott and Crosby (2001) explain, "The chemically dependent patient requires psychological, physiological, and spiritual frameworks to guide him or her through the recovery process. Contracts are an essential part of this external structure" (p. 127). These contracts provide the client with a detailed road map of the daily actions needed to deal with life stress and to reduce distractions.

An effective recovery contract has seven key components: (1) Presentation of the contract in a serious and compassionate manner, preferably with the significant other and any program representatives in attendance; (2) Releases of information—the patient must sign off on privacy releases for family members, coworkers, and others to be involved in contract reporting; (3) Leverage through clearly understood consequences when expectations are not met (behaviors should be highly specific); (4) Organization of a client's support system; (5) Statement of short treatment time frame so that the client feels capable of compliance. Most contracts are designed to cover a 5-year span, but they are renewed annually, biannually, or even quarterly; (6) Contract review, which should take place formally at least every 6 months and informally on an ongoing basis; and (7) A "slip" relapse clause. Clients should be educated regarding warning signs so they can seek help *before* they head into a full-blown relapse (Talbott & Crosby, 2001).

Additional Resources

For a detailed chapter on this topic, see Talbott, G. D., & Crosby, L. R. (2001). Recovery contracts: Seven key elements. In R. H. Coombs (Ed.), *Addiction recovery tools: A practice handbook.* Thousand Oaks, CA: Sage.

PSYCHOSOCIAL TOOLS

These treatment modalities focus on strengthening and reinforcing the network of a client's social support network.

FAMILY STRENGTHENING

Family members typically enable the client's addictive behaviors. This codependence, an adaptation paralleling addiction, needs to be identified and treated. Brown and her colleagues (S. Brown, Lewis, & Liotta, 2000; Schmid & Brown, 2001) use a developmental model that consists of four addictive stages:

1. *Active addiction:* In this stabilizing phase, all family members are screened and treated for their own addictions or dual diagnosis issues.
2. *Transition:* Family members accept there is an addicted person in the family and come to terms with the need to take action.
3. *Early recovery:* Family members start to act differently and no longer act on impulse. The focus is on education and the development of new behavior that supports the family; the addictive family member no longer controls the family.
4. *Ongoing recovery:* The family is out of denial and is no longer emotionally, cognitively, and behaviorally trapped. This is a crucial stage for each family member in healing from the trauma of living with an addict.

Additional Resources

For more on this subject, see Schmid, J., & Brown, S. (2001). Family treatment: Stage-appropriate psychotherapy for the addicted family. In R. H. Coombs (Ed.), *Addiction recovery tools: A practical handbook.* Thousand Oaks, CA: Sage.

GROUP THERAPY

Group therapy is an effective tool for two basic reasons: (1) Group interaction helps penetrate "the addict's massive wall of denial," (Washton, 2001, p. 240) and (2) recovering addicts need a strong social support system (Coombs, 2001). When you group several addicts together in a therapeutic atmosphere, they call each other's bluffs even as they provide an encouraging recovery environment.

Washton (2001) suggests arranging different types of groups for progressive stages of recovery: (1) Self-evaluation groups for clients who are not yet ready to commit to abstinence and need motivational enhancement; (2) Early recovery groups, lasting from several months to a year, where members work on acknowledging their addiction, achieve abstinence, and stabilize their lives; and (3) Relapse prevention groups for those in advanced recovery who have maintained abstinence for some time and are ready to focus specifically on those issues that make them more vulnerable to relapse.

Additional Resources

For an effective resource on group treatment planning, see Jongsma, A. E., Jr., & K. M. Paleg. (1999). *Group therapy treatment planner.* New York: Wiley.

PEER SUPPORT

Peer groups provide hope and give recovering addicts a much needed social support system in lieu of their network of drug-using friends. Social support groups, common in 12-step programs, help break down denial and encourage participants to change and take personal responsibility for their actions. For high impact, Alcohol Anonymous (AA) suggests that newcomers attend 90 meetings in 90 days (Kurtz, 2001).

At these meetings—whether 12-step oriented or a 12-step alternative—members share their recovery stories, discuss insights and concerns, or study pertinent literature. Recovery is greatly enhanced when a group member working the program can call a sponsor—a senior member of the group who is assigned to assist addicted individuals outside meetings any time of day or night for help in resisting the urge to relapse.

Additional Resources

See "Addiction Recovery Programs" later in Part V for detailed specifics.

LIFESTYLE PLANNING AND MONITORING

The two key features in the big-picture approach to addiction recovery are getting off drugs and creating a healthy, drug-free way of life (Zackon, McAuliffe,

& Chien, 1993). Zackon (2001) identifies three common barriers to success: (1) the people problem (building a satisfying new social network); (2) the work problem (finding rewarding employment); and (3) the pleasure problem (acquiring new means of entertainment and excitement). He points out that the drug lifestyle, with its immediate gratification and highs, is not easily replaced by a straight life, which may seem inherently dull and unsatisfying to drug users.

Howatt (1999) explains that clients who wish to gain a healthy lifestyle must balance five elements: money, career, relationships, self, and health. Zackon (2001), suggests that a recovery lifestyle needs eight vital elements: (1) Participation in a community that supports abstinence and nourishes moral or spiritual values; (2) productive work (or appropriate training or education) that yields sustenance and social approval; (3) social activities with friends who offer drug-free recreation and support; (4) a home setting that is comforting and relatively free of strong "triggers" (incitements to use); (5) personal growth activities in any or all of the preceding; (6) standard practices for avoiding high-risk (trigger-laden) situations; (7) standard practices for coping with unavoidable high-risk situations, and (8) regularity in personal routines and schedules.

Additional Resources

For resources on how to implement life management skills, see Kern, M., & Lenon, L. (1994). *Take control now! Life management.* Los Angeles: Management Skills. A user-friendly book on life coaching is provided by Curly, M. (2001). *The life coaching handbook.* London: Crown House. For more information on coaching training, visit Coach U at www.coachinc.com.

HOLISTIC TOOLS

Traditionally used by nonmedical specialists, these treatment modalities address the health of the entire body, not just a specific body part or malady. Clinicians trained in Western medicine philosophy and techniques have been incorporating these elements of Eastern medicine into their treatment arsenals.

ACUPUNCTURE

Some 1,000 treatment programs use acupuncture in treating addictions, both to ease withdrawal symptoms and to prepare clients for psychosocial recovery (M. O. Smith & White, 2001). Acupuncture has a calming effect and improves treatment retention; in addition, it is safe and cost-efficient (Brewington, Smith, & Lipton, 1994).

During treatment, needles are inserted smoothly and shallowly and other than a brief pinching sensation, pain or bleeding are rarely experienced. The technique generally produces an immediate sense of relaxation. Clients may also feel warmth, tingling, electrical movement, or heaviness either in the application area (usually the ears) or some other part of the body (M. O. Smith & White, 2001). Touch, movement, heat, and electricity can also stimulate the points. Related acupuncture procedures include acupressure, shiatsu, reiki, and tai ji chaun.

In addition to treating the obvious needs for relaxation and relief of withdrawal symptoms, acupuncture addresses the addict's general state of physiological imbalance and ill health. Holistic treatment can also support treatment of coexisting psychiatric disorders ranging from depression to paranoia. The Lincoln Recovery Center has found a group setting to be most successful, and has trained clinicians to administer this treatment. The National Acupuncture Detoxification Association (NADA) assists programs interested in applying this treatment modality (www.acudetox.com).

Additional Resources

For information on certified and licensed clinicians, visit the American Association of Oriental Medicine (www.aaom.org) and the National Certification Commission for Acupuncture and Oriental Medicine (www.nccaom.org). Also, see Knaster (1996). *Discovering the body's wisdom.* New York: Bantam Books.

SPIRITUALITY ENHANCEMENT

Though spirituality has long been a central focus of 12-step programs, only recently has Western medicine acknowledged its importance. Spirituality cannot be measured scientifically, but its consequences can. Research has documented that praying for strength has health-enhancing benefits (Dossey, 1997). Even atheist nations like the former USSR, turned to spirituality-based programs to deal with rampant alcoholism in their society.

Efforts to develop spiritually can open doors of opportunity for clients who are willing to experiment. A large literature is developing on the relationship between spirituality and health.

Additional Resources

To learn more about the application of spirituality and addiction counseling, visit the Centre for Spiritual Awareness (www.csa-davis.org) and read Kus, R. J. (Ed.). (1995). *Spirituality and chemical dependency.* New York: Harrington. This excellent resource provides a strategy for implementing spirituality into recovery. See also Carl Jung's classical writings described in Part IV of this book.

MEDITATION

Meditation, "a specific state of attending to a particular focus while withdrawing one's attention from the outside world," (Snarr, Norris, & Fahrion, 2001, p. 307), is used effectively to support recovery. An alternative to the addictive state, meditation slows the mind and body to achieve a restful state normally achieved by addicts only through their addictive elixir. By slowing down the central nervous system, the client calms the mind and reduces stress. When the brain rhythms are slowed, the brain produces mind-altering and brain-healing substances, such as neuropeptides, enkephalins, and endogenous opiates that reduce craving and promote abstinence (Blum & Payne, 1991). Through mastering a meditative state, clients are better able to connect their conscious and unconscious mind for the purpose of healing (Benson & Stark, 1997).

Breathing and hand temperature training are two basic meditation techniques. Regulating breathing is the first skill learned by beginning students of meditation. The goal is to replace shallow thoracic breathing with deeper diaphragmatic breathing, a calming practice. Hand temperature training, in which clients learn to adjust the warmth and blood flow in their hands, is an example of biofeedback which also integrates the mind/body connection.

Additional Resources

For tools to learn more about meditation and its application to addiction, see Schaub, B., & Schaub, R. (1997). *Healing addiction.* New York: Delmar; Davis, M., Eshelman, E. R., & McKay, M. (1995). *The relation and stress reduction workbook* (4th ed.). Oakland, CA: New Harbinger; and Lohman, R. (1999). Yoga techniques applicable within drug and alcohol rehabilitation programmes. *Therapeutic Communities: International Journal for Therapeutic and Supportive Organizations, 20*(1), 61–72.

This Internet resource provides a user-friendly application for how to meditate: www.how-to-meditate.org.

NUTRITIONAL COUNSELING

Many addicts become malnourished and have a severe imbalance in their body's biochemistry. Adding nutritional counseling to your repertoire will close what tends to be a glaring gap in the addict's treatment needs (Gordis, 1993).

Early animal studies showed that well-nourished subjects demonstrated "wisdom of the body" by rejecting alcohol in favor of water, while malnourished subjects were more likely to consume alcohol (Williams et al., 1955, cited in Beasley, 2001). In another study, even bacterial cultures were better able to resist the toxic effects of alcohol when they were better nourished (Ravel et al., 1955, cited in Beasley, 2001). Three decades later, Guenther (1983) treated two groups of addicts, differentiating in her approach only by incorporating a nutritional component into one program. A follow-up at 6 months found that 81% of the nutrition groups were not drinking, as opposed to 38% of the control group (Guenther, 1983). Patients in the nutrition group also claimed to experience fewer cravings.

Building on Guenther's (1983) work in their program for 111 patients in New York, Beasley (2001, p. 294) found, "[All] had severe and chronic alcoholism. All had long and difficult histories of alcohol and drug abuse, with many failed treatment attempts. . . . All their diets were deficient; 80% were overtly clinically malnourished, almost two thirds had liver disease, and almost half were also addicted to other drugs." After 12 months in his treatment program that included a strong nutritional component, 91 patients were still participating, and 74% of these patients were sober (Beasley, 2001, p. 294).

Addiction counselors should develop core competencies in nutritional counseling. Simple basics such as eating regular healthy meals and drinking lots of bottled water (2 liters a day) are only two examples.

Additional Resources

To support your client's nutritional needs while in recovery, an excellent guide is Beasley, J. D., & Knightly, S. (2001). *Food for recovery: The complete nutrition companion for recovering from alcoholism, drug addiction, and eating disorders* (2nd ed.). New York: Crown Books. Center for Food Safety and Applied Nutrition, 5100 Paint Branch Parkway, College Park, MD 20740-3835, http://vm.cfsan.fda.gov/list.html.

Clemens Library, Internet Resources for Nutrition: www.csbsju.edu/library /internet/nutrition.html.

Coombs, Robert H. (Ed.). (2001). *Addiction recovery tools: A practical handbook.* Thousand Oaks, CA: Sage. This edited book offers more extensive elaboration on each of the recovery tools briefly reviewed in this chapter. It also discusses ways to match clients with recovery tools.

ADDICTION RECOVERY PROGRAMS

RESIDENTIAL AND OUTPATIENT TREATMENT PROGRAMS

Long-term residential treatment provides 24-hour care, generally in nonhospital settings. Therapeutic communities are probably the best-known residential treatment model; however, other residential treatment facilities may employ other approaches, such as the 12-step and/or cognitive-behavioral therapy approaches.

THERAPEUTIC COMMUNITIES

A therapeutic community (TC) is a residential program with planned lengths of stay of 6 to 12 months. It is highly structured and usually confrontational. Utilizing a "resocialization" approach, a TC uses the entire community (sometimes called "family") of residents as the active treatment component. Although addiction is viewed within the context of an individual's learned deficits, treatment focuses on the community helping change dysfunctional traits to healthy ones.

SHORT-TERM RESIDENTIAL TREATMENT

These live-in programs, often based on a modified 12-step approach, provide intensive but relatively brief (28 days) treatment programs. Originally designed to treat alcohol problems, many of these programs diversified during the cocaine epidemic of the mid-1980s to treat addictions to illicit drugs as well as alcohol.

The original residential treatment approach developed by Hazelden consisted of a 3- to 6-week hospital-based inpatient treatment phase followed by extended outpatient therapy and participation in a self-help group, such as Alcoholics Anonymous (see *Principles of Drug Addiction Treatment,* National Institute on Drug Abuse, 1999b, pp. 28–30).

TREATMENT FACILITIES DIRECTORIES

The following directories provide excellent sources for locating residential treatment facilities.

Substance Abuse Treatment Facility Locator

This online searchable directory lists more than 11,000 drug and alcohol treatment facilities at various locations. It identifies services for different populations and those manifesting various drug problems (http://findtreatment .samhsa.gov).

The National Directory of Drug Abuse and Alcoholism Treatment and Prevention Programs (DHHS Pub. No. SMA 01-3243)

This publication, offered free by calling the National Clearinghouse for Alcohol and Other Drug Information at (800) 729-6686, lists federal, state, local, and private providers of alcoholism and drug abuse treatment and prevention services. It gives the location and selected characteristics of substance abuse service providers and offers information about state authorities and prevention contacts. Each facility is identified by name, with address, telephone number, hotline (if applicable), and codes for types of service providers, facility location, and third-party payments.

SoberRecovery.com: www.soberrecovery.com/links/dualdiagnosis.html

An online program based in Southern California supported by sponsors, affiliates, and donations from visitors and members, it lists more than 2,500 resources (all with links of their own). This web site provides information on AA, NA, Sober Living Homes, Al-Anon and NarAnon, Detox Centers, Treatment Facilities, Eating Disorders, and Mental Health Resources.

Additional Resources

Leukefeld, C. G., Pickens, R. W., & Schuster, C. R. (1991). Improving drug abuse treatment: Recommendations for research and practice. In R. W. Pickens, C. G. Leukefeld, & C. R. Schuster (Eds.), *Improving drug abuse treatment* (NIDA Research Monograph Series, DHHS Pub No. ADM 91-1754). Washington, DC: U.S. Government Printing Office.

Lewis, B. F., McCusker, J., Hindin R., Frost, R., & Garfield, F. (1993). Four residential drug treatment programs: Project IMPACT. In F. M. Tims, J. A. Inciardi,

B. W. Fletcher, & A. MacNeill Jr. (Eds.), *Innovative approaches in the treatment of drug abuse* (pp. 45–60). Westport, CT: Greenwood Press.

Sacks, S., Sacks, J., De Leon, G., Bernhardt, A., & Staines, G. (1998). Modified therapeutic community for mentally ill chemical abusers: Background, influences, program description, preliminary findings. *Substance Use and Misuse, 32*(9), 1217–1259.

OUTPATIENT PROGRAMS

Outpatient drug-free treatment varies according to the types and intensity of services offered. Programs typically cost less than residential treatment and are more suitable for those with extensive social supports. Some low-intensity programs offer little more than drug education and admonition, whereas others emphasize group counseling. Some are also designed to treat clients who, in addition to alcohol and other drug problems, also have medical or mental health problems (see *Principles of Drug Addiction Treatment, A Research-Based Guide.* National Institute on Drug Abuse/NIH Pub. No. 99-4180, 1999).

To locate an appropriate outpatient program, see the national directory of AOD treatment programs (http://findtreatment.samhsa.gov).

Additional Resources

Obert, J., Weiner, A., Stimson, J., & Rawson, R. A. (2004). Treating substance use disorders. In Robert H. Coombs (Ed.), *Handbook of addictive disorders: A practical guide to treatment and diagnosis.* Hoboken, NJ: Wiley.

SUPPORT GROUPS

12-STEP SUPPORT GROUPS

Unlike some recovery programs, self-help programs lack a professional cadre of employed staff to direct and supervise activities. A small gathering of individuals who share similar struggles meet regularly (usually weekly) to share their experiences, strength, support, encouragement, and hope with one another. Larger groups may have a common opening session and then break into small groups to allow more intimate fellowship and sharing. Ideally, support groups are strictly confidential, and typically anonymous, so that participants can speak freely.

Twelve-step programs typically follow the same format and guidelines. Alcoholics Anonymous, the grandfather of all 12-step programs, began in 1935 with an informal meeting of two alcoholics, a New York stockbroker and an Ohio surgeon (both now deceased), who had been hopeless drunks.

Many other mutual-help programs are based on the 12-step AA model (e.g., Narcotics Anonymous, Cocaine Anonymous, Smokers Anonymous, Pills Anonymous, Marijuana Addicts Anonymous, and others discussed in this section). Family members and friends have Al-Anon, Alateen, and Nar-Anon groups, similarly based on this model.

The most popular mutual help recovery group in the United States and throughout the world, AA, as well as other 12-step groups, seeks to help chemically dependent people stay sober "one day at a time." Nonreligious but highly spiritual, the 12-step approach requires only that its members demonstrate "a desire to stop drinking [or drugging]."

Participants attend regular, free group meetings for support and often assist—"sponsor"—another participant alcoholic as an advisor and confidant. The sponsor, someone of the same gender who has been sober longer, provides peer support, and is available for emotional support 24 hours a day. By helping others, sponsors also help themselves.

Encouraged to admit that they are "powerless" over alcohol and other psychoactive substances, AA participants follow these 12 steps (Alcoholics Anonymous World Services, Inc., 2001):

1. We admit we were powerless over alcohol—that our lives had become unmanageable.
2. Came to believe that a Power greater than ourselves could restore us to sanity.
3. Made a decision to turn our will and our lives over to the care of God, as we understood Him.
4. Made a searching and fearless moral inventory of ourselves.
5. Admitted to God, to ourselves and to another human being the exact nature of our wrongs.
6. Were entirely ready to have God remove all these defects of character.
7. Humbly asked him to remove our shortcomings.
8. Made a list of all persons we had harmed, and became willing to make amends to them all.
9. Made direct amends to such people wherever possible, except when to do so would injure them or others.
10. Continued to take personal inventory and when we were wrong promptly admitted it.
11. Sought through prayer and meditation to improve our conscious contact with God, as we understood Him, praying only for knowledge of His will for us and the power to carry that out.
12. Having had a spiritual awakening as the result of these steps, we tried to carry this message to alcoholics and to practice these principles in all our affairs.

Twelve-step programs do not keep membership records, case histories, or engage in research projects. Twelve-step rituals are followed, and social rewards are given to members who reach recovery milestones. In some groups, newcomers receive a purple poker chip that they keep in the same pocket with the money they used to buy alcohol—reminding them to stay sober for just that day. After a month's sobriety, a white chip replaces the purple one, and so on. Other groups give medallions with sobriety length engraved on one side and the "Serenity Prayer" on the other.

The latter, slightly revised from theologian Reinhold Niebuhr's original, is recited in concert at each meeting: "God grant me the serenity to accept the things I cannot change, the courage to change the things I can, and the wisdom to know the difference."

Slogans remind alcoholics and addicts of principles essential to living chemical-free. "First things first" emphasizes that staying sober is the most important priority. "One day at a time" encourages focus on the here and now. "Easy does it" reminds one to be patient, not frustrated or discouraged, or try to accomplish too many things at once. "Keep it simple" encourages one to do the simple things: go to meetings, read *Alcoholics Anonymous* (AA's *Big Book*, 2001, which sets forth the basic principles of the recovery program), work the steps, and reach out to others who suffer from chemical dependence. "HOW"—standing for *Honesty, Openness,* and *Willingness*—reminds AA members to be honest in sharing what they feel and experience; open in considering new ideas; and willing to look at and change their destructive habits. "HALT" warns alcoholics to avoid being *Hungry, Angry, Lonely,* or *Tired,* since an excess of any one may lead to relapse. Twelve-step programs do not require any particular religious belief as a condition of membership.

The effectiveness of 12-step programs has been noted by many, including William E. Mayer, MD, former director of the Substance Abuse and Mental Health Services Administration (SAMHSA), "AA by and large works better than anything we have been able to devise with all our science and all our money and all our efforts. AA has shown the way and presented us with a model of long-term care that is really not care. It is participatory self-management. It is an assertion of the autonomy of the individual. Instead of his thinking of himself of a victim, a helpless person . . . AA gives a person a kind of sense of self-worth and along with it the kind of humility and reality testing that are absolutely essential in the management of alcohol problems" (Mayer, 1982).

The most significant 12-step programs are listed alphabetically:

Alcoholics Anonymous (AA) World Services, Inc.
General Service Office
P.O. Box 459, Grand Central Station
New York, NY 10163
Telephone: (212) 870-3400
Fax: (212) 870-3137
Web site: www.aa.org

AA, an international fellowship of over two million men and women who presently have or previously had a drinking problem, is a voluntary, nonprofessional, self-supporting, nondenominational, multiracial, apolitical fellowship with more than 100,000 groups that meet regularly in 150 countries.

There are no dues or fees for AA membership and no age or education requirements; membership is open to anyone who wants to do something about his or her drinking problem. A total abstinence program, members simply stay away from one drink, one day at a time. Sobriety is maintained through sharing experiences and following the Twelve Steps.

AA offers two types of meetings: (1) *Open meetings* that anyone may attend, usually consisting of talks by a leader and two or three speakers who share their experience of alcoholism and their recovery in AA; and (2) *Closed meetings*, limited to addicts who need to privately and confidentially share with one another.

AA groups can be located in any telephone directory or on the Internet. Staffed mainly by volunteers, they will either answer your questions or put you in touch with someone who can.

An electronic variation of AA, the Online Intergroup of Alcoholics Anonymous (OIAA) offers worldwide online participation (www.AA-intergroup.org).

Chemically Dependent Anonymous (CDA)
P.O. Box 423
Severna Park, MD 21146-0423
Telephone: (888) CDA-HOPE
Web site: www.cdaweb.org

CDA makes no distinction between substances, believing that the addictive-compulsive usage of *any* mood-altering chemical is the core of addictive disease and their use of *any* of them will result in relapse. CDA uses the Twelve Steps and Twelve Traditions of AA and is not affiliated with any political, religious, or commercial organizations or institutions.

CDA helps the drunk, junkie, acid head, speed or Valium freak, coke snorter and/or shooter, pill head, glue nose, needle nut, Sterno Joe, prescription-drug abuser, "recreational" pot smoker, or one who is all or a combination of any of the preceding. Neither does CDA rule out gamblers, sex addicts, overeaters, or others with strictly behavioral problems.

Meetings are held in several states (check their Internet web site for locations).

Cocaine Anonymous (CA)
World Service Office
3740 Overland Avenue, Suite C
Los Angeles, CA 90034-6337
Telephone: (310) 559-5833
Fax: (310) 559-2554
International referral line: (800) 347-8998
Web site: www.ca.org
Click on Local Phones & Links for a complete listing of telephone numbers in
    the United States, Canada, United Kingdom, and the Netherlands.
E-mail: publicinfo@ca.org

CA uses the 12-step approach to help those addicted to cocaine. The only requirement for membership is a desire to stop using cocaine, including "crack" cocaine, and all other mind-altering substances.

CA had its first meeting in Hollywood, California, in 1982 and has since expanded to over 2,000 groups throughout the United States and Canada (groups are also now forming in Europe). CA literature, available in English, French, and Spanish, includes *Hope, Faith and Courage: Stories from the Fellowship of Cocaine Anonymous*, published in 1994. While guided by the *Twelve Traditions of Cocaine Anonymous*, each group conducts its business as it sees fit.

CA offers these services to the general public: (1) Speakers (in both professional and educational settings) describing the organization and its program of recovery, (2) speaker panels for addicts confined in hospitals or other closed institutions, (3) *books* and other literature for members of the professional community and their clients or patients, and (4) *referrals* to local chapters.

Crystal Meth Anonymous (CMA)
CMA General Services
8205 Santa Monica Blvd. PMB 1-114
West Hollywood, CA 90046-5977
Telephone information line: (213) 488-4455
Web site: www.crystalmeth.org

A 12-step fellowship that advocates complete abstinence from crystal meth, alcohol, inhalants, and all other mind-altering substances, CMA is open to anyone with a desire to stop using drugs. A young program, CMA is not yet active all over the country; a listing of CMA meeting locations in the United States and Canada can be found by clicking on "Schedules" on the CMA web site.

Debtors Anonymous (DA)
P.O. Box 920888
Needham, MA 02492-0009
Telephone: (781) 453-2743
Fax: (781) 453-2745
Web site: www.debtorsanonymous.org

Debtors Anonymous—first called the "Penny Pinchers" and later "Capital Builders"—started in 1968 when a core group of AA members held their first meeting to discuss their money problems. After 2 years, the group disbanded, then regrouped in 1976 and Debtors Anonymous was born. Today, more than 500 meetings are held in the United States and in 13 other countries throughout the world.

Participants in DA meet together to help solve their common problem of compulsive debting. Their one requirement for membership is a desire to stop incurring unsecured debt (taken from *Preamble of Debtors Anonymous*). After a member has gained some familiarity with the DA program through attendance at meetings, he or she organizes a Pressure Relief Group, a meeting to relieve any financial or other kinds of pressure the member may be feeling and provide support for recovery. Meetings consist of the new member plus two other members of the fellowship who have been solvent for 3 months and who usually have more experience in the program. The group meets periodically to review the new member's financial situation.

To obtain publications helpful in working with a debtor, contact the General Service Office or your local DA office/intergroup. D.A. General Service Conference-Approved Literature include, *Currency of Hope, Pressure Relief Groups and Pressure Relief Meetings* pamphlet, and *Ways and Means Newsletter.* To find a DA meeting, go to their web site and click on "Find A DA Meeting."

Domestic Violence Anonymous (DVA)
c/o Baylaw
P.O. Box 29011
San Francisco, CA 94129
Telephone: (415) 681-4850
Web site: www.baylaw.com
E-mail: Baylaw1@ix.netcom.com

DVA is a 12-step program for any victim of domestic violence (emotional, physical, or mental)—whether the person experienced domestic violence as an adult or as a child. Meetings are held in the United States, New Zealand, Russia, Australia, Poland, and Spain. Sponsored by *Baylaw,* a nonprofit organization that exists to serve the victims of domestic violence, all officers and staff are unpaid volunteers. For more information, click on *Domestic Violence Anonymous Meetings.*

Eating Addictions Anonymous (EAA)
General Service Office
P.O. Box 8151
Silver Spring, MD 20907-8151
Telephone: (202) 882-6528
Web site: http://dcregistry.com/users/eatingaddictions/main.html

A 12-step program, EAA is made up of overeaters, anorexics, bulimics, undereaters, binge eaters, grazers, and exercise bulimics who have negative relationships with their bodies or a distorted body image. EAA's only requirement is the members' desire to stop abusing food and their own bodies. This program is built on the SANE principles of recovery: (1) **S**piritual Surrender, (2) **A**bsolute Commitment, (3) **N**ecessary Action, and (4) **E**motional Healing.

EAA focuses on internal growth and finding lifelong recovery, not just from eating disorders but also from the shame and self-hatred that accompanies these addictions. Not run by therapists, doctors, or other professionals, EAA comprises only recovering addicts who seek holistic, balanced recovery, encouraging members to address their body image issues specifically. EAA believes that in recovery, obese persons *do* lose weight, and emaciated persons *do* gain, but that body size and eating abuses are merely symptoms of an addictive way of dealing with deeper problems.

> Gamblers Anonymous (GA)
> P.O. Box 17173
> Los Angeles, CA 90017
> Telephone: (213) 386-8789
> Fax: (213) 386-0030
> Web site: www.gamblersanonymous.org
> E-mail: isomain@gamblersanonymous.org

Gamblers Anonymous was founded in 1957 when two men, each with a baffling history of obsessive gambling, met and, after having regular meetings, neither returned to gambling. They concluded that relapse could be avoided by changing character traits within themselves. To accomplish this, they adopted the 12-step principles used by others recovering from compulsive addictions. Since then, the fellowship has grown steadily with groups now flourishing throughout the world.

> Jewish Alcoholics, Chemically Dependent Persons and Significant
>   Others (JACS)
> Web site: www.jacsweb.org

Founded in 1979, JACS has grown to serve thousands of Jewish addicts. A voluntary 12-step, mutual-help group for Jews in recovery from the abuse of alcohol and other chemicals, JACS offers participants and their families an opportunity to connect with one another, explore their Jewish roots, and discover resources within Judaism to enhance their recovery. JACS members represent the entire spectrum of Jewish experience, background, affiliation, and observance.

JACS volunteers work to (1) encourage and assist Jewish alcoholics, other chemically dependent persons and their families, friends, and associates to explore recovery in a nurturing Jewish environment by conducting retreats and other events that provide support to Jews in recovery; (2) promoting knowledge and understanding of the disease of alcoholism and chemical dependency as it involves the Jewish community; and (3) acting as a resource center and information clearinghouse on the effects of alcoholism and drug dependency on Jewish family life.

> Marijuana Anonymous (MA)
> World Services
> P.O. Box 2912
> Van Nuys, CA 91404
> Telephone: (800) 766-6779
> Web site: www.marijuana-anonymous.org

Although MA uses the Twelve Steps, meeting formats vary and are autonomous. Sometimes there is a speaker; other times the Steps or other literature are discussed. Anonymity is the foundation of this program as it strives for progress, not perfection. MA teaches three important ideas: (1) We are marijuana addicts and cannot manage our own lives, (2) probably no human power can relieve our addiction, and (3) our Higher Power can and will if sought.

Click on the MA web site (www.marijuana-anonymous.org) to obtain a pamphlet, *Detoxing from Marijuana,* which reviews the experiences of many MA members who completed an extensive questionnaires regarding their own early days of abstinence from their drug of choice. To find a meeting, go to the MA web site, click on Meetings and bring up "On Land Meetings," find your state and click.

Narcotics Anonymous (NA)
World Service Office
P.O. Box 9999
Van Nuys, CA 91409
Telephone: (818) 773-9999; (818) 700-0700
Web site: www.na.org
E-mail: FSTeam@na.org

An international, community-based association of recovering drug addicts, NA has more than 28,000 weekly meetings in 113 countries. Its first meetings were held in Los Angeles in 1953. NA books and information pamphlets are currently available in 22 languages, with translations in process for nine languages, NA's earliest self-titled pamphlet, known among members as the "White Booklet," states, "We are not interested in what or how much you used . . . but only in what you want to do about your problem and how we can help." Membership is open to any drug addict, regardless of the particular drug or combination of drugs used. (When adapting AA's First Step, the word "addiction" was substituted for "alcohol," thus removing drug-specific language and reflecting the disease concept of addiction.)

Highly informative, the NA web site offers bulletins, books and A-Vs, events, and NA World Services News (in five languages). Contacts links you directly to any e-mail address required to set your client up with a NA meeting.

Nicotine Anonymous World Services (NicA)
419 Main Street, PMB# 370
Huntington Beach, CA 92648
Telephone: (415) 750-0328
Web site: http://nicotine-anonymous.org
E-mail: info@nicotine-anonymous.org

This nonprofit fellowship welcomes those seeking freedom from nicotine addiction, including those using cessation programs and nicotine withdrawal aids. This support group also uses the Twelve Steps, as adapted from AA.

Overeaters Anonymous (OA)
World Service Office
P.O. Box 44020
Rio Rancho, NM 87174-4020
Telephone: (505) 891-2664
Fax: (505) 891-4320
Web site: www.overeatersanonymous.org
E-mail: info@overeatersanonymous.org

OA's purpose is to help members abstain from compulsive overeating and to carry this message of recovery to those who still suffer. OA welcomes everyone who wants to stop eating compulsively.

Sex Addicts Anonymous (SAA)
ISO of SAA
P.O, Box 70949
Houston, TX 77270
Telephone: (713) 869-4902; (800) 477-8191
E-mail: info@saa-recovery.org
Web site: www.sexaa.org

SAA, open to all who share a desire to stop addictive sexual behavior, is a spiritual program indebted to AA's 12-step approach. "Our common goals are to become sexually healthy and to help other sex addicts achieve freedom from compulsive sexual behavior "

Sex and Love Addicts Anonymous (SLAA)
P.O. Box 338
Norwood, MA 02062-0338
Telephone: (781) 255-8825; (866) 836-7522; or in the Hartford, CT, area
    (860) 246-4009
Web site: www.slaact.org

A 12-step, 12-tradition oriented fellowship, SLAA members reach out to others to counter the destructive consequences of sex addiction; love addiction; dependency on romantic attachments; emotional dependency; and sexual, social, and emotional anorexia. "We find a common denominator in our obsessive, compulsive patterns which renders any personal differences of sexual or gender orientation irrelevant."

Sexual Compulsives Anonymous (SCA)
P.O. Box 1585
Old Chelsea Station
New York, NY 10011
Telephone: (800) 977-HEAL
E-mail: info@sca-recovery.org
Web site: www.sca-recovery.org

Open to anyone with a desire to recover from their sexual compulsion, SCA is a spiritual program that provides a safe environment for working on problems of sexual addiction and sexual sobriety. Encouraged to develop a sexual recovery plan, members define sexual sobriety for themselves: "We believe we are not meant to repress our God-given sexuality, but to learn how to express it in ways that will not make unreasonable demands on our time and energy, place us in legal jeopardy, or endanger our mental, physical or spiritual health."

Sexaholics Anonymous (SA)
P.O. Box 111910
Nashville, TN 37222
Telephone: (615) 331-6230
Fax: (615) 331-6901
Web site: www.sa.org
E-mail: saico@sa.org

The only requirement for membership to SA is a desire to stop lusting, to become and stay sexually sober, and to help others achieve sexual sobriety.

Workaholics Anonymous (WA)
World Service Organization
P.O. Box 289
Menlo Park, CA 94026-0289
Telephone: (510) 273-9253
Web site: www.workaholics-anonymous.org/#wso

WA offers support for those seeking to recover from workaholism. The only requirement for membership is the desire to stop working compulsively and to carry the message of recovery to other workaholics.

12-STEP ALTERNATIVES

These support groups, put off by AA's emphasis on spirituality, retain some AA program features, but omit AA's emphasis on spirituality and reliance on a higher power.

LifeRing Secular
Oakland, CA
Telephone: (510) 763-0779
E-Mail: service@lifering.org
Web site: www.unhooked.com

Acknowledging that 12-step recovery programs help many, LifeRing points out, "People who want to maintain abstinence from alcohol and other addictive substances deserve a choice." Meetings are free of any religious content and belief in a higher power. Relying on human efforts instead of on divine intervention or faith healing, meetings offer peer support with feedback in a "secular setting and open architecture (i.e., members structure their own programs)." There are no steps or sponsors.

"Not for everyone, LifeRing is for the more rebellious client who thinks more outside the box by questioning authority." Members give and take with other people in small talk circles with a conversational format that focuses on current events in participants' lives. Feedback (crosstalk) is encouraged and meetings end with a round of applause for progress.

LifeRing uses the 3-S philosophy—Sobriety, Secularity, and Self-Help. *Sobriety* always means abstinence. The basic membership requirement is a sincere desire to remain abstinent from alcohol and drugs. The motto is "We do not drink or use, no matter what." *Secularity* means that "You get to keep whatever religious beliefs you have, and you are under no pressure to acquire any if you don't. Participants' spiritual or religious beliefs or lack thereof remain private." *Self-help* means that motivation and effort are the keys to recovery. The main purpose of the group process is to reinforce the individual's own inner strivings to stay clean and sober.

Moderation Management (MM)
22 W. 27th Street
New York, NY 10001
Telephone: (212) 871-0974
Fax: (212) 213-6582
E-mail: mm@moderation.org
Web site: www.moderation.org

Founded in 1995, MM is a behavioral change program and national support network for people who have decided to reduce their drinking and make other positive lifestyle changes. A program for "problem drinkers" who are trying to control or reduce their drinking, MM is not intended for heavily alcohol-dependent patients or those who have already achieved abstinence.

Rational Recovery Systems (RR)
P.O. Box 800
Lotus, CA 95651
Telephone: (800) 303-CURE
Web site: www.rational.org

An abstinence-based, non-12-step recovery program with no religious or spiritual content, RR provides orientation in Addictive Voice Recognition Technique (AVRT):

> Observe your thoughts and feelings, positive and negative, about drinking or using. Thoughts and feelings which support continued use are called the Addictive Voice (AV); those that support abstinence are you. When you recognize and understand your AV, it becomes not-you, but "it," an easily defeated enemy that has been causing

you to drink. All it wants is pleasure. "I want a drink," becomes, "It wants a drink." Think to yourself, "I will never drink again," and listen for its reaction. Your negative thoughts and feelings are your AV talking back to you. Now, think, "I will drink/use whenever I please." Your pleasant feelings are also the AV, which is in control. Recovery is not a process; it is an event. The magic word is "Never," as in, "I will never drink/use again." Recognition defeats short-term desire, and abstinence soon becomes effortless. Complete separation of "you" from "it" leads to complete recovery and hope for a better life. The only time you can drink is now, and the only time you can quit for good is right now. "I will never drink/use again," becomes, "I never drink now." It's not hard; anyone can do it. (www.rational.org/Crash.html).

Secular Organizations for Sobriety (SOS)
(Save Our Selves)
4773 Hollywood Blvd,
Hollywood, CA 90027
Telephone: (323) 666-4295
E-mail: SOS@CFIWest.org
Web site: www.secularsobriety.org

A not-for-profit network of autonomous, nonprofessional groups dedicated solely to helping individuals achieve and maintain sobriety, SOS offers group meetings in many cities throughout the United States and other countries. SOS encourages members to acknowledge their addiction, accept each day that drinking or using are off limits, and make sobriety a priority.

SOS takes a self-empowerment approach to recovery. Sobriety (abstinence) is "Priority One, no matter what!" The individual is credited with achieving and maintaining his or her own sobriety. Although SOS does not have the spiritual component of the 12-step programs, it does use AA's "one day at a time" approach.

Not opposed to or in competition with any other recovery programs—SOS respects recovery in any form, regardless of the path by which it is achieved—supports healthy skepticism and encourages the use of the scientific method to understand alcoholism.

SMART Recovery
7537 Mentor Avenue, Suite #306
Mentor, OH 44060
Telephone: (440) 951-5357
Fax: (440) 951-5358
E-mail: srmail1@aol.com
Web site: www.smartrecovery.org

An abstinence-based recovery program without the spiritual components of AA and the other 12-step groups, SMART recovery is a self-help program for those having problems with drinking who reject AA's idea that addicts have no control or power over their condition, and therefore do not rely on a higher power.

RECOVERY PROGRAMS FOR SELECTED POPULATIONS

Some recovery programs exist exclusively for special populations—women, adolescents, family members, psychiatric patients, persons with HIV/AIDS and gays and lesbians. The following reviews these resources.

WOMEN

Although women use illicit substances less frequently than men, those who do suffer from more acute and chronic problems. Female alcoholics are more likely to die from suicides, alcohol-related accidents, circulatory disorders, and liver cirrhosis. Due to gender differences in body water content, women experience higher blood alcohol concentration levels with a lower alcohol intake, and long-term problem drinking takes a greater health toll.

Female-specific support groups are important because (1) women in coed groups tend to take a backseat to men and talk less, (2) women in treatment need to focus on specific issues such as low self-esteem, sexual abuse, battering, and child abuse (questions not easily discussed in coeducational settings) and, (3) women in treatment, more often abused in childhood and marriage than men, need to discuss physical, sexual, and emotional violence issues.

Women for Sobriety (WFS)
P.O. Box 618
Quakertown, CO 18951
Telephone: (215) 536-8026; (800) 333-1606
Hotline: (800) 333-1606
Fax: (215) 538-9026
Web site: www.womenforsobriety.org

A self-help alternative to 12-step programs, WFS is based on cognitive therapy. Founded by Dr. Jean Kirkpatrick, WFS holds that female alcoholics and addicts often have special needs and issues not addressed by recovery programs founded largely by and for men. The program strives to build self-esteem as well as help women recover from addiction. Both an organization and a self-help recovery program, WFS offers a 13-statement program of positive principles that encourage emotional and spiritual growth:

1. I have a life-threatening problem that once had me; I now take charge of my life. I accept the responsibility.
2. Negative thoughts destroy only myself. My first conscious act must be to remove negativity from my life.
3. Happiness is a habit I will develop. Happiness is created, not waited for.
4. Problems bother me only to the degree I permit them to. I now better understand my problems and do not permit problems to overwhelm me.

5. I am what I think. I am a capable, competent, caring, compassionate woman.
6. Life can be ordinary or it can be great. Greatness is mine by a conscious effort.
7. Love can change the course of my world. Caring becomes all important.
8. The fundamental object of life is emotional and spiritual growth. Daily I put my life into a proper order, knowing which are the priorities.
9. The past is gone forever. No longer will I be victimized by the past, I am a new person.
10. All love given returns. I will learn to know that others love me.
11. Enthusiasm is my daily exercise. I treasure all moments of my new life.
12. I am a competent woman and have much to give life. This is what I am and I shall know it always.
13. I am responsible for myself and for my actions. I am in charge of my mind, my thoughts, and my life (WFS, n.d.; www.womenforsobriety.org).

WFS holds that addiction results from attempts to cope with stress and emotional deprivation and that recovery occurs from self-knowledge and abstinence.

Other Resources for Women

Although the following are not treatment resources, they provide helpful information for women:

National Organization on Fetal Alcohol Syndrome (NOFAS)
Hotline: (800) 638-BABY
Web site: www.nofas.org

NOFAS is dedicated to spreading the message that drinking and pregnancy do not mix.

National Women's Health Information Center (NWHIC)
8550 Arlington Blvd., Suite 300
Fairfax, VA 22031
Telephone: (800) 994-9662
TDD: (888) 220-5446
Web site: www.4woman.org (included here is Office of Women's Health)

NWHIC's mission is to provide current, reliable, commercial and cost-free health information to women and their families. A gateway to the vast array of federal and other women's health information resources, NWHIC serves as the Office of Women's Health's Clearinghouse. It provides information to help women link to, read, and download a wide variety of health-related material developed by the

Department of Health and Human Services, the Department of Defense, other federal agencies, and private sector resources.

National Women's Health Network
514 10th Street NW, Suite 400
Washington, DC 20004
Telephone: (202) 237-1140
Web site: www.womenshealthnetwork.org

The mission of the National Women's Health Network is to advocate national policies that protect and promote all women's health and to provide evidence-based, independent information to empower women to make fully informed health decisions. To accomplish this mission, they:

- Act as an independent voice for women's health and thus accept no money from companies that sell pharmaceuticals, medical devices, dietary supplements, alcohol, tobacco, or health insurance.
- Represent and are supported by our individual and organizational members.
- Research and analyze women's health issues from a feminist, critical perspective free from the influence of corporate interests.
- Create and disseminate evidence-based information on women's health issues to consumers, advocates, health care professionals, media, and policymakers.
- Monitor and educate Congress and federal agencies to ensure that laws and policies as well as research and regulatory decision making reflect the interests of all women.
- Monitor information provided by companies that sell or promote pharmaceuticals, medical devices, and dietary supplements.
- Link activists and community groups nationwide.
- Address the interconnections among social, racial, economic, and gender equity.

Click on "Substance Abuse" in the *SAMHSA Locator*. www.findtreatment.SAMHSA.gov/facilitylocatordoc.htm. Click on your state and provide the requested information to locate the treatment facility nearest you (look for Women under Special Programs/Groups).

ADOLESCENTS

These resources target children and teenagers affected by substance abuse:

Al-Anon/Alateen Family Group Headquarters, Inc.
1600 Corporate Landing Parkway
Virginia Beach, VA 23454-5617
Telephone: (757) 563-1600; (800) 356-9996; (888) 4AL-ANON
Fax: (757) 563-1655
Web sites: www.al-anon.org; www.al-anon.alateen.org

Al-Anon, a fellowship of relatives and friends of alcoholics who believe their lives have been affected by someone else's drinking, is an anonymous program based on the Twelve Steps of Alcoholics Anonymous (AA). Its purpose is to help families and friends of alcoholics recover from the effects of living with the problem drinking of a relative or friend.

Alateen, the recovery program for young people, is sponsored by Al-Anon members (see Adolescent Programs). Al-Anon (and its Alateen teenage members) is an established community resource for anyone whose life has been affected by a problem drinker, whether the alcoholic is still drinking or not.

Betty Ford Center (BFC) Family Programs
(Main Campus)
39000 Bob Hope Drive
Rancho Mirage, CA 92270
Telephone: (760) 773-4100; (800) 854-9211 and
Dallas-Ft. Worth Metroplex Children and Family Programs
1320 Greenway Drive, Suite 105
Irving, TX 75038
Telephone: (972) 753-0552; (972) 751-0363
E-mail: FamilyProgram@bettyfordcenter.org
Web site: www.BettyFordCenter.org

The BFC Family program offers a recognized form of therapeutic education and support for family members and others significant to the addicted person. Based on the 12-step program of Al-Anon, the program for family members consists of a 5-day intensive process for adolescents and adults designed to help family members and friends begin their own recovery from the effects of another's addiction. Participants attend lectures, films, group therapy sessions, discussion groups, and other activities.

Children of Alcoholics Foundation
164 W. 74th Street
New York, NY 10023
Telephone: (212) 595-5810, ext. 7760
E-mail: coaf@phoenixhouse.org
Web site: www.coaf.org

A national nonprofit organization, the Foundation provides a range of educational materials and services to help professionals, children, and adults break the intergenerational cycle of parental substance abuse.

Just like children of alcoholics, children of substance abusers (called COSAs) are harmed by drugs, whether marijuana, prescription pills, cocaine, heroin, or whatever.

TEEN-ANON Groups
267 Lester Avenue, Suite 104
Oakland, CA 94606
Telephone: (510) 444-6074 9 A.M. to 11 A.M. PST; 12 P.M. to 2 P.M. EST
Web site: www.teen-anon.com

A national 12-step recovery fellowship for teens dealing with substance abuse of all kinds, TEEN-ANON is a behavioral and spiritual program for teens 12 to 19, supervised by experienced recovering adults. Site lists meeting locations and contains literature geared for teens to access.

National Association for Children of Alcoholics (NACoA)
11426 Rockville Pike, #100
Rockville, MD 20852
Telephone: (301) 468-0985
Hotline: (888) 554-COAS
Fax: (301) 468-0987
E-mail: NACoA@nacoa.org
Web site: www.nacoa.org

NACoA maintains that vulnerable children should not grow up in isolation and without support. A national nonprofit membership organization working on behalf of children of alcohol- and drug-dependent parents, NACoA advocates for all children and families affected by alcoholism and other drug dependencies—they help kids hurt by parental alcohol and drug use by:

- Working to raise public awareness
- Providing leadership in public policy at the national, state, and local levels
- Advocating for appropriate, effective, and accessible education and prevention services
- Facilitating the advancement of professional knowledge and understanding of substance abuse
- Publishing a bimonthly newsletter
- Creating videos, booklets, posters and other educational materials
- Hosting an Internet site with information about and ways to help children of alcoholics
- Sending out information packets to anyone who asks
- Maintaining a toll-free phone available to all.

GamblingSolutions
9A Munroe Court
Peabody, MA 01960
Telephone: (978) 532-5885
Fax: (978) 897-4804
Web site: www.gamblingsolutions.net
E-mail: service@GamblingSolutions.net

GamblingSolutions provides training and consultation to colleges and high schools to help minimize the corrosive effects of problem gambling. It trains school administrators, faculty and resident advisors, school counselors/clinicians, and students.

Other Adolescent Resources Available on the Internet

Monitoring the Future Study
Web site: http://monitoringthefuture.org

Although not a clinical resource, these sequential reports provide the most recent prevalence and incidence rates of adolescent substance abuse. Monitoring the Future is an ongoing study of the behaviors, attitudes, and values of American secondary school students, college students, and young adults. Each year, some 50,000 8th-, 10th-, and 12th-grade students are surveyed. In addition, annual follow-up questionnaires are mailed to a sample of each graduating class for a number of years after their initial participation. News releases, publications, and the most recent prevalence and incidence rates of adolescent substance abuse are at your fingertips.

Center on Addiction and Substance Abuse (CASA)

This Columbia University paper (1997) provides information on risk and protective factors for alcohol as well as other substances of abuse.

Substance abuse and the American adolescent. New York, NY: Hogue & Liddle. Available at the following web site: www.casacolumbia.org/publications1456/publications_form.htm.

The Clinical Toolbox Series

This Internet web site provides links to information about treatments for adolescent drug abuse, including treatment manuals and articles on effective approaches to treatment. See www.drugabuse.gov/TB/Clinical/ClinicalToolbox.html.

Additional Resources

Bukstein, O. G. (1995). *Adolescent substance abuse: Assessment, prevention, and treatment.* New York: Wiley. This book provides general descriptions of the various types of treatment and prevention approaches for adolescent substance abuse.

Center on Addiction and Substance Abuse (CASA) at Columbia University. (2000). *No place to hide: Substance abuse in mid-size cities and rural America.* New York: Hogue & Liddle. This report provides information on subgroup and geographic trends in rates of adolescent substance use.

Center on Addiction and Substance Abuse (CASA) at Columbia University. (2001). *Malignant neglect: Substance abuse and America's schools.* New York: Hogue & Liddle. This report provides statistics on drug use among adolescents as well as information on consequences of adolescent substance use.

Center on Addiction and Substance Abuse (CASA) at Columbia University. (2002). *Teen tipplers: America's underage drinking epidemic.* New York: Hogue & Liddle. This report provides recent statistics on alcohol use among adolescents.

Ozechowski, T. J., & Liddle, H. A. (2000). Family-based therapy for adolescent drug abuse: Knowns and unknowns. *Clinical Child and Family Psychology Review,* 3(4), 269–298. This article provides an overview of the current state of knowledge regarding family-based approaches for treating adolescent drug abuse, as well as areas in which research is lacking.

Tarter, R. E. (2002). Etiology of adolescent substance abuse: A developmental perspective. *American Journal on Addictions, 11,* 171–191. This article provides information on the etiology of adolescent substance abuse.

Wagner, E. F., & Waldron, H. B. (2001). *Innovations in adolescent substance abuse interventions.* Amsterdam: Pergamon. This book provides an overview of the main types of treatment for adolescent substance abuse that have received empirical support. Descriptions of the treatments as well as outcome research are described.

FAMILY MEMBERS

These recovery resources, previously described, assist family members of addicted persons: (1) Al-Anon/Alateen Family Group Headquarters, Inc.; (2) Betty Ford Center (BFC) Family Programs; and (3) Children of Alcoholics Foundation. In addition, see:

Codependents of Sex Addicts (COSA)
National Service Organization
P.O. Box 14537
Minneapolis, MN 55414
Telephone: (763) 537-6904
E-mail: info@cosa-recovery.org
Web site: www.cosa-recovery.org

An anonymous 12-step fellowship program open to those whose lives have been affected by compulsive sexual behaviors, COSA is self-supported through members' weekly voluntary contributions and is not affiliated with any outside treatment centers, religions, or therapeutic approach. One can find a meeting site in almost every state.

Co-Anon Family Groups World Services
P.O. Box 12722
Tucson, AZ 85732-2722
Telephone: (520) 513-5028; (800) 898-9985
E-mail: info@co-anon.org
Web site: www.co-anon.org

Co-Anon Family Groups, consisting of husbands, wives, parents, relatives, or close friends of someone who is chemically dependent, share a common bond—they feel their lives have been deeply affected by another person's drug abuse. Co-Anon helps relieve feelings of hurt, fear, anger, resentment, and guilt. By practicing the 12 steps of recovery, members develop coping skills to deal with difficulties and find a more serene approach to life.

Families Anonymous, Inc. (FA)
P.O. Box 3475
Culver City, CA 90231-3475
Infoline: (800) 736-9805
Fax: (310) 815-9682
E-mail: famanon@FamiliesAnonymous.org
Web site: www.familiesanonymous.org

A 12-step, self-help, recovery support group for relatives and friends of those who have alcohol, drug, or behavioral problems, FA provides mutual support and a safe place to share experiences and concerns. Attending meetings helps members adopt an honest and consistent approach toward addicts and come to terms with their problems.

Gam-Anon
P.O. Box 157
Whitestone, NY 11357
Telephone: (718) 352-1671
Fax: (718) 746-2571
Web site: www.gam-anon.org

A support group for the spouses, family, and/or close friends of compulsive gamblers, Gam-Anon's purposes are threefold: (1) to learn acceptance and understanding of the gambling illness; (2) to use the program and its problem-solving suggestions in rebuilding their lives, and (3) to give assistance to those who suffer.

Gam-Anon offers help in working through and in resolving feelings and helps participants refuse to be responsible for the gambler's behavior. Its members experience relief from anxiety by accepting the fact of powerlessness over the family problem.

Meeting schedules are available as well as literature sources and general information about gambling addiction with a Questions/Answer section.

Hazelden's Family Center
15245 Pleasant Valley Road
P.O. Box 11
Center City, MN 55012-0011
Telephone: (651) 213-4000; (800) 257-7810
Fax: (651) 213-4411
Web site: www.Hazelden.org

Hazelden's Family Center, open to anyone whose life has been affected by a loved one's drinking or drug use, offers information about (1) how families function when coping with chemical dependency, (2) help in identifying the signs of unhealthy versus healthy relationships, (3) skills to change responses to family situations, (4) an introduction to self-help groups like Al-Anon, and (5) education about the disease of chemical dependency and recovery.

Nar-Anon Family Group
P.O. Box 2562
Palos Verdes Peninsula, CA 90274
Telephone: (310) 547-5800
Web site: www.syix.com/mleahey/United

Nar-Anon Family Group, a worldwide self-help organization, helps members learn about drug abuse as an illness, share problems, seek help, replace despair with hope, improve family attitudes, and regain self confidence. Primarily for people who know a feeling of desperation concerning the addiction of someone very near to them, the program is based on the 12 suggested steps of Narcotics Anonymous.

DUAL DIAGNOSIS CLIENTS

An addicted client may have more than a straightforward chemical dependency problem. Although it may not be obvious, the client may also have one or more coexisting psychiatric disorders, another addictive disorder, or both (see Dual Diagnosis in Part III). As this may complicate treatment, it is essential to assess all new clients for such problems. If you suspect the client might also have a psychiatric disorder, refer him or her for psychiatric evaluation.

To order a copy of the ASAM Patient Placement Criteria for the Treatment of Substance-Related Disorders, contact the *ASAM Publications Distribution Center* (800) 844-8948 (www.asam.org/ppc).

Dual Diagnosis Recovery Network (DRN)
220 Venture Circle
Nashville, TN 37228
Telephone: (615) 742-1000; (888) 869-9230
Fax: (615) 742-1009

The DRN, an organization with regional chapters, offers individuals in dual recovery, their families, and service providers, a means of working together to enhance recovery. Regional chapters allow those involved in dual recovery to contact one another, assess the needs in their own community, ease the stigma, and raise the level of care.

The DRN mission is to enhance recovery opportunities for individuals and families in dual recovery by (1) participating with community-based mental health, chemical dependency, and consumer advocate organizations; (2) offering in-service and workshop presentations to increase public awareness and to reduce stigma that is associated with dual disorders; and (3) providing a speakers bureau of individuals with expertise in dual disorders and recovery.

National Alliance for the Mentally Ill
Colonial Place Three
2107 Wilson Blvd., Suite 300
Arlington, VA 22201-3042
Telephone: (703) 524-7600
Toll-Free Help Line: (800) 950-NAMI
Web site: www.nami.org

National studies commissioned by the federal government estimate that 10 to 12 million Americans have co-occurring mental and addictive disorders. This research confirms that integrated treatment for co-occurring disorders is much more effective than treating these illnesses separately. Researchers agree that integrated treatment means mental illness and addictive disorders services and interventions are delivered simultaneously at the same treatment site, ideally with cross-trained staff. What is not considered integrated treatment is *sequential treatment* (treat one disorder first, then the other) or *parallel treatment* (in which two treatment providers at separate locations use separate treatment plans to treat each condition separately, but at the same time).

Substance abuse complicates almost every aspect of care for the person with mental illness. These individuals are very difficult to engage in treatment. Diagnosis is difficult because it takes time to unravel the interacting effects of substance abuse and the mental illness. They may have difficulty being accommodated at home and may not be tolerated in community residences or rehabilitation programs. They lose their support systems and suffer frequent relapses and hospitalizations. Violence is more prevalent among the dually diagnosed population. Both domestic violence and suicide attempts are more common. Of the mentally ill who wind up in jails and prisons, a high percentage are drug abusers.

National Mental Health Association (NMHA)
2001 N. Beauregard Street, 12th Floor
Alexandria, VA 22311
Telephone: (703) 684-7722; (800) 969-NMHA
Fax: (703) 684-5968
TTY: (800) 433-5959
Web site: www.nmha.org

The country's oldest and largest nonprofit organization addressing all aspects of mental health and mental illness, NMHA has more than 340 affiliates nationwide. NMHA works to improve the mental health of all Americans, especially the 54 million individuals with mental disorders, through advocacy, education, research, and service. NMHA has educated millions about mental illnesses and reduced barriers to treatment and services. As a result of these efforts, many Americans with mental disorders have sought care and now enjoy fulfilling, productive lives in their communities.

Useful Dual-Diagnosis Internet Sites
Sciacca Comprehensive Service Development for MIDAA
New York, NY
Telephone: (212) 866-5935
Web site: http://users.erols.com

This site, designed to provide information and resources for service providers, consumers, and family members who are seeking assistance and/or education in this field, seeks to improve service delivery systems which usually address only singular/discrete disorders instead of comprehensive services.

See the Dual Diagnosis E-mail Group web site at www.angelfire.com/journal/bipolaralcoholic. This dual diagnosis e-mail group for those with alcoholism/addictions and mental illness reviews AA principles, spirituality, mental health, medications, and just about anything that relates to dual diagnosis and how it affects life.

HIV/AIDS-Afflicted Persons

Sharing syringes or using dirty needles may lead to severe infections such as HIV and hepatitis. These resources are specifically designed to address these health problems.

For information on addiction and HIV/AIDS, access the American Society of Addiction Medicine (see Professional Organizations) at their web site: www.asam.org/conf/aids.htm.

National AIDS Treatment Advocacy Program (NATAP)
580 Broadway
New York, NY 10012
Telephone: (212) 219-0106
Fax: (212) 219-8473
Web site: www.natap.org
E-mail: info@natap.org

NATAP's mission is to educate individuals about HIV and hepatitis treatments and to advocate on the behalf of all people living with HIV/AIDS and hepatitis C virus (HCV). Efforts in these areas are conducted on local, national, and international levels.

NATAP collaborates with other organizations as well as city and state agencies. Nationally, NATAP works with federal agencies such as the Food and Drug

Administration and the National Institute of Health and advocates on policy and treatment issues. Jules Levin, executive director, is a community representative to the AIDS Clinical Trials Group (ACTG) and the HIV Disease Research Agenda Committee (RAC) of the ACTG, where the federal government conducts its HIV research.

GAYS AND LESBIANS

Lesbian, gay, bisexual, and transgender (LGBT) clients are, according to some studies, more likely to smoke, drink, and use other drugs than their nonlesbian/gay peers. Also, they reportedly are less likely to abstain and more likely to continue heavy drinking into later life (www.nalgap.org).

Although frequently reported that LGBT clients experience increased risk for substance use and abuse—some reports indicate one out of every three gay men and lesbians (over 8 million LGBT men and women) struggle with alcohol and drug-related problems—other studies disagree, reporting moderate alcohol use rates similar to those of the mainstream populations. The later reports indicate, however, that the LGBT population is overrepresented on both ends of the spectrum—those who abstain and those who are heavy drinkers. More research is needed in order to implement effective prevention and treatment programs (see *CSAP cultural competence series #4: Cultural competence for social workers, etc.,* DHHS Pub. No. SMA 95-3075, p. 197, 1995).

Specific resources for LGBT clients with alcohol and drug problems can be accessed at this government web site (www.health.org/features/lgbt/subtreat.aspx). Also see Alcoholics Anonymous web site: Http://www.alcoholics-anonymous.org.

Many cities offer meetings for gay, lesbian, bisexual, and transgender people. Check your local listings, or call the General Office: telephone (212) 870-3400.

Alternatives
Web site: www.alternativesinc.com/contact_frame.html

This organization, dedicated to providing dual-diagnosis treatment services to lesbian, gay, bisexual, and transgender adults, strives to create an atmosphere free from judgment, fear, and discrimination to help their patients recover from emotional, mental, and addictive disorders.

See the web site for Bicultural competence: A mediating factor affecting alcohol use practices and problems among lesbian social drinkers at http://sadatabase.health.org/ida/html2/ida52340.aspx.

CSAP RADAR Network Center, Project Connect: Lesbian and Gay
    Community Services Center
208 W. 13th Street
New York, NY
Telephone: (212) 620-7310
Web site: www.gaycenter.org

A comprehensive, community-based, multiservices organization that is a local and national resource providing education, consultation, and direct services relevant to the needs of gay and lesbian people.

Addiction Recovery Services of the Los Angeles Gay and Lesbian Center
1625 N. Schrader Blvd.
Los Angeles, CA 90028-9998
Telephone: (323) 993-7655
Web site: www.laglc.org/home.aspx

This center, receiving 15,000 to 20,000 individual visits each month, provides such services as legal aid, addiction recovery, counseling, primary medical care, comprehensive youth services and housing, education and enrichment courses, employment training and placement, seniors programming, cultural programming, computer skills training, Internet access in a state-of-the-art CyberCenter, civil rights advocacy, HIV prevention/education, and extensive AIDS-related services.

Fenway Community Health Center
7 Haviland Street
Boston, MA 02115
Telephone: (617) 267-0900
Web site: www.fenwayhealth.org

The Fenway Center, one of many such agencies in various U.S. cities, provides quality medical and mental health care to Boston's lesbian, gay, bisexual, and transgender communities.

Gay and Lesbian Medical Association (GLMA)
459 Fulton Street, Suite 107
San Francisco, CA 94102
Telephone: (415) 255-4547
Web site: www.glma.org

The largest organization of its kind, GLMA was founded in 1981 to combat homophobia within the medical profession and in society at large. Today, GLMA promotes quality health care for LGBT and HIV-positive people, fosters a professional climate in which its diverse members can achieve their full potential, and supports members challenged by discrimination on the basis of sexual orientation.

Hetrick-Martin Institute
2 Astor Place
New York, NY 10003
Telephone: (212) 674-2400
Web site: www.hmi.org

This Institute provides education, recreation, counseling, training, and outreach to gay, lesbian, bisexual, transgender, and questioning youth.

Lambda Treatment and Recovery Program
Web site: www.thelambdacenter.com
E-mail: LAMBDA@Human-Service-Centers.org

The Lambda Center, committed to providing high-quality behavioral health care programs to the gay, lesbian, bisexual and transgender communities, provides clinical services and an atmosphere of diversity in a safe and comfortable environment.

International Advisory Council for Homosexuals
Men and Women in Alcoholics Anonymous (IAC)
P.O. Box 18212
Washington, DC 20036-8212
Web site: www.iac-aa.org

The IAC serves the gay and lesbian members of AA. According to their mission statement, "Our sole purpose is to provide our experience, strength and hope to any arm of AA when called upon to do so, and to work in the spirit of *UNITY* and *SERVICE* with AA for the betterment of the gay and lesbian members, and AA as a whole. Our function is not that of a policy or decision-making board in matters affecting gay and lesbian members of AA, nor is our function to isolate or separate ourselves from the mainstream of AA."

National Association of Lesbian and Gay Addiction Professionals (NALGAP)
c/o NAADAC
1911 N. Ft. Meyer Drive, Suite 900
Arlington, VA 22209
Telephone: (703) 465-0539
Fax: (703) 741-7698
Web site: www.prta.com/lgbtpa~1.html and its history
    www.prta.com/nalgaphistory.html

In July 1979, the National Association of Lesbian and Gay Alcoholism Professionals (now the National Association of Lesbian and Gay Addiction Professionals, NALGAP), was formed to fight an epidemic: alcohol and other drug addiction in the gay and lesbian communities, and homophobia in the alcoholism and drug addiction treatment communities.

New Leaf Services for Our Community
1853 Market Street
San Francisco, CA 94103
Telephone: (415) 626-7000
Web site: www.newleafservices.org

A community-based, nonprofit, multipurpose outpatient-counseling center, this service is one of the largest counseling centers for the lesbian, gay, bisexual, and transgender communities.

Pride Institute
www.pride-institute.com

An accredited inpatient facility devoted exclusively to treating alcohol- and drug-dependent lesbian, gay, and bisexual persons, the Pride Institute is dedicated to the idea that lesbians and gay men have the same need for freedom from society's prejudices and pressures as every other patient in treatment.

Stonewall Recovery Services
430 Broadway Avenue East
Seattle, WA 98102
Telephone: (206) 461-4546
Web site: www.stonewallrecovery.org

This service provides a safe and compassionate environment for recovery and prevention programs that respond to the mental, physical, spiritual, emotional, and financial well-being of the children, youth, adults, and families of lesbian, gay, bisexual, and transgender individuals in their area.

The Stepping Stone
3425 Fifth Avenue
San Diego, CA 92103
Telephone: (619) 295-3995
Web site: www.steppingstonesd.org

The Stepping Stone creates, sustains, and extends life-enhancing alcohol and other drug recovery and prevention services primarily to gays and lesbians in San Diego County.

HARM REDUCTION PROGRAMS

Harm reduction (HR), a public-health approach to drug-related issues, emphasizes reducing the negative consequences of drug use. The emergence of AIDS, linked to drug use through needle sharing, was the primary catalyst for the surge of HR programs in Europe and the United States.

"At its heart," notes Dr. Patt Denning, Director of Clinical Services and Training at San Francisco's Harm Reduction Therapy Center, "harm reduction is a public health philosophy which uses a multitude of strategies to reduce drug-related harm, ranging from syringe exchange to drug substitution therapies, to abstinence, to controlled use. These methods have proven effective in helping people make lasting changes in a variety of health related behaviors" (Denning, 2005).

Reasoning that the spread of AIDS from needle-sharing drug users to the general population posed a greater health threat than the drug abuse itself, public health officials in western European countries (notably The Netherlands, Great Britain, and Switzerland) led the way in substituting this public health-based approach for the usual punitive model (see Denning, 2005, for a history of the harm-reduction movement).

"Dead addicts don't recover" is the clarion call of HR activists who avoid setting the threshold for addiction treatment too high. Respecting people's choices, HR offers such "low threshold treatment" as helping addicts obtain childcare and overcoming obstacles like requiring abstinence prior to entering treatment (Denning, 2005).

HR counselors accept addicted clients where they are and help them minimize the risk of their addictive behaviors. DanceSafe (dancesafe.org), provides information about "club drugs" and gives technical assistance to club owners by testing samples of the club drug Ecstasy to determine its purity. They also give instructions for "safe use" while dancing. Many club owners offer free water and a "cool down" room to prevent accidental deaths from overheating (Denning, 2005).

Harm reduction programs are an important option in the treatment of addictions, provided the client is a good candidate and the HR program suits the treatment goals (Wormer & Davis, 2003). Before recommending a HR protocol, always consider the severity of the client's addiction and the client's ability to adhere to any HR protocols (Gossop, Griffith, Powis, & Strang, 1993). Although HR protocols reduce harm, they are not for everyone, especially those with more serious dependency issues.

The Harm Reduction Coalition (HRC) in New York and Oakland, California, reportedly the world's largest peer-based, consumer-led, harm reduction group, promotes (1) policy and advocacy, (2) street outreach, and (3) treatment revision. HRC publishes newsletters and drug information brochures, and holds annual conferences to disseminate the latest research and policies (Denning, 2000, 2005). Visit www.harmreduction.org.

In some circles, the mention of "harm reduction," raises ire. "The very mention of harm reduction often causes more heat than light," Denning (2005, p. 491) notes, "with people taking sides for or against. But when you think about it, it is almost impossible to be *against* harm reduction. It's what we do every day. We all find ways to reduce the risks of life. When I drive to work each day, for example, I reduce my risk by wearing a seat belt. Abstaining behavior may sometimes be the best harm reduction strategy, and yet most of us choose, for a multitude of reasons, to practice other harm reduction methods."

ADDITIONAL RESOURCES

For a detailed analysis of current government policies and strategies congruent with HR models (e.g., drug courts), visit National Association of Drug Court Professionals at www.nadcp.org. Also see Wormer and Davis (2003).

CHARACTERISTICS OF HARM REDUCTION PROGRAMS

Effective HR programs have these characteristics (Marlatt, Abrams, & Lewis, 2002):

- *Pragmatism:* From a community perspective, containment and amelioration of drug-related harms may be a more pragmatic or feasible option than efforts to eliminate drug use entirely.
- *Humanistic values:* The dignity and rights of the client are respected.
- *Focus on harms:* The first priority is to decrease the negative consequences of the client's behavior to both the client and to others, as opposed to focusing on decreasing the behavior itself. HR neither excludes nor presumes the long-term treatment goal of abstinence.
- *Balancing costs and benefits:* Identifying, measuring, and assessing the relative importance of drug-related problems, their associated harms, and costs/benefits of intervention are carried out to focus resources on priority issues.
- *Priority of immediate needs:* Most HR programs have a hierarchy of goals, with the immediate focus on proactively engaging clients, target groups, and communities to address their most pressing needs first.

HARM REDUCTION GOALS

These 10 goals characterize viable HR programs (Blume, Anderson, Fader, & Marlatt, 2001):

1. Teach clients how to decrease their risk and increase their safety when using drugs/alcohol.
2. Teach and educate clients how to reduce the negative consequences of drug and alcohol use.
3. Provide clients with education and knowledge so they can make more informative choices while using.
4. Work with clients to design an effective intervention and treatment plan that will improve their current overall well-being.
5. Be flexible and creative with clients, but without losing sight of the main objective: to improve health.
6. Focus on decreasing drug use to increase health and continue to reduce drug use as required.
7. Make healthy choices the criteria and work toward them.
8. Become a stepping-stone when appropriate to decrease use potentially to abstinence.

9. Take advantage of interventions that work and reduce harm.
10. Partner with clients in the development of their treatment plan and goals.

HARM REDUCTION TECHNIQUES

The following HR techniques and programs, borrowed from western Europe and Canada, are highlighted here.

NEEDLE EXCHANGE

The purpose of syringe exchanges is to reduce the risk of spreading HIV infection. Easy to do and inexpensive, it provides drug users' outreach services via mobile vans or street workers that deliver clean needles to drug scenes or to users' homes (Erickson, Riley, Cheung, & O'Hare, 1997; Inciardi, Horowitz, & Pottieger, 1993; www.caps.ucsf.edu/publications/needlereport.html).

Canada has a progressive network of more than one hundred syringe exchanges. In some provinces, pharmacists are actively involved in these exchange programs. Evidence shows that syringe exchange programs decrease risk of harm. The less needle sharing, the fewer HIV infections.

Additional Resources

To learn more about needle exchange programs, visit Drug Sense at www.drugsense.org/nep.htm.

DRUG SUBSTITUTION THERAPIES

Most drug substitution strategies are for opiate dependence. Legal and stringently controlled by federal law, methadone, LAAM, and buprenorphine are used as drug substitutes but remain a controversial part of traditional drug treatment programs. The majority of clients who use methadone dramatically reduce their use of opiates and of other drugs as well. The inconvenience, stigma, and expense of going to federally licensed methadone facilities keeps many heroin addicts from using this life-saving treatment.

Methadone Maintenance

Developed in Germany at the end of World War II, methadone has been used since the early 1960s to treat addictions to Demerol, heroin, morphine and Dilaudid. Administered orally as a syrup, it has the same properties as heroin and morphine. This effective HR tool brings drug users into the community instead of treating them like criminal outsiders. Unlike heroin addicts, methadone users are not involved in antisocial behaviors (Mattick, Ward, & Hall, 1998).

Methadone, administered by physicians, decreases not only opiate cravings, but also cravings for other abused drugs such as alcohol, benzodiazepins, cocaine, and THC (Mattick et al., 1998). The client avoids withdrawals as methadone has a long half-life (one dose per day prevents withdrawal symptoms).

Additional Resources

The Drug Policy Alliance provides reviews of trends in Drug Substitution Therapies at www.drugpolicy.org/reducingharm/maintenancet.

For a useful overview of a typical methadone program and its application, see www.methadone.org/intro.html.

CONTROLLED DRINKING

According to the National Institute on Alcohol Abuse and Alcoholism (NIAAA), the United States has four times as many problem drinkers as alcoholics. Yet very few programs specifically target *early* problem drinkers.

Controlled drinking programs target clients whose drinking seriously interferes with their lives (e.g., disrupting close relationships, causing health problems, and impairing driving) and attempts to teach clients to consume alcohol in a moderate or sensible manner. Other prevention techniques include server intervention programs that moderate intake through third-party control and designated driver programs to prevent impaired driving.

Empirical studies show that harm reduction approaches to alcohol problems are as effective as abstinence-oriented programs in reducing alcohol-related consequences (Heather, 1995). Although these studies show that moderation-based treatments may be preferred over abstinence-only approaches, the public opinion of alcohol treatment still supports zero-tolerance (Marlatt & Witkiewitz, 2002).

Additional Resources

See Rotgers, F., Kern, M., & Hoeltzel, R. (2002). *Treating drug problems.* New York: Wiley; Rotgers, F. (in press). *Book series in treating addictions,* New York: Wiley; and Stanley Peele's web site for more information about controlled drinking: www.peele.net/lib/index09.html. Also see DeLuca, A., *The controlled drinking debates: A review of four decades of acrimony,* www.doctordeluca.com /Library/AbstinenceHR/FourDecadesAcrimony.htm.

SKILLS TRAINING

A large body of empirical evidence points to a lack of basic life skills among people with addictive disorders. Vital and important skills that help clients get a job, pay bills, make a doctor's appointment, and look after themselves are critical. Skills training may at first appear simplistic, yet its importance becomes clear when the counselor realizes that the client does not know how to call a taxi. Often these deficits contribute to continuing addiction (Monti, 1989). Training in skills that most take for granted assists addicted clients in reducing their risk for future harm and go a long way toward improving their quality of life.

Additional Resources

This web site offers an excellent resource to help clients develop employment skills at www.blueprint4life.ca.

To help clients learn about the core skills for personal health, see the Personal Health Zone at www.personalhealthzone.com and the American Public Health Association at www.apha.org.

COMPUTERIZED INTERVENTIONS

User-friendly treatment planning guides on CD ROMs and online sites are ideal for informing addicted clients about the dynamics of addiction and recovery. A quick and easy way to obtain vital information, they provide clients with a private, nonthreatening way to explore and contemplate their situation and options.

Additional Resources

See Rice, Christopher P. (2001). Computer-assisted interventions: Mouse as cotherapist. In R. H. Coombs (Ed.), *Addiction recovery tools: A practical handbook* (pp. 35–60). Thousand Oaks, CA: Sage.

CONDOM DISTRIBUTION

Many agencies distribute condoms to teens, many of whom are sexually active while intoxicated. Besides reducing pregnancies, they also decrease cross-infection of sexually transmitted diseases (STDs).

BLEACH KITS

Bleach kits (containing bleach and instructions for cleaning equipment) are distributed to make drug injection less dangerous. Bleach does not kill the pathogen that causes hepatitis and is also not totally effective in eliminating HIV; however, such kits do reduce the likelihood of other infections being passed through sharing of dirty equipment.

OTHER HARM REDUCTION TECHNIQUES

Latecomers to the HR movement, U.S. clinicians have begun to develop new techniques. Two are illustrated here: psychotropic medications and substance use management. Currently, most treatment centers avoid these methods (Denning, 2005).

PSYCHOTROPIC MEDICATIONS

The use of these medications in addiction treatment is controversial. Even clients diagnosed as having psychiatric problems may be denied access to some medications. Although antipsychotic and antidepressant medications are often allowed, antianxiety drugs are typically banned.

Many physicians require that a client be at least 30 days "clean and sober" before prescribing antidepressants, since depressive symptoms may clear up with detoxification. Yet some patients receive significant relief from depression, if not complete remission, when they take these medications prior to a period of abstinence. If relieving emotional pain is a primary reason clients have become addicted to psychoactive substances, providing and monitoring appropriate prescribed drugs may ameliorate their addiction. This decision should be made in consultation with a medical doctor.

Additional Resources

For more information about the different kinds of psychotropic medication being used and their applications, access the Healthfind.org web site at www.findhealthproducts.com/health/psychiatric+medications.

SUBSTANCE USE MANAGEMENT

The following techniques, described by Denning (2005) involve changing the amount of the substance used, the numbers/types of drugs used together, the frequency of use, the route of administration, and the situation (alone versus with others). A great deal of planning is needed to achieve success using this method.

Changing the Amount

This helps clients realize that, because of tolerance, less is more. "You are more likely to actually enjoy your drug experience if you don't do it all the time or in large quantities." The general rule of thumb is "start low and slow until you know." This means cutting down a little at a time to reduce the stress on the body. Clients are encouraged to stay at each new level until it feels comfortable or normal to them.

Changing the Number/Types of Drugs Mixed Together

Many of the short-term adverse effects of drug use are related to taking more than one drug at a time. Some drugs cancel out the action of another. Other drugs may actually slow down the metabolism of another drug, so there is more danger of overdose even if the quantities are small.

Changing the Frequency

Daily use causes problems. If the addict has tried to cut down on the amount of drugs used without consistently good results, changing the frequency of use might be more satisfying. The less often one uses, the less chance a user will experience harm over the long run. Paying attention is the fundamental rule of harm reduction. If drug use is automatic (a habit), the user is not thinking.

Changing the Route of Administration

Some ways of getting drugs into a body are riskier than others. In general, eating a drug is the safest route and shooting into a vein is the most dangerous.

Changing the Situation

Sometimes changing the environment—bar, street corner, or home—will auto-matically change a person's drug use. Clients decide what they want and don't want to use. Where they use and with whom can either increase or decrease the risk of using the same drug. Shooting drugs under the freeway or in a bathroom makes it harder to take time and use good hygiene. Clients can be encouraged to arrange places and times when they can have some privacy, light, access to water, and so on and can see what they are taking.

Planning to Use

Clients can maximize the benefits and minimize the harms of drug use by fol-lowing these guidelines:

- *Get a designated driver.* Have someone drive the client and others who are using, or someone to guide the experience and make sure no one gets hurt (and to call 911 if they do).
- *Have clean equipment.* Clients should pack up their stuff ahead of time if they are going out, or get extra syringes at the exchange when they go. They should make sure they have enough cotton, cookers, pipes, and so on before people come over so no one has to share.
- *Clients should know who they are with and where (especially for psychedelic use).* Being with friends or being alone in a place that feels good can make an enor-mous difference, and save clients from a traumatic trip.
- *Have enough water and food.* Clients should start their fun out with some food and water, and keep more handy.
- *Clients should not eat too much if they are using psychedelics that can make them vomit.*
- *Alternate alcohol with something else.* If clients start by drinking a glass of water or juice, then an alcoholic beverage, they can space things out a bit. Then have a glass of water in between each drink. Clients will feel better the next day for sure.

Additional Resources

To learn more about the history of this HR program, see Hammon, J. P., *How to run a substance use management group,* at www.harmreduction.org/news/fall97/hammond.html.

For additional information about harm reduction, visit the Harm Reduction Coalition at (www.harmreduction.org/prince.html).

See Denning, P. (2000). *Practicing harm reduction psychotherapy.* This excellent book, the first to describe a comprehensive treatment model using the principles of harm reduction. It begins with a critique of existing treatments, then takes the reader step-by-step through assessment and treatment protocols. Many ex-tensive case histories are used to describe the approach.

Also see Marlatt, G. A., & Gordon, J. R. (1985). *Relapse prevention: Maintenance strategies in the treatment of addictive behaviors.* This is a groundbreaking book on relapse prevention.

PART VI
Professional Management

Part VI discusses professional management skills and responsibilities. Sample record-keeping forms are provided, and clinical issues are discussed. Practical information is given for managing such challenging issues as clinical crises and difficult clients, and for avoiding legal and ethical dilemmas.

RECORD KEEPING

CRISIS MANAGEMENT

Crisis Types
Crisis Reactions
Crisis Management Goals
Crisis Intervention Principles
Crisis Management Steps
Chronically Relapsing Clients

DIFFICULT CLIENTS

Safety Issues
When Threats Occur
Clients with Weapons
Client Who Appear Dangerous to Self
Suicide Prevention
Critical Incident Stress Debriefing

LEGAL AND ETHICAL RESPONSIBILITIES

Universal Professional Values
Ethical Codes
Ethical Decision Making
Confidentiality
Informed Consent
Dual Relationships

> Duty to Warn
> Referral Obligation
> Rights of Minors
> Malpractice
> Ethical Dilemmas

RECORD KEEPING

Documentation of therapy sessions is required by law to protect both the client and counselor. Failing to keep adequate records opens the way for possible lawsuits and puts clients' well-being at risk (*Record Keeping,* 2004).

All clinical records—whose confidentiality must be ensured and protected—should be comprehensive, objective, current, and organized. The Haight-Ashbury Free Medical Clinic in San Francisco offers a detailed list of forms for interview and intake, assessment, care planning, implementation, follow-up and monitoring, reassessment, and transfer and discharge (*Standards of Practice for Client-Centered Case Management,* www.hafmc.org/casemgmt/intake.html#reggie).

Examples of documents are:

- *Intake forms:* Basic information about the client, the reasons for referral, and the client's primary concerns
- *Histories:* Personal and family histories as well as histories of previous interventions or treatments
- *Evaluations and assessments:* Clinical assessments, previous evaluations, and any testing
- *Diagnoses and case formulations:* Formal diagnosis and a case formulation
- *Treatment plan:* Documentation of the treatment plan, including the target problems, methods of intervention, reviews, and outcomes
- *Progress notes:* Regular summaries of treatment sessions
- *Termination summary:* Summary of treatment provided, progress achieved, any remaining problems, a prognosis, the reasons for termination, and any clinical recommendations
- *Correspondence:* Correspondence and records from past treatment providers, notes on all nontrivial phone calls with the client or with other professionals about the client

- *Financial records:* A signed agreement to pay; dates of sessions; charges and payments; and any notes to the client or insurance companies about bills and payments
- *Legal documents:* Any releases signed by the client and documentation of informed consent and other contracts

Specific record-keeping formats established by employers must conform to legal requirements. For private practitioners, refer to Finley and Lenz's book *The Chemical Dependence Treatment Documentation Sourcebook* (1998).

These are the key items that should be covered in clinical documentation:

- Self-Help Program Review/Critique form
- Initial Client Information
- Consent for Treatment
- Release of Information
- Confidentiality in Therapy
- Client Rights Form
- Financial Information Form
- Master Treatment Plan
- Individual/Family Session Progress Notes

Figures VI.1 through VI.9 show sample forms, each of which is reprinted by permission from Finley, J. R., & Lenz, B. S. (1998). *The Chemical Dependence Treatment Documentation Sourcebook.* New York: Wiley.

Self-Help Program Meeting Review/Critique Form

Directions: DO NOT TAKE THIS FORM WITH YOU TO THE MEETING, and please do not write information that would violate anyone's anonymity or confidentiality!

1. Meeting Information:
   Group Name:_____
   Program (AA, NA, etc.): _____ Location: _____ Date/Time:_____
   Meeting format: _____ Tag/Open sharing _____ Speaker _____ Book/Step study
   Other (please describe): _____
   _____ All-male or all-female _____ Mixed   Number of people present: _____

2. What was the main topic of the meeting?_____

3. What were your general thoughts and feelings on that topic? _____
   _____
   _____
   _____
   _____

4. In what ways could you relate to the experiences and feelings shared by others at this meeting? Were you unable to relate to some people, and if so what was the difference between them and you that made you unable to relate? _____
   _____
   _____
   _____
   _____

5. What other thoughts and feelings did this meeting cause you to have? _____
   _____
   _____
   _____
   _____

6. How many people at the meeting did you know? _____

7. Please state your level of participation in this meeting: _____
   _____
   _____
   _____
   _____

8. What did you gain from this meeting? _____
   _____
   _____
   _____

FIGURE VI.1   Self-Help Program Meeting Review/Critique Form. *Source:* From *The Chemical Dependence Treatment Documentation Sourcebook* (p. 5.9), by J. R. Finley and B. S. Lenz, 1998, New York: Wiley. Reprinted with permission.

Initial Client Information

Name: _____   Birth date: ____/____/____
Address: _____   Today's Date: ____/____/____
         _____   Phone: (H) _____
Employer: _____   Phone: (W) _____
Address: _____   SSN: _____

Family Information

Marital status: _____ Married _____ Yrs _____ Never married _____ Separated
                _____ Divorced _____ Yrs _____ Widowed _____ Yrs
Children (Names and ages): _____
_____
Household: ___Live alone _____ Live w. partner and/or children _____ Live w. parents/other family
           ___ Homeless _____ Live w. roommate(s)/other _____ Group home/residential treatment center
           ___ Incarcerated
Will family or others participate in your counseling? _____ If so, who will participate?
Name:_____ Relationship: _____
Name:_____ Relationship: _____

Work/Education Information

Profession/type(s) of work: _____
Years in current field of work: _____ Years in other fields: _____ Years formal education: _____
Work/education goals: _____

Medical and Other Information

Please list any medical problem you are being treated for: _____
Please list any medications you take: _____
In case of a medical or other emergency, please tell us who you would like us to call:
Name: _____ Phone: _____
Address: _____ Relationship _____

Substance Abuse Information

Do you feel you have a drug or alcohol problem? _____ If yes, why? _____
What is your drug of choice (the drug, including alcohol, you use most often)? _____
How often have you used this drug in the past? _____ How much do you usually use? _____
When was the first time you used it? _____ When was the last time you used this drug? _____
What is the longest you have voluntarily gone without this drug? _____ Why? _____
What other drugs have you used in the past 6 months? _____
Please briefly describe the drug or alcohol related event that caused you to come to treatment: _____
_____

Counseling Information

Reason for coming to counseling/desired services: _____
Have you been in treatment or counseling before? _____ If so, please give us the following information:
Purpose/Issues: Name of Counselor: When & for How Long: Results:

_____ _____ _____ _____
What are your goals for the outcome of counseling? Please describe how you hope your life will be
different:_____

FIGURE VI.2   Initial Client Information. *Source:* From *The Chemical Dependence Treatment Documentation Sourcebook* (p. 4.3), by J. R. Finley and B. S. Lenz, 1998, New York: Wiley. Reprinted with permission.

Consent for Treatment

1. I have been fully informed of my rights as a client of this agency, the extent and limits of confidentiality in therapy, and the goals associated with this therapy. With that knowledge, I request and consent to receive therapy from qualified personnel of this agency. Initials: _____

2. I understand that the staff of this agency may not disclose information about my therapy to anyone outside this agency without my written consent, except as required by law to comply with a court order, to prevent suicide/self-harm or harm to others, or to stop or prevent abuse of a child, senior, or disabled person. However, I also understand that my participation in treatment may require my written consent to allow staff of this agency to provide some information about my therapy to a referring agency and/or an insurance company or other payer, and that if this is the case, the form provided for my written consent for this disclosure will state what specific types of information will be disclosed. Initials: _____

3. I understand that my therapist may work with me at this agency, in my home, or in other settings based on his/her professional judgement. I further understand that my therapy may involve my participation in individual, couple, family, and/or group counseling, and may involve homework assignments for me to do outside of therapy sessions. I agree to participate actively in my therapy, to cooperate with my therapist, and to complete required homework assignments or other activities included in my therapy. Initials: _____

4. I understand that if I participate in group counseling, a condition of my doing so is that I protect the privacy and confidentiality of other participants. I agree that if I participate in group counseling, I will not disclose information about the identity, words, or actions of other group counseling participants to anyone outside the therapy group. Initials: _____

5. I understand that my therapy may include my attendance at meetings of independent self-help support groups including Alcoholics Anonymous, Narcotics Anonymous, and/or other programs. I agree to participate in such programs if assigned and to abide by the practices of those programs regarding protecting the privacy and anonymity of other program participants. Initials: _____

Client/Guardian's Name: _____ Signature: _____ Date: ____/____/____

Agency Representative Name: _____ Signature: _____ Date: ____/____/____

FIGURE VI.3   Consent for Treatment. *Source:* From *The Chemical Dependence Treatment Documentation Sourcebook* (p. 4.6), by J. R. Finley and B. S. Lenz, 1998, New York: Wiley. Reprinted with permission.

Release of Information

I, _____ , hereby authorize the release and disclosure of the following clinical and/or therapeutic records for the following purpose(s):

[ ] Authorization to release information regarding counseling and therapy care and treatment.

[ ] Authorization to release information held under the Drug Office and Treatment Act of 1972 (PL-92255) and the Comprehensive Alcohol Abuse and Alcoholism Prevention Treatment and Rehabilitation Act Amendments of 1974.

[ ] Authorization to release information related to Human Immunodeficiency Virus (HIV) and Acquired Immune Deficiency Syndrome (AIDS).

Please release authorized information between (your agency name here) and:

_____

_____

_____

_____

_____

Specific information to be released (client's initials to approve release):

_____ Assessments and evaluations   _____ Psychosocial history

_____ Continued care & treatment   _____ Discharge summary

Correspondence (specify): _____

Other (specify): _____

_____

Purpose(s) for which information is to be released: _____

_____

_____

_____

_____

_____

Revocation/Expiration: This Release of Information is subject to revocation by the under-signed at any time except to the extent that information has already been disclosed based on authorization contained herein. Unless further limited by a date stated here, _____ , this Release of Information will automatically expire after a period of 180 days from the date signed. I have the right to receive a copy of this Release of Information upon my request.

Client/Guardian's Name: _____ Signature: _____ Date: ____/____/____

Therapist Name: _____ Signature: _____ Date: ____/____/____

FIGURE VI.4   Release of Information. *Source:* From *The Chemical Dependence Treatment Documentation Sourcebook* (p. 4.17), by J. R. Finley and B. S. Lenz, 1998, New York: Wiley. Reprinted with permission.

Confidentiality in Therapy

Before you tell your therapist about yourself, you have the right to know what information can and cannot be kept confidential. Please read this and initial each item only if you understand and agree to the conditions described. If there is anything you don't understand, your therapist will explain it in more detail.

General Extent and Limits of Confidentiality

The laws and ethics governing therapy require that therapists keep all information about clients confidential except for certain types of information and situations. Those exceptions are:

1. *Client's desire:* If you want your therapist or this agency to give information about your case to anyone outside this agency, you must sign a Release of Information giving written permission for this disclosure.

Acknowledgment: **I understand that if I want my therapist or this agency to give information about my case to any outside person or agency, I must sign a Release of Information. Initials: _____**

2. *Safety:*
   a. *Risk of self-harm:* If your words or behavior convince your therapist that you are likely to harm yourself, either deliberately or because you are unable to keep yourself safe, your therapist must do whatever he or she can to prevent you from being harmed. This means the therapist must take action up to and including hospitalizing you with or without your consent. If this situation comes up, your therapist will discuss it with you before taking action unless it appears that this would be unsafe or immediate action is needed to keep you from being harmed.

   b. *Risk of harm to others:* If you threaten serious harm to another person, your therapist must try to protect that person. He or she would report your threat to the police, warn the threatened person, and try to prevent you from carrying out your threat. If this situation comes up, your therapist will discuss it with you before taking action unless it appears that this would be unsafe or immediate action is needed to keep you from acting on your threat.

Acknowledgment: **I understand that if my therapist believes there is a serious risk that I will hurt or kill myself or another person, my therapist is legally required to report this, warn the endangered person if someone other than myself, and take whatever action seems needed in his or her professional judgement to prevent harm to myself or others. Initials: _____**

   c. *Emergencies:* In an emergency when your health or your life is endangered, your therapist must provide medical personnel or other professionals any information about you that is needed to protect your life, but only information that is needed for that purpose. If possible your therapist would discuss it with you and get your permission first. If not, he or she would talk with you about it afterward.

Acknowledgment: **I understand that in an emergency when my health or life is in danger, my therapist must give other professionals any information about me that is needed to protect my life. Initials: _____**

FIGURE VI.5 Confidentiality in Therapy. *Source:* From *The Chemical Dependence Treatment Documentation Sourcebook* (p. 4.18), by J. R. Finley and B. S. Lenz, 1998, New York: Wiley. Reprinted with permission.

3. *Abuse:* If your therapist obtains information leading him or her to believe or suspect that someone is abusing a child, a senior citizen, or a disabled person, the therapist must report this to a state agency. To "abuse" means to neglect, hurt, or sexually molest another person. The therapist cannot investigate and decide whether abuse is taking place: if the suspicion is there, the therapist must report it. The state agency will investigate. If you are involved in a situation of this kind, you should discuss it with a lawyer before telling your therapist anything about it unless you are willing to have the therapist make such a report. If this situation comes up, your therapist will discuss it with you if possible before making a report.

Acknowledgment: I understand that if my therapist believes or suspects that a child, a senior citizen, or a disabled person is being abused or neglected, my therapist must report this to a state agency who will then investigate the situation. Initials: _____

4. *Therapy of children, families, and couples:*

a. *Children and adolescents:* It is the policy of this agency, when a therapist treats children and adolescents, to ask their parents or guardians to agree that most details of what their children or adolescents tell the therapist will be treated as confidential. However, parents or guardians do have the right to *general* information about how therapy is going. The therapist may also have to tell parents or guardians about information if their children or others are in any danger. If this situation comes up, the therapist will discuss it with the child or adolescent first before talking to the parents or guardians.

Acknowledgment: I understand that if my child or adolescent is in therapy, the therapist will give me as the parent or guardian only general information about therapy, except that the therapist will tell me if he or she finds out from my child or adolescent that they or others are in danger. Initials: _____

b. *Families:* At the start of family therapy all participants must have a clear understanding of any limits on confidentiality that may exist. The family must also specify which members of the family must sign Release of Information forms if necessary for the records of family therapy.

Acknowledgment: I understand that in family therapy, all members of the family must understand the limits of confidentiality and must agree on which family members will have the power to sign Release of Information forms authorizing disclosure of information about the family's history or treatment.
Initials: _____ Initials: _____ Initials: _____ Initials: _____ Initials: _____ Initials: _____

c. *Couples:* If one member of a couple tells a therapist something the other member does not know, and not knowing this could harm him or her, the therapist cannot promise to keep it confidential from the other person. If this occurs the therapist will discuss it with you before doing anything else.

Acknowledgment: I understand that if I am in couples therapy and tell the therapist something my partner does not know, and not knowing this could harm my partner, the therapist and this agency cannot promise to keep that information confidential from my partner. Initials: _____ Initials: _____

FIGURE VI.5   (Continued)

5. *Group therapy:* In group therapy, the other members of the group are not therapists. They are not bound by the ethical rules and laws governing therapists. To avoid problems in this area, it is this agency's policy to ask all members of therapy groups to agree to protect one another's confidentiality, and to remove from the group any member who does violate another member's confidentiality. Still, this agency cannot be responsible for such disclosures by other clients, and it may be better for you to discuss information you feel must be legally protected in an individual session with your therapist than in a therapy group session.

Acknowledgment: I understand that in group therapy, I do not have the same degree of confidentiality in group sessions that I have in individual sessions with my therapist, and that other group members are not therapists and are not bound by the ethical rules and laws governing therapists. Initials: _____

6. *Professional consultation:* Your therapist may consult with a clinical supervisor or another colleague about your treatment. The other therapist must give you the same confidentiality as your therapist.

If this fellow therapist is employed at this agency, no written authorization from you is required. If your therapist discusses your case with a professional outside this agency, such as a therapist who treated you in the past, he or she must get your written permission (a Release of Information form) first. If another professional asks your therapist for information about you during or after your treatment, your therapist cannot provide any information unless that other professional provides a Release of Information which you have signed authorizing your therapist to provide that information.

Acknowledgment: I understand that my therapist may discuss my history and treatment with other therapists for professional purposes, and that if these other therapists are not employed at this same agency my therapist must get my specific written permission in advance. Initials: _____

7. *Legal proceedings:* If a judge orders your therapist to provide information about your history or your treatment, the therapist must do so.

Acknowledgment: I understand that if ordered by a judge, my therapist must give the court whatever information about my case the judge rules to be necessary. Initials: _____

8. *Debt collections:* If you fail to pay for services as agreed, and other methods of resolving the problem fail, this agency may have to use a collection agency or other legal means to collect the fees you owe. The only information the agency would disclose for this purpose would be your name and address, the dates you received services, and the amount of your unpaid balance.

Acknowledgment: I understand that if I fail to meet my financial obligation to this agency and it becomes necessary to use legal means to collect my fees, the agency may disclose my name, address, dates of services, and balance due for this purpose. Initials: _____

9. *Recording therapy:* This agency will not record therapy sessions on audiotape or videotape without your written permission. If you give permission for such recording, you have the right to know who will see or hear the recording, for what purpose(s) it will be used, and when it will be erased or destroyed.

Acknowledgment: I understand that my therapy will not be recorded on audiotape or videotape without my written permission. Initials: _____

FIGURE VI.5 (Continued)

10. *Referring agencies and conditions of treatment:* If you have been involuntarily referred for treatment by a court or a government agency such as a probation department or Child Protective Services, your treatment may include requirements that you comply with conditions including reporting of information about your therapy to the agency that referred you for treatment, or reporting to that agency if you appear to have violated laws regarding substance abuse or agency rules regarding satisfactory participation in this program. If such reporting requirements exist, your therapist will tell you about them before you start therapy, and will notify you when making any such required reports.

Acknowledgment: **I understand that if I have been involuntarily referred for treatment by a court or government agency, the conditions of my therapy may include mandatory reporting to the referring authority about my therapy and/or any violations I commit of laws regarding substance abuse or of agency rules regarding my conduct while in this program. Initials: _____**

11. *Independent disclosure by client:* Any information that you yourself share outside of therapy, willingly and publicly, will not be considered protected or confidential by a court.

Acknowledgment: **I understand that if I myself willingly and publicly disclose information about my therapy, that information is no longer confidential or legally protected. Initials: _____**

Our signatures here show that we have read, understand, and agree to the conditions presented above.

Client Name(s): _____   Date: ____/____/____

Signature: _____

Parent/Guardian Name: _____   Date: ____/____/____

Signature: _____

Therapist Name: _____   Date: ____/____/____

Signature: _____

FIGURE VI.5 (Continued)

Client Rights Form

1. I understand that I have the right to decide not to enter therapy (although depending on my situation there may be legal or other consequences for not entering or completing therapy), not to participate in any particular type of therapy, and to terminate therapy at any time. If I wish to terminate therapy here and continue therapy elsewhere, I will be given a list of providers with whom I can continue. Initials: _____

2. I understand that I have the right to a safe environment during therapy, free from physical, sexual, and emotional abuse. Initials: _____

3. I understand that I have the right to complete and accurate information about my treatment plan, goals, methods, potential risks and benefits, and progress. Initials: _____

4. I understand that I have the right to information about the professional capabilities and limitations of any clinician(s) involved in my therapy, including their certification/ licensure, education and training, experience, specialization, and supervision. I have the right to be treated only by persons who are trained and qualified to provide the treatment I receive. Initials: _____

5. I understand that I have the right to written information about fees, payment methods, co-payments, length and duration of sessions and treatment. Initials: _____

6. I understand that my confidentiality will be protected, and information regarding my treatment will not be disclosed to any person or agency without my written permission except under circumstances where the law requires such information to be disclosed. I understand that I have the right to know the limits of confidentiality, the situations in which the therapist or agency is legally required to disclose information about my case to outside agencies, and the types of information which must be disclosed. Initials: _____

7. I understand that I have the right to know if my therapist will discuss my case with supervisors or peers. I understand that no portion of my therapy may be recorded in audio or video form without my informed written consent, and that if I consent to have any portion of my therapy recorded I have the right to know who will see or hear the recording(s), for what purpose(s) the recording(s) will be used, and when and how the recording(s) will be erased or destroyed. Initials: _____

8. I understand that I have the right to request a summary of my treatment, including diagnosis, progress in treatment, prognosis, and discharge status. Initials: _____

9. I understand that I have the right to request the release of my clinical information to any agency or person I choose. Initials: _____

Client/Guardian's Name: _____ Signature: _____ Date: ____/____/____

Therapist Name: _____ Signature: _____ Date: ____/____/____

FIGURE VI.6   Client Rights Form. *Source:* From *The Chemical Dependence Treatment Documentation Sourcebook* (p. 4.22), by J. R. Finley and B. S. Lenz, 1998, New York: Wiley. Reprinted with permission.

Financial Information Form

Client's Name: _____ Date: ____/____/____ Case File #: _____

Address: _____ Phone: _____ Work Phone: _____

_____ SSN: _____ Date of Birth: ____/____/____

Name of Employer: _____

Address of Employer: _____ Position/Title: _____

_____ Supervisor: _____

Do you have health insurance coverage?   Yes _____   No _____

Do you intend to use it to pay for services?   Yes _____   No _____

If no, how do you intend to pay for services? _____

_____

If yes, please complete the following:

Insurance Information:

Insurance Company: ____ Blue Cross/Blue Shield   ____ CHAMPUS/TriCare   ____ Medicare

____ Aetna   ____ Cigna   ____ Premier   ____ Health Partners

____ Other: _____

Policy #: _____ Enrollment/plan/group number:_____ Effective date: ____/____/____

Calendar year deductible: $ _____   Deductible year starts: _____

Deductible met for year? Yes _____ No _____

Co-payment required: Is outpatient group therapy covered? Yes _____ No _____

Must referrals be made by a primary care physician or other gatekeeper? Yes _____ No _____

Any exclusions or limitations affecting this therapy, including number of sessions, types of therapy excluded from coverage, monetary caps, conditions not covered: _____

_____

Name of policyholder, if different from client: _____

Client's relationship to policyholder: _____

Provider's address: _____   Provider's phone: _____

_____

_____

Pre-approval or pre-authorization required? Yes _____ No _____

Pre-approval for specific provider? Yes _____ No _____

Pre-approval authorization number: _____

Number/Type sessions pre-approved: _____

I grant this agency permission to release any information obtained during assessments or treatment which is necessary to support insurance claims for my/our treatment. I understand that I am responsible for all charges, regardless of insurance coverage.

Client/Guardian's Name: _____ Signature: _____ Date: ____/____/____

FIGURE VI.7   Financial Information Form. *Source:* From *The Chemical Dependence Treatment Documentation Sourcebook* (p. 4.23), by J. R. Finley and B. S. Lenz, 1998, New York: Wiley. Reprinted with permission.

Master Treatment Plan

Identification Data

Client Name: _____ Admit Date: ____/____/____ Clinician: _____

Client ID#: _____ Age: _____ Gender: _____ Birth Date: ____/____/____

Initial Sessions Authorized: _____ Anticipated Length of Treatment: _____

Status upon Admission: _____ Vol _____ Invol (DTS ____ DTO ____) _____ Mandatory

Treatment Modality(ies): ____ Indiv/Fam ____ Psychoed. Group ____ Aftercare ____ Psychiatric

_____ Intensive Outpatient _____ Day Treatment _____ Residential _____ Other: _____

Problem List

Problem #1: _____

    Review Date: ____/____/____ Status: ___ Resolved ___ Improved ___ Unchanged ___ Worse

Problem #2: _____

    Review Date: ____/____/____ Status: ___ Resolved ___ Improved ___ Unchanged ___ Worse

Problem #3: _____

    Review Date: ____/____/____ Status: ___ Resolved ___ Improved ___ Unchanged ___ Worse

DSM-IV Diagnostic Impression

	Code	Description with Qualifiers
Axis I:	_____	_____
	_____	_____
	_____	_____
Axis II:	_____	_____
	_____	_____
	_____	_____
Axis III:	_____	_____
	_____	_____
	_____	_____
Axis IV:	_____	_____
	_____	_____
	_____	_____

Axis V: Current functioning: _____

           Past year functioning: _____

Primary Diagnosis: _____ Manifested by: _____

_____

_____

Client Strengths: _____

_____

Potential Obstacles to Treatment: _____

_____

_____

FIGURE VI.8 Master Treatment Plan. *Source:* From *The Chemical Dependence Treatment Documentation Sourcebook* (p. 5.3), by J. R. Finley and B. S. Lenz, 1998, New York: Wiley. Reprinted with permission.

Treatment Goals and Interventions

Overall/Long-Term Goal #1 (Related to Problem # _____):
    Target date: ____/____/____ Date resolved: ____/____/____
Measurable Objective 1.A: _____
Intervention 1.A.1: _____
Frequency: _____ Start date: ____/____/____ Completion date: ____/____/____
Intervention 1.A.2: _____
Frequency: _____ Start date: ____/____/____ Completion date: ____/____/____
Intervention 1.A.3: _____
Frequency: _____ Start date: ____/____/____ Completion date: ____/____/____
Measurable Objective 1.B: _____
Intervention 1.B.1: _____
Frequency: _____ Start date: ____/____/____ Completion date: ____/____/____
Intervention 1.B.2: _____
Frequency: _____ Start date: ____/____/____ Completion date: ____/____/____
Intervention 1.B.3: _____
Frequency: _____ Start date: ____/____/____ Completion date: ____/____/____
Measurable Objective 1.C: _____
Intervention 1.C.1: _____
Frequency: _____ Start date: ____/____/____ Completion date: ____/____/____
Intervention 1.C.2: _____
Frequency: _____ Start date: ____/____/____ Completion date: ____/____/____
Intervention 1.C.3: _____
Frequency: _____ Start date: ____/____/____ Completion date: ____/____/____

Overall/Long-Term Goal #2 (Related to Problem # _____):
    Target date: ____/____/____ Date resolved: ____/____/____
Measurable Objective 2.A: _____
Intervention 2.A.1: _____
Frequency: _____ Start date: ____/____/____ Completion date: ____/____/____
Intervention 2.A.2: _____
Frequency: _____ Start date: ____/____/____ Completion date: ____/____/____
Intervention 2.A.3: _____
Frequency: _____ Start date: ____/____/____ Completion date: ____/____/____
Measurable Objective 2.B: _____
Intervention 2.B.1: _____
Frequency: _____ Start date: ____/____/____ Completion date: ____/____/____
Intervention 2.B.2: _____
Frequency: _____ Start date: ____/____/____ Completion date: ____/____/____
Intervention 2.B.3: _____
Frequency: _____ Start date: ____/____/____ Completion date: ____/____/____
Measurable Objective 2.C: _____
Intervention 2.C.1: _____
Frequency: _____ Start date: ____/____/____ Completion date: ____/____/____
Intervention 2.C.2: _____
Frequency: _____ Start date: ____/____/____ Completion date: ____/____/____
Intervention 2.C.3: _____
Frequency: _____ Start date: ____/____/____ Completion date: ____/____/____

FIGURE VI.8   (Continued)

Overall/Long-Term Goal #3 (Related to Problem # _____):
      Target date: ____/____/____ Date resolved: ____/____/____
Measurable Objective 3.A: _____
Intervention 3.A.1: _____
Frequency: _____ Start date: ____/____/____ Completion date: ____/____/____
Intervention 3.A.2: _____
Frequency: _____ Start date: ____/____/____ Completion date: ____/____/____
Intervention 3.A.3: _____
Frequency: _____ Start date: ____/____/____ Completion date: ____/____/____
Measurable Objective 3.B: _____
Intervention 3.B.1: _____
Frequency: _____ Start date: ____/____/____ Completion date: ____/____/____
Intervention 3.B.2: _____
Frequency: _____ Start date: ____/____/____ Completion date: ____/____/____
Intervention 3.B.3: _____
Frequency: _____ Start date: ____/____/____ Completion date: ____/____/____
Measurable Objective 3.C: _____
Intervention 3.C.1: _____
Frequency: _____ Start date: ____/____/____ Completion date: ____/____ /
Intervention 3.C.2: _____
Frequency: _____ Start date: ____/____/____ Completion date: ____/____/____
Intervention 3.C.3: _____
Frequency: _____ Start date: ____/____/____ Completion date: ____/____/____

Discharge Plan

Projected Date for Resolution of Problems: ____/____/____ Projected No. of Sessions Required: ____
Criteria for Discharge from Treatment: _____
_____
_____
_____

Aftercare Plan: _____
_____
_____
_____

Comments: _____
_____
_____
_____

My/our signature(s) here indicate(s) that I/we have participated in designing this treatment plan, understand it, and accept responsibility to carry out my/our portion(s) of this plan.

Client/Guardian's Name: _____ Signature: _____ Date: ____/____/____

Program staff's Name: _____ Signature: _____ Date: ____/____/____

FIGURE VI.8   (Continued)

Individual/Family Session Progress Note

Client Name: _____ Client ID#:: _____ Birth Date:____/____/____

Program: _____ Session Date: ____/____/____ Session #: _____

Present in Session: _____ Length of Session: _____

Modality of Treatment: _____

Problem: _____

Objectives of Session: _____

Data (self-report, observations, interventions, current issues/stressors, functional impairment,
interpersonal behavior, motivation, progress): _____

_____

_____

_____

_____

_____

_____

_____

_____

Assessment (progress, evaluation of intervention, obstacles or barriers): _____

_____

_____

_____

_____

_____

_____

Plan (tasks to be completed between sessions, objectives for next session, changes, recommendations,
sessions remaining, date of next session, plan for termination): _____

_____

_____

_____

_____

_____

_____

_____

Clinician Name: _____ Signature: _____ Date: ____/____/____

FIGURE VI.9   Individual/Family Session Progress Note. *Source:* From *The Chemical
Dependence Treatment Documentation Sourcebook* (p. 5.8), by J. R. Finley and B. S. Lenz, 1998,
New York: Wiley. Reprinted with permission.

Additional Resources

www.practiceplanners.wiley.com is an excellent web site for finding more resources for the treatment of addiction.

Berghuis, D. J., & Jongsma, A. E., Jr. (2002). *The addiction progress notes planner* (2nd ed.). Hoboken, NJ: Wiley. This resource contains complete prewritten session and patient presentation descriptions for each behavioral problem in the Addiction Treatment Planner. The prewritten progress notes can be easily and quickly adapted to fit a particular client need or treatment situation (www.practiceplanners.wiley.com).

Finley, J. R., & Lenz, B. S. (1998). *The chemical dependence treatment documentation sourcebook: A comprehensive collection of program management tools, clinical documentation, and psychoeducational materials for substance abuse treatment professionals.* New York: Wiley. *The Chemical Dependence Treatment Document Sourcebook* provides addiction counselor with a library of forms that are used in day-to-day addiction counseling. (www.practiceplanners.wiley.com).

CRISIS MANAGEMENT

Since crisis situations rarely offer any warning, all counselors should develop a crisis management plan, become certified in first aid and cardiopulmonary resuscitation (CPR), and develop a critical contact list with the key community resources (police, fire, poison control, mental health, hospitals).

CRISIS TYPES

All crises have two components: (1) the client's perception that the stressful situation will eventually lead to significant distress and (2) the client's inability to work out the stressful situation with previously effective coping skills (Roberts, 2000).

James and Gilliland (2002) identify these differing kinds of crises:

- *Developmental:* Crises connected with normal life progression (e.g., retirement)
- *Situational:* Crises that occur randomly (e.g., overdosing), each with a different level of intensity and danger
- *Existential:* Crises that occur when an individual begins questioning the meaning and purpose of life and why he or she is here (e.g., client turns 50 and is stressed about his life accomplishments)

- *Environmental:* Crises caused by nature (e.g., hurricane) or humans' actions (e.g., economic or political upheaval)
- *Chronic:* Crises that continue and are self-perpetuating (e.g., client continues to overdose and put self at risk)
- *Combination:* Any two or more of the crises previously listed

CRISIS REACTIONS

A typical crisis reaction has three main features: (1) distorted thinking and overwhelming feelings; (2) failure of the usual coping mechanisms to resolve the situation and feelings that the situation is out of control, and (3) impairment of normal functioning, especially among alcohol and other drug (AOD) clients who already have performance and emotional control problems (Mitchell, 2005).

Crisis reactions usually include one or more of the following symptoms: helplessness, mental confusion, and disorganization; decision-making and problem-solving difficulties; intense anxiety, shock, denial, and disbelief; anger, agitation, and rage; lowered self-esteem, fear, withdrawal from others, subdued emotion; depression, grief, apathy; physical reactions such as nausea, shakes, headaches, intestinal disturbance, chest pain, or difficulty breathing (Mitchell, 2005).

CRISIS MANAGEMENT GOALS

The five main goals of crisis intervention are: (1) to stabilize, confine, and control both the crisis situation and the reactions to it; (2) to mitigate the impact of the distressing event on those involved; (3) to mobilize the resources necessary to manage the traumatic experience; (4) to normalize (i.e., "demedicalize" and "depathologize") the person's reaction to the traumatic experience; and (5) to restore the person to an acceptable level of adaptive function (Mitchell, 2005).

CRISIS INTERVENTION PRINCIPLES

Mitchell (2005, paraphrased) suggests that counselors consider these principles when dealing with a client in crisis:

- *Proximity:* The best crisis response is often provided in surroundings familiar to the victim.
- *Immediacy:* People in crisis cannot wait long for help.
- *Expectancy:* Early in the intervention, the crisis intervener has to instill hope that the situation can be resolved.
- *Brevity:* No one in crisis or crisis management has the luxury of abundant time.
- *Simplicity:* The intervention should be well thought out.
- *Creativity:* The intervener can be innovative in unusual and disturbing circumstances.
- *Practical:* Impractical solutions are no solutions at all.

Crisis interveners should stay within their training level and call for help when lacking the necessary experience. Most importantly, do not "unbox" anything that cannot be "reboxed" in the available time (Mitchell, 2005).

CRISIS MANAGEMENT STEPS

To manage any crisis, follow these steps:

- *Define the problem:* Ascertain the problem and risks. Try to determine the magnitude and scope of the problem.
- *Ensure safety:* Never put yourself or your client into a dangerous situation. Ask yourself: Is the client a threat to you, himself, or others? Then take appropriate steps to ensure the safety of those at risk.
- *Provide support:* After assessing and doing what is needed to ensure safety, provide personal support or arrange a support system (e.g., family members), and make sure that the client is fully aware of these support systems.
- *Provide alternatives:* Be prepared with a variety of skills. Read, practice, and avail yourself of professional development workshops and other learning opportunities.
- *Make plans:* Quickly organize the most appropriate resources into an effective action plan. Confidently apply different intervention combinations until the situation is resolved. Be very direct with clients who are in serious crisis and cannot cope.
- *Get a commitment:* Ensure that clients will address the problem and follow through to the best of their ability with the knowledge and skills they have available (James & Gilliland, 2001).

CHRONICALLY RELAPSING CLIENTS

Relapses are the most typical crises among recovering addicts. Since most clients relapse at one point or another in the recovery process (Saunders & O'Connor, 1996), consider these strategies:

- During the initial contact, educate the client about the risk of relapse.
- Examine and discuss past relapses.
- Discuss the risks involved when the client is exposed to potentially threatening situations.
- With the client, design and implement relapse prevention techniques (Doweiko, 2002).

Chronic relapse implies that one or more of these relapse management techniques should be taught to the client: refusal skills, social skills, assertiveness training, relaxation training, stress management, problem-solving skills, criticism skills, negotiation skills, and relationship enhancement skills (Saunders & O'Connor, 1996). See the section on recovery tools in Part V.

Additional Resources

James, B., & Gilliland, B. E. (2001). *Crisis intervention strategies* (4th ed.). Belmont, CA: Brooks/Cole is a helpful resource.

The following web site also provides a bibliography of 62 books on the topic of crisis management: www.fetchbook.info/Crisis_Intervention.html.

Rape-crisis programs offered by medical centers, community mental health centers, women's counseling centers, crisis clinics, and police departments provide crisis intervention, advocacy, support, education, and referrals to community resources (Roberts, 1990).

For disasters (such as earthquake damage), contact the Federal Emergency Management Agency (FEMA) at www.fema.gov.

These hotline numbers offered by the Municipality, Abuse and Healing Network may be helpful:

- SAFE Alternatives (800-DONT-CUT, 366-8288) helps prevent people from cutting themselves.
- Child Help USA (800-4A-Child) focuses on the treatment and prevention of child abuse.
- Gay and Lesbian National Hotline (888) THE-GLNH (843-4564) provides support for this population.
- Missing Children Information (800-843-5678) helps in the search for missing children.
- The National Domestic Violence Hotline (800-656-HOPE), staffed 24 hours a day by trained counselors, provides crisis assistance and information about shelters, legal advocacy, health care centers, and counseling. Callers will be transferred to the rape crisis center closest to their geographic area.
- National Domestic Violence Hotline: (800) 799-7233.
- Rape, Abuse, and Incest National Network (RAINN): hotline: (800) 656-HOPE; web site: www.rainn.org.
- For Poison Control, contact the American Association of Poison Control Centers (AAPCC) at hotline number (800) 222-1222, or at www.aapcc.org.
- Additional national hotline numbers (other than those provided here) can be found at www.m-a-h.net/support/hotlines.htm.

DIFFICULT CLIENTS

Nearly half the psychotherapists included in a recent study had been harassed, threatened, or physically attacked by a client (Saunders & O'Connor, 1996). Violent behaviors may include verbal threats, destruction of office contents, physical attacks, threats against loved ones, and destruction of property (Morrissey, 1998).

If you suspect a client is a potential threat to him- or herself or others, do a full risk assessment and implement appropriate intervention. Determine the roots of the acting-out behavior by completing a thorough medical history and mental status exam. It is imperative to document the client's psychological frame of reference for the acting-out behavior (loss, disappointment, or failure) and define how rage fits into the client's belief system.

The best indicator for predicting whether a client is dangerous is a past history of impulsive violence and volatile temper such as fighting, hurting others (or animals), suicide threats, aggression toward authority, and property destruction. Recent or frequent violent acts particularly indicate a potential for the client to act out (Berkowitz, 1993).

Other correlates of violence are (1) a belief in justified revenge or the appropriateness of violence, (2) being male, (3) being between the ages of 15 and 30, (4) being unemployed, (5) moving frequently or experiencing residential insecurity, (6) living or growing up in a violent subculture or family, (7) abusing substances, (8) having low intelligence, (9) having access to weapons and potential victims, and (10) living with multiple stressors that may lessen frustration tolerance (4therapy.com, 2004).

Although overt aggression is unmistakable, passive aggression is not. Common signs of the latter among clients include arriving late to the session, saying very little, giggling when the counselor speaks, and chronically drawing attention to themselves (when in a group environment). Nonverbal signs are raising eyebrows, frowning, sighing, shaking their head, and looking bored (M. S. Corey & Corey, 1998).

SAFETY ISSUES

When faced with an angry or violent client, personal safety is the first concern. Immediately leave if the situation escalates out of your control and get help (e.g., call 911). Always have a precautionary plan in mind, such as arranging the office chairs so that you are the closest to the door and will be able to pull the fire alarm while getting up and calmly walking out of the office.

Here are some helpful tips for reducing vulnerability (Morrissey, 1998):

- Be prepared. If you know that the client has a previous history of violence, arrange to have a coworker close by who is aware of the potentially dangerous situation.
- Work in groups with other coworkers.
- Make sure the counseling facility is always well lighted.
- Avoid unwise risks such as going to a client's home.
- Build a good relationship with the local police and have emergency phone numbers available.
- Never chase after a client who storms out of a session.
- Remain calm. Keep a calm tone and present a calm presence with the client.
- Do not tell the client to calm down because this may inadvertently suggest that you do not understand why the client is upset.
- Speak clearly. Be sure that clients are able to hear what you are saying through the anger they may be feeling.

- Declare your boundaries when appropriate—unless you are in danger of physical harm, stand your ground and tell the client that you will listen but will not be intimidated.
- Avoid blaming. Do not tell clients that they have no reason to be angry.
- Avoid being the expert. Do not act like a "know-it-all"; be careful how you offer your opinion and how you try to help clients.
- Voice inflections. Work to match the clients' tone and volume of voice and then slow down and lower your voice in the hope that they will follow your lead.
- Listen. Be attentive and let the angry person explain him- or herself without interruption.
- Do not argue. View the situation from the client's point of reference and do not try to persuade the client to see it your way.
- Paraphrase. Repeat in you own words what you think the client is trying to say to reassure the client that you understand.
- Show empathy and respect; let clients know that you understand their viewpoint and use phases like "You seem frustrated."
- Be honest. If a mistake has been made, acknowledge it and determine how and when to resolve it.
- Be clear about your own responsibilities and explain to the client what your limitations are.
- Offer a time-out or reschedule. Allow the client options such as taking a time-out to cool down or rescheduling.
- Be patient. It takes 30 to 40 minutes to physiologically calm down from anger, so even if the situation appears calmer, realize that things can still escalate.

WHEN THREATS OCCUR

If a client identifies a victim and mentions a time, method, location, and other contingencies, you are *required* to take protective action to prevent harm to another. By law, you *must* report the potential threat to a supervisor or responsible colleague and to authorities. When in doubt, consult with a legally savvy colleague to ensure that you follow ethical and legal guidelines (see "Legal and Ethical Responsibilities" later in Part VI).

Assess if the threat is real or manipulative. Is it self-justifying or self-protecting, or is it intended to avoid some consequence? Be especially alert to threats issued with specific detail. Consider the following advice:

- Focus on anger, consequences, and alternatives to violence.
- Pay close attention to even minor threats.
- Work with your client to attend to the triggers of violent behaviors and to change them. Be aware, however, that the client may lie to you about his or her changes in thoughts or intentions.
- Try to increase and strengthen the therapeutic alliance.
- Implement protective interventions.
- Develop a safety plan for the potential victim, the perpetrator, and yourself.

- Know your community's resources for victims (shelters, support groups, etc.).
- Collaborate with family members who can more closely observe the client.
- Consider hospitalization or police actions that can temporarily incapacitate the dangerous client.

CLIENTS WITH WEAPONS

A weapon (any object that can be used to harm) may range from a knife or gun to a letter opener or a paperweight. Be aware and have a plan to minimize risk and avoid harm. Consider the following:

- Set up your office so you have easy access to the exit should a client confront you with a weapon.
- Have a plan to get help (e.g., pull the fire alarm) if experiencing trouble during a session.
- Adhere to ethical guidelines for dual relationships and do not meet clients outside the counseling environment.
- With high-risk clients, co-facilitate groups with another colleague.
- Avoid sudden movements that can activate a client's startle response.
- Remain calm—use pacing to match or mirror the client's movements to lower the client's tension and anxiety.
- Keep objects that could be used to harm (e.g., paperweight or stapler) off your desk.
- Maintain eye contact as long as you can, but if told to look away, do so.
- Keep hands in the "stop position," out and away from the body, and slowly, while maintaining eye contact and while talking, walk away from the person with the weapon.
- When sensing danger, move slowly to get physical separation and exit.
- Do not be a hero and take dangerous risks. Do not attempt to wrestle the weapon from the client (Howatt, 2003a).

CLIENTS WHO APPEAR DANGEROUS TO SELF

Predicting suicide risk is not a perfect science, but when you suspect this, whether the risk is high or low, immediately and decisively implement every appropriate precautionary measure. First, do a standard suicide intervention such as Robert Wubbolding's (1989) five-step approach (approved by the National American Association of Suicidology) that asks these questions to assess risk:

1. Are you thinking of killing yourself?
2. Have you tried before?
3. Do you have a plan?
4. Do you have the means?
5. Will you promise yourself not to hurt yourself accidentally or on purpose? For how long?

A "yes" answer to any of these questions indicates great risk.

If the client is at risk, contact help (a supervisor, parents, police, or medical personnel). Under no circumstances should a client be left alone; ensure that the client is safely in the care of another (agency or personal support system such as parent or spouse).

To protect yourself against legal action when clients refuse to follow your recommendations, you might have them sign a written waiver of responsibility indicating that they have been fully informed and, despite your warning, have chosen to refuse your recommendations.

SUICIDE PREVENTION

Some clinicians have good success with suicide-prone clients by discussing the irreversibility of suicide. "What if you change your mind?" they ask. Additional prevention tactics are to:

- Build rapport and trust as soon as possible; the client needs to feel anchored, less helpless, and more hopeful.
- Develop with the client a "no-suicide contract" that best suits the client's situation. For example, "I Jane Doe promise myself not to hurt myself accidentally or on purpose for the next 12 hours. I also agree to contact my mother and Dr. Smith and ask for their assistance. I will stay at this office and wait for my mother to pick me up." Have Jane Doe sign and date. Do not naively rely on this contract to prevent client suicide. The main purpose of the contract is to ensure all the vital, suicide ideational issues are fully discussed, not left unsaid.
- Assist clients to understand their ambivalence, that they may want to give up while they also want to survive.
- Focus on obtaining the client's safety as well as any others who may be targets of violence.
- Help clients realize that only they have control over their feelings, thoughts, and behaviors, and that they can make the best choices. Make clear what options exist other than death.
- Explain referral services and available assistance (e.g., contacts, phone numbers, and plans to follow to assist the client during this crisis) (Howatt, 2000, 2003a).

CRITICAL INCIDENT STRESS DEBRIEFING

These debriefing meetings provide a way to discuss stressful client encounters with colleagues. Ideally held within eight hours of the incident, these meetings (typically 25 to 40 minutes) help counselors process difficult or unusual events (James & Gilliland, 2001). Led by a colleague who is not directly involved with the client(s) but is trained in critical-incident techniques, these sessions provide for exchange of information about stressful episodes and reinforce professional support.

Additional Resources

Preventing and Managing Violence, a detailed online resource, provides important information about managing violence: www.oxleas.nhs.uk/foi /PreventingManagingViolenceAggression.pdf.

For more information on critical incident stress, go to the International Critical Incident Stress Foundation, Inc. (ICISF) at www.icisf.org.

The Crisis Prevention Institute, Inc. helps counselors control their anxieties and maintain a professional manner when dealing with violent clients by teaching verbal, nonverbal, and physical intervention techniques for dealing with violent situations. Contact them at www.crisisprevention.com.

Information about 40 online *self-defense* web sites can be found at www .dynamicselfdefence.com/links.htm Also check the yellow pages in your area and ask for three referrals to contact before committing yourself.

The 24-hour a day National Suicide Hotline number is (800) SUICIDE.

The Suicide Prevention and Crisis Centers can be accessed by contacting the American Association of Suicidology (AAS) at www.suicidology.org.

LEGAL AND ETHICAL RESPONSIBILITIES

UNIVERSAL PROFESSIONAL VALUES

The following professional values need to be honored in the treatment of clients (White & Popovits, 2001, p. 28):

- *Autonomy:* Freedom over one's destiny.
- *Obedience:* Obey legal and ethically permissible directives.
- *Conscientious refusal:* Disobey illegal or unethical directives.
- *Beneficence:* Do good; help others.
- *Gratitude:* Pass good along to others.
- *Competence:* Be knowledgeable and skilled.
- *Justice:* Be fair; distribute by merit.
- *Stewardship:* Use resources wisely.
- *Honesty and candor:* Tell the truth.
- *Fidelity:* Keep your promises.
- *Loyalty:* Do not abandon the client.
- *Diligence:* Work hard.

- *Discretion:* Respect confidence and privacy.
- *Self-improvement:* Be the best that you can be.
- *Nonmalfeasance:* Do not hurt anyone.
- *Restitution:* Make amends to persons injured.
- *Self-interest:* Protect yourself.
- *Other culture:* Specific values.

Here are some concrete ways to protect yourself from ethical and legal problems (Popovits, 2005):

- *Take care of yourself:* Effective self-care, an essential precursor to ethical conduct, prevents counselors from using a client to meet their physical, emotional, and spiritual needs (White & Popovits, 2001, p. 28).
- *Get ethically educated:* Ethical decision making involves learned skills as well as good character. Seek training workshops and self-instructional reading to help you maintain an ethically safe environment for practicing your basic ethical decision-making skills.
- *Utilize mentors:* Develop a small group of consultants or peers who will provide a sounding board and objective advice on how to deal with difficult choices.
- *Know thyself:* Practice rigorous self-analysis to avoid breaches in ethical conduct when you are personally vulnerable in your relationship with one or more clients.
- *Ask for help:* Seek formal consultation when you feel vulnerable and when there appears to be an exception to the normal ethical prescriptions.
- *Protect yourself:* Don't be alone. Create a paper trail (e.g., a journal) that documents your ethical decision-making processes and decisions.
- *Respect your clients, your coworkers, your craft, and yourself:* Adhere to the ultimate ethical mandate, "First, do no harm."

ETHICAL CODES

Counselors are accountable for knowing local and federal laws as well as professional ethical codes. Ethical principles codified by the Association of Addiction Professionals (NAADAC, 1994) include these areas:

- Nondiscrimination
- Responsibility (for objectivity and integrity)
- Competence
- Legal and moral standards
- Public statements
- Publication credit
- Client welfare
- Confidentiality
- Client relationships
- Interprofessional relationships

- Remuneration
- Societal obligations

Ethical codes of conduct for addiction counselors, are specified by these three professional organizations: (1) the International Certification and Reciprocity Consortium/Alcohol and Other Drug Abuse, Inc. (ICRC; www.icrcaoda.org), (2) The Association for Addiction Professionals' ethical standards for counselors (www.naadac.org), and (3) the Canadian Addiction Counselor Certification Board (CCCB; www.caccb.ca).

ETHICAL DECISION MAKING

Making ethical decisions is a critical skill for all addiction counselors. To help navigate through the quagmire of policies, ethical codes, and laws, here are some helpful pointers (White & Popovits, 2001):

- Analyze the situation in terms of who will potentially benefit and who could potentially be harmed. This requires detailing both the probability and degree of *benefit* and *harm*. In this first step, you also examine whose interests in the situation might be in conflict (e.g., what is best for the client in a particular situation may not be what is best for you, the counselor, or your agency).
- Examine whether universal or culturally relevant values dictate the best direction to take (e.g., an action that could be beneficial in one cultural context might do harm or injury in another context).
- Explore how existing ethical codes, laws, regulations, organizational policies, or historical practices apply to the situation in question.

CONFIDENTIALITY

Client confidentiality, an imperative for counselors, is commonly breached in three ways (White, 2005):

- *Internal confidentiality:* Discussing information with peers who are not involved in the case and really do not need to know;
- *Casual interagency encounters:* Sharing information with other agencies that are working with the same client and family; and
- *Casual encounters with clients in public:* Talking to clients about their personal issues outside the treatment environment.

Since few addiction counselors are trained about legal issues related to their profession, it is important to become familiar with the ethical codes that govern counseling organizations, as well as federal regulations for confidentiality and privacy. Any time a counselor is faced with an unfamiliar situation, it is of paramount importance to seek supervision and consultation (Popovits, 2005).

Additional Resources

Federal regulations established to protect client privacy and confidentiality can be reviewed online. To read the entire legislation of 42 CFR Part 2 (confidentiality of Alcohol and Drug Abuse Patient Records), see www.access.gpo.gov/nara/cfr/waisidx_00/42cfr2_00.htm.

Also access the Health Insurance Portability and Accountability Act of 1996 (HIPAA) at www.cms.hhs.gov/hipaa.

INFORMED CONSENT

Client consent must be obtained before offering any kind of service. This involves informing the client of:

- The nature and purpose of the procedure/treatment.
- The risks and consequences.
- The alternatives.
- The risks of no treatment. This is the most common source of legal liability (Popovits, 2005).

Most agencies have standardized forms and policies outlining the procedures to follow and requirements to gain consent.

DUAL RELATIONSHIPS

A Dual Relationship, the simultaneous or sequential involvement in two or more roles between a counselor and a client, occurs when a counselor agrees to counsel someone with whom he or she has another relationship that might compromise the counselor's objectivity or the client's comfort (White, 2005). The NAADAC prohibits its members from entering into counseling relationships with family members, current or former intimate partners, friends, close associates, and others whose welfare might be jeopardized by such a dual relationship.

White (2005) points out four relationships that should be avoided:

1. Preexisting relationships
2. Social/business relationships
3. Recovery peer relationships
4. Sexual relationships

DUTY TO WARN

Without exception, addiction professionals are legally bound by state and federal regulations to report child abuse. Any breach of this regulation can result in fines and jail time.

The counselor also has a duty to report any clients who are potentially dangerous to themselves or others, or who threaten to commit a crime (see the section Difficult Clients). Because the client's confidentiality is protected under federal regulations (42 CFR overrides ethical guidelines), this may create a dilemma for the counselor about reporting, yet maintaining confidentiality. First, the counselor can ask clients to give written permission to report the incident (perhaps as a self-report) as part of their treatment or, second, get a court order. If unsure what action to take, seek the advice of a legally and ethically sophisticated colleague (Popovits, 2005).

REFERRAL OBLIGATION

Addiction counselors are required to refer a client whose problems lie beyond their core competencies to a professional with appropriate training and credentials to assist the client. In addition, clients have the right at any time to request a referral to another counselor.

RIGHTS OF MINORS

In some cases, a minor has special rights to information, such as counseling about birth control without parental consent. It is important for addiction counselors to be aware of the rights specified in the geographic area of practice.

MALPRACTICE

Malpractice suits result when counselors fail to render the services normally expected of professionals in clinical situations, especially if the client experiences injury or loss. These perceived behaviors may include (but are not limited to) negligence, breach of contract, intentional misconduct, invasion of privacy, failure to prevent injury, and defamation (Bhat, 2001). Many malpractice situations can be avoided with continual ethical due diligence and practice. The following malpractice complaints (and their frequency as a percentage of all such complaints) occur in hospital practice (Kenneth Pope, http://kspope.com/ethics/index.php):

Sexual impropriety	20.0%
Incorrect treatment (i.e., treatments by an inexperienced, untrained, or unqualified practitioner)	13.2%
Loss to the client due to inaccurate and/or incomplete psychological evaluation	8.5%
Breach of confidentiality or privacy	6.4%
Countersuit for fee collection (improper fee setting, billing, or fee collection methods)	6.2%
Suicide of patient	5.8%
Incorrect diagnosis	5.4%
Defamation (libel or slander)	4.4%

Wrongful death	3.2%
Violation of legal regulations	2.6%
Loss of child custody or visitation	2.2%

ETHICAL DILEMMAS

A national survey identified these ethical dilemmas in clinical practice (Kenneth S. Pope & Valerie Vetter, *Ethical Dilemmas Encountered by Members of the American Psychological Association: A National Survey*, http://kspope.com/ethics/ethics2.php):

- *Confidentiality* concerning child abuse reporting, treating clients with human immunodeficiency virus (HIV) or suffering from acquired immunodeficiency syndrome (AIDS), clients who threaten to commit or have committed a violent act, and elder abuse;
- *Dual relationships:* dealing with boundary issues around roles;
- *Payment sources:* the challenge of working with clients who do not have the resources to pay and are in great need for help;
- *Conduct of colleagues:* addressing peers who are not acting professionally;
- *Sexual involvement:* setting a standard and not becoming sexually involved with a client under any circumstances.

Since any of these factors can be career ending if not handled correctly, immediately seek guidance from a supervisor or peer if confronted with one of these dilemmas.

Additional Resources

For a wealth of information on ethics and malpractice, visit Ken Pope's web site at http://kspope.com/ethics/ethical.php.

Also see, Hedges, L., Hilton, R., Hilton, V., & Caudill, O. B. (1996). *Therapists at risk*. Northvale, NJ: Aronson, addresses how counselors can avoid ethic violations.

To view NAADAC 12 core principles, the pillars for NAADAC Ethical Standards, go to http://naadac.org/documents/display.php?DocumentID=11.

For an excellent overview about confidentiality issues, see Popovits (2005). "Disclosure dilemmas: Legal compliance for counselors." In R. H. Coombs (Ed.), *Addiction counseling review: Preparing for comprehensive, certification of licensing exams*. Mahwah, NJ: Erlbaum.

For a excellent overview of professional ethics, see White (2005) in the same volume.

PART VII

Career Enhancement Resources

Part VII provides information to enhance the careers of addiction counselors. The first section tells counseling aspirants about the basic knowledge, skills, and attitudes expected of addiction counselors; gives information about selecting a good training program; provides an overview about certification and licensing requirements; explains how to meet continuing education requirements; and gives contact information for continuing education providers.

After discussing such business decisions as setting and discussing fees and making referrals, the remaining sections give pointers for developing a personal wellness plan and obtaining malpractice insurance.

EDUCATIONAL RESOURCES

    Basic Knowledge, Skills, and Attitudes Expected of Addiction Counselors
    Selecting a Training Program
    Certification and Licensing
    Continuing Education

BUSINESS PLAN

    Setting Fees
    Discussing Fees
    Home-Based Practices
    Referrals
    Multidisciplinary Teams

> WELLNESS PLAN
>> Burnout
>> Avoiding Burnout
>
> MALPRACTICE INSURANCE

EDUCATIONAL RESOURCES

BASIC KNOWLEDGE, SKILLS, AND ATTITUDES EXPECTED OF ADDICTION COUNSELORS

ADDICTION COUNSELOR COMPETENCIES

In 1993, the Center for Substance Abuse Treatment (CSAT) created the Addiction Technology Transfer Center (ATTC) Program to foster improvements in the preparation of addiction treatment professionals. Comprising 11 geographically dispersed centers in 24 states and Puerto Rico, the ATTC National Curriculum Committee defined the competencies essential to the effective practice of counseling for psychoactive substance use disorders.

Addiction Counselor Competencies (DHHS Pub. No. SMA 00-3468, 2000) lists the knowledge, skills, and attitudes taught in reputable alcohol and other drugs (AOD) training programs that characterize the competent practice of addictions counseling.

Understanding Addiction

- Understand a variety of models and theories of addiction and other problems related to substance use.
- Recognize the social, political, economic, and cultural context within which addiction and substance abuse exist, including risk and resiliency factors that characterize individuals and groups and their living environments.
- Describe the behavioral, psychological, physical health, and social effects of psychoactive substances on the user and significant others.
- Recognize the potential for substance abuse disorders to mimic a variety of medical and psychological disorders and the potential for medical and psychological disorders to coexist with addiction and substance abuse.

Treatment Knowledge

- Describe the philosophies, practices, policies, and outcomes of the most generally accepted and scientifically supported models of treatment, recovery, relapse prevention, and continuing care for addiction and other substance-related problems.
- Recognize the importance of family, social networks, and community systems in the treatment and recovery process.
- Understand the importance of research and outcome data and their application in clinical practice.
- Understand the value of an interdisciplinary approach to addiction treatment.

Application to Practice

- Understand the established diagnostic criteria for substance use disorders and describe treatment modalities and placement criteria within the continuum of care.
- Describe a variety of helping strategies for reducing the negative effects of substance use, abuse, and dependence.
- Tailor helping strategies and treatment modalities to the client's stage of dependence, change, or recovery.
- Provide treatment services appropriate to the personal and cultural identity and language of the client.
- Adapt practice to the range of treatment settings and modalities.
- Be familiar with medical and pharmacological resources in the treatment of substance use disorders.
- Understand the variety of insurance and health maintenance options available and the importance of helping clients access those benefits.
- Recognize that crisis may indicate an underlying substance use disorder and may be a window of opportunity for change.
- Understand the need for and the use of methods for measuring treatment outcome.

Professional Readiness

- Understand diverse cultures and incorporate the relevant needs of culturally diverse groups, as well as people with disabilities into clinical practice.
- Understand the importance of self-awareness in one's personal, professional, and cultural life.
- Understand the addiction professional's obligations to adhere to ethical and behavioral standards of conduct in the helping relationship.
- Understand the importance of ongoing supervision and continuing education in the delivery of client services.
- Understand the obligation of the addiction professional to participate in prevention as well as treatment.
- Understand and apply setting-specific policies and procedures for handling crisis or dangerous situations, including safety measures for clients and staff.

STATE-MANDATED TRAINING IN ALCOHOL AND OTHER DRUGS

Because many AOD counselors came from the recovering community, a competency-based standard was formerly utilized with counselors expected to master a set of core functions. As states move to regulate AOD counselors through licensure, educational standards rise. Credentialing/licensing requirements now require specific academic coursework, supervised training experience, and a passing grade in college-based and state or organizational certification and licensure exams.

Our Internet review of course offerings in AOD programs at community colleges and master's degree programs found great uniformity. However, some programs offer more comprehensive programs that include courses in eating disorders, compulsive gambling, and sex addiction.

The California Association of Alcohol and Drug Abuse Counselors (CAADAC, 2001), an affiliate of NAADC, requires 315 academic hours (21 semester units) of formal classroom sessions in five performance domains: (1) assessment; (2) counseling; (3) case management; (4) client, family, and community education; and (5) professional responsibility. The academic content related to these professional domains includes the following:

Introduction and Overview

- The history of alcohol and other mood-changing drugs in the United States, the myths and stereotypes of alcohol use, the sociocultural factors that contribute to drug use, and the patterns and progressions of alcoholism.
- *Cultural/lifestyle norms and differences:* Issues specific to special populations (i.e., ethnic minorities, women, youth, elderly, gays/lesbians, physically impaired); the nature and extent of alcoholism/drug dependency problems among target population.
- *Human behavior:* Theories of personality and human development, emotional states (e.g., dependency, resentment, guilt), theories of human needs and motivation, the denial process.
- *Family dynamics:* Recognition of family roles, modalities of treatment, communication issues, role playing.
- *Recovery program approaches and program planning strategies:* Recovery/treatment modalities, psychiatric, psychosocial, Alcoholics Anonymous (AA), aversion therapy, social, behavior modification, drug driving program.
- *Program planning and client education:* Goals and objectives, program policies and procedures, program strengths and limitations, service delivery planning, social model and community model approaches, client education, lecture groups, and inpatient/outpatient.

Physiology and Pharmacology of Alcohol and Other Drugs

- Examination of the effects of alcohol and psychoactive drugs on the body and behavior, damage to the brain, liver, and other major organs.
- Tolerance, cross-tolerance, and synergistic effects.

- Male versus female differences.
- *The disease of alcoholism:* Signs and symptoms; THIQ research, endocrine research, AMA definition, Jellinek's "The Disease Concept of Alcoholism."
- *Chemical dependency/addiction:* The pharmacology of alcohol and other psychoactive drugs and their interaction; the pharmacology of addiction and cross-addiction; how blood alcohol concentration (BAC) affects behavior; dependency/addiction stages and patterns; diagnostic laboratory results (e.g., blood lab, EEG, liver function).
- *Human sexuality:* Nomenclature/nosology as related to pharmacology (e.g., Antabuse therapy).
- *Pharmacological and physiological treatment/recovery strategies:* Methadone maintenance; chemotherapy; individual counseling, group exercise; nutritional consideration; leisure skills; aftercare planning; vocational training, self-help groups, ongoing health care.
- HIV-AIDS education.

Laws and Ethics, Community Prevention, Education, Outreach, and Referral

- *Current legal sanctions:* Liabilities regarding death, automobile accidents, party hosts/hostesses, bars, restaurant, liquor stores, alcohol and traffic laws.
- Special issues related to employment problems.
- Patient's rights; professional liability.
- *Legal and regulatory restrictions:* Federal confidentiality regulations, state regulations; potential hazards resulting from noncompliance with regulations; state agencies, federal agencies.
- *Professional ethics and responsibilities:* Legal issues; client welfare as primary concern; professional competence; supervision and development; financial issues; personal wellness; and relationships to other counselors and institutions.
- *Community prevention and education:* The concepts of prevention, community education and community outreach, education and prevention models and the role of community groups in these models; the effectiveness of alternative prevention strategies; education and training methods including adult education techniques.
- *Outreach:* Businesses and clubs that can be used as identification and referral sources; sources of information about the needs of target populations, how to assess needs for training and/or technical assistance; the purposes, methods, and outcomes of technical assistance; how to package and publicize data on community needs to obtain support; information to be included in a consultant/service agreement with other agencies; encouraging potential clients to initiate treatment.
- *Screening techniques:* Communication theories and techniques; interviewing techniques; what to consider in assessing client needs, resources, strengths, and limitations; consideration of the denial process (e.g., appropriate and eligible).
- *Intervention and referral:* Emphasis on the disease and recovery processes of addiction in relation to the community continuum of care. Areas of particular emphasis are employee assistance programs; information and referral;

detoxification; the various treatment modalities; recovery homes; the 12-step programs; third-party payments; and intervention.

- *Crisis intervention:* The signs and symptoms of potential suicide, aggression, and self-destructive behaviors.
- *Crisis counseling techniques and theories:* How to take a history relative to a crisis; the signs and symptoms that indicate crisis reduction; the action necessary to calm the situation when immediate crisis incident is over; how to use the crisis situation to assist the client in making desired changes.

Case Management: Assessment, Orientation, Treatment Planning, and Relapse Prevention (Aftercare Planning)

- *Initial intake and case management:* Administration requirements for admission; interpersonal dynamics and their potential influence on client behavior (e.g., family functioning/relationships, and relationships with authority figures); the normal range of vital signs; signs and symptoms of physical violence; the signs and symptoms of physical disabilities; activities that bring services, agencies, resources, or people together within a planned framework of action toward the achievement of established goals.
- *Initial assessment:* Information needed to complete the intake interview—alcohol/drug history; educational background; vocational information; cultural information; socioeconomic information; lifestyle information; living situation; medical status; strengths and weaknesses; problems and needs for development of a treatment plan.
- *Orientation:* General nature and goals of the program—rules governing client conduct and infractions that can lead to disciplinary action or discharge from the program; hours during which services are available in a nonresidential program; treatment costs to be borne by the client, if any; client's rights.
- *Recovery planning:* The components of a recovery plan; problem-solving models and processes; theories and behavioral components of change; techniques used in behavioral contracting; the stages of recovery from alcoholism and other drug dependencies; how to identify and rank problems needing resolution; realistic and unrealistic treatment goals at various stages of recovery; the value of participant concurrence; expressed disagreement in the therapeutic process; how to organize client information for presentation to professional colleagues; case presentation procedures.
- *Reports and record keeping:* Charting the results of the assessment and treatment plan; writing reports, progress notes, discharge summaries, and other related client data.
- *Practice exercise.*
- *Aftercare and follow-up:* The role of aftercare in the treatment process; the role and importance of client follow-up; relapse dynamics; self-help groups and their programs of recovery; the relationship of AA's Twelve Steps and traditions to the recovery progress.
- *Consultation and referral:* Alternative resources available to provide treatment and support services; roles and functions of individuals in resource agencies

and their position in the decision-making process; advocacy techniques; assessing need for referral and consultation; identifying limits of counselor practice and appropriate referral or consultation.

Individual, Group, and Family Counseling

Counseling, basically, is a relationship in which the counselor helps clients mobilize resources to resolve their problem and modify attitudes and values.

- *Objectives of counseling:* Exploration of a problem and its ramifications; examination of attitude and feelings; consideration of alternative solutions; decision making; therapeutic approaches (e.g., reality therapy, rational emotive therapy, behavior therapy, systematic therapy, transactional analysis).
- *Family counseling:* Theories of family codependency; techniques for motivating family involvement in the treatment process; techniques of multifamily group counseling; limitations of the chemical dependency counselor; working with the family therapist; selecting an appropriate family therapist for ongoing family work; role-playing.
- *Group counseling:* Purpose and function of different types of counseling groups (open versus closed; members with similar characteristics versus members who are different); models of groups, counselor intervention (specific variables to observe, considerations in timing an intervention, and types of intervention); therapeutic factors in group counseling (getting feedback from others, having permission to express strong feelings, feelings of belonging to a group); client behaviors that may affect group participation outcome (minimum length of participation in the group, regular and timely attendance, commitment to sobriety, commitment to participate); process group versus didactic/training group; theories about the stags of group development; the role of the group counselor at various stages of group development; the difference between individual-oriented and group-oriented behavior; group techniques and exercises (their purposes, and possible consequences); group orientation process (group ground rules, expectations of group members, and purposes of the group).
- *Practical exercise.*

Personal and Professional Growth

- *Counselor burnout:* Signs and Symptoms: early warning signs; unique needs of the recovering counselor; prevention techniques.
- *Personal growth:* Recognizing personal strengths and limitations and using that knowledge to promote personal and professional growth; the importance of stress management; relaxation techniques; leisure time skills; physical exercise; proper nutrition; the importance of discussing personal feelings with other professionals, AA sponsor, friends, and significant others; "practicing what we preach."
- *The recovering counselor:* Attending self-help meetings; personal programs for sobriety—the job will not keep you sober.

- *Professional growth:* Ethical and professional standards, the relationship of consultation to counselor support and performance; the skills of a successful helper (empathy, self-disclosure, concreteness); resources for personal and professional growth (training, education, time management, consultation); the value of periodic self-assessment to professional growth (career planning); sources for secure information on current trends and developments in alcoholism and related fields (professional associations, related groups, trade journals); translating the code of ethics into sources of supervision/consultation; impaired counselor organizations.
- *Certification and credentialing requirements:* The California system for certification of alcoholism and drug counselors.
- *Professional associations.*

Supervised Practicum (Internship)

This course consists of forty-five (45) classroom hours. The course instructor ensures that the student completes 255 hours at an approved agency setting where a "qualified staff person" provides direct supervision. The instructor is available for consultation with the student should a problem arise at the agency. The instructor also is an intermediary among the agency, the student, and the educational institution. The Practicum of 255 hours is to begin during the 45-hour course of the Practicum class/classes and be completed within 1 year of the Practicum class.

SELECTING A TRAINING PROGRAM

When selecting a training program, look for one that teaches the knowledge, skills, and attitudes just mentioned.

Junior College Training

Some junior colleges, such as the Nova Scotia Community College (Annapolis Valley Campus), offer training programs in addiction counseling services. Graduates of the Human Services program who, during their second year complete a concentration in addictions counseling, graduate with an Addictions Counseling Diploma and find employment in crisis centers, hospitals, addiction centers, detox centers, community services, group homes, halfway houses, or outpatient services.

Core requirements in this particular 2-year program are:

- *Counseling Theories and Theorists in Addictions:* This one-semester course is designed to introduce the student to a comprehensive overview of counseling theories and the application of the theories to the field of addictions.
- *Introduction to Substance Abuse:* This one-semester course is designed to introduce the student to the physiological and psychological effects of alcohol, drugs, and gambling.

- *Assessment Issues in Addictions:* This one-semester course introduces students to the essentials of assessments in the addictions field.
- *Introduction to Addictions Counseling:* This is a one-semester course that introduces students to the foundation skills of individual counseling.
- *Cross-Cultural Counseling:* This course introduces the basic personal qualities, attitudes, values, and skills needed for competence in individual counseling, at the paraprofessional level, in a multicultural society.
- *Professional Development:* The purpose of this course is to address areas of professional development that are specific to the human services field.
- *Issues in Addictions:* This one-semester course is designed to introduce the student to the issues and trends surrounding substance abuse and gambling.
- *Group Skills for Addicted Populations:* Students will demonstrate through presentation and role-playing, their understanding of group counseling with people who have issues related to addictions.
- *Crisis Theory and Interventions:* This is a one-semester course that is designed to introduce students to fundamental skills of crisis intervention.
- *Introduction to Ethical Issues:* This course explores how to resolve ethical dilemmas in counseling through ethical decision-making processes.
- *Health and Physical Awareness for Addicted Populations:* This course develops an awareness of universal precautions so that the student will be able to demonstrate self-care.
- *Gambling and Compulsive Behavior.*
- *Drug Abuse Prevention.*
- *Work Experience:* Students have a work experience for a total of 9 weeks including consolidation.

Visit www.caade.org/colleges.htm for a list of 2-year accredited programs in chemical dependency studies.

GRADUATE TRAINING PROGRAMS

Students with bachelor's degrees who have achieved strong academic records can apply to a graduate program that leads directly or indirectly to clinical licensure. These web sites provide more information about these graduate training options:

- Clinical social work (www.socialworker.com/career.htm)
- Human resource development (www.shrm.org/jobs)
- Law (www.lawcareers.net/lcn.asp)
- Marriage and family therapy (www.aamft.org and Go to Career and Practice Information)
- Medicine (www.aamc.org/students/cim/start.htm)
- Psychology (www.uni.edu/walsh/linda4.html)
- Public Health (www.sph.umich.edu/career_Networking/students/career)

Every university and college has an Internet address. Type in the name in the URL address box and hit enter to access the matching web site e-address.

If you are interested in a graduate degree in psychology, see the Psychology Graduate School Information at www.uni.edu/walsh/linda2.html. This site provides a sampling of information about preparing for and applying to graduate school. Also, Psychology Online Resource Central found at www.psych-central.com provides "one-stop shopping" in psychology, with such information as Areas of Specialization, Career Center, Conventions, Discussion and News Groups, Graduate School Information, Interactive Web Sites, Library Links, Licensure Links, Mega Sites, Miscellaneous Web Links, Online Journals, Online Surveys, Online Writing Tutor, Organizations on the Web, Psych Fun, Psychology Departments on the Web, Psychology Store, Psychology Students Home Page, Professors Home Page, Research Links, Study Tips for Students, Teaching Links and Undergraduate Publications.

Also see the *Insider's Guide to Graduate Programs in Clinical and Counseling Psychology: 2002–2003 Edition* (Guilford Press, 2002, $22.95). This excellent guide presents up-to-date facts on more than 300 accredited programs in the United States and Canada. Each program's in-depth profile includes admissions criteria, acceptance rates, research areas, specialty clinics, and more. The techniques outlined in the book will help you match your skills and interests to a program's strengths and resources. Access web resources to gather information and download application materials. Now in its tenth edition, this reference contains vital information in three major areas: Detailed information on each of more than 500 graduate level departments with more than 1,000 counselor preparation programs; Statistical treatment with interpretations of composite national research on the six largest types of entry level (master's and sixth year) and four doctoral level counseling programs; trends based on comparison of 1999 data with longitudinal data collected periodically since 1970 (Hollis, 1999). All master's and doctoral level counselor and therapist preparation programs in the United States are listed, including community, marriage/family, mental health, pastoral, gerontological, rehabilitation, school, career, and student affairs counseling.

The following American Psychological Association (APA) career guidance publications and other related topics are available at www.psycCareers.com:

- *Is Psychology the Major for You? Planning for Your Undergraduate Years* provides practical advice for the undergraduate student.
- *Career Paths in Psychology* describes the vast range of work available to psychologists. The book shows that psychologists now work in all areas of education, government, and private industry.
- *Getting in: A Step-by-Step Plan for Gaining Admission to Graduate School in Psychology* provides applicants with manageable goals and the tools to achieve them. Applicants are taught how to define their training goals, what to look for in a program, and why.
- *Graduate Study in Psychology* offers students complete practical information on more than 500 psychology programs in the United States and Canada. It provides information about programs and degrees offered, admission requirements, application information, financial aid, and tuition.

- *The Psychologist's Guide to an Academic Career* is filled with advice on all stages of academic professional life.
- *Psychology/Careers for the Twenty-First Century* provides an overall view and explanation of the field and subfields (free publication):

American Psychological Association
Education Directorate
750 First Street, NE
Washington, DC 20002-4242
Telephone: (202) 336-5970
APA Order Department: (800) 374-2721, ext. 5510

RECOMMENDED READING

There are many books to help one contemplating a career in counseling. Some focus exclusively on AOD counseling and others discuss counseling in general. The following books provide a sampling:

Bissell, L., & Royce, J. E. (1994). *Ethics for addiction professionals.* Center City, MN: Hazelden.

Boren, J. J., Onken, L. S., & Carroll, K. M. (2000). *Approaches to drug abuse counseling.* Washington, DC: NIDA, Division of Treatment and Research Development, Behavioral Treatment Development Branch.

Clinebell, H. J. (1998). *Understanding and counseling persons with alcohol, drug and behavioral addictions: Counseling for recovery and prevention using psychology and religion.* New York: Albingdon Press.

Coombs, R. H. (Ed.). (2005). *Addiction counseling review: Preparing for comprehensive, certification and licensing exams.* Mahwah, NJ: Erlbaum.

Deitch, D. & Carleton, S. (1997). Education and training of clinical personnel. In J. Lowinson, P. Ruiz, R. Millman, & J. Langrod (Eds.), *Substance abuse: A comprehensive textbook* (3rd ed.). Baltimore: Williams & Wilkins.

Harrison, T. C., & Fisher, G. L. (1999). *Substance abuse: Information for school counselors, social workers, therapists, and counselors.* Boston: Allyn & Bacon.

Laban, R. J. (1997). *Chemical dependency treatment planning handbook.* Springfield, IL: Charles C Thomas.

Lawson, G. W., Lawson, A. W., & Rivers, P. C. (2000). *Essentials of chemical dependency counseling* (3rd ed.). Rockville, MD: Aspen Press.

Levin, J. D. (1995). *Introduction to alcoholism counseling: A biopsycho-social approach* (2nd ed.). New York: Taylor & Francis.

Lewis, J. A., Dana, R. Q., & Blevins, G. A. (2001). *Substance abuse counseling: An individualized approach* (3rd ed.). Belmont, CA: Wadsworth.

Meyers, R. J., & Smith, J. E. (1995). *Clinical guide to alcohol treatment.* New York: Guilford Press.

Miller, G. (2005). *Learning the language of addiction counseling.* Hoboken, NJ: Wiley.

Myers, P. L., & Salt, N. R. (2000). *Becoming an addictions counselor: A comprehensive text.* Boston: Jones and Bartlett.

Perkinson, R. R. (1997). *Chemical dependency counseling.* Thousand Oaks, CA: Sage.

Pita, D. D. (1994). *Addictions counseling: A practical guide to counseling people with chemical and other addictions.* New York: Crossroad.

Powell, D. J., & Brodsky, A. (2004). *Clinical supervision in alcohol and drug abuse counseling: Principles, models, methods.* San Francisco: Jossey-Bass.

CERTIFICATION AND LICENSING

Although certification standards for alcohol counselors were established in the 1970s, it was not until the following decade that addiction specialists began to define alcoholism as a chemical addiction. At that time, AOD counseling began to be considered under a single set of standards, and various professional boards were created to establish and maintain standards for assessing clinical competencies.

Prior to the 1970s, alcoholism and other drug dependencies were considered separate problems, and remnants of this cleavage still exist today. Two federal agencies, not one, sponsor addiction programs—one for alcohol (the National Institute on Alcoholism and Alcohol Abuse) and the other for other drugs (the National Institute on Drug Abuse). Although progress has been slow in viewing alcohol as a mood-altering drug, the designation "alcohol and other drug dependencies" (AOD) now conveys a more correct designation.

STATE LICENSING

Each state sets its own laws defining professional standards and regulates licensing of physicians (psychiatrists), psychologists, marriage and family therapists, professional counselors, substance abuse counselors, and social workers. For a specific state, see www.stopbadtherapy.com/main/boards.html. Many have a tiered system that allows for two or three levels of licensure. Independent practice usually requires a master's degree, whereas other counselors are required to work under supervision.

These two books provide information about state and federal licensing, registration, and certification programs in various occupations:

- David P. Bianco, Amanda Moran, and David J. Bianco (Eds.), 1996, *Professional and Occupational Licensing Directory: A Descriptive Guide to State and Federal Licensing, Registration, and Certification Requirements,* Gale Group.
- Phillip A. Barnhart, 1997, *Guide to Professional Certification Programs,* Boca Raton, FL: CRC Press.

STATE CERTIFICATION

Each state also offers a variety of certifications. The following certifications are offered in California:

- *Registered Student (RS):* Enrolled in alcohol and drug studies program/Sign a Code of Ethics
- *Registered Recovery Worker (RRW):* Currently working in an state Department of Alcohol and Drug Programs licensed facility/Sign a Code of Ethics
- *Registered Alcohol and Drug Intern (RADI):* 315 hours of approved alcohol and drug formal education/Supervised Practicum (supervised by at least a CADC-I): including classroom participation (45 hours) and completion of 255 hours at an approved agency/Pass ICRC written examination/Sign a Code of Ethics and Scope of Practice
- *Registered Alcohol and Drug Technician (RADT-I):* 100 hours of approved alcohol and drug formal education/1,000 hours of supervised training (supervised by at least a CADC-I)/Sign a Code of Ethics and Scope of Practice
- *Registered Alcohol and Drug Technician II (RADT-II):* 300 hours of approved alcohol and drug formal education/3,000 hours of supervised training (supervised by at least a CADC-I)/Sign a Code of Ethics and Scope of Practice
- *California Certified Prevention Specialist (CCPS):* 100 hours approved prevention training (50 hours ATOD specific)/120 hours of practicum experience/2,000 hours of supervised ATOD prevention experience/Sign a Code of Ethics and/ Pass ICRC written examination (see manual for additional information and requirements)/supervision by a qualified prevention professional
- *Certified Alcohol and Drug Counselor-I (CADC-I):* Meet all requirements of a RADI/Provide documentation of 4,000 hours or 2 years full-time supervised work experience (supervised by at least a CADC-II)/Pass ICRC Case Presentation Method of Oral Review Examination
- *Certified Alcohol and Drug Counselor-II (CADC-II):* Meet all requirements of CADC-I/Provide documentation of 6,000 hours or 3 years full-time supervised work experience (supervised by at least a CADC-II)
- *Certified Clinical Supervisor (CCS):* Meet all requirements of CADC-II/Provide documentation of 10,000 hours or 5 years of counseling experience as a CADC-II/Provide verification of 4,000 hours or 2 years of clinical supervisory experience in the AODA field (these 2 years may be included in the 5 years of counseling experience)/Verification of 30 hours of didactic training in clinical supervision/Pass ICRC written examination

NATIONAL CERTIFYING STANDARDS

Since standards and laws differ widely from state to state, professional associations have stepped up to establish national standards. In 1981, the International Certification and Reciprocity Consortium/Alcohol and Other Drug Abuse, Inc. (ICRC/AODA) was formed to standardize the certification of AOD counselors. A not-for-profit, voluntary membership organization in Research Triangle Park, North Carolina, ICRC/AODA's members include 70 AOD counselor certification boards and more than 35,000 AOD certified counselors. Located in 41 states and the District of Columbia, these boards include five branches of the U.S. Armed Services and seven Indian Health Services.

In addition to the IRRC/AODA, two other certifying bodies (each described in this section) constitute the three major AOD certifying bodies in the United States: (1) the IRRC/AODA, (2) the National Association of Alcohol and Drug Abuse Counselors (NAADAC), and (3) the American Academy of Health Care Providers in the Addictive Disorders.

International Certification and Reciprocity Consortium/Alcohol and Other
    Drug Abuse (IC&RC/AODA)
6402 Arlington Blvd. #1200
Falls Church, VA 22042-2356
Telephone: (703) 294-5827
Fax: (703) 875-8867
E-mail: info@crcaada.org
Web site: www.icrcaoda.org

The IC&RC, a not-for-profit voluntary membership organization, comprises certifying agencies that credential alcohol and drug abuse counselors, clinical supervisors, and prevention specialists.

Committed to public protection, IC&RC and its members provide quality, competency-based certification programs for professionals engaged in the prevention and treatment of addictions and related problems. The organization also promotes the establishment and recognition of minimum standards to provide reciprocity for certified professionals.

The IC&RC offers five reciprocal certifications: (1) Alcohol and Drug Counselor, (2) Advanced Alcohol and Drug Counselor, (3) Certified Clinical Supervisor, (4) Criminal Justice Addictions Professional, and (5) Certified Prevention Specialist.

National Association of Alcohol and Drug Abuse Counselors (NAADAC)
901 N. Washington Street, Suite 600
Alexandria, VA 22314
Telephone: (703) 741-7686; (800) 548-0497
Fax: (800) 741-7698 or (800) 377-1136
Web site: www.naadac.org

The NAADAC, also known as the "Association for Addiction Professionals," has nearly 14,000 members and 47 state affiliates representing more than 80,000 addiction counselors. Founded in 1972, it is the nation's largest network of alcohol and drug abuse treatment professionals. NAADAC began with a primary focus on alcohol and drug addiction counselors but now recognizes tobacco and gambling addiction counseling.

Among the organization's national certification programs are the National Certified Addiction Counselor and the Masters Addiction Counselor designations (more than 15,000 counselors in the past 8 years have been credentialed).

Two other credentials are Tobacco Addiction Specialist Certification and Substance Abuse Professional (SAP).

American Academy of Health Providers in the Addictive Disorders (AAHPAD)
314 West Superior Street, Suite 702
Duluth, MN 55802
Telephone: (218) 727-3940
Fax: (218) 722-0346
E-mail: info@americanacademy.org
Web site: www.americanacademy.org

This international nonprofit credentialing body, organized to maintain quality standards for treating addictive disorders, provides competency standards for addiction treatment professionals throughout the world.

The Academy's Certified Addiction Specialist (CAS) credential unites clinicians from various disciplines—nurses, doctors, psychologists, psychiatrists, social workers, and counselors—under a single standard of health care. The CAS credential covers such addictive disorders as alcoholism, other drug addictions, eating disorders, compulsive gambling, and sex addiction. Those specializing in gambling disorders receive the designation "Gambling Specialist Certification."

The AAHPAD recently implemented a national Tobacco Cessation Specialist (TCS) certification in response to the U.S. Department of Health and Human Services, Office of the Surgeon General and the U.S. Public Health Services' report, *Treating Tobacco Use and Dependence: A Clinical Practice Guideline* (n.d.), which recommends the adoption of a uniform standard of competence in tobacco dependence treatment. At the time of this writing, certification requirements were being developed.

CERTIFICATION REQUIREMENTS

Certifying standards for the three largest certifying organizations include IC&RC/AODC, NAADAC, and AAHPAD.

IC&RC/AODC

- *Experience:* Three years (6,000 hours) of documented supervised work experience with a certified AOD counselor in a paid or voluntary capacity providing direct counseling services to AOD clients. One year may be exchanged with a BA or advanced degree in behavioral science.
- *Education:* A total of 270 hours of documented formal classroom education, with 6 of these hours in professional ethics and responsibilities.
- *Training:* 300 hours in a formal, systematic program that focuses on skill development and integration of knowledge in a setting where AOD counseling is provided.
- *International written exam:* All certification boards must use IC&RC's international written exam in their processes of certifying new applicants.

- *Case presentation method (CPM):* A standardized process to measure applicant competence in the 12 core functions by peers through an oral examination.
- *Code of ethics:* Each applicant must sign a code to give the board a written enforcement and appeals mechanism to maintain ethical standards.
- *Recertification standards:* 40 hours of continuing education earned every 2 years.

NAADAC

Three certifications are offered:

1. The National Certified Addiction Counselor Level 1 requires a current state certification/licensure as an AOD counselor, 3 years' full-time or 6,000 hours of supervised AOD counseling, 270 contact hours of AOD class work or related counseling topics including 6 hours of ethics, and 6 of HIV/AIDS, and a passing score on national exam.
2. Level 2 requires a bachelor's degree, current state certification/licensure as an AOD counselor, 5 years' full-time or 10,000 hours of supervised AOD counseling, 450 contact hours in AOD classes including 6 hours of ethics and 6 of HIV/AIDS, and a passing score on national exam.
3. Master Addiction Counselor (MAC) requires a master's degree in the healing arts of an AOD-related field, 500 contact hours of AOD class work, 3 years of supervised AOD clinical experience, 2 at post master's degree level, and passing score on the national exam.

AAHPAD

Minimal eligibility requirements for certification include:

- A master's or doctorate degree from an accredited health care training program.
- Three years of postgraduate, supervised experience providing direct health care services to clients who have an addictive disorder. Predoctoral or pre-master's internship at an approved site may be applied toward 1 year of training.
- A portfolio of clinical training with a minimum of 120 hours in basic counseling skills including assessment, interviewing, and diagnosis, and a minimum of 60 hours of training in each area of specialization.
- Three professional recommendations, at least one of which must be a supervisor who is personally familiar with the applicant's work and can document his or her health care experience.
- A completed application with the application fee. Continuing education annual renewal requirement is 20 hours in addiction-related coursework.

Minimal eligibility requirements for professionals with other degrees (or without degree) are:

- A high school diploma;
- Five years of supervised experience providing direct health care services to addictive disordered clients; and
- Clinical training that includes a minimum of 120 hours in basic counseling skills including assessment, interviewing, and diagnosis, and a minimum of 60 hours of training in each area of specialization.

Table VII.1 (on pages 238–239) shows a chart prepared by James Henderson (2005). It provides an easy overview of certifying organizations and their requirements.

INTERNATIONAL CERTIFYING AGENCIES

Other countries certify AOD professionals as well. In Canada the Canadian Addiction Counsellors Certification Board certifies alcohol and drug counselors:

Canadian Addiction Counsellors Certification Board
236 Victoria Street North, Unit 2
Kitchener, Ontario N2H 5C8
Canada
Telephone: (866) 624-1911
Toll Free: (519) 772-0533
Fax: (519) 772-0535
E-mail: info@caccb.ca
Web site: www.caccb.ca

Formed in 1985, the AIA is a voluntary nonprofit organization affiliated with the International Certification and Reciprocity Consortium/Alcohol and Other Drug Abuse (IC&RC/AODA). The latter consists of over 70 alcohol and other drug certifying bodies in the United States and eight other countries. Each member board accepts, without qualification, the eligibility certificates of its sister boards. This process creates a level of mobility for the professional alcohol and drug abuse counselor.

Counselors certified by the AIA meet rigorous standards that include a combination of education, work experience, clinical supervision, knowledge, and skills specific to substance abuse disorders.

PROFESSIONAL ASSOCIATIONS

Several U.S. professional organizations also offer certifications in drug counseling. These include the American Society of Addiction Medicine (ASAM), the American College of Addictionology and Compulsive Disorders, the National Board for Certified Counselors, Inc. (NBCC), and the Substance Abuse Program Administrators Association (SAPAA):

TABLE VII.1 Certifying Organizations and Their Requirements

Organization	Program(s)	Education Requirements	Experience Requirements	Other Requirements	Types of Examination
American Academy of Health Care Providers in the Addictive Disorders	Certified Addiction Specialist	Advanced or doctoral degree from an accredited health care training program	Three years of postgraduate, supervised experience providing direct health care services to those identified with an addictive disorder	Portfolio of clinical training with 120 hours of training in basic counseling skills and a minimum of 60 hours of training in each area of specialization Three professional recommendations	200-item multiple-choice examination
	Gambling Specialist Certification	Minimum 60 hours of pathological gambling-specific clinical training	Documented clinically supervised experience in treating clients with a gambling addiction	Successfully completed all of the CAS minimum eligibility requirements, including passing the CAS examination	200-item multiple-choice examination
American Society of Addiction Medicine	Certification in Addiction Medicine	Graduation from a medical school in the United States	One year of full-time involvement in the field of alcoholism and other drug dependencies 50 hours of Category I credit toward the AMA Physician Recognition Award	License to practice medicine Three letters of recommendation Certification through a member board of the American Board of Medical Specialties	350 to 400 multiple-choice questions
CASTLE Worldwide, Inc.	Examination for Counselors of Problem Gamblers	Established by credentialing authority	Established by credentialing authority	Established by credentialing authority	150 multiple-choice questions
International Certification & Reciprocity Consortium	AODA Counselors	270 hours of AODA-specific training	6,000 hours of supervised experience	300-hour practicum	150 multiple-choices questions and an oral examination

238

Organization	Credential	Education/Training	Experience	Other requirements	Examination
	Advanced AODA Counselors	Master's or equivalent 180 hours AODA specific training	2,000 hours of supervised experience	300-hour practicum	150 multiple-choice questions
	ATOD Prevention Specialists	100 contact hours in ATOD prevention	One year of experience in ATOD prevention		150 multiple-choice questions
	Clinical Supervisors	30 contact hours in clinical supervision	Five years as an AODA counselor and two years experience as a clinical supervisor	AODA counselor certification	150 multiple-choice questions
NAADAC: National Association for Addiction Professionals	Nationally Certified Addiction Counselor I	270 hours of AODA-specific training	6,000 hours of supervised experience	Current state licensure or certification References	250 multiple-choice questions
	Nationally Certified Addiction Counselor II	Bachelor's degree 450 hours of AODA-specific training	10,000 hours of supervised experience	Current state licensure or certification References	250 multiple-choice questions
NAADAC and National Board for Certified Counselors (Jointly Sponsored)	Master Addiction Counselor	Master's degree in the healing arts or related field; 500 contact hours of AODA-specific training	6,000 hours of experience (4,000 of which must be post masters)	References	200 multiple-choice questions
Substance Abuse Program Administrators Certification Commission	Substance Abuse Program Administrator	40 hours of substance abuse-related training	6,000 hours of experience (4,000 with bachelors degree)		15 multiple-choice questions
	Substance Abuse Providers [as defined in 49 CFR 40.281]	Training as required under 49 CFR 40.281		Current state licensure or certification under NAADAC or IC&RC	150 multiple-choice questions

Reprinted by permission from "Professional Examinations in Alcohol and Other Drug Abuse Counseling" (chap. 26), by James Henderson, in *Addiction Counseling Review: Preparing for Comprehensive, Certification and Licensing Exams*, R. H. Coombs (Ed.), 2005, Mahwah, NJ: Erlbaum.

American Society of Addiction Medicine
4601 N. Park Avenue
Upper Arcade #101
Chevy Chase, MD 20815
Telephone: (301) 656-3920
Fax: (301) 656-3815
E-mail: email@asam.org
Web site: www.asam.org

ASAM, the nation's medical specialty society dedicated to educating physicians and medical students in addiction treatment, seeks to improve the treatment of individuals suffering from alcoholism and other addictions, promotes research and prevention, and strives to enlighten and inform both the medical community and the public about these issues.

Since its inception in 1986, ASAM has certified more than 3,300 physicians in the specialty of addiction medicine. ASAM also offers a subspecialty for physicians interested in being certified as Medical Review Officers.

The American College of Addictionology and Compulsive Disorders
3303 Flamingo Drive
Miami Beach, FL 33140
Telephone: (305) 535-8803; (800) 490-7714
Fax: (800) 538-2204
Web site: www.acacd.com

"C. Ad," the credential offered, indicates that candidates are prepared with the skills required to be a primary resource in addiction intervention, treatment, and management. This certification allows the designee to function in hospitals, residential and outpatient treatment centers, federal, state, and county criminal justice programs as well as private practice.

National Board for Certified Counselors, Inc. (NBCC)
Telephone: (336) 547-0607
E-mail: eubanks@nbcc.org dilda@nbcc.org
Web site: www.nbcc.org

The NBCC® was initially created by a committee of the American Counseling Association (ACA) as an independent credentialing body. NBCC and ACA have strong historical ties and work together to further the profession of counseling. However, the two organizations are completely separate entities with different goals.

Since 1982, NBCC's certification program has recognized counselors who have met predetermined standards in their training, experience, and performance on the National Counselor Examination (NCE) for Licensure and Certification, the most portable credentialing examination in counseling. NBCC has over 31,000 certified counselors who work in more than 50 countries. These examinations are used by more than 40 states, the District of Columbia, and Guam to credential counselors on a state level.

NBCC's flagship credential is the National Certified Counselor (NCC). NBCC also offers specialty certification: (1) the National Certified School Counselor (NCSC), (2) the Certified Clinical Mental Health Counselor (CCMHC), and (3) the Master Addictions Counselor (MAC).

The NCC is a prerequisite or corequisite for the specialty credentials such as the Master of Addiction Counselor credential. In addition to holding the NCC credential, the requirements for the MAC credential include (1) documentation of a minimum of 12 semester hours of graduate coursework in the area of addictions which may include coursework in group and/or marriage and family counseling (up to 6 semester hours) or 500 CE hours specifically in addictions, (2) three years' supervised experience as an addictions counselor at no fewer than 20 hours per week. Two of the 3 years must have been completed after the counseling master's degree was conferred, and (3) A passing score on the Examination for Master Addictions Counselors (EMAC).

The Substance Abuse Program Administrators Association (SAPAA)
7220 SW Sylvan Ct.
Portland, OR 97225
Telephone: (866) 538-4788
Fax: (503) 297-4748
E-mail: president@sapacc.org
Web site: www.sapacc.org

SAPAA's mission is to establish, promote, and communicate high standards of quality, integrity, and professionalism in the administration of workplace substance abuse prevention programs through education, training, and the exchange of ideas. SAPAA's national standards are recognized as the credential for the substance abuse testing and program management industry professional. The Certified Substance Abuse Program Administrators' (C-SAPA) certifying examination, formalized in 1997, aids employment opportunities and has increased the professional stature of the many professionals who have earned it.

The Substance Abuse Program Administrators' Certification Comission (SAPACC), is the national certifying body for substance program administrators who have chosen to be recognized as specialists with demonstrated proficiency in their field. As a nonprofit corporation dedicated to enhancing the quality and level of professional knowledge and skills, SAPACC administers proficiency training, examination, and certification programs.

U.S. Armed Services Certifying Boards

Branches of the U.S. military services also offer certifying programs for enlisted personnel:

Army
Army Substance Abuse Prevention Board
Army Center for Substance Abuse Programs
4501 Ford Avenue, Suite 320
Alexandria, VA 22302
E-mail: none

United States Army Medical Command (USAMC)
Human Resources Management Division
2050 Worth Road
Fort Sam Houston, TX 78234-6000
E-mail: wanda.kuer@cen.amedd.army.mil

Air Force
Air Force Substance Abuse Counselor Certification Board (AFSACCB)
AFMOA/SGOC
Two Skyline Place
5203 Leesburg Pike, Suite 702
Falls Church, VA 22041
E-mail: tina.boothe@pentagon.af.mil

Navy
United States Navy Certification Board (USNCB)
Attn: Cert. Office
Naval Sub Base Bldg. 500
140 Sylvester Road
San Diego, CA 92106-3521
E-mail: TAJudson@nmcsd.med.navy.mil

STATE-SPECIFIC CREDENTIALING ORGANIZATIONS

Two examples of state credentialing agencies are (1) the California Association of Alcoholism and Drug Abuse Counselors (CAADAC) and (2) the California Association for Alcohol/Drug Educators (CAADE).

California Association of Alcoholism and Drug Abuse Counselors (CAADAC)
3400 Bradshaw Road, Suite A5
Sacramento, CA 95827
Telephone: (916) 368-9412
Fax: (916) 368-9424
Web site: http://caadac.org

With CAADAC's "Career Ladder" approach, career-minded addiction professionals are "covered" throughout their working lives—from beginning and volunteer staff, to seasoned, certified counselors, CAADAC offers professional

recognition, opportunities for career growth, a registry for employment verification, ethical standards enforcement, and networking that allows for an AODA treatment team approach.

California Association for Alcohol/Drug Educators (CAADE)
Credentialing Coordinator
P.O. Box 9152
Oxnard, CA 93031-7152
Telephone: (805) 485-5247
Web site: www.caade.org

CAADE, one of the credentialing organizations included in the California Department of Alcohol and Drug Programs Directory promotes and supports quality education in alcohol and drug studies through (1) the development and application of accreditation standards for alcohol and drug education, (2) certification of alcohol and drug treatment specialists, (3) provision for continuing education and professional development, and (4) participation in forums for examination, discussion, and debate on subjects related to alcohol and drug studies.

With 733 members, CAADE acts as a credentialing organization for over 60 college and university programs as part of the State of California Department of Alcohol and Drug Programs. Most states have similar, easily accessed, organizations.

CAADE and sister state organizations promote AOD studies programs, develop guidelines to assist colleges and universities in admitting students, selecting appropriate faculty, and developing courses to meet the training needs of program managers, counselors, mental health workers, nurses, employee assistance personnel, and a growing number of other professionals within the field of health and human services.

Certifying Agencies Specific to Gaming

Two organizations certify addiction counselors who specialize in compulsive gambling: (1) The American Compulsive Gambling Counselor Certification Board and (2) the National Council on Problem Gambling.

American Compulsive Gambling Counselor Certification Board
3635 Quakerbridge Road, Suite 7
University Office Plaza 1
Hamilton, NJ 08619
Telephone: (609) 588-9338
E-mail: CCGNJShirl@aol.com
Web site: www.certificationboard.com

The American Compulsive Gambling Counselor Certification Board, Inc., a nonpartisan, nonpolitical, and nonprofit organization, establishes standards for performance and competencies. Requirements for initial certification as a compulsive gambling counselor are:

- No history or evidence of addictive disorders involving gambling, drugs, or alcohol for a minimum of 2 years immediately prior to the date of application
- Completion of at least 142 hours within a 5-year period, referred to as the Core Curriculum
- A total of 180 supervised practical training hours under qualified supervision in a recognized treatment facility
- Completion of 750 hours paid, volunteer, or combination of paid and volunteer experience under qualified supervision within 3 years immediately prior to date of application
- Passing a written national examination, the *Professional Exam for Counselors of Problem Gamblers,* developed and administered through Columbia Assessment Services (CAS), a subsidiary of CASTLE Worldwide, Inc.

The National Council on Problem Gambling, Inc.
208 G Street NE
Washington, DC 20002
Telephone: (202) 547-9204
Web site: www.ncpgambling.org

This certification is designed to be a national minimal standard with each state encouraged to build on the requirements and add local criteria to best serve their client population.

Studying for Certifying Exams

Numerous companies offer exam preparation courses for a fee to certification candidates. The Association for Advanced Training in the Behavioral Sciences (AATBS) offers independent study materials, test-taking strategies and practice exams, glossaries, pretests, and toll-free expert telephone consultation:

Association for Advanced Training in the Behavioral Sciences (AATBS)
5126 Ralston Street
Ventura, CA 93003
Telephone: (800) 472-1931
Fax: (800) 676-3033
Web site: www.aatbs.com

Recommended Reading

Books on Credentialing for a Counseling License (Non-AOD Specific):

Barnhart, P. A. (1997). *The guide to national professional certification programs.* Amherst, MA: HRD Press.
Bradley, F. (Ed.). (1991). *Credentialing in counseling.* Alexandria, VA: American Counseling Association.

Mobley, C. S., & Deutsch, S. K. (1999). *The credentialing handbook.* Rockville, MD: Aspen Press.

Pare, M. A. (Ed.). (1998). *Certification and accreditation programs directory: A descriptive guide to national voluntary certification and accreditation programs for professionals and institutions* (Certification and Accreditation Programs Directory, 2nd ed.), Gale Group. This publication supplies comprehensive national, voluntary certification and accreditation information for about 1,600 programs for individuals and over 200 for educational programs, institutions, businesses, and service providers. Compiled from various sources, this easy-to-use book contains separate sections for certification and accreditation programs. The chapter on certification offers information arranged by job category and then alphabetically by title, and within the accreditation chapter alphabetically according to specialty area. Entries detail titles awarded; number of individuals certified or institutions accredited; full contact data; requirements in terms of education, experience or other; exam information; application, reapplication, accreditation, and renewal procedures; fees; and endorsements. A third section provides alphabetical profiles of certifying bodies with contact data and titles awarded. A wide audience of individuals seeking professional advancement, consumers searching for highly qualified professionals, persons checking the standards of educational institutions, and professionals interested in certification and accreditation will find this reliable compilation useful (description from Amazon.com).

Rosenthal, H. (1993). *Encyclopedia of counseling: Master review and tutorial.* Bristol, PA: Accelerated Development.

Wallace, S. A., & Lewis, M. D. (1998). *Becoming a professional counselor: Preparing for certification and comprehensive exams.* Thousand Oaks, CA: Sage.

CONTINUING EDUCATION

Licensing boards and professional organizations typically require their members to obtain regular, specified continuing education units (CEUs). These educational requirements help counselors stay up-to-date on professional advances.

CEU REQUIREMENTS

All boards specify a certain number of required hours. To maintain licensure as a Certified Addiction Specialist (CAS), the American Academy of Health Providers in the Addictive Disorders requires 20 CEU hours of addiction-related education every year (through Academy approved CEU provider or state/national accrediting bodies). Continuous collegiate teaching hours equal half of the required 20 hours.

The California Association for Alcohol/Drug Educators (CAADE; see Certification and Licensing section for more information on this organization) renewal requirements for the Certified Addictions Treatment Specialist require a total of 30 hours of continuing education during the period covered by the certification.

Some boards require core requirements and specify a given number of CEU hours (e.g., Ethics or Hypnosis) and permit additional hours in associated areas.

Each state licensing board has its own continuing education requirements. Although many states accept at least one of the national certifying board's approvals, there is still some variance in the approval and acceptability of audiotapes and home study, even with the national approvals. To check on the variances in state CE requirements (e.g., whether they allow home study credits), see www.ongoodauthority.com.

CEU PROVIDERS

The provision of CEUs has become a cottage industry serving health care providers who must earn continuing education credits. Educational formats for these CEU offerings include on-site workshops, meetings of professional organizations, training by certification agencies, and instruction at colleges and universities. Some agencies offer independent study courses (mainly on the Internet). Examples of CEU providers follow:

The *American Psychological Association* offers CEUs to their conference attendees, where more than 50 Continuing Professional Education workshops are typically offered. These workshops, offering a broad array of CEU topics, are scheduled either for half (four hours) or full day (seven hours).

CEU programs offered by APA include over 60 Independent Study Programs that allow self-directed study based on APA publications, as well as online exams and instant grading. On their web site, click on the title, order the book, and take the examination either electronically or via hardcopy. On completion of your examination, with a score of at least 75% accuracy, you will receive documentation of your CE credit by mail. Contact information is as follows:

American Psychological Association
Continuing Education in Psychology
750 First Street NE
Washington, DC 20002-4242
Telephone: (800) 374-2721, ext. 5991
Fax: (202) 336-6151
Web site: www.apa.org/ce/online.html

The Breining Institute, a 4-year nationally recognized college, is one of many that offers CEU degree and certificate programs in the addictions:

College for the Advancement of Addictive Disorders
8880 Greenback Lane
Orangevale, CA 95662
Telephone: (916) 987-2007
Fax: (916) 987-8823
Web site: www.breining.edu

Another source is university-based CEU programs offered as workshop weekends. One example is the *University of California, Los Angeles Extension Program* course, "Pharmacotherapy in the Treatment of Mental Illness," a 6-hour Marriage and Family Therapist/Licensed Clinical Social Worker (MFT/LCSW) credit course that meets one full day on Saturday.

These evening or weekend extension courses can be taken either individually or as part of a larger certification program. The UCLA certificate program in alcohol/drug abuse studies consists of 17 units of study providing an overview of social, clinical, and treatment issues of alcohol and other forms of drug abuse. The UCLA Extension program in alcohol/drug counseling, a 36-unit program designed for prospective substance abuse counselors, combines theory with applications and practical experience and includes in-depth training in counseling skills.

These courses cater to health professionals; human service and mental health providers (especially those with an interest in substance abuse training); counselors; teachers; nurses; spiritual counselors; and law enforcement, government, and other personnel working in the criminal justice system:

UCLA Extension
10995 Le Conte Avenue
Los Angeles, CA 90024-2883
Web site: www.uclaextension.org

Distance learning courses, such as those offered by the Distance Learning Center for Addiction Studies (DLCAS), LLC, an affiliate of the Betty Ford Center, are another popular form of independent study program. An Internet-based educational service that provides current and comprehensive information about addiction-related topics, DLCAS helps professionals maintain their credentials while staying current with the advances of the field. The distance education format may save you considerable time and money by allowing you to do your training in your own home or office:

Distance Learning Center for Addiction Studies
Telephone: (866) 0471-1742
Web site: www.dlcas.com

Another company that offers home study distance learning courses is:

Institute of Addiction Awareness
24881 Alicia Parkway, #E-519
Laguna Hills, CA 92653-4696
Telephone: (888) 333-CEUS
Fax: (949) 716-5923
Web site: www.CEUInstitute.com

These home study programs provide low-cost independent study courses and are NAADAC approved.

Many other quality providers can be found on the NAADAC web site (www.naadac.org) or in the magazines cited in the Recommended Reading section.

Selecting Quality CEU Programs

Check the *APA Sponsor Approval System* to ensure that the program is approved by your licensing board for CEU credit. This system provides organizations offering CEU credit to psychologists an opportunity to earn the APA sponsor approval status that is given to quality organizations. Check the approximately 600 organizations listed on their web site (www.apa.org/ce/online.html) that currently hold approval status.

State professional organizations such as the California Association of Alcoholism and Drug Abuse Counselors (CAADAC) also list approved continuing education providers in the education section of their web site (www.caadac.org).

Recommended Reading

Enos, G. A. (Ed.). (2003). *Behavioral healthcare tomorrow/addiction professional buyer's guide.* Manisses Communications Group, Inc. This magazine lists organizations accepted by the NAADAC Certification Commission as approved education and training providers for NCAC and MAC recredentialing requirements (All are NAADAC Approved Education Providers). Moreover, many of the organizations and companies in this directory include an extended description of their services. Copies of this magazine guide are distributed to the members of numerous associations. To obtain a copy for $20, phone (800) 333-7771 or e-mail manissescs@manisses.com.

BUSINESS PLAN

As you develop your business and financial policies (e.g., how much to charge, how to handle insurance coverage, and how to address delinquent accounts), choose options that are fair, enforceable, and protective of both you and your client.

SETTING FEES

Since there is no one standard method for setting fees, the following considerations and options may be helpful (Parvin & Anderson, 1999):

- If you are a fee-for-service provider, determine appropriate fees after consulting with your professional organization about industry standards for your qualifications and location.
- Determine the length of the sessions you will provide (e.g., 30 minutes, 50 minutes, 90 minutes) and the fees you will charge for each.
- Decide what your fees will be for individuals, couples, families, and other groups.
- When a client cannot afford your fee, decide if you will offer a sliding scale based on ability to pay. If so, what minimum are you willing to accept? If a client is unable to afford *any* fee, decide if your services will be offered pro bono.
- Decide about a payment schedule. Many addiction counselors have clients pay after each session, whereas others may accept insurance reimbursement after the client pays the deductible fee required by the insurance company. If your fees are more than the insurance covers, be sure clients know they will be responsible for the difference.
- Decide on a cancellation policy (e.g., canceling at least 24 hours prior to scheduled appointment) and if there will be a late fee for not paying on time. If you are going to charge a cancellation or late fee, inform clients in writing and have them sign a letter of understanding.

Additional Resources

An excellent resource for managing financial billing is the Therapist Helper at www.helper.com.

DISCUSSING FEES

Before beginning treatment, addiction counselors should openly address financial policies with all prospective clients. This practice allows clients time to make an informed decision. If they cannot afford your fee, you may offer a lower amount (from a sliding scale) that adjusts for their financial circumstances. If you accept a lower payment or provide pro bono service, document your rationale in your notes.

If another person (or agency) is paying the client's fee, make sure that this person (or agency) has agreed to this responsibility. To ensure there are no miscommunications around expectations, obtain a formal written agreement before providing services that specifies the terms of payment and the kinds of services that will be offered.

As mentioned, most professional organizations provide recommendations for appropriate billing. Whatever strategy you use, disclose your fees and billing specifics prior to counseling. Informed consent is essential.

HOME-BASED PRACTICES

Although working at home will not suit every therapist's practice, there are some significant advantages (aside from saving travel time and expense):

- Overhead is lower.
- There are tax advantages (e.g., writing off office space. Discuss with your tax advisor what is allowed and not).
- You have fewer people to supervise (e.g., receptionists).
- Location is convenient.
- It is easier to be available when clients have after-hours emergencies.
- It is easy for your family to gain access to you.
- "No shows" are less irritating since more options are readily available for spending time productively (adapted from 4Therapy.com Network, www .4therapy.com /professional/research/lawandethics/item.php?uniqueid=6523 &categoryid=503&).

If you are thinking about a home-based practice, consider the following recommendations (4Therapy.com Network):

- If possible, arrange for a separate entrance and close off the office area from the rest of your home.
- Ensure the privacy of both your clients *and* your family.
- Consider keeping the door that leads into your home closed and locked when you are in sessions.
- If the layout of your home allows, provide a separate bathroom for clients.
- Check the local zoning restrictions to make sure that you can follow all legal statutes pertaining to an at-home health care practice.
- Check the local business and zoning ordinances to ensure that you have adequate insurance coverage for business liabilities.
- Finally, and most important, consider whether your practice lends itself to a home setting.

Additional Resources

For further information, see Buelow, Hebert, and Buelow (1999).

REFERRALS

Counselors have both a professional and an ethical responsibility to meet the needs of their clients. A referral to another professional (e.g., psychiatrist) should be made when client needs exceed the training and competencies of the addiction counselor or agency. Clients with severe mental health problems, such as schizophrenia, will need additional psychiatric support.

Counselors may refer simply because clients' progress is slow or they may be better served by another counselor. Referrals help build multidisciplinary teams (e.g., social worker, physician, school counselor, and pastor) that come together to assist the client.

Clients have the right to request such referrals. When this occurs, follow up to ensure that an appropriate match has been made. To find and develop collegial relationships in your area:

- Review local yellow pages to identify agencies in your area and build your own referral phone table.
- Send letters of introduction to other professionals in the community (e.g., medical doctors, social workers, psychologists, and other counselors) to inform them about who you are and what you do.
- Network with local professionals (e.g., attend local chapter meetings of professional organizations).
- Ask appropriate colleagues to share their organizational directories (a listing of all the professionals, agencies, and services) in your area.
- From these activities, build your own master directory.

Additional Resources

Buelow, G. S., Hebert, S., & Buelow, S. (1999). *Psychotherapist's resource on psychiatric medications: Issues of treatment and referrals* (2nd ed.). Belmont, CA: Wadsworth.

MULTIDISCIPLINARY TEAMS

Multidisciplinary teams, comprising individuals with various skills and professional training, come together to assist clients in need. By integrating complementary information and resources, these teams magnify the treatment knowledge and skills brought to bear in helping the client.

Additional Resources

For a wealth of information on ethics and malpractice, visit Ken Pope's web site: http://kspope.com/ethics/ethical.php.

Another powerful tool is Hedges, L., Hilton, R., Hilton, V., & Caudill, O. B. (1996). *Therapists at risk.* Northvale, NJ: Aronson. This addresses how counselors can avoid ethics violations.

WELLNESS PLAN

Daily contact with emotionally taxing clients puts counselors at risk for becoming physically and emotionally drained. Counter this occupational stress by developing and maintaining a personal wellness plan.

BURNOUT

Burnout, Vecchio (1991) explains, is the physical, emotional, and mental exhaustion that results from prolonged exposure to stressful situations. Symptoms include absenteeism, decreased productivity, and mounting psychological distress.

Burnout often has these characteristics (James & Gilliland, 2001):

- The onset is slow and insidious.
- Multiple incidents, not a single one, instigate burnout.
- Work piles up with no relief in sight.
- There are stressful changes in one's personal life that add stress at work.
- A lack of clarity exists concerning rights, responsibilities, methods, goals, status, and accountability to self and work situations.
- The person is experiencing incompatible conflicts, facing demands that are inappropriate or inconsistent with personal values and ethics.
- There is a feeling of helplessness since no matter how hard one works, the outcome is the same.

The burnout process typically includes these stages (James & Gilliland, 2001):

Stage 1: Enthusiasm: Individuals begin the job with high hopes and often-unrealistic expectations.

Stage 2: Stagnation: They begin to feel that their personal, financial, and career needs are not being met. If chronically unfulfilled, they move to the next stage.

Stage 3: Frustration: Self-doubts accumulate in the face of ever-mounting obstacles; workers start questioning their effectiveness, value, and impact.

Stage 4: Apathy: Demoralized, and in a state of chronic indifference, workers are unable to control emotions or cognitions and are unable to work up to their potential. Likely in a state of denial, they have little objective understanding of what is occurring. Therapy may be necessary to reverse this unhealthy condition.

Type A personalities are more burnout prone than Type B personalities (Vecchio, 1991). *Type A* individuals tend to be impatient, competitive, and feel that they are constantly under time pressure. In addition, they are also aggressive, try to accomplish several things at the same time, and have difficulty relaxing—traits that put the individual at high risk for stress. *Type B* personalities, by contrast, are more capable of staying calm in challenging situations and are less likely to be aggressive. Awareness of their personality type may help workers be realistic about potential burnout and take appropriate preventive action.

AVOIDING BURNOUT

These 10 tips may reduce the burnout risk (Howatt, 1999, 2003b):

1. Develop a list of *stress-reduction techniques* you will implement, such as deep breathing, journaling, and visualization.
2. Write down your *personal and professional goals*—ideally a 12-month plan and monitor progress weekly.

3. *Deal with conflicts as they arise;* do not let them build up.
4. Enlist a *professional mentor* to assist you.
5. Develop and maintain *interests and hobbies* outside work; spend time every day having fun outside the workplace.
6. Make *exercise, rest, relaxation,* and *diet* the four pillars of each day.
7. Maintain healthy *interpersonal relationships* outside work.
8. Design a *rewarding environment:* Arrange the work environment with soothing colors, uplifting pictures, and conveniences. When possible, seek positive peers and avoid negative ones.
9. Reduce *negative thinking:* Replace harsh self-evaluations and negative self-talk with positive reminders. A "good things list," frequently updated and reviewed helps you focus on uplifting events and accomplishments.
10. Learn about *your personality:* If you are a Type A personality, you probably accomplish more than others. But, compared with others, you also produce 40 times more cortisol (a stress hormone), 4 times more adrenalin (another stress hormone), and pump 3 times more blood into your muscles (Vecchio, 1991). Learn how to filter and process events to avoid becoming chronically stressed and fatigued.

   Diaphragmatic breathing: Take three slow breaths to slow things down. Count silently and slowly to three when you breathe in (through your nose) and push your stomach out instead of your chest. Diaphragm breathing has a calming influence and gets oxygen to the brain.

Additional Resources

This web site—www.mindtools.com—provides an outstanding resource for professionals seeking to maintain personal and professional wellness.

Another rich resource for developing a wellness plan and helping clients deal with stress is Davis, M., Eshelman, E. R., & McKay, M. (1995). *The relaxation and stress reduction workbook* (4th ed.). Oakland, CA: New Harbinger.

MALPRACTICE INSURANCE

All addiction counselors need their own professional liability insurance; an employer's insurance plan is not always comprehensive enough to protect individual interests as institutional coverage tends to have many restrictions and limitations. In today's litigious society, malpractice claims are on the rise so liability insurance is a necessity.

Malpractice insurance—professional liability coverage that insures the counselor in cases of lawsuits alleging negligence—will cover legal fees as well as possible damages. Most professional organizations align themselves with a preferred vendor.

These insurance companies provide health care professionals with liability protection against malpractice claims and lawsuits. Also note that many professional associations recommend particular companies for their members.

American Professional Agency, Inc.
95 Broadway
Amityville, NY 11701
Telephone: (631) 691-6400; (800) 421-6694
Web site: www.americanprofessional.com

American Professional Agency, Inc. (APA) began operations in 1940 focusing on professional liability insurance with special emphasis in the mental health field. Today, APA is the largest writer of mental health professional liability insurance in the United States with over 100,000 policyholders (it ranks in the top 100 insurance brokerages in the country). The National Association of Social Workers refers their members to this company.

APA's insurance partners include Chubb, Gulf Insurance Group, TDC (The Doctor Company), and AIG. To get an insurance premium quote, click on their home page to see limits of liability and rates.

Professional Risk Management Services, Inc.
The Psychiatrists' Program
1515 Wilson Blvd., Suite 800
Arlington, VA 22209-2404
Telephone: (800) 245-3333
Web site: www.prms.com

Professional Risk Management Services, Inc., specializes in professional liability insurance and risk management services for health care professionals—from individual psychiatrists to multistate corporate health care providers. Their Psychiatrists' Program (APA sponsored) specializes in professional liability insurance coverage for psychiatrists and mental health professionals. They maintain a staff of psychiatric professional liability specialists to provide these services.

The Van Wagner Group
21 Maple Avenue
P.O. Box 5710
Bayshore, NY 11706-0503
Telephone: (888) 383-3512; (800) 735-1588
Fax: (888) 525-9072
Web site: www.vanwagnergroup.com/home.asp

Click on "Program Highlights and Quotes" to directly access the Van Wagner Group premium rates.

Since 1985, the NAADAC (Association for Addiction Professionals) has referred its members to the Van Wagner Group/Behavioral Health Management Corp./Behavioral Health Purchasing Group. This company has written coverage through four of the leading carriers of professional liability, all of which are rated "A" or higher by A.M. Best and Company.

Healthcare Providers Service Organization
159 East County Line Road
Hatboro, PA 19040-1218
Telephone: (800) 982-9491
Web site: www.hpso.com

For the past 25 years, Healthcare Providers Service Organization (HPSO) has provided services to over 700,000 health care providers from 70 groups. HPSO is a division of Affinity Insurance Services, Inc., a subsidiary of Aon Services Group.

PART VIII
Information Resources

Part VIII describes and gives contact information about organizations that offer services related to drug abuse and addiction. It offers an overview of federal, state, educational, professional, and grassroots organizations that deal with addictions.

It also identifies and describes grant-funding resources and addiction publications. A final section provides information about policy organizations whose views differ from the federal government.

NATIONAL AND INTERNATIONAL ORGANIZATIONS
> Federal Substance Abuse Agencies
> Regional Substance Abuse Agencies
> State Substance Abuse Agencies
> Educational and Training Institutions
> Professional Addiction-Related Organizations
> Canadian Agencies
> International Substance Abuse Organizations
> Grassroots Alcohol and Other Drugs Information

GRANT-FUNDING RESOURCES
> Federal Granting Agencies
> International Granting Agencies
> Private Granting Agencies
> Other Funding Databases

PUBLISHING RESOURCES
> Academic and Professional Journals
> Addiction Magazines and Web Sites
> Addiction Newsletters and Web Sites

DRUG POLICY ADVOCATES

The Drug Policy Alliance
National Organization for the Reform of Marijuana Laws
Ham Reduction Coalition
Law Enforcement against Prohibition
Multidisciplinary Association for Psychedelic Studies
Religious Leaders for a More Just and Compassionate Drug Policy
Educators for Sensible Drug Policy
Canadian Foundation for Drug Policy

NATIONAL AND INTERNATIONAL ORGANIZATIONS

Governmental and professional organizations provide key resources for addiction counselors. This section provides descriptions and contact information for the following organizations:

- Federal substance abuse agencies
- State substance abuse agencies
- Educational and training institutions
- Professional addiction related organizations
- Canadian AOD organizations
- International AOD organizations
- Grassroots AOD information

FEDERAL SUBSTANCE ABUSE AGENCIES

The following agencies provide a wealth of information useful to AOD counselors.

Substance Abuse and Mental Health Services Administration (SAMHSA)
U.S. Department of Health and Human Services (DHHS)
5600 Fishers Lane
Parklawn Building, Suite 13C-05
Rockville, MD 20857
E-mail: info@samhsa.gov
Web site: www.samhsa.gov

Established by Congress in 1992, SAMHSA seeks to strengthen the nation's health care capacity in prevention, diagnosis, and treatment services for substance abuse and mental illness by working in partnership with states, communities, and private organizations. With annual budgets of more than $2.5 billion, SAMHSA includes the Center for Mental Health Services (CMHS); the Center for Substance Abuse Prevention (CSAP), the Center for Substance Abuse Treatment (CSAT), and the Office of Applied Studies (OAS).

> Center for Mental Health Services (CMHS)
> 5600 Fishers Lane
> Parklawn Building, Room 17-99
> Rockville, MD 20857
> The Knowledge Exchange Network (KEN)
> Information clearinghouse for CMHS
> Telephone: (800) 789-2647
> Web site: www.mentalhealth.org

CMHS works to create community-based mental health service infrastructures to improve the availability and accessibility of high-quality care for people with, or at risk for, mental illnesses, as well as their families. The largest portion of the Center's annual appropriation supports individual state programs through the Community Mental Health Services Block Grant Program. However, CMHS also maintains a portfolio of grant programs to develop and apply knowledge about community-based practices that reach those at greatest risk: adults with serious mental illness and children with serious emotional disturbances. The Center collects and disseminates national mental health services data designed to inform future services policy and program decision making.

> Center for Substance Abuse Prevention (CSAP)
> Telephone: (800) 729-6686
> Web site: http://prevention.samhsa.gov

CSAP identifies and promotes methods to prevent illicit drug use, misuse of legal medications, tobacco use, and excessive or illegal use of alcohol. CSAP seeks to strengthen families and communities, and to develop knowledge about prevention techniques for different populations at risk. The Center's grant programs promote the development, application, and dissemination of new knowledge in substance abuse prevention. CSAP also supports the National Clearinghouse for Alcohol and Drug Information (NCADI), the nation's primary information source on substance abuse research, treatment, and prevention.

The Regional Alcohol and Drug Awareness Resource (RADAR) Network, established by CSAP, provides immediate access to substance abuse prevention and treatment resources (see State Substance Abuse Agencies). Formed in partnership with state governments and national constituency groups, the RADAR Network provides local support to prevention practitioners and other community members addressing alcohol, tobacco, and other drug problems.

Center for Substance Abuse Treatment (CSAT)
5600 Fishers Lane
Rockwall II
Rockville, MD 20857
Telephone: (301) 443-5052
Referral to treatment center: (800) 662-HELP
Telecommunications Device for the Deaf: (800) 487-4889
    Spanish: (877) 767-8432
    Referrals to: (800) ALCOHOL; (800) COCAINE
    Web site: www.samhsa.gov/centers/CSAT2002

The federal government's agency to enhance the quality of substance abuse treatment services, CSAT was created by Congress in 1992 to identify, develop, and support policies and programs that enhance and expand science-based treatment services for substance-abusing individuals. CSAT administers the state block grant program for substance abuse prevention and treatment. CSAT also administers (1) the Addiction Technology Transfer Centers (ATTC), (2) the Office of Applied Studies (OAS), (3) the National Household Survey on Drug Abuse (NHSDA), (4) the Drug Abuse Warning Network (DAWN), and (5) the Drug and Alcohol Services Information System (DASIS).

Addiction Technology Transfer Centers (ATTC)
National Office
University of Missouri—Kansas City
5100 Rockhill Road
Kansas City, MO 64110-2499
Telephone: (816) 482-1200
Fax: (816) 482-1101
Web site: www.nattc.org
E-mail: no@nattc.org

A nationwide program consisting of 14 independent regional centers and a national office, the ATTC is a multidisciplinary resource that draws on the knowledge, experience, and latest work of recognized addiction experts. Its three key objectives are (1) to increase the knowledge and skills of addiction treatment practitioners from multiple disciplines by facilitating access to state-of-the-art research and education; (2) to heighten the awareness, knowledge, and skills of all professionals who have the opportunity to intervene in the lives of people with substance use disorders; and (3) to foster regional and national alliances among practitioners, researchers, policymakers, funders, and consumers for support and implementation of best treatment practices. A primary ATTC goal is to promote collaboration among disciplines and influence the education and credentialing requirements for treatment professionals. See, for example, the ATTC publications, *Addiction Counseling Competencies: The Knowledge, Skills* and *Attitudes of Professional Practice—Technical Assistance Publication #21; The Change Book:*

A Blueprint for Technology Transfer; and *Systems Change Project* (accessed via their web site at www.nattc.org).

Office of Applied Studies (OAS)
Web site: www.drugabusestatistics.samhsa.gov

OAS gathers, analyzes, and disseminates data on substance abuse practices in the United States. OAS provides the latest national data on (1) alcohol, tobacco, marijuana, and other drug abuse, (2) drug-related emergency room episodes and medical examiner cases, and (3) the national substance abuse treatment system. OAS is responsible for the annual *National Household Survey on Drug Abuse* (recently renamed the National Survey on Drug Use and Health), *the Drug Abuse Warning Network, and the Drug and Alcohol Services Information System,* among other studies. OAS also coordinates evaluation of the service-delivery models within SAMHSA's knowledge development and application programs.

National Survey on Drug Use and Health (prior name: Household Survey on
    Drug Abuse [NHSDA])
Web site: www.samhsa.gov/oas/nhsda.htm

This annual survey provides the primary source of information on the prevalence, patterns, and consequences of alcohol, tobacco, and illegal drug use and abuse in the United States among the civilian, noninstitutionalized population, age 12 and older.

Drug Abuse Warning Network (DAWN)
Web site: www.samhsa.gov/oas/dawn.htm

DAWN, an ongoing drug abuse data collection system, collects data from two sources: (1) hospital emergency departments (EDs) and (2) medical examiners (MEs). The *DAWN ED component,* a national representative sample of hospital EDs, produces information on the number and characteristics of drug abuse related visits to EDs in U.S. metropolitan areas. The *DAWN mortality component* provides information about drug abuse related deaths, based on reports from participating medical examiners. DAWN cases (drug-related ED visits or deaths) include detailed information about the abuse of illegal drugs or legal drugs used for nonmedical purposes.

Drug and Alcohol Services Information System (DASIS)
Web site: www.samhsa.gov/oas/dasis.htm

DASIS, the primary source of national data on substance abuse treatment, is conducted by the Office of Applied Studies, and has three components:

1. *The Inventory of Substance Abuse Treatment Services* (I-SATS), a listing of all known public and private substance abuse treatment facilities in the United States and its territories.
2. The *National Survey of Substance Abuse Treatment Services* (N-SSATS), an annual survey of all facilities in the I-SATS that collects information on location, characteristics, services offered, and utilization. Information from the N-SSATS is used to compile and update the *National Directory of Drug and Alcohol Abuse Treatment Programs* and the online *Substance Abuse Treatment Facility Locator*. The N-SSATS includes a periodic survey of substance abuse treatment in adult and juvenile correctional facilities.
3. *The Treatment Episode Data Set* (TEDS) is a compilation of the demographic and substance abuse characteristics of admissions to substance abuse treatment. Information on treatment admissions is routinely collected by state administrative systems and then submitted to SAMHSA.

National Clearinghouse for Alcohol and Drug Information (NCADI)
11426-28 Rockville Pike, Suite 200
Rockville, MD 20852
P.O. Box 2345
Rockville, MD 20847-2345
Telephone: (800) 729-6686 (available 24 hours a day, 7 days a week to take calls)
Web site: www.ncadi.samhsa.gov

The world's largest resource for current information and materials concerning substance abuse, NCADI is a one-stop resource for the most current and comprehensive information about substance abuse prevention and treatment. NCADI offers thousands of items to the public, many free of charge. These include fact sheets, brochures, pamphlets, monographs, posters, and videotapes as well as the latest studies and surveys, guides, videocassettes, and other types of information and materials on substance abuse developed by such federal agencies as CSAP, the Center for Substance Abuse Prevention, the Center for Substance Abuse Treatment, the National Institute on Alcohol Abuse and Alcoholism, and the National Institute on Drug Abuse, and the U.S. Departments of Education and Labor.

The NCADI library has more than 80,000 journals, newspapers, magazines, and reference books, plus equipment for reviewing audiotapes and videotapes. It also has access to the Prevention Materials database (PMD) including over 8,000 prevention-related materials and the Treatment Resources Database, available to the public in electronic form, and provides rapid dissemination of federal grant announcements for ATD prevention, treatment, and research funding opportunities.

Staff includes both English- and Spanish-speaking specialists skilled at recommending appropriate publications, posters, and videocassettes, conducting customized searches, providing grant and funding information, and referring people to appropriate organizations.

National Institutes of Health (NIH)
9000 Rockville Pike
Bethesda, MD 20892
Telephone: (301) 496-4000
E-mail: execsec1@od.nih.gov
Web site: www.nih.gov

The NIH conducts research in its own laboratories; supports the research of non-federal scientists in universities, medical schools, hospitals, and research institutions throughout the country and abroad; helps train research investigators; and fosters communication of medical information.

The NIH goals are to (1) foster fundamental creative discoveries, innovative research strategies, and their applications as a basis to advance significantly the nation's capacity to protect and improve health; (2) develop, maintain, and renew scientific human and physical resources that will assure the nation's capability to prevent disease; (3) expand the knowledge base in medical and associated sciences to enhance the nation's economic well-being and ensure a continued high return on the public investment in research; and (4) amplify and promote the highest level of scientific integrity, public accountability, and social responsibility in the conduct of science.

Among the 19 institutes sponsored by NIH, two deal exclusively with substance abuse—the National Institute on Alcohol Abuse and Alcoholism (NIAAA) and the National Institute on Drug Abuse (NIDA)—and one other, the National Institute on Mental Health (NIMH), sometimes has related issues when discussing comorbid disorders.

National Institute on Alcohol Abuse and Alcoholism (NIAAA)
6000 Executive Blvd.—Willco Building
Bethesda, MD 20892-7003
Web site: www.niaaa.nih.gov

NIAAA supports and conducts biomedical and behavioral research on the causes, consequences, treatment, and prevention of alcoholism and alcohol-related problems. It also provides national leadership to reduce the severe and often fatal consequences of these problems by (1) conducting and supporting research directed at determining the causes of alcoholism, discovering how alcohol damages the organs of the body, and developing prevention and treatment strategies for application in the nation's health care system; (2) supporting and conducting research across a wide range of scientific areas including genetics, neuroscience, medical consequences, medication development, prevention, and treatment through the award of grants and within the NIAAA's intramural research program; (3) conducting policy studies that have broad implications for alcohol problem prevention, treatment, and rehabilitation activities; (4) conducting epidemiological studies such as national and community surveys to assess risks for and magnitude of alcohol-related problems among various population groups; (5) collaborating with other research institutes and federal programs relevant to alcohol abuse and alcoholism, and providing coordination for federal alcohol abuse and alcoholism research activities; (6) maintaining continuing relationships with institutions and professional associations, with international, national, state and local officials, and with voluntary agencies and organizations engaged in alcohol-related work; and (7) disseminating research findings to health care providers, researchers, policymakers, and the public.

National Institute on Drug Abuse (NIDA)
6001 Executive Blvd., Room 5213
Bethesda, MD 20892-0561
E-mail: information@lists.nida.nih.gov
Hotline: (800) 622-HELP
Web site: www.nida.nih.gov

Established in 1974, NIDA became part of the NIH in 1992. NIDA supports over 85% of the world's research on the health aspects of drug abuse and addiction, including the most fundamental and essential questions about drug abuse, ranging from the molecule to managed care, and from DNA to community outreach research.

NIDA not only seeks to further public understanding of how drugs of abuse affect the brain and behavior, it also works to ensure the rapid and effective transfer of scientific data to policymakers, drug abuse practitioners, other health care practitioners, and the general public. The NIDA web page is an important part of this effort.

The *NIDA Clinical Toolbox*, a compilation of publications based on NIDA-supported research, includes the first three in a series of drug treatment therapy manuals; the most recent publication, *Principles of Drug Addiction Treatment: A Research-Based Guide*, provides a science-based foundation in clinical practice settings. As new materials become available, NIDA will continue to distribute them for inclusion in the *Toolbox*. Free copies of the *NIDA Clinical Toolbox* are available from the National Clearinghouse for Alcohol and Drug Information (800-729-6686) or can be viewed on this Internet web site: www.drugabuse.gov/TV/Clinical/ClinicalToolbox.htm.

National Institute of Mental Health (NIMH)
6001 Executive Blvd., Room 8184, MSC 9663
Bethesda, MD 20892-9663
Telephone: (301) 443-4513; (866) 615-NIMH (6464)
TTY: (301) 443-8431
Fax: (301) 443-4279
E-mail: nimhinfo@nih.gov
Web site: www.nimh.nih.gov

The National Institute of Mental Health (NIMH), one of 27 components of the National Institutes of Health (NIH), is the federal government's principal biomedical and behavioral research agency. NIMH's mission is to reduce the burden of mental illness and behavioral disorders through research on mind, brain, and behavior.

The Institute (1) conducts research on mental disorders and the underlying basic science of brain and behavior; (2) supports research on these topics at universities and hospitals around the United States; (3) collects, analyzes, and disseminates information on the causes, occurrence, and treatment of mental illnesses; (4) supports the training of more than 1,000 scientists to carry out basic and clinical research; and (5) communicates information to scientists, the public, the news media, and primary care and mental health professionals about mental illnesses, the brain, mental health, and research in these areas.

Office of National Drug Control Policy (ONDCP)
Drug Policy Information Clearinghouse
P.O. Box 6000
Rockville, MD 20849-6000
Telephone: (800) 666-3332
Fax: (301) 519-5212
E-mail: ondcp@ncjrs.org
Web site: www.whitehousedrugpolicy.gov

A component of the Office of the President, ONDCP establishes policies, priorities, and objectives for the nation's drug control program. The goals of ONDCP are to reduce illicit drug use, manufacturing, and trafficking, drug-related crime and violence, and drug-related health consequences. The ONDCP is charged with producing the National Drug Control Strategy that directs the nation's antidrug efforts and establishes a program, a budget, and guidelines for cooperation among federal, state, and local entities. By law, the ONDCP also evaluates, coordinates, and oversees both the international and domestic antidrug efforts of executive branch agencies and ensures that such efforts sustain and complement state and local antidrug activities.

National Highway Traffic Safety Administration (NHTSA)
400 Seventh Street SW
Washington, DC 20590
Telephone: (202) 366-9550; (202) 366-0123 (DC area); (888) DASH-2-DOT or
    (888) 327-4236; (800) 424-9153 or (202) 366-7800 (hearing impaired)
Auto safety hotline: (800) 424-9393
Web site: www.nhtsa.dot.gov

NHTSA enforces safety performance standards for motor vehicles and motor vehicle equipment, and through grants to state and local governments to enable them to conduct effective local highway safety programs. NHTSA and its partners offer an array of tool kits and resources to help plan and implement comprehensive programs to make communities a safer and healthier place.

REGIONAL SUBSTANCE ABUSE AGENCIES

For location of the nearest Regional Alcohol and Drug Awareness Resource (RADAR) Network Center, contact:

National Clearinghouse for Alcohol and Drug Information (NCADI)
P.O. Box 2345
Rockville, MD 20847-2345
Telephone: (800) 729-6686
TDD: (800) 487-4889
Web site: www.health.org/about/radar

A far-reaching resource established by the federal government's Center for Substance Abuse Prevention, RADAR provides immediate access to substance abuse prevention and treatment resources. The RADAR Network provides local support to prevention practitioners and other community members interested in addressing alcohol, tobacco, and other drug problems. The RADAR Network consists of (1) state clearinghouses, (2) prevention resource centers (currently there are over 750 centers), (3) Department of Education Regional Training Centers; and (4) national, international, and local organizations supporting substance abuse prevention activities.

The RADAR Network Centers gather, share, and exchange information responding to both the immediate and the long-term substance abuse prevention needs of their communities and operate as an integral part of NCADI's distribution system.

STATE SUBSTANCE ABUSE AGENCIES

Each state has an easily accessible office that deals with AOD issues. The following alphabetic list provides relevant contact information:

Alabama
Dept. of Mental Health and Retardation
Substance Abuse Services Division
P.O. Box 301410
100 N. Union Street
Montgomery, AL 36130-1410
Telephone: (334) 242-3961
Fax: (334) 242-0759
Web site: www.mh.state.al.us/services/sa/sa-main.html

Alaska
Division of Alcoholism and Drug Abuse
Dept. of Health and Social Services
240 Main Street, Suite 700
Juneau, AK 99801
Telephone: (907) 465-2071
Fax: (907) 465-2185
Web site: www.health.hss.state.ak.us/dada

American Samoa
Dept. of Human and Social Services
American Samoa Govt.
P.O. Box 997534
Pago Pago, AS 96799
Telephone: (684) 633-2609
Fax: (684) 633-7449

Arizona
Behavioral Health Services
Div. of Substance Abuse/General Mental Health
2122 East Highland Street, Suite 100
Phoenix, AZ 85016
Telephone: (602) 381-8999
Fax: (602) 553-9143
Web site. www.hs.state.az.us/bhs

Arkansas
Bureau of Alcohol and Drug Abuse Prevention
5800 West 10th Street
Freeway Medical Center, Suite 907
Little Rock, AR 72204
Telephone: (501) 280-4505
Fax: (501) 280-4519
E-mail: pwagner@healthyarkansas.com

California
Dept. of Alcohol and Drug Programs
1700 K Street
Sacramento, CA 95814-4037
Telephone: (800) 879-2772
Fax: (916) 323-1270
Web site: www.adp.ca.gov

Colorado
Alcohol and Drug Abuse Division
Dept. of Human Services
4055 S. Lowell Blvd.
Denver, CO 80236-3120
Telephone: (303) 866-7480
Fax: (303) 866-7481
Web site: www.cdhs.state.co.us/ohr/adad/index.html

Connecticut
Dept. of Mental Health and Addiction Services
410 Capitol Avenue, 4th Floor
P.O. Box 341431, Mail Stop #14COM
Hartford, CT 06134
Telephone: (860) 418-7000
Fax: (860) 418-6691
Web site: www.dmhas.state.ct.us

Delaware
Alcohol and Drug Treatment Services
Div. of Substance Abuse and Mental Health
1901 North DuPont Highway
Adm. Building, First Floor
New Castle, DE 19720
Telephone: (302) 577-4460
Fax: (302) 577-4486
Web site: www.state.de.us/dhass/dsamh/dmhhome.htm

District of Columbia
Addiction Prevention and Recovery Administration
Dept. of Health
825 N. Capitol Street NE, Suite 3132
Washington, DC 20002
Telephone: (202) 442-9152
Fax: (202) 442-4827
Web site: www.dchealth.com/apra/welcome.htm

Florida
Substance Abuse Program Office
Florida Dept. of Children and Families
1317 Winewood Blvd.
Building 6, Room 334
Tallahassee, FL 32399-0700
Telephone: (850) 487-2920
Fax: (850) 487-2239
Web site: www5.myflorida.com/cf_web myflorida2/healthhuman
    /substanceabusementalhealth

Georgia
Division of Mental Health/Mental Retardation & Substance Abuse
Two Peachtree Street NW
23rd Floor, Suite 23.204
Atlanta, GA 30303-3171
Telephone: (404) 657-2135
Fax: (404) 657-2160
Web site: www.dmh.dhr.state.ga.us

Guam
Drug and Alcohol Treatment Services
Clinical Services Division
790 Governor Carlos Camacho Road
Tamuning, GU 96911
Telephone: (671) 647-5440
Fax: (671) 649-6948

Hawaii
Dept. of Health
Alcohol and Drug Abuse Division
Kakuhihewa Bldg.
601 Kamokila Blvd., Room 360
Kapolei, HI 96707
Telephone: (808) 692-7506
Fax: (808) 692-7521
Web site: www.hawaii.gov/health/resource/drug_abuse.html

Idaho
Bureau of Mental Health and Substance Abuse
Dept. of Health and Welfare
450 W. State Street, 5th Floor
P.O. Box 83720
Boise, ID 83720-0036
Telephone: (208) 334-5935
Fax: (208) 334-6699
Web site: www2.state.id.us/dhw/mentalhealth/index.htm

Illinois
Dept. of Alcoholism and Substance Abuse
100 West Randolph, Suite 5-600
Chicago, IL 60601
Telephone: (312) 814-3840
Fax: (312) 814-2419
Web site: www.state.il.us/agency/dhs/newsasanp.html

Indiana
Div. of Mental Health and Addiction
Family and Social Services Administration
402 W. Washington Street, Room W353
Indianapolis, IN 46204-2739
Telephone: (317) 232-7800
Fax: (317) 233-3472
Web site: www.in.gov/fssa

Iowa
Div. of Health Promotion, Prevention, and Addictive Behaviors
Dept. Public Health
Lucas State Office Building, 4th Floor
321 East 12th Street
Des Moines, IA 50319-0075
Telephone: (515) 281-4417
Fax: (515) 281-4535
Web site: www.idph.state.ia.us/sa.htm

Kansas
Substance Abuse/Mental Health and Developmental Disabilities
Substance Abuse Treatment Recovery Unit
DSOB 5th Floor North
915 Harrison Street
Topeka, KS 66612
Telephone: (785) 296-7272
Fax: (785) 296-0494
Web site: www.srskansas.org/hcp/mhsatr/mhsatr.htm

Kentucky
Dept. for Mental Health/Mental Retardation Services
Division of Substance Abuse
100 Fair Oaks Lane, 4E-D
Frankfort, KY 40621
Telephone: (502) 564-2880
Fax: (502) 564-7152

Louisiana
Dept. Health and Hospitals
Office for Addictive Disorders
1201 Capitol Access Road
P.O. Box 2790 BIN 18
Baton Rouge, LA 70821-2790
Telephone: (410) 402-8600
Fax: (410) 342-3875
Web site: www.dhh.state.la.us/oada

Maine
Office of Substance Abuse
Dept. of Behavioral and Developmental Services
AMHI Complex, Marquardt Bldg.
SHS #159, 3rd Floor
Augusta, ME 04333-0159
Telephone: (800) 499-0027
Fax: (207) 287-4334

Maryland
Dept. of Health and Mental Hygiene
Alcohol and Drug Abuse Administration
55 Wade Avenue
Catonsville, MD 21228
Telephone: (410) 402-8600
Fax: (410) 402-8602
Web site: www.maryland-adaa.org

Massachusetts
Bureau of Substance Abuse Services
Dept. of Public Health
250 Washington Street, 3rd Floor
Boston, MA 02108-4619
Telephone: (617) 624-5111
Fax: (617) 624-5185
Web site: www.state.ma.us/dph/bsas/bsas.htm

Michigan
Div. of Substance Abuse Quality and Planning
Dept. of Community Health
3423 N. Martin Luther King Blvd.
P.O. Box 30195
Lansing, MI 48909
Telephone: (517) 335-0278
Fax: (517) 241-2611
Web site: www.mdch.state.mi.us

Minnesota
Dept. of Human Services
Chemical Dependency Division
Human Services Building
444 Lafayette Road
Saint Paul, MN 55155-3823
Telephone: (651) 582-1832
Fax: (651) 585-1808

Mississippi
Div. of Alcohol and Drug Abuse
Dept. of Mental Health
Robert E. Lee Office Bldg., 11th Floor
239 North Lamar Street
Jackson, MS 39201
Telephone: (877) 210-8513
Fax: (601) 359-6295
Web site: www.dmh.state.ms.us/alcohol_and_drug_abuse_services.htm

Missouri
Dept. of Mental Health
Division of Alcohol and Drug Abuse
1706 East Elm Street
P.O. Box 687
Jefferson City, MO 65101
Telephone: (573) 751-4942
Fax: (573) 751-7814
Web site: www.modmh.state.mo.us/ada

Montana
Addictive and Mental Disorders Division
Dept. of Public Health and Health Services
555 Fuller
P.O. Box 202905
Helena, MT 59620-2905
Telephone: (406) 444-3964
Fax: (406) 444-9389
Web site: www.oraweb.hhs.state.mt.us/stats/dph_r3a.htm

Nebraska
Dept. of Health and Human Services System
Div. of Alcoholism and Drug Abuse
Lincoln Recreation Center, Campus Bldg. 14
Lincoln, NE 68509-4728
Telephone: (402) 479-5583
Fax: (402) 479-5162
Web site: www.hh.state.ne.us/beh/behindex.htm

Nevada
Bureau of Alcohol and Drug Abuse
Dept. of Human Resources, Health Division
505 E. King Street, Room 500
Carson City, NV 89701
Telephone: (775) 684-4190
Fax: (775) 684-4185
Web site: www.health2k.state.nv.us/bada

New Hampshire
Div. of Alcohol, Drug Abuse Prevention and Recovery
Dept. of Health and Human Services
105 Pleasant Street
Concord, NH 03301
Telephone: (800) 804-3345
Fax: (603) 271-6116
Web site: www.dhhs.state.nh.us/Index.nsf?Open

New Jersey
Div. of Addiction Services
Dept. of Health and Senior Services
120 S. Stockton Street, 3rd Floor
P.O. Box 362
Trenton, NH 08625-0362
Telephone: (609) 292-5760
Fax: (609) 292-3816
Web site: www.state.nj.us/health/as/abuse.htm

New Mexico
Behavioral Health Services Division
Dept. of Health
1190 Saint Francis Drive
Harold Runnels Bldg., Room 3300 North
Santa Fe, NM 87502
Telephone: (505) 827-2601
Fax: (505) 827-0097
Web site: www.health.state.nm.us

New York
State Office of Alcoholism and Substance Abuse Services
1450 Western Avenue
Albany, NY 12203-3526
Telephone: (518) 473-3460
Fax: (518) 457-2335
Web site: www.oasas.state.ny.us

North Carolina
Substance Abuse Services
Div. of Mental Health/DD/Substance Abuse Services
325 North Salisbury Street, Suite 1156-P
3007 Mail Center
Raleigh, NC 27699-3007
Telephone: (701) 328-8920
Fax: (701) 733-9455
Web site: www.dhhs.state.nc.us/mhddssas

North Dakota
Div. of Mental Health and Substance Abuse Services
Dept. of Human Services
600 South 2nd Street, Suite 1E
Bismarck, ND 58504-5729
Telephone: (701) 328-8920
Fax: (701) 328-8969
Web site: www.Inotes.state.nd.us/dhs/dhsweb.nsf

Ohio
Dept. of Alcohol and Drug Addiction Services
280 North High Street, 12th Floor
Two Nationwide Plaza
Columbus, OH 43215-2537
Telephone: (614) 644-8440
Fax: (614) 752-8645
Web site: www.statc.oh.us/ada/odada:htm

Oklahoma
Substance Abuse Program
Dept. of Mental Health and Substance Abuse Services
1200 NE 13th, 2nd Floor
P.O. Box 53277
Oklahoma City, OK 73152-3277
Telephone: (405) 522-3877
Fax: (405) 522-0637
Web site: www.odmhsas.org/subab.htm

Oregon
Office of Alcohol and Drug Abuse Programs
Dept. of Human Services
500 Summer Street NE, E86
Salem, OR 97301-1118
Telephone: (503) 945-5763
Fax: (503) 378-8467
Web site: www.oadap.hr.state.or.us

Pennsylvania
Dept. of Health
Bureau of Drug and Alcohol Programs
02 Kline Plaza, Suite B
Harrisburg, PA 17104
Telephone: (717) 783-8200
Fax: (717) 787-6285
Web site: www.health.state.pa.us/php/sca/default.htm

Puerto Rico
Dept. of Mental Health and Anti-Addiction
Services Administration
Barboza Ave.
P.O. Box 21414, Hato Rey Station
Hato Rey, PR 00928-1414
Telephone: (787) 764-3795
Fax: (787) 764-3670

Republic of Palau
Ministry of Health
P.O. Box 6027
Koror, Palau, PW 96940
(680) 488-2913; (680) 488-1211

Rhode Island
Div. of Substance Abuse/Dept. of MHRH
Barry Hall Bldg. 052
14 Harrington Road
Cranston, RI 02920
Telephone: (401) 462-4680
Fax: (401) 462-6078
Web site: www.mhrh.state.ri.us/Divisions.htm

South Carolina
Dept. of Alcohol and Other Drug Abuse Services
101 Business Park Blvd.
Columbia, SC 29203-9498
Telephone: (803) 896-5555
Fax: (803) 896-5557
Web site: www.daodas.org

South Dakota
Dept. of Human Services
Div. of Mental Health and Substance Abuse
East Highway 34, Hillsview Plaza
c/o 500 East Capitol
Pierre, SD 57501-5070
Telephone: (605) 773-3123
Fax: (605) 773-7076
Web site: www.state.sd.us/dhs/ada

Tennessee
Dept. of Health
Bureau of Alcohol and Drug Abuse Services
3rd Floor, Cordell Hull Bldg.
425 5th Avenue North
Nashville, TN 37247-4401
Telephone: (615) 741-1921
Fax: (615) 532-2419
Web site: www.State.tn.us/health/links.html

Texas
Commission on Alcohol and Drug Abuse
9001 N. IH 35, Suite 105
P.O. Box 80529
Austin, TX 78708-0529
Telephone: (512) 349-6600
Fax: (512) 821-4490
Web site: www.tcada.state.tx.us

Utah
Div. of Substance Abuse
Utah Dept. of Human Services
120 N 200 West
2nd Floor, Room 201
Salt Lake City, UT 84103
Telephone: (801) 538-3939
Fax: (801) 538-4696
Web site: www.Utahdsa.com

Vermont
Dept. of Health
Div. of Alcohol and Drug Abuse Programs
108 Cherry Street
P.O. Box 70
Burlington, VT 05402
Telephone: (802) 651-1550
Fax: (802) 651-1573

Virgin Islands
Charles Harwood Hospital
Dept. of Mental Health
3500 Richmond Street
Christiansted Saint Croix, VI 00820-4370
Telephone: (809) 773-1311
Fax: (809) 733-7900

Virginia
Office of Substance Abuse Services
Dept. of MH/MR & SAS
P.O. Box 1797
109 Governor Street
Richmond, VA 23218
Telephone: (804) 786-3906
Fax: (804) 786-4320
Web site: www.dmhmrsas.state.va.us

Washington
Dept. of Social and Health Services
Div. of Alcohol and Substance Abuse
P.O. Box 45330
612 Woodland Square Loop SE, Bldg. C
Olympia, WA 98504-5330
Telephone: (877) 301-4557
Fax: (877) 438-8078
Web site: www-app2.wa.gov/dshs/dasa/index.htm

West Virginia
Div. on Alcoholism and Drug Abuse
Dept. of Health and Human Resources
350 Capitol Street, Room 350
Charleston, WV 25301-3702
Telephone: (304) 558-2276
Fax: (304) 558-1008
Web site: www.wvdhhr.org/obhs/dad.htm

Wisconsin
Bureau of Substance Abuse Services
Div. of Supportive Living
Dept. of Health and Family Services
P.O. Box 7851
Madison, WI 53707-7851
Telephone: (608) 266-2717
Fax: (608) 266-1533
Web site: www.dhfs.state.wi.us/substabuse/index.htm

Wyoming
Substance Abuse Division
2424 Pioneer Avenue, Suite 306
Cheyenne, WY 82002-0480
Telephone: (307) 777-6494
Fax: (307) 777-7006
Web site: www.sa.state.wy.us

State Gaming Councils

Some states also sponsor programs to assist compulsive gamblers and their families. These state councils offer certification programs for health care professionals who counsel these individuals. The certification model utilizes standards of training and treatment procedures as set forth by the National Council on Problem Gambling.

Arizona Council on Compulsive Gambling
2922 North 7th Avenue
Phoenix, AZ 85013
Telephone: (602) 212-0278
Fax: (602) 212-1725
Crisis Helpline: (800) 777-7207
Web site: www.azccg.org

California Council on Problem Gambling
121 S. Palm Canyon Drive, Suite 225
Palm Springs, CA 92262
Telephone: (800) FACTS4U; (800) 322-8748; (760) 320-0234
Fax: (760) 416-1349
Helpline: (800) GAMBLER
E-mail: info@calproblemgambling.org
Web site: www.calproblemgambling.org

Connecticut Council on Problem Gambling
47 Clapboard Hill Road
Guilford, CT 06437
Telephone: (203) 453-0138
Fax: (203) 453-9142
Helpline: (800) 34 NOBET
Web site: www.ccpg.org

Massachusetts Council on Compulsive Gambling
190 High Street, Suite 5
Boston, MA 02110-3031
Telephone: (617) 426-4554
Helpline: (800) 426-1234 (MA only)
Fax: (617) 426-4555
Web site: www.masscompulsivegambling.org

Minnesota Council on Compulsive Gambling
See the North American Training Organization under
    "Professional Organizations"
Web site: www.nati.org

Mississippi Council on Problem and Compulsive Gambling
E-mail: mcpcg@netdoor.com
Helpline: (888) 777-9696
Web site: www.msgambler.org

New Jersey Council on Compulsive Gambling
3635 Quakerbridge Road, Suite 7
Hamilton, NJ 08619
Telephone: (609) 588-5515
Fax: (609) 588-5665
Helpline: 800-GAMBLER©
E-mail: ccgnj@800gambler.org
Web site: www.800gambler.org

EDUCATIONAL AND TRAINING INSTITUTIONS

The following leading universities offer AOD training and research programs:

Brown University
Center for Alcohol and Addiction Studies
Butler Hospital Campus
345 Blackstone Blvd.
Providence, RI
Telephone: (401) 444-1800
Fax: (401) 444-1850
E-mail: CAAS@brown.edu
Web site: http://center.butler.brown.edu

The center promotes the identification, prevention, and treatment of alcohol and other drug use problems through research, education, training, and policy advocacy. Postdoctoral research training is offered in the behavioral, medical, and social sciences and for health care professionals who wish to pursue careers in AOD research.

Project ADEPT, established in 1986, was the first teaching package of its kind for medical schools. It provides instructional materials for basic knowledge and treatment skills regarding AOD. The first two volumes have become the foundation of medical school curricula, currently being used in 80% of the medical schools in the United States, as well as in Canada, Australia, England, and the Netherlands.

Columbia University
National Center on Addiction and Substance Abuse (CASA)
633 Third Avenue, 19th Floor
New York, NY 10017-6706
Telephone: (732) 445-2190
Fax: (732) 956-8020
Web site: www.casacolumbia.org

Organized in four divisions—Health and Treatment Research and Analysis, Policy Research and Analysis, and Program Demonstration and Communications— CASA conducts comprehensive evaluations of AOD treatment programs across the country, assesses the effects of AOD on the nation, focuses on children at risk, ex-offender/ex-addicts, and substance-abusing women on welfare, and annually surveys the attitudes of teenagers, their parents, teachers, and principals.

Gemini Research
P.O. Box 1390
Northampton, MA 01061-1390
Telephone: (413) 584-4667
Web site: www.geminiresearch.com

The only international organization that specializes in managing and reporting on studies of gambling and problem gambling, Gemini Research, Ltd., has extensive experience with survey development, questionnaire design, and sampling methods as well as statistical analysis and interpretation.

Harvard Medical School, Division on Addictions
350 Longwood Avenue, Suite 200
Boston, Massachusetts 02115
Telephone: (617) 432-0058
Fax: (617) 432-0057
E-mail: doa@hms.harvard.edu
Web site: www.hms.harvard.edu/doa

The Division seeks to strengthen worldwide understanding of addiction through innovative research, education, and the global exchange of information. The ultimate goal is to alleviate the individual, social, medical, and economic burdens of addictive behaviors. The Division offers encouragement, education, and training to both the next generation of health care workers and to scientists who study addiction, and provides information to public policymakers and the public.

Missouri Alcoholism Research Center (MARC)
Department of Psychiatry
Campus Box 8134
Washington University School of Medicine
St. Louis, MO 63108
Telephone: (314) 286-2206
E-mail: andrew@matlock.wustl.edu
Web site: www.missouri.edu/~marc/program

A collaborative program of researchers at Washington University School of Medicine, St. Louis University, the University of Missouri, Columbia, the Palo Alto Veterans Administration Medical Center, and Queensland Institute of Medical

Research in Australia, MARC focuses on the etiology and course of alcohol problems and associated comorbidity in community samples of adolescents and youth. Center-wide research themes involve testing three classes of mediational models for alcoholism risk: (1) pharmacological vulnerability; (2) negative affect-regulation; (3) deviance proneness—in a series of prospective behavioral, genetic, and family studies, as well as laboratory-based studies.

> North American Training Institute
> 314 West Superior Street, Suite 702
> Duluth, MN 55802
> Telephone: (218) 722-1503; (888) 989-9234
> Fax: (888) 722-0346
> E-mail: info@nati.org
> Web site: www.nati.org

Established in 1988, the NATI is a private, not-for-profit, Minnesota-based corporation that recently merged with the American Academy of Health Providers in the Addictive Disorders. It develops and presents professional training programs and courses, research facilitation, and distributes research-based information on the topics of pathological and underage gambling. It also operates a problem gambling helpline service, convenes public policy think tanks to discuss concerns and strategies for the management of problem gambling, designs responsible gaming programs for the gaming and wagering industries, and serves the medical community by providing continuing medical education (CME) programs.

> Rutgers University, Center of Alcohol Studies (CAS)
> 607 Allison Road
> Piscataway, NJ 08854-8001
> Telephone: (732) 445-2190
> Fax: (732) 445-3500
> Web site: www.rci.rutgers.edu/~cas2

A multidisciplinary institute, CAS is dedicated to acquisition and dissemination of knowledge on psychoactive substance use, with primary emphasis on alcohol use and consequences. It uses five central themes: (1) to conduct research (basic, clinical, and applied) on the nature, development, etiology, and treatment of psychoactive substance use, misuse, abuse, and dependence by employing relevant biological, psychological, and sociocultural paradigms; (2) to develop, implement, and evaluate theory-driven prototypical clinical, prevention, and educational programs and services for appropriate target populations and constituent communities; (3) to facilitate the transfer and utilization of the Center's expertise by providing educational and training experiences for undergraduate, graduate, and postgraduate students and professionals in basic knowledge, the conduct of research, and the delivery of clinical and prevention services; and to adapt and extend this expertise and knowledge to other individuals, groups, organizations, and agencies in the community; (4) to provide broad access to the knowledge base essential to students, researchers, clinicians, prevention, and education specialists, and concerned others by identifying, organizing, and disseminating the fundamental empirical, theoretical, and practical literature of the field through a multiformatted collection; and (5) to assist agencies and organizations, public and private, charged with the responsibility to formulate policy in the analysis of issues related to psychoactive substance use, misuse, abuse, and dependence.

> University at Buffalo, The State University of New York, Research Institute
>   on Addictions (RIA)
> 1021 Main Street
> Buffalo, NY 14203-1016
> Telephone: (716) 887-2566
> Web site: www.ria.org

The RIA contributes to the following broad areas of addictions research: the etiology, prevention, and treatment of addictions; the role of alcohol and other drugs in violence needs of special populations, including minorities, women, and youth; family functioning and its relationship to alcohol and substance use; the assessment and treatment of persons arrested for driving while intoxicated; and the social, medical, psychological, and neurophysical aspects of addictions gambling.

> University of California, Los Angeles
> Integrated Substance Abuse Programs (ISAP)
> 1640 S. Sepulveda Blvd., Suite 200
> Los Angeles, CA 90025
> Telephone: (310) 445-0874 or
> 11050 Santa Monica Blvd., Suite 100
> Los Angeles, CA 90025
> Telephone: (310) 312-0500
> Web site: www.npi.ucla.edu/center/isap

The ISAP coordinates substance abuse research and treatment within the Department of Psychiatry and Biobehavioral Sciences at the UCLA School of Medicine. One of the largest substance abuse research groups in the United States (including more than 300 researchers, clinicians, and support personnel), its network of activities extends from highly sophisticated and specialized laboratory research (including molecular genetics, brain imaging, and medication testing), to pharmacological and behavioral clinical research, to community-based research, research on public health policy, and substance abuse treatment services. The seven basic categories of ISAP activities are (1) Substance Abuse Treatment Services, (2) Biobehavioral Research, (3) Clinical Trials Network, (4) Treatment Outcomes and Health Services Research, (5) Substance Abuse Policy and International Issues, (6) Practice Improvement and Research-to-Practice Efforts, and (7) Training and Education.

> University of California, San Diego
> Addiction Training Center
> 565 Pearl Street, Suite 306
> La Jolla, CA 92037-5051
> Telephone: (858) 551-2944
> Web site: www.attc.ucsd.edu

A training center in the Department of Psychiatry, their mission is to assist service systems and institutions develop capacities for addressing substance use disorders within populations they serve.

> University of Connecticut Health Center, Psychiatry
> The Gambling Treatment and Research Center
> 263 Farmington Avenue, Suite LG006
> Farmington, CT 06030-3944
> Telephone: (860) 679-2177; (877) 400-0570
> Fax: (860) 679-1312
> E-mail: gambling@psychiatry.uchc.edu
> Web site: http://gamblingtreatment.net

The Center conducts treatment studies that offer opportunities for gamblers to receive free and confidential treatment. New England adults 18 years or older may be eligible for one of several treatment studies (compensation is provided).

> University of Miami
> Center for Treatment Research on Adolescent Drug Abuse (CTRADA)
> E-mail: mpotoczniak@med.miami.edu
> Web site: www.med.miami.edu/ctrada

Founded in 1991, CTRADA was the first NIDA-funded clinical research center to focus on adolescent drug abuse treatment. Studying the development, refinement, and evaluation of family-oriented treatments for drug-abusing adolescents, its mission is to (1) create a scientific climate of discovery and rigor that will facilitate the expansion of knowledge in ADA treatment through basic and applied studies; (2) improve family-oriented treatments for drug-abusing adolescents; (3) test the efficacy and effectiveness of family-oriented as well as existing treatments for drug-abusing adolescents; (4) develop a greater understanding of treatment factors, and patient and family characteristics that increase or decrease the likelihood of treatment success; (5) create the opportunity for synergism among treatment studies and researchers targeting a broad range of ADA populations: dually diagnosed, ethnically diverse, gender specific; (6) disseminate information on successful treatment models to the local and national drug abuse community; (7) serve as a national resource to the National Institute on Drug Abuse (NIDA) for matters related to the treatment of ADA, and (8) promote translation of findings from basic to applied research practice and policy.

University of Michigan
Addiction Research Center (ARC)
400 E. Eisenhower, Suite 2A
Ann Arbor, MI 48108-0740
Telephone: (734) 615-6060
Fax: (734) 615-6085
Web site: www.med.umich.edu/psych/sub/research

The ARC conducts research into the causes, costs, and treatment of substance abuse. Ongoing research projects examine essential aspects of substance abuse ranging from genes to health care use. Areas currently being explored include *Neuropsychopharmacology, Developmental Psychopathology and Genetics, Treatment,* and *Health Services.*

The university also publishes *Monitoring the Future,* an ongoing study of the behaviors, attitudes, and values of American secondary school students, college students, and young adults. Each year, it surveys 50,000 8th-, 10th-, and 12th-grade students and also mails yearly follow-up questionnaires to a sample of each graduating class for a number of years after their initial participation. News releases, publications, and the most recent prevalence and incidence rates of adolescent substance abuse are at your fingertips. See http://monitoringthefuture.org.

University of Minnesota
Center for Addiction Studies (CAS)
Telephone: (218) 726-6261
Fax: (218) 726-6386
E-mail: jlaunde3@d.umn.edu

CAS conducts addictions research and provides campus coordination of teaching and addictions curricula. Established in 1990, the CAS assesses the prevalence and treatment of problem gambling in Minnesota.

University of Nevada, Reno
The Institute for the Study of Gambling & Commercial Gaming
College of Business Administration
Reno, NV 89557-1057
Telephone: (775) 784-1442
Fax: (775) 784-1057
Web site: www.unr.edu/gaming

Established in 1989, the Institute seeks to broaden the understanding of gambling and the commercial gaming industries. It aims to encourage and promote research and learning about the multifaceted issues surrounding gambling and commercial gaming and how they affect individuals and society.

University of New Mexico
Center on Alcoholism, Substance Abuse, and Addictions (CASAA)
2650 Yale SE
Albuquerque, NM 87106
Telephone: (505) 925-2350
Fax: (505) 925-2351
Web site: http://casaa.unm.edu

The CASAA mission is to generate new knowledge about alcoholism, substance abuse, and other addictive behaviors, and to foster communication and collaboration among researchers in multiple disciplines, and between researchers in applied areas.

University of North Carolina at Chapel Hill
Bowles Center for Alcohol Studies
CB#7178, Thurston Bowles Bldg.
Chapel Hill, NC 27599-7178
Telephone: (919) 966-5678
Fax: (919) 966-5679
Web site: www.med.unc.edu/alcohol

The Bowles Center conducts, coordinates, and promotes basic and clinical research on the causes, prevention, and treatment of alcoholism and alcohol abuse. It is one of 14 Alcohol Research Centers supported by the NIAAA.

University of Washington
Addictive Behaviors Research Center
Department of Psychology
Guthrie Annex III
P.O. Box 351525
Seattle, WA 98195-1525
Telephone: (206) 685-1200
Fax: (206) 685-1310
Web site: abrc@u.washington.edu

Established in 1981, its primary mission is to provide research, training, and evaluation in the development and dissemination of interventions to prevent and treat addictive behaviors.

PROFESSIONAL ADDICTION-RELATED ORGANIZATIONS

Significant professional organizations offer useful programs to addiction counselors.

Academy for Eating Disorders
6728 Old McLean Village Drive
McLean, VA 22101
Telephone: (703) 556-9222
Fax: (703) 556-8729
Web site: www.aedweb.org

Founded in 1995, the Academy is a multidisciplinary association of academic and clinical professionals with expertise in eating disorders. Its goals are to (1) promote the effective treatment and care of patients with eating disorders and associated disorders; (2) develop and advance initiatives for the primary and secondary prevention of eating disorders; (3) provide for the dissemination of knowledge regarding eating disorders to members of the Academy, other professionals, and the general public; (4) stimulate and support research in the field; (5) advocate for the field on behalf of patients, the public, and eating disorder professionals; (6) assist in the development of guidelines for training, practice, and professional conduct within the field; and (7) identify and reward outstanding achievement and service in the field.

Academy of Organizational and Occupational Psychiatry
717 Princess Street
Alexandria, VA 22314
Telephone: (877) 789-2667; (703) 683-4999
Fax: (877) 789-6050
E-mail: staff@aoop.org
Web site: www.aoop.org

The Academy's mission is to (1) enhance psychiatry's contribution to the well-being and productivity of workers, leaders, and work organizations; (2) enhance the knowledge and skills of its members through various training opportunities and professional networking; (3) liaison with other professional groups concerned with workplace health and mental health; and (4) encourage and support the practice of organizational and occupational psychiatry.

African American Family Services (AAFS)
2616 Nicollet Avenue South
Minneapolis, MN 55408
Telephone: (612) 871-7878
Fax: (612) 871-2567
Web site: www.aafs.net

Founded in 1975, the goal is to help the African American individual, family, and community reach a greater state of well-being through the delivery of community-based, culturally specific chemical health, mental health, and family preservation services. Originally called the Minnesota Institute on Black Chemical Abuse and then the Institute on Black Chemical Abuse, it became known as an effective treatment, prevention, and aftercare center. As it grew, its services expanded to encompass other issues that often coexist with chemical dependency.

American Academy of Addiction Psychiatry
7301 Mission Road, Suite 252
Prairie Village, KS 66208
Telephone: (913) 262-6161
Fax: (913) 262-4311
E-mail: Addicpsych@aol.com
Web site: www.aaap.org

The Academy's six goals are to (1) promote accessibility to the highest quality treatment for all who need it; (2) promote excellence in clinical practice in addiction psychiatry; (3) educate the public to influence public policy regarding addictive illness; (4) provide continuing education for addiction professionals; (5) disseminate new information in the field of addiction psychiatry; and (6) encourage research on the etiology, prevention, identification, and treatment of the addictions.

American Academy of Child and Adolescent Psychiatry (AACAP)
3615 Wisconsin Avenue NW
Washington, DC 20016-3007
Telephone: (202) 966-7300
Fax: (202) 966-2891
Web site: www.aacap.org

Established in 1953, AACAP is dedicated to treating and improving the quality of life for children, adolescents, and families affected by psychiatric disorders. A not-for-profit organization, its membership includes over 6,500 *child and adolescent psychiatrists* and other interested physicians.

American Academy of Health Care Providers in the Addictive Disorders
314 West Superior Street, Suite 702
Duluth, MN 55802
Telephone: (218) 727-3940
Fax: (218) 722-0346
E-mail: info@americanacademy.org
Web site: www.americanacademy.org

Established in 1989, the Academy is an international certification organization for addiction specialists. A nonprofit credentialing organization, it merged with the North American Training Institute to maintain quality standards for the treatment in the addictive disorders. The most comprehensive credential for AOD counseling, it covers AOD, eating disorders, compulsive gambling, and sex addiction. It unites clinicians from several disciplines (nurses, doctors, psychologists, psychiatrists, social workers, and counselors) under a single standard, all committed to providing the highest quality of health care to individuals suffering from addiction.

American Association for the Treatment of Opioid Dependence (AATOD)
217 Broadway, Suite 304
New York, NY 10007
Telephone: (212) 566-5555
Web site: www.aatod.org

Founded in 1984 as the Northeast Regional Methadone Treatment Coalition, Inc., its goals are to support the legitimacy of methadone maintenance as a valuable treatment for opioid dependence, to increase the availability of comprehensive treatment services to people in need of care, and to organize the national treatment community. AATOD works with federal and state agencies to assist members in complying with national and state standards, improving the quality of health care in member facilities, increasing the legitimacy of the treatment system, and greatly reducing the stigma often associated with the field.

American Council on Alcoholism (ACA)
P.O. Box 25126
Arlington, VA 22202
Telephone: (703) 248-9005
Fax: (703) 248-9007
E-mail: aca2@earthlink.net
Web site: www.aca-usa.org

Formed in Baltimore, Maryland, in 1976, it is a national agency that provides a cohesive, realistic, and coordinated approach to understanding alcoholism. A national voice that advocates a well-informed public as the best long-term defense against alcohol abuse and alcoholism, its objectives are to (1) increase public awareness and understanding of the disease of alcoholism and related issues; (2) provide a national information network of resources on prevention, treatment, research, education, and rehabilitation of alcoholism; (3) oppose restrictive approaches for controlling the disease of alcoholism that infringe on the freedom of many for the claimed betterment of a few; (4) emphasize the critical importance of early detection of alcoholism through education in schools, businesses, and communities; (5) promote improved services and facilities for the treatment of alcoholism; and (6) promote innovative early identification, treatment, and rehabilitation approaches that ensure continuity of care and delivery of quality services to persons with alcoholism.

American Counseling Association
5999 Stevenson Avenue
Alexandria, VA 22304
Telephone: (800) 347-6647
TDD: (703) 823-6862
Fax: (800) 473-2329
Web site: www.counseling.org

Founded in 1952 as a not-for-profit professional and educational organization dedicated to the growth and enhancement of the counseling profession, it is the world's largest counselors' association. By providing leadership training, publications, continuing education opportunities, and advocacy services to nearly 52,000 members, ACA helps counseling professionals develop their skills and expand their knowledge base. Instrumental in setting professional and ethical standards for the counseling profession, the ACA offers accreditation, licensure, and national certification and represents the interests of the profession before Congress and federal agencies.

American Lung Association (ALA)
61 Broadway, 6th Floor
New York, NY 10006
Telephone: (212) 315-8700
Web site: www.lungusa.org

Founded in 1904 to fight tuberculosis, the ALA comprises a National Office and constituent and affiliate associations around the country. It is funded by contributions from the public, along with gifts and grants from corporations, foundations, and government agencies. The ALA achieves its many successes through the work of thousands of committed volunteers and staff. It has been instrumental in persuading Congress to increase federal funding for lung-related biomedical research, as well as domestic health programs such as tuberculosis control activities. It offers smoking control and prevention programs targeted to specific groups.

American Osteopathic Academy of Addiction Medicine
142 E. Ontario Street, Suite 1023
Chicago, IL 60611
Telephone: (312) 202-8163
Fax: (312) 202-8463
No e-mail

A small academy of paid members, it seeks to enhance knowledge about substance abuse and addiction issues for the osteopathic profession.

American Psychiatric Association
1000 Wilson Blvd., Suite 1825
Arlington, VA 22209-3901
Telephone: (703) 907-7300; (888) 35-PSYCH
American Psychiatric Press, Inc. (APPI) order lines: (800) 368-5777
Fax: (703) 907-7322
Web site: www.psych.org

A medical specialty society composed of 37,000 U.S. and international member physicians dedicated to ensuring humane care, accessible quality psychiatric diagnosis, and effective treatment for all persons with mental disorders, including substance-related disorders.

American Psychological Association
750 First Street, NE
Washington, DC 20002-4242
Telephone: (202) 336-6123; (800) 374-2721
E-mail: Apacollege@apa.org
Web site: www.apa.org

Based in Washington, DC, the APA represents over 83,000 psychologists in the United States. Two divisions deal with AOD issues. Division 50 (Addictions) promotes advances in research, professional training, and clinical practice about addictive behaviors, including problematic use of alcohol, nicotine, and other drugs and disorders involving gambling, eating, sexual behavior, or spending. It also publishes the quarterly journal, *Psychology of Addictive Behaviors* and a newsletter, the *Addictions Newsletter* (three issues per year). Homepage: www.apa.org/divisions/div50. Division 28 (Psychopharmacology and Substance Abuse) is involved with teaching, research, and dissemination of information on the behavioral effects of medicine, drugs, and chemicals in both the laboratory and the clinic. The Division publishes the quarterly *Psychopharmacology Newsletter*. Homepage: www.apa.org/divisions/div28.

American Psychological Society
1010 Vermont Avenue NW, Suite 1100
Washington, DC 20005-4907
Telephone: (202) 783-2077
Fax: (202) 783-2083

Founded in 1988, the Society promotes, protects, and advances the interests of scientifically oriented psychology in research, application, teaching, and the improvement of human welfare. It publishes (1) *Psychological Science* (a scientific journal of authoritative articles across all of scientific psychology's subdisciplines); (2) *Current Directions in Psychological Science* (concise reviews written by leading experts that span all of scientific psychology and its applications), and (3) *Psychological Science in the Public Interest* (definitive assessments of topics where psychological science may have the potential to inform and improve the well-being of society).

American Society of Addiction Medicine (ASAM)
4601 North Park Avenue, Arcade Suite 101
Chevy Chase, MD 20815-4520
Telephone: (301) 656-3920
Fax: (301) 656-3815
E-mail: Email@asam.org
Web site: www.asam.org

New York Office:
12 West 21st Street
New York, NY 10010
Telephone: (212) 206-6776
Fax: (212) 627-9540

ASAM represents physicians from all medical specialties and subspecialties. The AMA recognizes addiction medicine (ADM) as one of its designated specialties.

American Sociological Association (ASA)
1307 New York Avenue NW, Suite 700
Washington, DC 20005
Telephone: (402) 479-5574
TDD: 872-0486
Fax: (402) 638-0882

Founded in 1905, the ASA is a nonprofit membership association dedicated to advancing sociology as a scientific discipline. Its Section on Alcohol and Drugs encourages research, teaching, and the examination of professional concerns in the study of alcohol and drugs and promotes communication and collaboration among scholars in the AOD field.

Association of Problem Gambling Service Administrators (APGSA)
Gamblers Assistance Program Manager
P.O. Box 94728
Lincoln, NE 68509-4728
Telephone: (402) 479-5574
Fax: (402) 479-5162
E-mail: tim.christensen@hhss.state.ne.us
Web site: www.apgsa.org

Formed in 2000, the APGSA serves as a forum for improving data gathering, reporting, research, and public awareness efforts relative to problem gambling. It provides (1) a unified voice to advocate for problem gamblers; (2) gambling services; (3) establishment of cohesive and appropriate best practices models for problem gambling service delivery in the public sector; (4) an environment in which accurate and timely information is easily disseminated; (5) research focusing on prevention, treatment, and public awareness efforts relative to problem gambling; and (6) a contact for those seeking information on publicly funded problem gambling efforts.

Center for Internet Studies (web site)
www.virtual-addiction.com

The Center's goal is to prevent the negative behaviors that result from Internet abuse and addiction. It provides consultation, training, and research services to the business community, schools and universities, mental health providers, and families.

Clinical Social Work Federation (CSWF)
239 N. Highland Street
Arlington, VA 22201
Telephone: (703) 560-4042
Fax: (703) 560-4232
Web site: www.cswf.org

A confederation of 31 state societies for clinical social work, the CSWF is a voluntary association that promotes professional education and clinical practice by (1) advocating on behalf of members of the state societies with the federal government and other national organizations; (2) assisting state societies in education, marketing, reimbursement, research, image building, promoting standards and competence, legislation and regulation, and related areas at the state and national levels; (3) providing the means for clinicians with common interests to work collectively on a national level; and (4) providing information to and advocacy for client populations who need and can benefit from clinical social work services.

Institute for Problem Gambling (IPG)
955 South Main Street
Middletown, CT 06457
Telephone: (860) 343-5500, ext. 2130
Fax: (860) 347-3183
Web site: www.gamblingproblem.net

A not-for-profit institute founded in 1997, the IPG provides science-based information on the study, prevention, and treatment of problem gambling. It offers

(1) training, (2) professional expertise concerning treatment, prevention, and research on problem gambling, (3) an Internet resource offering current information, products, and services, (4) a reference and resource library, and (5) the development of public service announcements, educational videos, and instructional manuals.

International Nurses Society on Addictions (IntNSA)
P.O. Box 10752
Raleigh, NC 27605
Telephone: (919) 821-1292
Fax: (919) 833-5743
Web site: www.intnsa.org

A professional specialty organization for nurses interested in the prevention, intervention, treatment, and management of addictive disorders including AOD, nicotine dependencies, eating disorders, dual and multiple diagnosis, and process addictions such as gambling. IntNSA advances addictions nursing practice through advocacy, collaboration, education, research, and policy development, and seeks to be a global leader in addictions nursing.

Johnson Institute (JI)
1273 National Press Building
Washington, DC 20045
Telephone: (202) 662-7104

Minnesota Office:
10001 Wayzata Blvd.
Minnetonka, MN 55305
Telephone: (952) 582-2713
Web site: www.johnsoninstitute.org

Since the 1960s, the JI has addressed barriers to AOD prevention, treatment, and recovery by promoting "intervention," a method that penetrates denial and helps addicts accept professional help. From a church study group, JI's founders challenged the idea that alcoholics could not get help until they reached a "bottom" (a state of surrender after family, job, finances, or other supports had evaporated). JI has trained thousands of counselors, pioneered in workplace employee assistance programs, and addressed family and youth aspects of AOD.

Join Together (JT)
One Appleton Street, 4th Floor
Boston, MA 02116-5223
Telephone: (617) 437-1500
Fax 437-9394
Web site: www.jointogether.org
E-mail: info@jointogether.org

Founded in 1991, JT supports community-based efforts to reduce, prevent, and treat substance abuse across the nation. It is primarily funded by the Robert Wood Johnson Foundation, and the Boston University School of Public Health, JT's scope includes gun violence prevention, supported by grants from the Joyce Foundation and the David Bohnett Foundation.

National Association of Addiction Treatment Providers (NAATP)
313 W. Liberty Street, Suite 129
Lancaster, PA 17603-2748
Telephone: (717) 392-8480
Fax: (717) 392-8481
Web site: www.naatp.org

NAATP promotes, assists, and enhances the delivery of ethical and effective research-based treatment for alcoholism and other drug addictions by (1) providing its members and the public with accurate, responsible information and other resources related to the treatment of these diseases; (2) advocating for increased access to and availability of quality treatment for those who suffer from alcoholism and other drug addictions; and (3) working in partnership with other organizations and individuals that share NAATP's mission and goals.

National Association of Alcoholism and Drug Abuse Counselors (NAADAC)
The Association for Addiction Professionals
901 N. Washington Street, Suite 600
Alexandria, VA 22314
Telephone: (703) 741-7686; (800) 548-0497
Fax: (800) 741-7698; (800) 377-1136
E-mail: naadac@naadac.org
Web site: www.naadac.org

Founded in 1972, NAADAC serves counselors who specialize in addiction treatment. With nearly 14,000 members and 47 state affiliates representing more than 80,000 addiction counselors in the United States, it recently changed its name to the Association for Addiction Professionals to reflect the recognition of other addictions such as tobacco and gambling. Its national certification programs include the National Certified Addiction Counselor and the Masters Addiction Counselor designations. In the past 8 years, NAADAC has credentialed more than 15,000 counselors.

National Association of Drug Court Professionals (NADCP)
4900 Seminary Road, Suite 320
Alexandria, VA 22311
Telephone: (703) 575-9400
Fax: (703) 575-9402
Web site: www.nadcp.org

Founded in 1994, the NADCP seeks to reduce substance abuse, crime, and recidivism by promoting and advocating the establishment and funding of Drug Courts and providing collection and dissemination of information, technical assistance, and mutual support for association members. It seeks to alter how the criminal justice system adjudicates offenders with AOD problems to ensure short-term accountability in the criminal adjudication process and a long-term reduction in recidivism. Instead of incarceration, it offers a therapeutic approach whereby offenders are required to undergo drug treatment, frequent drug testing, and close monitoring with regular court visits. There were initially only 12 drug courts, now there are more than 1,000.

National Association of Social Workers (NASW)
750 First Street NE, Suite 700
Washington, DC 20002-4241
Telephone: (202) 408-8600; (800) 638-8799
Web site: www.naswdc.org

Comprising nearly 150,000 social workers, NASW works to enhance the growth and development of its members, to create and maintain professional standards, and to advance sound social policies. They offer various publications, advocacy resources, and opportunities for professional development. The *NASW Press* is a leading scholarly publication in the social sciences that serves faculty, practitioners, agencies, libraries, clinicians, and researchers throughout the United States and abroad.

National Center for Responsible Gaming (NCRG)
P.O. Box 14323
Washington, DC 20044-4323
(No telephone number exists.)
E-mail: contact@ncrg.org
Web site: www.ncrg.org

Founded in 1996, the NCRG is devoted exclusively to funding independent, peer-reviewed scientific research on pathological and youth gambling. Its mission is to help individuals and families affected by gambling disorders by supporting peer-reviewed research; encouraging the application of new research findings to improve prevention, diagnostic, intervention, and treatment strategies; and enhancing public awareness. A tax-exempt, nonprofit organization, NCRG is governed by a volunteer board of directors.

National Coalition against Legalized Gambling (NCALG)
100 Maryland Avenue NE, Room 311
Washington, DC 20002
National Information Telephone Center: (800) 664-2680
Fax: (307) 587-8082
Web site: www.ncalg.org

Concerned with the rapid expansion of gambling and its effect on youths, families, and governments, the NCALG, since 1994, has opposed the gambling industry in every forum at every level with every educational tool available. Its goals are to (1) provide information, research, and technical support to state groups battling the expansion of gambling; (2) travel to states across the country to provide knowledge on how to organize at the grassroots level; (3) reach out to other national, state, and local groups for support, especially in retail business, entertainment, mental health, and law enforcement; (4) act as a clearinghouse through its National Information Center and antigambling Internet site.

National Commission Against Drunk Driving (NCADD)
8403 Colesville Road, Suite 370
Silver Spring, MD 20910
Telephone: (240) 247-6004
Fax: (240) 247-7012
Web site: www.ncadd.com

The NCADD continues the efforts of the Presidential Commission on Drunk Driving to reduce impaired driving and its tragic consequences. By uniting a broad-based coalition of public and private sector organizations and other concerned individuals, they identify strategies and programs that show promise in reducing the incidence of driving impaired, especially among 21- to 34-year-old adults; chronic drunk drivers, and underage drinkers.

National Council on Alcoholism and Drug Dependence, Inc. (NCADD)
20 Exchange Place, Suite 2902
New York, NY 10005-3201
Telephone: (212) 269-7797; 800-NCA-CALL
Fax: (212) 269-7510
E-mail: national@ncadd.org
Web site: www.ncadd.org

Founded in 1944, NCADD is a voluntary health organization with a nationwide network of affiliates that provides education, information, help, and hope in the fight against AOD. Advocating prevention, intervention, research, and treatment, NCADD is dedicated to ridding AOD of its stigma and its sufferers from their denial and shame. A hope line is open 24 hours a day to provide information and refer calls to local NCA affiliates.

National Council on Problem Gambling, Inc. (NCPG)
208 G Street NE
Washington, DC 20002
Telephone: (202) 547-9204
Helpline: (800) 522-4700 (national 24-hour)
Fax: (202) 547-9206
E-mail: ncpg@ncpgambling.org
Web site: www.ncpgambling.org

A tax-exempt, nonprofit organization that maintains a neutral stance on gambling, NCPG currently has 34 state affiliate chapters, and numerous corporate and individual members. Its mission is to increase public awareness of pathological gambling, ensure the widespread availability of treatment for problem gamblers and their families, and encourage research and programs for prevention and education. It publishes the *Journal of Gambling Studies,* offers a 24-hour confidential Help line, provides regional, national, and international conferences, distributes literature, works with other organizations involved in problem gambling issues, and offers a gambling-specific certification program for treatment professionals.

National Council on Sexual Addiction and Compulsivity (NCSAC)
P.O. Box 725544
Atlanta, GA 31139
Telephone: (770) 541-9912
Web site: www.ncsac.org

A private, nonprofit organization that promotes public and professional recognition, awareness, and understanding about sexual addiction, compulsivity, and offending. NCSAC goals are to (1) promote public and professional access to information and resources about the disorders of sexual addiction, sexual compulsivity, and sexual offending; (2) support research about these disorders; (3) promote diagnosis of these disorders; (4) promote appropriate training and education conducive to prevention, intervention, and treatment of these disorders; (5) encourage communication and collaboration among treatment models and available resources; (6) provide international educational opportunities through newsletters, journals, conferences, and the media; and (7) discern and respond to the stigmatization of these disorders.

National Families in Action (NFA)
2296 Henderson Mill Road, Suite 204
Atlanta, GA 30345
Telephone: (404) 934-6364
Web site: www.emory.edu/NFIA

Founded in 1977, NFA is a national drug education, prevention, and policy center based in Atlanta, Georgia, whose mission is to help families and communities prevent drug abuse among children by promoting science-based policies. It maintains a drug-information center for public use, an Internet web site, and publishes a quarterly digest, *Drug Abuse Update,* plus numerous articles, pamphlets, and books.

National Inhalant Prevention Coalition (NIPC)
2904 Kerbey Lane
Austin, TX 78703
Telephone: (512) 480-8953; (800) 269-4237
Fax: (512) 477-3932
E-mail: nipc@io.com
Web site: www.inhalants.org

Founded in 1992, The NIPC serves as an inhalant referral and information clear-inghouse, stimulates media coverage about inhalant issues, develops informa-tional materials, produces *ViewPoint* (a quarterly newsletter), provides training and technical assistance, and leads a week-long national grassroots inhalant ed-ucation and awareness campaign. Working with state agencies, schools, busi-nesses, trade associations, media, civic organizations, law enforcement, Poison Control Centers, and interfaith groups throughout the country, NIPC offers mul-tifaceted awareness and prevention campaigns designed to educate youth and adults about the debilitating effects of these dangerous gateway drugs. NIPC also provides in-service training for educators.

National Mental Health Association (NMHA)
2001 N. Beauregard Street, 12th Floor
Alexandria, VA 22311
Telephone: (703) 684-7722; (800) 969-NMHA (6642)
TTY: (800) 433-5959
Fax: (800) 684-5968
Web site: www.nmha.org

The country's oldest and largest nonprofit organization addressing all aspects of mental health and mental illness, the NMHA has more than 340 affiliates na-tionwide working through advocacy, education, research, and service to improve the mental health of all Americans, especially the 54 million individuals with mental disorders.

National Organization on Fetal Alcohol Syndrome (NAFOS)
216 G Street NE
Washington, DC 20002
Telephone: (202) 785-4585
Fax: (202) 466-6456
E-mail: information@nofas.org
Web site: www.nofas.org

A nonprofit organization founded in 1990, NAFOS seeks to eliminate birth de-fects caused by alcohol consumption during pregnancy and to improve the qual-ity of life for those individuals and families affected. The mission is to raise public awareness of fetal alcohol syndrome (FAS)—the leading known cause of mental retardation—and to develop and implement innovative ideas in prevention, intervention, education, and advocacy in communities throughout the nation. NOFAS activities include national and community-based public awareness campaigns, a curriculum for medical and allied health students, training workshops for professional and lay audiences, peer education and youth outreach initiatives, and the NOFAS information, resource, and referral clearinghouse.

> Partnership for a Drug-Free America (PDFA)
> 405 Lexington Avenue, Suite 1601
> New York, NY 10174
> Telephone: (212) 922-1560
> Fax: (212) 922-1570
> Web site: www.drugfreeamerica.org

Created in 1986 with seed money provided by the American Association of Advertising Agencies, the PDFA is a nonprofit coalition of professionals from the communications industry that sponsors a national drug-education advertising campaign and other forms of media communication to help kids and teens reject substance abuse. Consisting of a small staff and hundreds of volunteers from the communications industry, PDFA receives major funding from the Robert Wood Johnson Foundation and more than 200 corporations and companies. Strictly nonpartisan, PDFA accepts no funds from manufacturers of alcohol and/or tobacco products. The national advertising campaign, the largest public service campaign in the history of advertising, seeks to reduce overall drug use in the United States.

> Problem Gambling
> 10443 Noontide Avenue
> Las Vegas, NV 89135
> Telephone: (800) 522-4700 (plus Canadian provinces)
> Fax: (702) 363-7934
> E-mail: webmaster@problemgambling.com
> Web site: www.problemgambling.org

For those concerned with problem gambling, this online resource provides the gaming industry, government organizations, researchers, counselors, treatment centers, and the public at large with information, assistance, training, consulting, products, services, news, and views on problem gambling. The primary goal is to reduce the impact of problem gambling on individuals, families, business, and society. Products for purchase (A-Vs, manuals, books) are listed, as are treatment and training centers, subject matter experts, interventionists, and counselor certification agencies.

CANADIAN AGENCIES

A number of governmental and private Canadian organizations contribute to the prevention of chemical dependence and compulsive gambling.

Addictions Foundation of Manitoba (AFM)
1031 Portage Avenue
Winnipeg, MB R3G 0R8
Telephone: (204) 944-6200
Fax: (204) 786-7768
Web site: www.afm.mb.ca

AFM serves Manitoba through its 26 offices and three regions—Winnipeg, Western, and Northern. Through education, prevention, rehabilitation, and research, they seek to lead the way to an addiction-free society that improves the health and well-being of Manitobans by addressing the harm associated with addictions.

Alberta Alcohol and Drug Abuse Commission (AADAC)
24-hour Helpline: (866) 332-2322
Web site: www.aadac.com

An agency funded by the provincial government to assist Albertans in achieving freedom from the harmful effects of alcohol, drugs, and gambling, AADAC provides cost-effective, holistic alternatives to hospital-based and medical services. It delivers services in four areas: (1) community outpatient and prevention (2) crisis intervention, (3) residential treatment; and (4) research, information, and monitoring.

Canadian Addiction Counsellors Certification Board
236 Victoria Street, Unit 2
Kitchener, Ontario N2H 5C8
Canada
Telephone: (866) 624-1911
Toll Free: (519) 772-0533
Fax: (519) 772-0535
E-mail: info@caccb.ca
Web site: www.caccb.ca

Formed in 1985, AIA is a voluntary nonprofit organization that has regional representation across the Canadian provinces and territories. AIA is an active member of the International Certification and Reciprocity Consortium/Alcohol and Other Drug Abuse (IC&RC/AODA). Counselors certified by the AIA meet rigorous standards that include education, work experience, clinical supervision, knowledge, and skills specific to substance abuse disorders.

Canadian Centre on Substance Abuse (CCSA)
75 Albert Street, Suite 300
Ottawa, ON Canada K1P 5E7
Telephone: (613) 235-4048
Fax: (613) 235-8101
Web site: www.ccsa.ca

A national center to reduce health, social, and economic harm associated with substance abuse and addictions, the CCSA is funded by *Canada's Drug Strategy* and promotes informed debate on substance abuse issues and encourages public participation in reducing the harm associated with drug abuse; disseminates information on the nature, extent, and consequences of substance abuse; and supports and assists organizations involved in substance abuse treatment, prevention, and educational programming.

Canadian Council for Tobacco Control (CCTC)
75 Albert Street, Suite 508
Ottawa, Ontario
K1P 5E7 Canada
Telephone: (613) 567-3050; (800) 267-5234
Fax: (613) 567-2730
E-mail: info-services@cctc.ca
Web site: www.cctc.ca

Formerly the Canadian Council on Smoking and Health (CCSH), the CCTC was founded in 1974 by nongovernmental organizations such as the Canadian Cancer Society, the Heart and Stroke Foundation of Canada, and the Canadian Lung Association concerned with the tobacco epidemic. The CCTC goals are preventing tobacco use among young people; persuading and helping smokers to stop using tobacco products; protecting Canadians by eliminating exposure to secondhand smoke; and educating Canadians about the marketing strategies and tactics of the tobacco industry and the adverse effects the industry's products have on the health of Canadians.

The Centre for Addiction and Mental Health
33 Russell Street
Toronto, ON M5S 2S1
Telephone: (416) 979-4250
Information Centre: (416) 595-6111
Telephone: (800) 463-6273

The Centre offers a wide range of clinical programs, support, and rehabilitation to meet the diverse needs of people who are at risk. Services include assessment, brief early interventions, residential programs, continuing care, and family support. The Centre is also a research facility, an education and training institute, and a community-based organization providing health promotion and prevention services across the province.

The Canadian Women's Health Network (CWHN)
419 Graham Avenue, Suite 203
Winnipeg, Manitoba
Canada R3C 0M3
Telephone: (204) 942-5500
Fax: (204) 989-2355
E-mail: cwhn@cwhn.ca
Clearinghouse: (888) 818-9172
Web site: www.cwhn.ca

Launched in May 1993 by women representing over 70 organizations from every Canadian province and territory, CWHN seeks to provide easier access to health information, resources and research, produce user-friendly materials and re-sources, promote and develop links to information and action networks, provide forums for critical debate, act as a watchdog on emerging issues and trends that may affect women's health, work to change inequitable health policies and prac-tices, encourage community-based participatory research models, and promote women's involvement in health research.

The Ontario Drug and Alcohol Registry of Treatment (DART)
Within Ontario: (800) 565-8603
Outside Ontario: (519) 439-0174
Fax: (519) 439-0455
Web site: www.dart.on.ca

A toll-free, province-wide, treatment information and referral service located in Ontario, Canada, DART is available to professional and public callers. Since 1991, it has been linking callers with suitable treatment options tailored to their individual needs and with local assessment and referral sources. DART provides comprehensive, up-to-date information on a wide range of drug and alcohol treatment services such as withdrawal management, assessment, outpatient, day/evening, short-term residential, and long-term residential. DART utilizes a computerized database, updated regularly and includes information on over 220 drug and alcohol treatment agencies in Ontario and the nearly 1,300 different services they provide.

The Responsible Gambling Council, Ontario (RGCO)
3080 Yonge Street, Suite 4070 Box 90
Toronto, Ontario
Canada M4N 3N1
Telephone: (416) 499-9800
Fax: (416) 499-8260; (888) 391-1111
Web site: www.responsiblegambling.org

Since 1983, the RGCO has created innovative programs to promote responsible gambling, educated the public on avoiding problem gambling, informed people with a gambling problem where they can find help, promoted changes in public policy, and undertaken research.

The Substance Abuse Network of Ontario (SANO)
Web site: http:\\sano.camh.net

An online presence targeted at those working in the substance use and addiction field, SANO makes a wide range of information related to substance use available in an electronic format and provides a forum for communication. Begun in 1994 under the Ontario Action for Substance Abuse Information Services (OASIS) project, its goal is to support community action aimed at creating healthy communities. Ongoing goals are to provide a tool to foster electronic information exchange to those working in the field of substance abuse in the province of Ontario, to improve public access to addiction-specific information through the innovative use of information technologies, to provide a means for global dissemination of addiction-related information and research findings, and to utilize the latest technology.

The Women's Addiction Foundation
4500 Oak Street, E500B
Vancouver, BC v6H 3N1
Telephone: (604) 875-3756
Fax: (604) 875-2039
E-mail: info@womenfedn.org
Web site: www.womenfdn.org

The Women's Addiction Foundation is a public foundation committed to the physical, mental, emotional, and spiritual wellness of women whose lives have been affected by their misuse of, or dependency on, alcohol or other drugs. The Foundation works to ensure all women have access to programs that value women and recognize their unique needs. The Foundation works independently and in partnership with other providers to support research, education, and treatment programs.

INTERNATIONAL SUBSTANCE ABUSE ORGANIZATIONS

Here are some other key international organizations involved with chemical dependency issues.

Alcohol and Public Health Research Unit
Faculty of Medicine and Health Science
University of Auckland
Private Bag 92 019
Auckland 1020, New Zealand
Telephone: (64) 9 373 7524
Fax: (64) 9 373 7057
E-mail: l.morice@auckland.ac.nz
Web site: www.aphru.ac.nz

A World Health Organization Collaborating Centre on Alcohol and Other Drugs, the Unit is an independent peer-reviewed research organization based at the University of Auckland, New Zealand. As a multidisciplinary unit, it undertakes a range of descriptive research, policy analysis, community action research, and evaluation research. Much of their alcohol research focuses on harm prevention through national policy and community action.

European Monitoring Centre for Drugs and Drug Addiction
Rua da Gruz de Santa Apolonia 23-25
PT-1149-045 Lisbon
Portugal
Telephone: (+351) 21 811 3000
Fax: (+351) 21 813 1711
E-mail: info@emcdda.eu.int
Web site: www.emcdda.org

The European Union's (EU) drug agency, its mission is to provide the community and its member states with objective, reliable, and comparable information concerning drugs and drug addiction and their consequences. The agency also plays a key role in implementing the EU joint action on new synthetic drugs as well as monitoring national and community strategies and policies and their impact on the drug situation.

Institute of Alcohol Studies (IAS)
Alliance House, 12 Caxton Street
London, United Kingdom
Web site: www.ias.org.uk
E-mail: info@ias.org.uk

The Institute of Alcohol Studies (IAS) is an educational body with the basic aims of increasing knowledge of the social and health consequences of alcohol misuse and encouraging and supporting the adoption of effective measures for the management and prevention of alcohol-related problems. The Institute is financially independent of both government and the alcoholic beverage industry and is sponsored by the United Kingdom Temperance Alliance Ltd, a registered educational charity. The IAS provides information and education to the general public, the helping professions, and industry, commerce, and trade unions. These services are available by request. The Institute provides fact sheets, leaflets, reports, and discussion papers; conferences and seminars; education and training courses for members of the helping professions; consultative assistance to industry and commerce in relation to occupational policies on alcohol problems; and accompanying education and training courses and assistance with workplace alcohol education programs.

International Coalition for Addiction Studies Education (INCASE)
P.O. Box 3492
Brockton, MA 02304
Telephone: (617) 287-6260
E-mail: joseph.bebo@umb.edu
Web site: www.incase.org

Founded in 1990, INCASE is a professional association of individuals, programs, and students specializing in addiction studies, including the use and abuse of alcohol and other drugs, other addictions, counselor preparation, prevention and treatment, research, and public policy. Its purpose is to provide a global forum for the examination and debate of issues concerning postsecondary education in addiction studies, and to enhance the quality of training and education in addiction studies, to disseminate professional knowledge and share ideas regarding addition studies and scholarship, and to develop standards and implement an accreditation process for addictions studies programs within and between nations, states, and provinces.

International Council on Alcohol and Addictions (ICAA)
Case Postale 189
1001 Lausanne, Switzerland
Web site: www.icaa.de/index2.htm

The ICAA is a nongovernmental organization created in Stockholm, Sweden, in 1907 that brings together many national bodies and a wide range of professionals in different disciplines who exchange knowledge, ideas, advice, guidance, expertise, and research, facilitated by conferences and other activities in the field of dependencies. The mission is to provide an international forum and network for all concerned with the prevention and/or alleviation of harm resulting from the use of alcohol and other drugs; to enhance and develop, through the expertise of its worldwide membership, appropriate responses to addiction problems; and to offer advice, guidance, and assistance in the development of relevant policies, strategies, programs, and research.

Pan American Health Organization (PAHO)
Regional Office of the World Health Organization
525 Twenty-third Street NW
Washington, DC 20037
Telephone: (292) 974-3000
Fax: (292) 974-3663
Web site: www.paho.org

PAHO is an international public health agency with more than 90 years of experience in working to improve health and living standards of the countries of the Americas. It serves as the specialized organization for health of the Inter-American System. It also serves as the Regional Office for the Americas of the World Health Organization and enjoys international recognition as part of the United Nations system. Click on Public Health Topics: Tobacco, Alcohol and Drugs to locate publications covering Alcoholism, Smoke-free Spaces, Substance Abuse Prevention and Control, Tobacco and Alcohol and Drugs, and Tobacco Prevention and Control.

United Nations Office on Drugs and Crime (UNODC)
Postal Address
United Nations Office on Drugs and Crime
Vienna International Centre
P.O. Box 500
A-1400 Vienna, Austria

Street Address
United Nations Office on Drugs and Crime
Vienna International Centre
Wagramer Strasse 5
A-1400 Vienna, Austria
Telephone: (+43) 1 26060 0
Fax: (+43) 1 26060 5866
Web site: www.undcp.org

A global leader in the fight against illicit drugs and international crime, UNODC was established in 1997. Consisting of the Drug Program and the Crime Program, UNODC has approximately 350 staff members worldwide. Its headquarters are in Vienna, and it has 22 field offices as well as liaison offices in New York and Brussels. UNODC relies on voluntary contributions, mainly from governments, for 90% of its budget. Founded in 1991, the Drug Program works to educate the world about the dangers of drug abuse. The Program aims to strengthen international action against drug production, trafficking, and drug-related crime through alternative development projects, crop monitoring, and anti-money-laundering programs. UNODC also provides accurate statistics through the Global Assessment Program (GAP) and helps to draft legislation and train judicial officials as part of its legal advisory program.

The Commission on Narcotic Drugs (CND), established in 1946 by the Economic and Social Council of the United Nations, is the central policy-making body within the UN system for dealing with all drug-related matters. The Commission analyzes the world drug abuse situation and develops proposals to strengthen international drug control.

World Health Organization (WHO)
Avenue Appia 20
1211 Geneva 27
Switzerland
Telephone: (+ 41 22) 791 21 11
Fax: (+ 41 22) 791 3111
Telex: (+ 41 22) 415 416
Telegraph: UNISANTE GENEVA
E-mail: info@who.int
Web site: www.who.int/en
Click on Health Topics: Substance Abuse

WHO, the United Nations' specialized agency for health, was established on April 7, 1948, with the objective of attaining the highest possible level of health for all people. (Health is defined in WHO's Constitution as a state of complete physical, mental, and social well-being and not merely the absence of disease or infirmity.) Governed by 192 member states through the World Health Assembly, the Assembly is composed of representatives from those member states, WHO's Secretariat is staffed by health professionals, other experts, and support staff working at headquarters in Geneva, in the six regional offices, and in countries. WHOs regional offices are scattered throughout the world.

GRASSROOTS ALCOHOL AND OTHER DRUGS INFORMATION

These private sources provide interesting information about addiction control and prevention.

American Medical Association Alliance, Inc. (AMA)
515 N. State Street
Chicago, IL 60610
Telephone: (312) 464-4470
Fax: (312) 464-5020
E-mail: AMAA@ama-assn.org
Web site: www.ama-assn.org

The proactive volunteer arm of the AMA, the Alliance, launched in 1995, seeks to promote better public health, ensure sound health care legislation, and raise funds for medical education. Its SAVE program seeks to Stop America's Violence Everywhere. Click on "Patients" to find Health Information and then go into this medical information site and click on Substance Abuse and Addictions to find information on Alcohol Abuse, Illicit Drug Abuse, Inhalant Abuse, and Nicotine Dependence.

Boaters Against Drunk Driving, Inc. (BADD)®
344 Clayton Avenue
Battle Creek, MI 49017-5218
Telephone and fax: (269) 963-7068
E-mail: NationalBADD@ameritech.net
Web site: www.badd.org

Founded in 1989 to combat drinking and operating a watercraft, BADD advocates that all persons complete an approved basic boating safety course before launching a craft for the first time, and endorses a national Blood Alcohol Level (BAL) for those operating a watercraft. BADD has monitored over 300 cases of individuals charged with boating under the influence (BUI).

Drug Policy Alliance (DPA)
Washington, DC Office (one of seven national offices)
925 15th Street NW, 2nd Floor
Washington, DC 20005
Telephone: (202) 216-0035
Fax: (202) 216-0803

Formed in 1994, the Alliance was formerly known as the Lindesmith Center, the leading independent drug policy reform institute in the United States. It is a nonprofit membership organization that relies entirely on private donations. It seeks to broaden the public debate on drug policy and to promote realistic, sensible, humane alternatives to the war on drugs based on science, compassion, health, and human rights. The guiding principle of the Alliance is harm reduction, an alternative approach to drug policy and treatment that focuses on minimizing the adverse effects of both drug use and drug prohibition.

Mothers Against Drunk Driving (MADD)
1025 Connecticut Avenue NW, Suite 1200
Washington, DC 20036
Telephone: (202) 974-2497; 800-GET-MADD (438-6233)
Web site: www.madd.org

A grassroots organization with more than 600 chapters nationwide, MADD's mission is to stop drunk driving, support the victims of this violent crime, and prevent underage drinking. Since MADD's inception, alcohol-related traffic fatalities have declined 43%. Due in large part to MADD's efforts, more than an estimated 138,000 people are alive today and an untold number have received comfort, support, and assistance in dealing with the aftermath of a drunk driving crash.

Moyers on Addiction: Close to Home
P.O. Box 245
Little Falls, NJ 07424-0245
Web site: www.pbs.org/wnet/closetohome
To order ($399): (800) 257-5126 at www.films.com

An educational video, this is an original report by health journalist Janet Fir-shein on the science of understanding and treating addiction. It is a five-part series: (1) *Portrait of Addiction,* (2) *The Hijacked Brain,* (3) *Changing Lives,* (4) *The Next Generation,* and (5) *The Politics of Addiction.* Using animated scientific illustrations and real-life stories of people who talk about their struggles in recovery, it also provides editorials that debate controversial policy issues. A downloadable educational guide and discussion forum, it offers information on where to get help.

Recovery Zone
www.recoveryzone.org/docs/national.htm

The Recovery Zone lists national self-help organizations and provides the postal address, phone number, e-mail, and web site addresses (if available) for each.

Stanton Peele's Addiction Web Site
www.peele.net

Stanton Peele's book, *Love and Addiction* (1975) argues that addiction is not limited to narcotics, or to drugs at all, but is a pattern of behavior and experience best understood by examining an individual's relationship with his or her world. A nonmedical approach, he views addiction as a general pattern of behavior that nearly everyone experiences in varying degrees at one time or another.

GRANT-FUNDING RESOURCES

At some time in your professional career, you may want to apply for a research grant. The following provides information and contact information about major sources of grant support.

FEDERAL GRANTING AGENCIES

These federal agencies provide competitive grant opportunities:

National Institutes of Health (NIH)
Web site: http://grants1.nih.gov/grants/index.cfm

Go to "Grants" to learn about NIH grant and fellowship programs. The Office of Extramural Research provides information about how to apply for a grant or fellowship, policy changes, administrative responsibilities of awardees, peer review policies and procedures, and the number and characteristics of awards made.

National Science Foundation (NSF)
Web site: www.nsf.gov

Go to "Grants" for information about research and education grants in science and engineering. The NSF accounts for about 20% of federal support to academic institutions for basic research.

National Institute on Alcohol Abuse and Alcoholism (NIAAA)
Web site: www.niaaa.nih.gov

Go to "Extramural Research" to see funding opportunities.

National Institute on Drug Abuse (NIDA)
Web site: www.drugabuse.gov/funding

Go to "Funding" where the NIDA Office of Extramural Affairs coordinates the overall process for submitting requests for funding and for reviewing those requests.

National Institute of Mental Health (NIMH)
Web site: www.nimh.nih.gov

Go to "Funding" for information on NIMH grants and contracts programs including grant applications and review, ongoing program announcements, research training, and career development.

U.S. Department of Health and Human Services (DHHS)
Web site: www.hhs.gov

Go to "Grants and Funding" to find a plethora of Contract Information from all the various Health and Human Services (HHS) agencies.

Health Resources and Services Administration (HRSA)
Web site: www.hrsa.gov/grants.htm

The mission of the Health Resources and Services Administration is to expand access to quality health care for all Americans. Go to the "Grants," section at this web site.

INTERNATIONAL GRANTING AGENCIES

You may also want to check out these international agencies that provide grant opportunities:

World Health Organization (WHO)
Web site: www.who.int/tdr/grants/grants/default.htm

WHO is the specialized U.N. agency for health. Research opportunities are set out in the various scientific work plans, which you should study before submitting a grant application. In addition to the research opportunities outlined in the scientific work plans, specific calls for applications can be made at any time of year.

PRIVATE GRANTING AGENCIES

A few private foundations also provide competitive grants:

American Association for the Advancement of Science (AAAS)
Web site: www.aaas.org

The world's largest general scientific society and publisher of *Science,* the AAAS, seeks to "advance science and innovation throughout the world for the benefit of all people." Go to "Career in Science" to find GrantsNet, a resource to find funds for training in the sciences and undergraduate science education.

American Foundation of Addiction Research (AFAR)
Web site: www.addictionresearch.com

AFAR fosters scientific research, understanding, and disseminating knowledge of the causes and nature of addictive disorders. To learn about projects targeted for funding, go to "Research Funding Opportunities."

American Psychological Association (APA)
Web site: www.apa.org/science/awd.html

This site takes you directly to a list of APA Scientific Awards and Funding Programs.

MacArthur Foundation
Web site: www.macfdn.org/programs/index.htm

The John D. and Catherine T. MacArthur Foundation, a private, independent grant-making institution, seeks to foster lasting improvement in the human condition. The Foundation seeks the development of healthy individuals and effective communities, peace within and among nations, responsible choices about human reproduction, and a global ecosystem capable of supporting healthy human societies. The Foundation supports research, policy development, dissemination of information, education, training, and practice in support of these goals. The Foundation makes grants through four programs: (1) the Program on Human and Community Development; (2) the Program on Global Security and Sustainability; (3) the General Program (those that meet Foundation goals but do not fall under the other categories); and (4) the MacArthur Fellows Program (awards 5-year unrestricted fellowships to individuals across all ages and fields who show exceptional merit and promise of continued and enhanced creative work).

National Academy of Sciences (NAS)
Web site: www.nationalacademies.org

This institution, founded in 1863, eventually expanded in 1916 to include the National Research Council, the National Academy of Engineering, and in 1970, the Institute of Medicine. Collectively, these organizations are called the National Academies—the National Academy of Sciences and its sister organizations—the National Academy of Engineering, the Institute of Medicine, and the National Research Council. The Academies and the Institute are honorary societies that elect new members to their ranks each year. The Institute of Medicine also conducts policy studies on health issues.

These nonprofit organizations provide a public service by working outside the framework of government to ensure independent advice on matters of science, technology, and medicine. They enlist committees of the nation's top scientists, engineers, and other experts—all of whom volunteer their time to study specific concerns. They also provide a listing of ways to find granting opportunities. (Search "Grants" to find numerous possibilities for federal agency opportunities.)

The National Academies (via the National Research Council) provide Postdoctoral and Senior Research Awards through Associateship Programs, part of the *Policy and Global Affairs Division*. The Research Associateship Programs are sponsored by federal laboratories and NAS Research Centers at over one hundred locations in the United States and overseas (web site: www4.nationalacademies .org/pga/rap.nsf).

Awards are made to doctoral level scientists and engineers who can apply their special knowledge and research talents to research areas of interest to the NAS and to the host laboratories and centers. Awards are made to Postdoctoral Associates (within 5 years of the doctorate) and Senior Associates (normally 5 years or more beyond the doctorate). The Fellowship Office of Policy and Global Affairs (PGA) administers several predoctoral, dissertation, and postdoctoral fellowship programs. View specifics at their web site: www7.nationalacademies.org /fellowships

Social Science Research Council (SSRC)
Web site: www.ssrc.org

The SSRC, an independent, nongovernmental, not-for-profit international organization, seeks to advance social science throughout the world and supports research, education, and scholarly exchange on every continent. For more than 75 years, the SSRC has linked universities, foundations, social science disciplines, area studies associations, and government and nongovernmental organizations in exploring new intellectual paths and testing theories and methods against the challenges of contemporary and historical problems.

The SSRC sponsors fellowship and grant programs on a wide range of topics, and across many career stages. Most support goes to predissertation, dissertation, and postdoctoral fellowships, offered through annual competitions. Some programs support summer institutes and advanced research grants. Although most programs target the social sciences, many are also open to applicants from the humanities, the natural sciences, and relevant professional and practitioner communities. View by Type: *Predissertation—Dissertation—Postdoctoral—Other*

W. T. Grant Foundation
Web site: www.wtgrantfoundation.org

The William T. Grant Foundation seeks to help create a society that values young people and enables them to reach their full potential. It pursues this goal by investing in research that uses evidence-based approaches. The Foundation's three primary focus areas are (1) Youth Development, (2) Systems Affecting Youth, and (3) the Public's View of Youth. See the "Grants" and "Funding Opportunities" sections.

OTHER FUNDING DATABASES

Three services, by paid subscription, offer databases containing thousands of federal and nonfederal funding opportunities in the sciences, social sciences, arts, and humanities. Each provides program summaries that include sponsor names, program titles and descriptions, contact information, deadlines, and restrictions.

Community of Science (COS)
Web site: fundingopps.cos.com

The largest and most comprehensive research funding database on the Web, COS provides information about 4,270 Graduate Awards and 860 Postdoctoral Awards. Updated daily, COS Funding Opportunities includes more than 23,000 records, representing over 400,000 funding opportunities, worth over $33 billion.

Individual researchers and research administrators rely on COS Funding Opportunities to identify funding information as it relates to research, collaborative activities, travel, curriculum development, conferences, fellowships, postdoctoral positions, equipment acquisition, operating and capital expenses, and more.

Illinois Researcher Information Service (IRIS)
Web site: http://carousel.library.uiuc.edu/~iris/about_iris.html

A unit of the University of Illinois Library at Urbana-Champaign, IRIS offers three web-based funding and research services (1,930 Graduate Awards, 640 Postdoctoral Awards): (1) the IRIS Database of federal and private funding opportunities in all disciplines, (2) the IRIS Alert Service, and (3) the IRIS Expertise Service.

The *IRIS Database* contains over 8,000 active federal and private funding opportunities in the sciences, social sciences, arts, and humanities. Users can search IRIS by sponsor, deadline date, keyword, and other criteria. Most IRIS records contain live links to sponsor web sites, electronic forms, or Electronic Research Administration (ERA) portals. The IRIS Database is updated daily.

The *IRIS Alert Service* enables researchers at subscribing institutions to create their own IRIS search profiles. Researchers can select their preferred search frequency, delivery method (e-mail or Web), and keywords. The program runs the researcher's profile against the IRIS database and delivers the search results automatically.

The *IRIS Expertise Service* enables researchers at subscribing institutions to create detailed electronic CVs ("biosketches") and post them to a web-accessible database for review by colleagues at other institutions, program officers at federal and private funding agencies, and private companies. The biosketches can also be used in the electronic submission of grant proposals. There are no copyright or ownership restrictions on IRIS Expertise Service biosketches. Subscribing institutions can download their faculty members' biosketches at any time and use them to populate a local database—or even another online service.

IRIS is available to *colleges and universities* for an annual subscription fee. For more information, see the *IRIS Trial Period and Subscription Policy*. IRIS is not a funding agency. They do not offer grants, scholarships, or financial aid.

Sponsored Programs Information Network (SPIN)
Web site: www.infoed.org

SPIN provides up-to-date information on current national and international government and private funding sources, including fellowships, research grants, publication support, sabbatical support, curriculum development, and more. All of the data on SPIN is obtained directly from the sponsoring agencies to ensure the integrity of the information.

SPIN supplies all the information necessary to make an informed decision whether to pursue a funding opportunity. Programs are summarized in helpful abstracts, and links are provided to the details. The flexible search engine allows users to customize their queries and design their own reports on programs they choose. SPIN provides one-click access to new funding opportunities based on predefined queries. In addition, Quick Searches enables spontaneous free-text queries against the SPIN database.

PUBLISHING RESOURCES

ACADEMIC AND PROFESSIONAL JOURNALS

General—Covering All Addictions

- *Addiction:* A monthly, international peer-reviewed journal that publishes research reports on alcohol, illicit drugs, and tobacco. It features editorials, commentaries, reviews, historical articles, interviews with leading figures in addiction, letters, news, and a comprehensive book review section. Contact at:

Journal Customer Services U.S. Office
Blackwell Publishing
350 Main Street
Malden, MA 02148
Telephone: (781) 388-8206; (800) 835-6770
Fax: (781) 388-8232
E-mail: subscrip@blackwellpub.com
Web site: www.blackwellpublishing.com/cservices

- *Addiction Abstracts:* A quarterly, international journal published in print and online that spans all addictive substances and other compulsive behaviors. It includes abstracts in psychology, psychiatry, public health medicine, health behavior, treatment, and prevention. Contact at:

  Customer Services for Taylor & Francis Group Journals (United States)
  325 Chestnut Street, Suite 800
  Philadelphia, PA 19106
  Telephone: (800) 354-1420
  Fax: (215) 625-8914
  Web site: www.taylorandfrancis.com

- *Addiction Biology:* A quarterly, peer-reviewed journal that includes original scientific research, invited reviews, short communications, scientific letters and correspondence, book reviews, and a calendar of relevant scientific meetings and events. Contact at:

  Customer Services for Taylor & Francis Group Journals (United States)
  325 Chestnut Street, Suite 800
  Philadelphia, PA 19106
  Telephone: (800) 354-1420
  Fax: (215) 625-8914
  Web site: www.taylorandfrancis.com

- *Addiction Research and Theory:* A cross-disciplinary journal examining the effects of context on the use and misuse of substances, and on the nature of intoxications of all kinds. Topics range from substance-based addictions to problems such as gambling, sexual behavior, and eating disorders. It publishes research primarily psychological and social in origin (broad sense). Contact at:

  Customer Services for Taylor & Francis Group Journals (United States)
  325 Chestnut Street, Suite 800
  Philadelphia, PA 19106
  Telephone: (800) 354-1420
  Fax: (215) 625-8914
  Web site: www.taylorandfrancis.com

- *Addiction: An International Journal:* A monthly international peer-reviewed journal read in over 60 countries. It publishes peer-reviewed research reports on alcohol, illicit drugs, and tobacco. In addition to original research, the journal features editorials, commentaries, reviews, historical articles, interviews with leading figures in addiction, letters, news, and a comprehensive book review section. Contact at:

Blackwell Publishing
9600 Garsington Road
Oxford OX4 2DQ, United Kingdom
Telephone: (+44) 1865 776868
Fax: (+44) 1865 714591
Web site: www.addictionjournal.org

- *Addictive Behaviors:* A professional journal of original research and theoretical papers in the area of substance abuse and problems associated with eating. Two major types of research are featured: (1) descriptive studies in which functional relationships between a substance abuse and any combination of social factors are established, (2) clinical outcome data in which treatment or prevention procedures are systematically evaluated by controlled group research or single-case designs. Contact at:

Elsevier (go to www.elsevier.com for details)
Regional Sales Office (United States)
Customer Support Department
P.O. Box 945
New York, NY 10059-0945
Telephone: (212) 633-3730; for North American customers: (888) 437-4636
Fax: (212) 633-3680
E-mail: usinfo-f@elsevier.com

- *Addictive Disorders & Their Treatment:* A quarterly international journal devoted to practical clinical research and treatment issues related to the misuses of alcohol and licit and illicit drugs. The journal publishes original articles, in-depth reviews, short reports, case reviews, editorials, book reviews, meeting announcements, and letters to the editor. Contact at:

Publisher
Maria McMichael
E-mail: mmcmicha@lww.com

Managing Editor
Julie Porter
Addictive Disorders & Their Treatment
9327 W. Nova Avenue
Littleton, CO 80128
Telephone: (303) 978-9054
Fax: (303) 978-9037
E-mail: julieporter@kingfisherranch.com

- *American Journal of Drug and Alcohol Abuse:* A quarterly journal providing study and treatment of drug abuse and alcoholism with focus on the preclinical, clinical, pharmacological, administrative, and social aspects. Contact at:

  United States, Canada, and South America Customer Service and
      Distribution
  Marcel Dekker, Inc.
  Cimarron Road
  P.O. Box 5005
  Telephone: (845) 796-1919; (800) 228-1160
  Fax: (845) 796-1772

- *American Journal on Addictions:* Official quarterly journal of the American Academy of Addiction Psychiatry that covers topics ranging from codependence to genetics, epidemiology to dual diagnostics, and etiology to neuroscience. It features special overview articles, clinical or basic research papers, clinical updates, and book reviews. Contact at:

  Customer Service for Taylor & Francis Group Journals (United States)
  325 Chestnut Street, Suite 800
  Philadelphia, PA 19106
  Telephone: (800) 354-1420
  Fax: (215) 625-8914

- *CyberPsychology and Behavior:* Bimonthly peer-reviewed journal explores the impact of the Internet, multimedia, and virtual reality on behavior and society. Contact at:

  Mary Ann Liebert, Inc.
  2 Madison Avenue
  Larchmont, NY 10538
  Telephone: (914) 834-3100
  Fax: (914) 834-3688
  E-mail contacts: Editorial Department: editorial@liebertpub.com
  Manuscript submission: mark.d.wiederhold@saic.com
  Reprints: reprints@liebertpub.com

- *Drug and Alcohol Dependence:* Monthly international journal devoted to publishing original research, scholarly reviews, commentaries, and policy analyses in the area of drug, alcohol, and tobacco use and dependence. Articles include studies of the chemistry of substances of abuse, their actions at molecular and cellular sites, laboratory-based and clinical research in humans, substance abuse treatment and prevention research. Contact at:

Elsevier (go to www.elsevier.com for details)
Regional Sales Office (United States)
Customer Support Department
360 Park Avenue South
New York, NY 10010-1710
Telephone: (212) 633-3730; for North American customers: (888) 437-4636
Fax: (212) 633-3680
E-mail: usinfo-f@elsevier.com

• *Drug and Alcohol Review:* Quarterly, international meeting ground for the views, expertise, and experience of all those involved in the study of treatment of alcohol, tobacco, and drug problems. Contributors to the journal examine and report on alcohol and drug abuse from a wide range of clinical, biomedical, psychological, and sociological standpoints. Contact at:

Customer Service for Taylor & Francis Group Journals
325 Chestnut Street, Suite 800
Philadelphia, PA 19106
Telephone: (800) 354-1420
Fax: (215) 625-8914

• *Drug Dependence, Alcohol Abuse and Alcoholism:* Provides a careful selection of abstracts (and other bibliographic data) from the latest issues of 4,000 leading international biomedical journals on all aspects of the abuse of drugs, alcohol, and organic solvents and includes material relating to experimental pharmacology of addiction. Contact at:

Elsevier (go to www.elsevier.com for details)
Regional Sales Office (United States)
Customer Support Department
360 Park Avenue South
New York, NY 10010-1710
Telephone: (212) 633-3730; for North American customers: (888) 437-4636
Fax: (212) 633-3680
E-mail: usinfo-f@elsevier.com

• *Drugs: Education, Prevention & Policy:* Quarterly, refereed journal that provides a forum for communication and debate between policymakers, practitioners, and researchers concerned with social and health policy responses to legal and illicit drug use and drug-related harm. The quarterly publishes multidisciplinary research papers, commentaries, and reviews on policy, prevention, and harm reduction. It encourages submissions that reflect different cultural, historical, and theoretical approaches to the development of policy and practice. Contact at:

Customer Service for Taylor & Francis Group Journals (United States)
325 Chestnut Street, Suite 800
Philadelphia, PA 19106
Telephone: (800) 354-1420
Fax: (215) 625-8914

- *European Addiction Research:* Unique international forum for the exchange of interdisciplinary information and expert opinions on all aspects of addiction research. Contact at:

S. Karger Publishers, Inc. (United States)
26 West Avon Road
P.O. Box 529
Farmington, CT 06085
Telephone: (860) 675-7834; (800) 828-5479
Fax: (860) 675-7302
E-mail: karger@snet.net

- *Experimental and Clinical Psychopharmacology:* Quarterly journal publishes original empirical research involving animals or humans that spans (1) descriptive and experimental studies of drug abuse; (2) behavioral pharmacology research; and (3) controlled clinical trials. It publishes manuscripts in four categories: Original Research Reports, Reviews of the Literature, Innovations in Psychopharmacology, and Remarks. Contact at:

American Psychological Association
Subscriptions
750 First Street NE
Washington, DC 20002-4242
Telephone: (202) 336-5600
Fax: (202) 336-5568
E-mail: subscriptions@apa.org

- *Heroin Addiction and Related Clinical Problems:* The official journal of EUROPAD, this international peer-reviewed journal is published twice each year. It covers research and opinion on opiate misuse treatment in Europe and around the world. Contributors are a core group of researchers committed to the development of effective opiate addiction treatment. Contact at:

Subscriptions
Associazione per l'Utilizzo delle Conoscenze
Neuroscientifiche a Fini Sociali (onlus)
Via XX Settembre, 83-55045 Pietrasanta (Lucca), Italy
Telephone: (+39) 0584-700073
Fax: (+39) 0584-72081

- *International Journal of Drug Policy:* Publishes material on the social, political, legal, and health contexts of psychoactive substance use, licit and illicit, in a global context. Contact at:

  Elsevier (go to www.elsevier.com for details)
  Regional Sales Office (United States)
  Customer Support Department
  360 Park Avenue South
  New York, NY 10010-1710
  Telephone: (212) 633-3730; for North American customers: (888) 437-4636
  Fax: (212) 633-3680
  E-mail: usinfo-f@elsevier.com

- *Journal of Addictions and Offender Counseling:* Focuses on prevention and treatment programs, theoretical and philosophical rationales for these programs with juvenile and adult offenders, and descriptions of research conducted on rehabilitation programs with public offender counselors. It is published twice a year by the International Association of Addictions and Offender Counselors (IAAOC). Contact at:

  JAOC Editorial Office
  Dr. Jane J. Carroll, JAOC Editor
  CSPC, 5055 Colvard Bldg.
  The University of North Carolina at Charlotte
  Charlotte, NC 28223
  Telephone: (704) 547-4721
  Fax: (704) 547-2916
  E-mail: jacarrol@email.uncc.edu

- *Journal of Addictive Diseases:* Focuses on clinical research and treatment, featuring state-of-the-art research and clinical applications developed by prominent researchers and leaders in the substance abuse field. Contact at:

  Subscriptions
  The Haworth Medical Press
  10 Alice Street
  Binghamton, NY 13904-1580
  Voice: (800) 342-9678
  E-mail: Getinfo@Haworth.com

  Editor, Barry Stimmel, MD
  Dean for Graduate Medical Education
  Mount Sinai School of Medicine
  Annenberg 5-02G, Box 1193
  One Gustave L. Levy Place
  New York, NY 10029
  Telephone: (212) 241-6694
  Fax: (212) 426-7748

- *Journal of Alcohol and Drug Education:* Published three times a year, the journal serves as a forum for various educational philosophies and different points of view about alcohol and drugs. It reports teacher experience and experiments and provides a reference for teaching materials, prevention guides, techniques, and procedures; it also reports new, effective, and exciting programs of education appropriate for the community, the church, and the family. Contact at:

Editor
Manoj Sharma, PhD
School of HPER Univ. of Nebraska at Omaha
Omaha, NE 68182-0216
Telephone: (402) 554-2670
Fax: (402) 554-3693
E-mail: msharma@mail.unomaha.edu

- *Journal of Chemical Dependency Treatment:* This peer-reviewed journal presents leading-edge information on prevention, intervention, treatment, management, supervision, and programmatic issues in a broad range of disciplines (including psychology, social work, counseling, medicine, and education). Practical articles include best practices, current technologies, administrative issues, employee assistance program concerns, behavioral health care management, military chemical dependency issues, interventions for different settings, financing, and funding issues. Contact at:

Customer Service
The Haworth Press Inc.
10 Alice Street
Binghamton, NY 13904
Telephone: (800) 429-6784
Fax: (800) 895-0582
E-mail: getinfo@haworthpress.com
Web site: www.haworthpress.com/FAQ

- *Journal of Child & Adolescent Substance Abuse:* The journal is an interdisciplinary forum that provides a source for current information about state-of-the-art approaches to strategies and issues in assessment, prevention, and treatment of adolescent substance abuse. Clinical case reports and descriptions of new and innovative evaluation and treatment methods are encouraged. Contact at:

Customer Service
The Haworth Press Inc.
10 Alice Street
Binghamton, NY 13904
Telephone: (800) 429-6784
Fax: (800) 895-0582
E-mail: getinfo@haworthpress.com
Web site: www.haworthpress.com/FAQ

- *Journal of Drug Education:* Authoritative, peer-refereed, quarterly publication affording a wide-ranging coverage of important trends and developments in the drug field. It provides critical analyses, innovative approaches, scholarly standards, and clear, concise reports on theoretical, research, and programmatic issues. Contact at:

  Baywood Publishing Company, Inc.
  26 Austin Avenue
  P.O. Box 337
  Amityville, NY 11701
  Telephone: (631) 691-1270
  Fax: (631) 691-1770
  E-mail: info@baywood.com
  Orderline: (800) 638-7819

- *Journal of Drug Issues:* This refereed publication with international contributors and subscribers is dedicated to providing a professional and scholarly forum centered on the national and international problems associated with drugs, especially illicit drugs. Contact at:

  School of Criminology and Criminal Justice
  Florida State University
  P.O. Box 66696
  Tallahassee, FL 32313-6696
  Telephone: (850) 644-7368
  E-mail: jdi@garnet.fsu.edu

- *Journal of Ethnicity in Substance Abuse:* Formerly *Drugs & Society,* this journal covers research on ethnic and cultural variations in alcohol, tobacco, and other drug use and abuse. The journal is a clearinghouse and forum for culturally competent strategies for individual, group, and family treatment of alcohol, tobacco, and other drug abuse; program development and evaluation, prevention programming; and harm reduction. Contact at:

  Customer Service
  The Haworth Press Inc.
  10 Alice Street
  Binghamton, NY 13904
  Telephone: (800) 429-6784
  Fax: (800) 895-0582
  E-mail: getinfo@haworthpress.com
  Web site: www.haworthpress.com/FAQ

- *Journal of Maintenance in the Addictions: Innovations in Research, Theory and Practice:* This peer-reviewed journal focuses on bringing treatment to the vast untreated population while improving the quality, efficiency, and efficacy of care for opioid addiction. Other features include innovative models for methadone treatment programs, new and developing pharmacotherapies, and case study discussions in which two to three clinicians respond to a case presentation. Articles include original scientific papers based on clinical and laboratory studies; review and tutorial articles; personal, regional, national, and international articles; case studies; reports related to program administration activities; and articles dealing with established and innovative counseling techniques and strategies. Contact at:

Customer Service
The Haworth Press Inc.
10 Alice Street
Binghamton, NY 13904
Telephone: (800) 429-6784
Fax: (800) 895-0582
E-mail: getinfo@haworthpress.com
Web site: www.haworthpress.com/FAQ

- *Journal of Ministry in Addiction & Recovery:* The journal is designed for pastoral caregivers involved with services and programs for addicted clients and also for substance abuse treatment centers that are interested in expanding their services to include pastoral/ministry services as a part of the team approach. Contact at:

Customer Service
The Haworth Press Inc.
10 Alice Street
Binghamton, NY 13904
Telephone: (800) 429-6784
Fax: (800) 895-0582
E-mail: getinfo@haworthpress.com
Web site: www.haworthpress.com/FAQ

- *Journal of Online Behavior:* Peer-reviewed, behavioral science/social science journal, concerned with the study of human behavior in the online environment, and with the impact of evolving communication and information technology on individuals, groups, organizations, and society. It publishes full-length articles and research reports. Manuscripts must be submitted electronically. Contact at:

Editor
Joseph B. Walther
Department of Language, Literature, and Communication
Rensselaer Polytechnic Institute
Troy, NY 12180-3590
Telephone: (518) 276-2557
E-mail: jobeditor@behavior.net

- *Journal of Psychoactive Drugs:* Quarterly multidisciplinary periodical. The journal addresses the multiplex nature of substance use and abuse and has provided in-depth examination of a host of complex topics, including the disease concept of addiction, drug use and criminality, drug use and the elderly, drug use and sexual behavior, ethnographic drug research, the history of cocaine smoking, therapeutic communities, hallucinogens, stimulants, depressants, smokable drugs, drug dependence and the family, women and substance abuse, professional treatment and the 12-Step process, chemical dependence and AIDS, dual diagnosis, psychotherapy/counseling, adverse effects of tobacco smoking, understanding and preventing relapse, substance abuse in the workplace, drug testing, methadone treatment, prescription drug issues, and culturally relevant substance abuse treatment. Contact at:

Haight-Ashbury Publications
612 Clayton Street
San Francisco, CA 94117
Telephone: (415) 565-1904
Fax: (415) 864-6162
E-mail: hapjpd@>hafreeclinics.org

- *Journal of Social Work Practice in the Addictions:* This journal is designed to help social work practitioners stay abreast of the latest developments in the field of addictions. It publishes refereed articles on innovative individual, family, group work, and community practice models for treating and preventing substance abuse and other addictions in diverse populations. Contact at:

Customer Service
The Haworth Press Inc.
10 Alice Street
Binghamton, NY 13904
Telephone: (800) 429-6784
Fax: (800) 895-0582
E-mail: getinfo@haworthpress.com
Web site: www.haworthpress.com/FAQ

- *Journal of Substance Abuse Treatment:* Features peer-reviewed research articles pertinent to the treatment of nicotine, alcohol, and other drug dependence. Directed toward treatment practitioners in both private and public sectors. Contact at:

Elsevier (go to www.elsevier.com for details)
Regional Sales Office (United States)
Customer Services Department
6277 Sea Harbor Drive
Orlando, FL 32887-4800
Telephone: (877) 839-7126
Fax: (407) 363-1354
E-mail: usinfo-f@elsevier.com

- *Journal of Substance Use:* Quarterly international journal, publishing peer-reviewed articles on issues relating to the use of legal and illegal substances. Informs and supports those undertaking research in substance use, developing substance use services, and participating in, leading, and developing educational and training programs. Papers may explore legal issues, therapeutic interventions and treatments, and behavioral approaches. Contact at:

  Customer Services for Taylor & Francis Group Journals (United States)
  325 Chestnut Street, Suite 800
  Philadelphia, PA 19106
  Telephone: (800) 354-1420
  Fax: (215) 625-8914

- *Journal of Teaching in the Addictions:* The first journal dedicated to instructional/ educational issues for the drug and alcohol field. Test and assessment reviews, evaluations of audiovisual material, simulations, new computer and technology applications are discussed. Contact at:

  The Haworth Press Inc.
  10 Alice Street
  Binghamton, NY 13904 (United States)
  Telephone: (800) 429-6784
  Fax: (800) 895-0582
  E-mail: getinfo@haworthpress.com
  Web site: www.haworthpress.com/FAQ

- *Prevention & Treatment (Electronic Journal):* Peer-reviewed electronic journal sponsored by the American Psychological Association. Articles cover major empirical and theoretical research on prevention, the outcome of psychotherapy and social and environmental interventions, biologically oriented therapy, and the combination of such interventions. Contributions of different lengths are encouraged in the form of Brief Reports or Full Articles. Contact at:

  Editor
  Martin E. P. Seligman, PhD

  Manuscript Submission
  E-mail: admin@apa.org

- *Prevention File: Alcohol, Tobacco, and Other Drugs:* Reports on current research, field experiences, public policy applications, innovations, trends, and strategies concerned with reducing health and safety problems associated with alcohol, tobacco, and other drug use. It features exclusive Q&A interviews with prevention researchers and public health advocates, timely updates on alcohol and tobacco industry retailers and producers, an ongoing interpretive series on national and international research centers, media analysis, and resource reviews. Contact at:

Prevention File
4635 West Talmadge Drive
San Diego, CA 92116-4834
E-mail: tomc@silvergategroup.com

- *Psychology of Addictive Behaviors:* Published quarterly, the journal includes peer-reviewed full-length research reports, literature reviews, essays, brief reports, and comments related to the psychological aspects of addictive behaviors. Contact at:

American Psychological Association
Subscriptions
750 First Street NE
Washington, DC 20002-4242
Telephone: (202) 336-5600
Fax: (202) 336-5568
E-mail: subscriptions@apa.org

- *Science & Practice Perspectives:* A biannual, peer-reviewed journal for drug abuse researchers and treatment providers. Regular features include reviews of critical topics in the science of prevention and treatment, service providers' perspectives on what works in diverse treatment settings and priorities for future research. Contact at:

National Institute on Drug Abuse
National Institutes of Health
6001 Executive Boulevard, Room 5213
Bethesda, MD 20892-9561
Telephone: (301) 443-1124
E-mail: information@lists.nida.nih.gov

- *Substance Abuse:* A peer-reviewed journal, the official publication of AMERSA, offers wide-ranging coverage for medical professionals and addiction specialists in teaching, clinical care, and service delivery. The journal's multi-disciplinary Editorial Board represents the full strength and range of AMERSA's experience and teaching. Contact at:

Publishing Editor—Brain and Behavior
Sarah Williams
Kluwer Academic/Plenum Publishers
233 Spring Street
New York, NY 10013
Telephone: (212) 620-8003
Fax: (212) 463-0742
E-mail: Sarah.Williams@wkap.com

- *Substance Misuse Bulletin:* Concerned with all major aspects of substance misuse and related topics in the United Kingdom and overseas, this journal is published four times a year by the Centre for Addiction Studies. It welcomes contributions from practitioners, policymakers, academics, and researchers. Contact at:

Submissions
Alison Keating
Substance Misuse Bulletin
Centre for Addiction Studies
Department of Psychiatry of Addictive Behavior
St. George's Hospital Medical School
Cranmer Terrace
London SW17 0RE, United Kingdom
Fax: (+44) 181 725 2914

- *Substance Use & Misuse* (formerly the *International Journal of the Addictions*): Provides a unique international multidisciplinary environment for the exchange of facts, theories, viewpoints, and unresolved issues concerning substance use and misuse (licit and illicit drugs, alcohol, nicotine, and caffeine), "abuse," and dependency; eating disorders; and gambling. Founded and edited by Stanley Einstein, Institute for the Study of Drug Misuse, Inc., Jerusalem, Israel. Contact at:

United States, Canada, and South America Customer Service and Distribution
Marcel Dekker, Inc.
Cimarron Road
P.O. Box 5005
Monticello, NY 12701
Telephone: (845) 796-1919; (800) 228-1160
Fax: (845) 796-1772

ALCOHOL

- *Addiction:* See description in "General" section.
- *Alcohol:* For both practitioners and basic scientists, *Alcohol* is the major international journal devoted solely to biomedical research on alcohol and alcoholism. Peer-reviewed, this journal features original research, review, and theoretical articles, brief and rapid communications. Contact at:

Elsevier (go to www.elsevier.com for details)
Regional Sales Office (United States)
Customer Support Department
360 Park Avenue South
New York, NY 10010-1710
Telephone: (212) 633-3730; for North American customers: (888) 437-4636
Fax: (212) 633-3680
E-mail: usinfo-f@elsevier.com

- *Alcohol & Alcoholism:* Official bimonthly journal of the Medical Council on Alcoholism, the journal covers biomedical, psychological, and sociological aspects of alcoholism and alcohol research. Papers include new results obtained experimentally (including clinical or theoretical), or new interpretations of existing data. The following submissions are included in the journal: Full-length papers, Rapid communications, Letters to the Editors, Reviews, Commentaries, and Book Reviews. Contributors are strongly urged to be short and concise. Contact at:

  Oxford University Press
  2001 Evans Road
  Cary, NC 27513
  Telephone: (919) 677-0977, ext. 6686; (800) 852-7323
  Fax: (919) 677-1714
  E-mail: jnl.etoc@uop.co.uk

- *Alcohol Research & Health* (formerly *Alcohol Health and Research World*): A quarterly, peer-reviewed scientific journal, published by the National Institute on Alcohol Abuse and Alcoholism (NIAAA). Each issue focuses on a specific alcohol-related topic, presenting the latest research findings and developments. Available online starting from Volume 18 (1) 1994. Contact at:

  National Technical Information Service (NTIS)
  U.S. Department of Commerce
  5285 Port Royal Road
  Springfield, VA 22161
  Telephone: (800) 553-6847
  Fax: (703) 321-8547

- *Alcoholic Beverage Medical Research Foundation (ABMRF) Journal (online):* Publication covering 1991-2001 that features leading scientific articles on sociobehavioral and biomedical effects of alcohol consumption. Since 2002, the journal lists references to recently published alcohol research studies, organized into various behavioral and medical subjects, with links to available online abstracts. Contact at:

  Alcoholic Beverage Medical Research Foundation
  1122 Kenilworth Drive, Suite 407
  Baltimore, MD 21204
  Telephone: (410) 821-7066
  Fax: (410) 821-7065
  E-mail: info@abmrf.org

- *Alcoholism Treatment Quarterly:* The practitioner's quarterly for individual, group, and family therapy. The journal features articles specifically related to the treatment of alcoholism, details the "how to" approaches of intervention and therapy, presents case studies and commentaries by counselors and therapists, publishes original research and articles related to theory development. Contact at:

The Haworth Press Inc.
10 Alice Street
Binghamton, NY 13904
Telephone: (800) 429-6784 (United States and Canada); (607) 722-5857
    (outside the United States and Canada)
Fax: (800) 895-0582 (United States and Canada); (607) 771-0012 (outside the
    United States and Canada)
E-mail: getinfo@haworthpress.com
Web site: www.haworthpress.com/FAQ

- *Alcoholism: Clinical and Experimental Research:* A monthly multidisciplinary journal publishing original research that makes substantial contributions to the understanding of the etiology, treatment, and prevention of alcohol-related disorders. Issues include original, peer-reviewed articles, rapid communications, minireviews, and editorial commentaries. Contact at:

Publisher
John Ewers
Lippincott William & Wilkins
351 West Camden Street
Baltimore, MD 21201
Telephone: (410) 528-4088
E-mail: jewers@lww.com

- *Drug and Alcohol Dependence:* A peer-reviewed international journal sponsored by College on Problems of Drug Dependence (CPDD). The journal provides researchers, clinicians, and policymakers access to material from all perspectives in a single journal that has received rigorous editorial review. Articles include studies of the chemistry of substances of abuse, their actions at molecular and cellular sites, laboratory-based and clinical research in humans, substance abuse treatment, and prevention research. Contact at:

Elsevier (go to www.elsevier.com for details)
Regional Sales Office (United States)
Customer Support Department
P.O. Box 945
New York, NY 10159-0945
Telephone: (212) 633-3730; for North American customers: (888) 437-4636
Fax: (212) 633-3680
E-mail: usinfo-f@elsevier.com

- *Journal of Studies on Alcohol:* A bimonthly-refereed journal concerned with scientific research related to alcohol and drugs. Articles cover the uses and abuses from the perspectives of the behavioral, biological, medical, and sociocultural sciences. Contact at:

  Editor
  Marc A. Schuckit, MD
  Journal of Studies on Alcohol
  Department of Psychiatry (116A)
  VA San Diego Healthcare System
  3350 La Jolla Village Drive
  San Diego, CA 92161-2002
  Telephone: (858) 552-8585, ext. 7978
  E-mail: jsaeditor@ucsd.edu

- *Social History of Alcohol Review:* A refereed, international, and cross-disciplinary publication, this quarterly journal of the Alcohol and Temperance History Group promotes the exchange of ideas in any aspect of past alcohol use, abuse, production, and control within given societies or countries. Contact at:

  Subscriptions
  Jon Miller
  Secretary-Treasurer, Alcohol and Temperance History Group (ATHG)
  Department of English
  University of Akron
  Akron, OH 44325-1906
  Telephone: (330) 972-5717
  E-mail: mjon@uakron.edu

  Editor Contact
  E-mail: shar@athg.org

EATING DISORDERS

- *Addiction Research and Theory:* See description in "General" section.
- *Eating Behaviors:* Peer-reviewed, original behavioral research and reviews on the etiology, prevention, and treatment of obesity, binge eating, and other eating disorders in both adults and children. Two types of manuscripts are encouraged: (1) descriptive studies establishing functional relationships between obesity and/or eating behavior and one or a combination of social, cognitive, environmental, attitudinal, emotional, or biochemical factors; and (2) clinical outcome research evaluating the efficacy of prevention or treatment protocols. Contact at:

Elsevier (go to www.elsevier.com for details)
Regional Sales Office (United States)
Customer Support Department
P.O. Box 945
New York, NY 10159-0945
Telephone: (212) 633-3730; for North American customers: (888) 437-4636
Fax: (212) 633-3680
E-mail: usinfo-f@elsevier.com

- *Eating Disorders: The Journal of Treatment and Prevention:* A distinguished international editorial board ensures that articles reflect the current theories, effective therapies, and treatment approaches in eating disorders, from anorexia nervosa to bingeing to yo-yo dieting. Contact at:

Customer Services for Taylor & Francis Group Journals (United States)
325 Chestnut Street, Suite 800
Philadelphia, PA 19106
Telephone: (800) 354-1420
Fax: (215) 625-8914
Web site: www.taylorandfrancis.com

- *International Journal of Eating Disorders:* Publishes basic research, clinical, and theoretical articles on anorexia nervosa, bulimia, obesity, and other atypical patterns of eating behavior and body weight regulation. Full-length articles or brief reports are welcome. Contact at:

North, Central, South America
Subscription Inquiries
John Wiley & Sons, Inc.
Attn: Journals Admin Dept., United Kingdom
111 River Street
Hoboken, NJ 07030
Telephone: (201) 748-6645
E-mail: subinfo@wiley.com

Manuscript Submission
Michael Strober, PhD
Department of Psychiatry, UCLA
Neuropsychiatric Institute
760 Westwood Plaza
Los Angeles, CA 90024
E-mail: mstrober@npih.medsch.ucla.edu

- *Psychology of Addictive Behaviors:* See description in "General" section.
- *Substance Use & Misuse:* See description in "General" section.

GAMBLING

- *Addiction Research and Theory;* See description in "General" section.
- *Electronic Journal of Gambling Issues: eGambling (EJGI):* Peer-reviewed articles about gambling as a social phenomenon and the prevention and treatment of gambling problems are offered in an Internet-based forum for developments in gambling-related research, policy, and treatment as well as personal accounts about gambling and gambling behavior. The editor welcomes manuscripts submitted by researchers and clinicians, people involved in gambling as players, and family and friends of gamblers. Contact at:

  Editor
  Phil Lange
  The Electronic Journal of Gambling Issues: eGambling
  Centre for Addiction and Mental Health
  33 Russell Street
  Toronto, Ontario M5S 2S1, Canada
  Telephone: (416) 535-8501, ext. 6077
  E-mail: Phil_Lange@camh.net

- *International Gambling Studies:* Peer-reviewed interdisciplinary journal in gambling studies presenting work on the theory, methods, practice, and history of gambling. The journal encourages articles that offer a new theoretical argument, provide new data, or use an innovative methodological approach or mode of analysis. Contact at:

  Customer Services for Taylor & Francis Group Journals (United States)
  325 Chestnut Street, Suite 800
  Philadelphia, PA 19106
  Telephone: (800) 354-1420
  Fax: (215) 625-8914
  Web site: www.taylorandfrancis.com

- *Journal of Gambling Studies:* An interdisciplinary forum for information on gambling behavior, both controlled and pathological, problems attendant to, or resultant from, gambling behavior including alcoholism, suicide, crime, and mental health problems. Articles are representative of a cross-section of disciplines including psychiatry, psychology, sociology, political science, criminology, and social work, and are of interest to the professional and layperson alike. Contact at:

Publishing Editor
Kluwer Academic Publishers
Mr. Michael Williams
101 Philip Drive
Assinippi Park
Norwell, MA 02061
Telephone: (781) 681-0619
Fax: (781) 871-7507
E-mail: Michael.Williams@wkap.com

Manuscript Submission
Howard J. Shaffer, PhD, CAS
Harvard Medical School
Division on Addictions
350 Longwood Avenue, Suite 200
Boston, MA 02115

- *Psychology of Addictive Behaviors:* See description in "General" section.
- *Substance Use & Misuse:* See description in "General" section.

NICOTINE

- *Addiction:* See description in "General" section.
- *Nicotine and Tobacco Research:* A peer-reviewed journal devoted exclusively to nicotine and tobacco research from the biobehavioral, neurophysiological, epidemiological, prevention, and treatment arenas, this journal seeks submissions that are technically competent, but also are original and contain information or ideas of fresh interest to our international readership. Contact at:

Customer Services for Taylor & Francis Group Journals (United States)
325 Chestnut Street, Suite 800
Philadelphia, PA 19106
Telephone: (800) 354-1420
Fax: (215) 625-8914
Web site: www.taylorandfrancis.com

- *Psychology of Addictive Behaviors:* See description in "General" section.
- *Tobacco Control:* Provides a forum for research, analysis, commentary, and debate on policies, programs, and strategies that are likely to further the objectives of a comprehensive tobacco control policy. The journal studies the nature and consequences of tobacco use worldwide; the effect of tobacco use on health, the economy, the environment, and society; the efforts of the health community and health advocates to prevent and control tobacco use; and the activities of the tobacco industry and its allies to promote tobacco use. Contact at:

Editor
Professor Simon Chapman
Department of Public Health & Community Medicine
University of Sydney, Building A27
Sydney, NSW 2006, Australia
Telephone: (+61) 2 9351 5203
Fax: (+61) 2 9351 7420
E-mail: simonc@health.usyd.edu.au

Subscriptions (all inquiries and orders)
Telephone: (+44) (0) 20 7383 6270
Fax: (+44) (0) 20 7383 6402
E-mail: subscriptions@bmjgroup.com

Sex

- *Addiction Research and Theory:* See description in "General" section.
- *Archives of Sexual Behavior:* Official publication of the International Academy of Sex Research is dedicated to the dissemination of information in the field of sexual science, broadly defined. Contributions consist of empirical research, theoretical reviews and essays, clinical case reports, letters to the editor, and book reviews. Contact at:

Executive Publishing Editor
Kluwer Academic/Plenum Publishers
Ms. Carol Bischoff
233 Spring Street
New York, NY 10013-1578
Telephone: (212) 620-8085
Fax: (212) 463-0742
E-mail: bischoff@plenum.com

Manuscript Submission
Editor
Kenneth J. Zucker, PhD
Child and Adolescent Gender Identity Clinic
Child Psychiatry Program
Centre for Addiction and Mental Health—Clarke Division
250 College Street
Toronto, Ontario M5T 1R8, Canada

- *Deviant Behavior:* All aspects of deviant behavior are discussed, including crime, juvenile delinquency, alcohol abuse and narcotic addiction, sexual deviance, societal reaction to handicap and disfigurement, mental illness, and socially inappropriate behavior. Contact at:

Customer Services for Taylor & Francis Group Journals (United States)
325 Chestnut Street, Suite 800
Philadelphia, PA 19106
Telephone: (800) 354-1420
Fax: (215) 625-8914
Web site: www.taylorandfrancis.com

- *Journal of Sex and Marital Therapy:* Featured topics include sexual dysfunctions, therapeutic techniques, clinical considerations, theoretical issues, and marital relationships. Contact at:

Customer Services for Taylor & Francis Group Journals (United States)
325 Chestnut Street, Suite 800
Philadelphia, PA 19106
Telephone: (800) 354-1420
Fax: (215) 625-8914
Web site: www.taylorandfrancis.com

- *Journal of Sex Research:* Published quarterly by the Society for the Scientific Study of Sexuality, the journal is devoted to the publication of articles relevant to the disciplines involved in the scientific study of sexuality. It provides empirical reports, theoretical essays, literature reviews, methodological articles, historical articles, clinical reports, teaching papers, book reviews, and letters to the editor. Contact at:

The Society Office
Executive Director
David Fleming
P.O. Box 416
Allentown, PA 18105-0416
Telephone: (610) 530-2483
Fax: (610) 530-2485
E-mail: thesociety@inetmail.att.net

- *Sexual Abuse: A Journal of Research and Treatment:* Focuses exclusively on sexual abuse, thoroughly investigating its causes, consequences, and treatment strategies. It provides essential data for those working in both clinical and academic environments. Contact at:

Senior Editor Behavorial Sciences
Kluwer Academic/Plenum Publishers
Ms. Sharon Panulla
233 Spring Street
New York, NY 10013-1578
Telephone: (212) 620-8000
Fax: (212) 463-0742
E-mail: Sharon.Panulla@wkap.com

Manuscript Submission
Managing Editor
Connie Isaac
4900 SW Griffith Drive, Suite 274
Beaverton, OR 97005-3035
Telephone: (503) 643-1023
Fax: (503) 643-5084

- *Sexual Addiction and Compulsivity:* Quarterly, peer-reviewed journal that provides useful and innovative strategies for intervention and treatment from a multidisciplinary perspective. Conceptual issues regarding addiction, compulsivity, and sexual medicine will be explored as new research emerges, as well as the underlying challenges in public policy and prevention, and criteria for diagnosis and reimbursement. Contact at:

Customer Services for Taylor & Francis Group Journals (United States)
325 Chestnut Street, Suite 800
Philadelphia, PA 19106
Telephone: (800) 354-1420
Fax: (215) 625-8914
Web site: www.taylorandfrancis.com

- *Sexual and Relationship Therapy* (formerly *Sexual and Marital Therapy*): International refereed journal concerned with sexual and marital function. It features the results of original research, subject reviews, accounts of therapeutic and counseling practice, case studies, short communications, and book reviews. Contact at:

Customer Services for Taylor & Francis Group Journals (United States)
325 Chestnut Street, Suite 800
Philadelphia, PA 19106
Telephone: (800) 354-1420
Fax: (215) 625-8914
Web site: www.taylorandfrancis.com

ADDICTION MAGAZINES AND WEB SITES

General—Covering All Addictions

- *Addiction Professional:* The official magazine of NAADAC, The Association for Addiction Professionals. It is the addiction treatment and prevention field's clinical magazine outlining what's working in services for people with alcohol and drug use disorders. Contact at:

Editor
Gary A. Enos
Telephone: (401) 831-6020, ext. 3019
E-mail: genow@manisses.com

- *Counselor: The Magazine for Addiction Professionals:* A bimonthly publication featuring one cover story and six in-depth feature articles written by the top expert in a particular subject area of addiction treatment. Contact at:

A Health Communications, Inc. Publication
3201 SW 15th Street
Deerfield Beach, FL 33442-8190
Telephone: (954) 360-0909; (800) 851-9100
Fax: (954) 360-0034
E-mail: info@counselormagazine.com
Web site: www.counselormagazine.com

- *CrossCurrents: The Journal of Addiction and Mental Health:* The only magazine exploring issues in addiction and mental health in Canada. It provides a unique perspective on current mental health and addiction-related issues through professionally written stories, research summaries, news, and feature articles. Contact at:

The Editor
CrossCurrents
Centre for Addiction and Mental Health
33 Russell Street
Toronto, Ontario
Canada M5S 2S1
Telephone: (416) 595-6714
Fax: (416) 595-6892
E-mail: hema_zbogar@camh.net

- *Drug and Alcohol Findings:* The only magazine to publish evidence on the effectiveness of interventions to treat, prevent, or reduce drug and alcohol problems. It is produced in the United Kingdom by a partnership of leading national charities. Contact at:

Subscriptions
DrugScope
32-36 Loman Street
London SE1 0EE, London
Telephone: (020) 7928 1211
Fax: (020) 7928 1771
E-mail: findings@drugscope.org.uk

- *Drugs in Society:* A quarterly magazine produced by the Alcohol and Drug Foundation–Queensland. Contact at:

Alcohol and Drug Foundation–Queensland
Sureplan House, Level 3
133 Leichhardt Street
Spring Hill
Queensland, Australia
P.O. Box 332
Spring Hill Qld.
Australia 4004
Telephone: (+617) 3832-3798
Fax: (+617) 3832-5625
E-mail: dinie@adfq.org
Web site: www.adfq.org

* *Drug Watch:* Produced by the Alcohol and Drug Foundation–Queensland, the magazine highlights the issues relating to alcohol and other drug abuse. Contact at:

Alcohol and Drug Foundation–Queensland
Sureplan House, Level 3
133 Leichhardt St.
Spring Hill
Queensland, Australia
P.O. Box 332
Spring Hill Qld.
Australia 4004
Telephone: (+617) 3832-3798
Fax: (+617) 3832-5625
E-mail: dinie@adfq.org
Web site: www.adfq.org

* *Globe:* The Global Alcohol Policy Alliance's (GAPA) international magazine on alcohol. It features research and news related to alcohol and substance abuse issues. Contact at:

Publisher
Institute of Alcohol Studies
12 Caxton Street
London, SW1H 0QS
Telephone: (020) 7222-4001
Fax: (020) 7799-2510

* *HabitSmart (online):* This web site provides alternative theories (non-12-step focus) of addictive behavior and change, and provides addiction information in general. The site offers an abundance of information about addictive behavior: theories of habit endurance and habit change as well as tips for effectively managing problematic habitual behavior. Contact at:

Robert Westermeyer, PhD
E-mail: habtsmrt@cts.com

- *Medbroadcast.com (online):* A comprehensive, consumer-oriented online medical resource dedicated to providing (1) credible, relevant, mainstream information about health care concerns; (2) a safe, supportive, carefully managed community environment to communicate with others about similar health care issues; and (3) carefully selected health care products that enhance the quality of life of those dealing with illness. Contact at:

Web site: www.medbroadcast.com

- *Paradigm:* Magazine for professionals and individuals interested in addiction-related subjects. Each quarterly issue contains articles written by the staff of the Illinois Institute for Addiction Recovery and other experts in the field. Contact at:

Illinois Institute for Addiction Recovery (IIAR)
5409 N. Knoxville Avenue
Peoria, IL 61614
Telephone: (800) 522-3784
E-mail: eric.zehr@proctor.org

- *Recover Magazine:* Lifestyle magazine for people at all stages of addiction recovery. Every issue discusses therapeutic options for people in the recovery community. Distributed to hospitals, treatment centers, medical offices, and meeting facilities. Contact at:

Recover Magazine
P.O. Box 4078
Ft. Lauderdale, FL 33338
Telephone: (954) 764-1069; (outside Florida): (866) 273-2683

Editor-Publisher
Tara Coiro

- *Scientific American* (available online at www.ScientificAmerican.com): The oldest continuously published magazine in the United States, *Scientific American* has been bringing its readers unique insights about developments in science and technology for more than 150 years. Contact at:

Scientific American, Inc.
415 Madison Avenue
New York, NY 10017
Telephone: (212) 754-0550
Web site: www.sciam.com

Subscriptions
Telephone: (800) 333-1199
E-mail: subscriptons@sciam.com

Editors
E-mail: editors@sciam.com

ALCOHOL

- *Addiction Professional:* See description in "General" section.
- *Alcohol Alert:* Published three times a year by the Institute of Alcohol Studies, whose aims are to increase the knowledge of alcohol and the social and health consequences of its misuse and to encourage and support the adoption of effective measures for the management and prevention of alcohol-related problems. Contact at:

Institute of Alcohol Studies
1 The Quay, St. Ives
Cambridgeshire, PE27 5AR
Telephone: (+44) 1480 466766
Fax: (+44) 1480 497583
E-mail: info@ias.org.uk

- *Drug Watch:* See description in "General" section.
- *Globe:* See description in "General" section.
- *Medbroadcast.com (online):* See description in "General" section.
- *Straight Talk: The Alcohol Concern Quarterly Magazine:* Published quarterly, its principal aims are to reduce the incidence and costs of alcohol-related harm and to increase the range and the quality of the services available to people with alcohol-related problems. Alcohol Concern is the national voluntary agency on alcohol misuse and acts as the national umbrella for 500 local agencies. Alcohol Concern is a registered charity. Contact at:

Alcohol Concern's Office
Waterbridge House
32-36 Loman Street
London SE1 0EE, England
Telephone: (+020) 7928 7377
Fax: (+020) 7928 4644
E-mail: contact@alcoholconcern.org.uk

EATING DISORDERS

- *Medbroadcast.com (online):* See description in "General" section.

GAMBLING

- *Electronic Journal of Gambling Issues: eGambling (EJGI):* See description in "Gambling" section.
- *Wager (online):* A weekly, peer-reviewed research bulletin published by the Division on Addictions at Harvard Medical School in collaboration with the Massachusetts Council on Compulsive Gambling. The mission of the *Wager* is to gather, distill, and share gambling-related resources, providing readers with a direct pipeline to the latest information on pathological gambling. Submissions focus on gambling-related research, treatment, and public policy. Contact at:

The Wager
The Landmark Center
401 Park Drive, 2nd Floor East
Boston, MA 02215
Telephone: (617) 384-9030
Fax: (617) 384-9023
E-mail: wager@hms.harvard.edu

NICOTINE

- *Medbroadcast.com (online):* See description in "General" section.

SEX

- *Online Sexual Addiction:* To serve those struggling with sexual addiction, or compulsive sexuality, OSA provides easy access to relevant support, education, and resources. OSA provides free self-assessment and a free bulletin board that is monitored and kept free of pornography. Contact at:

Online Sexual Addiction
P.O. Box 181
Morro Bay, CA 93443

Membership
E-mail: member@onlinesexaddict.org

ADDICTION NEWSLETTERS AND WEB SITES

GENERAL—COVERING ALL ADDICTIONS

- *Addiction Treatment Forum (online):* Reports on substance abuse and addiction research, therapies, news, and events of interest to both health care professionals and patients. The focus has been on methadone used in opioid addiction treatment, although many other treatment options and topics of concern are regularly presented. Contact at:

Clinco Communications, Inc.
P.O. Box 685
Mundelein, IL 60060
Telephone: (847) 392-3937
Web site: www.atforum.com

- *Addictions Newsletter:* Official newsletter of the American Psychological Association, Division 50-Addictions, it promotes advances in research, professional training, and clinical practice within the broad range of addictive behaviors including problematic use of alcohol, nicotine, and other drugs and disorders involving gambling, eating, sexual behavior, or spending. Contact at:

Editor
Bruce S. Liese, PhD
KUMC Family Medicine
3901 Rainbow Blvd.
Kansas City, KS 66160-7370
E-mail: bliese@kumc.edu

- *ATTC Networker:* (Addiction Technology Transfer Center)—Dedicated to identifying and advancing opportunities for improving addiction treatment. It transmits the latest knowledge, skills, and attitudes of professional addiction treatment practice. ATTC's vision is to unify science, education, and services to transform the lives of individuals and families affected by alcohol and other drug addiction. Contact at:

ATTC National Office
Telephone: (816) 482-1200
E-mail: no@nattc.org

- *Alcoholism and Drug Abuse Weekly:* Offers significant news and analysis of public policy developments at the federal and state levels. ADAW is an indispensable resource for directors of addiction treatment centers, managed care executives, federal and state policymakers, and health care consultants. Topics include managed care's impact on behavioral health, integration of addiction services with mental health programs, national opinion pieces, and the latest findings in prevention and treatment. Contact at:

Manisses Customer Service
208 Governor Street
Providence, RI 02906
Telephone: (800) 333-7771
Fax: (401) 861-6370
E-mail: Manissescs@manisses.com

- *DATA: The Brown University Digest of Addiction Theory and Application:* A monthly news-style synopsis of critical research developments in the treatment and prevention of alcoholism and drug abuse, including dozens of research abstracts from over 75 medical journals. Provides professional commentary, treatment assessment, tips for measuring outcomes, examinations of co-occurring disorders, and suggested reading. Contact at:

Manisses Customer Service
208 Governor Street
Providence, RI 02906
Telephone: (800) 333-7771
Fax: (401) 861-6370
E-mail: Manissescs@manisses.com

- *Drug Policy Analysis Bulletin:* A quarterly bulletin that publishes concise articles bringing research and analysis to bear on the problems of drug abuse control. This applies to the currently licit drugs, alcohol and nicotine, as well as those substances now banned entirely or restricted to medical use. Contact at:

Drug Policy Analysis Bulletin
c/o Federation of American Scientists
1717 K Street NW, Suite 209
Washington, DC 20036

- *Freedom Newsletter:* CAADAC's official bimonthly publication, featuring news on legislative and regulatory issues, regional news, and other articles of interest relating specifically to addiction treatment in California. Contact at:

Freedom Newsletter Editor
Sherry Daley
California Association of Alcoholism & Drug Abuse Counselors (CAADAC)
3400 Bradshaw Road, Suite A-5
Sacramento, CA 95827
Telephone: (916) 368-9412
Fax: (916) 368-9424
E-mail: counselors@caadac.org

- *Hazelden Voice: News and Opinion for Recovering People and Professionals:* Published twice a year to help build recovery in the lives of individuals, families, and communities affected by alcoholism, drug dependency, and related diseases. Contact at:

Editor
Marty Duda
Hazelden BC 10
P.O. Box 11
Center City, MN 55012-0011
Telephone: (651) 213-4455; (800) 257-7800, ext. 4455
Fax: (651) 213-4590
E-mail: customersupport@hazelden.org
Web site: www.hazelden.org

- *ICADTS Reporter:* Published quarterly by the International Council on Alcohol, Drugs and Traffic Safety (ICADTS) with support from the U.S. National Highway Traffic Safety Administration. The goal of ICADTS is to reduce mortality and morbidity related to misuse of alcohol and drugs by operators of vehicles in all modes of transportation. Contact at:

Editors
Kathryn Stewart and Barry Sweedler
3798 Mosswood Drive
Lafayette, CA 94549 (United States)
Telephone: (925) 962-1810
Fax: (925) 962-1810
E-mail: Stewart@pire.ort or sweedlb@hotmail.com
Web site: www.icadts.org

- *NAMA Advocate:* This publication reports on diverse issues pertaining to methadone and other subjects of interest to patients in MMT programs. Contact at:

National Alliance of Methadone Advocates
435 Second Avenue
New York, NY 10010
Telephone: (212) 595-6262
Fax: (212) 595-6262
E-mail: NAMAnewsletter@AOL.com
Web site: www.methadone.org

- *NIDA Notes:* Covers drug abuse research in the areas of treatment and prevention, epidemiology, neuroscience, behavioral science, health services, and AIDS. The publication reports on research; identifies resources; and promotes communication among clinicians, researchers, administrators, policymakers, and the public. Contact at:

Subscriptions Department
MasiMax Resources, Inc.
1375 Piccard Drive, Suite 175
Rockville, MD 20850
Telephone: (240) 632-5614
Fax: (240) 632-0519
E-mail: nidanotes@masimax.com

- *Prevention Researcher:* See description in "General" section.
- *Web of Addictions (online):* This site provides information about alcohol and other drug addictions. It was developed because of concerns about the pro drug use messages in some web sites and in some use groups, and also about the extent of misinformation about abused drugs on the Internet. Contact at:

Dick Dillon
E-mail: Razer@ix.netcom.com

ALCOHOL

- *Alcoholism:* A bimonthly newsletter of the Medical Council on Alcohol (MCA), which was founded by doctors for "the benefit of the community to provide an organization of registered medical practitioners with a view to coordination of effort, the better understanding of alcoholism and its prevention and the treatment and after-care of alcoholics." Contact at:

The Medical Council on Alcohol
3 St. Andrew's Place
Regent's Park, London NW1 4LB
Telephone: (44) 20-7487-4445
Fax: (44) 20-7935-4479
E-mail: mca@medicouncilalcol.demon.co.uk

- *Alcoholism and Drug Abuse Weekly:* See description in "General" section.
- *DATA: The Brown University Digest of Addiction Theory and Application:* See description in "General" section.
- *ICADTS Reporter:* See description in "General" section.

EATING DISORDERS

- *Prevention Researcher:* See description in "General" section.

GAMBLING

- *National Center for Responsible Gaming (NCRG):* The first national organization devoted exclusively to funding independent, peer-reviewed scientific research on pathological and youth gambling. Contact at:

NCRG
P.O. Box 14323
Washington, DC 20044-4323
E-mail: contact@ncrg.org

- *Prevention Researcher:* See description in "General" section.
- *Responsible Gaming Quarterly:* A joint publication of the NCRG and the American Gaming Association (AGA). The publication highlights initiatives throughout the industry, government, academia, and the treatment community to address disordered gambling. Contact at:

American Gaming Association (AGA)
555 13th Street NW, Suite 1010 East
Washington, DC 20004
Telephone: (202) 637-6500
Fax: (202) 637-6507
E-mail: info@americangaming.org

- *Wager:* See description in "General" section.

SEX

- *Sexual Science* (formerly the *Society Newsletter*): The quarterly newsletter of the Society for the Scientific Study of Sexuality, the aim is to advance knowledge of sexuality. Contact at:

Editor
Sexual Science
Nancy Coiro
E-mail: ncoiro@yahoo.com

DRUG POLICY ADVOCATES

Many believe that the federal drug policy—the "War on Drugs"—has failed as a national policy. Like Prohibition of the 1920s, illegal drug sales fuel gangs and organized crime and millions of nonviolent drug offenders clog the judicial system creating an expensive and overcrowded correctional system.

The following organizations advocate new, creative approaches to managing the problems of drug abuse and addiction.

THE DRUG POLICY ALLIANCE

Founded in 1987, the Drug Policy Alliance is a nonprofit membership organization with 25,000 member supporters. Relying entirely on private donations from individuals and foundations, it advocates more sensible and humane drug policies. In July 2000, it merged with the Lindesmith Center, a leading independent drug policy institute, to form a national drug policy reform movement.

The mission of the Drug Policy Alliance is to advance policies and attitudes that best reduce the harm of both drug misuse and drug prohibition.

To find an Alliance Center near you, check their web site: www.drugpolicy.org or phone them at (212) 613-8020.

NATIONAL ORGANIZATION FOR THE REFORM OF MARIJUANA LAWS

Since its founding in 1970, National Organization for the Reform of Marijuana Laws (NORML) has sought the repeal of marijuana prohibition so the responsible use of cannabis by adults is no longer penalized. During the 1970s, NORML led successful efforts to decriminalize minor marijuana offenses in 11 states and significantly lowered marijuana penalties elsewhere. Today NORML continues to lead the fight to reform state and federal marijuana laws, whether by voter initiative or through the legislatures. For more information, see www.cannabis-news.com/news/thread17386.shtml. Contact at:

NORML
1600 K Street NW, Suite 501
Washington, DC 20006-2832
Telephone: (202) 483-5500
Web site: www.norml.org

HARM REDUCTION COALITION

The Coalition recognizes that families and communities (especially communities of color) are frequently devastated by addiction, arrest, incarceration, lack of available drug treatment, infectious disease, poor housing, and unemployment. The harm reduction movement grows from the need for a conscientious response to drug use that is less damaging to the social fabric of the United States' diverse communities.

Harm reduction is a set of practical strategies that reduce the negative consequences of drug use. These strategies range from safer use, to managed use, to abstinence. Harm reduction strategies also address the conditions of drug use. Contact at:

Harm Reduction Coalition
22 West 27th Street, 5th Floor
New York, NY 10001
Telephone: (212) 213-6376

And at:
1440 Broadway, Suite 510
Oakland, CA 94612
Telephone: (510) 444-696
Web site: www.harmreduction.org

LAW ENFORCEMENT AGAINST PROHIBITION

Founded on March 16, 2002 by current and former law enforcement personnel, Law Enforcement against Prohibition (LEAP) is a drug-policy reform organization founded on the belief that because drug policies have failed to save lives, lower the rate of addiction, and conserve tax dollars, drug prohibition must end.

LEAP's mission is (1) to educate the public, the media, and policymakers to the failure of current drug policy by presenting an alternate historical picture of the causes, and effects of drug abuse and drug-related crime; (2) to create a speakers bureau staffed with knowledgeable and articulate former drug-warriors who describe the impact of current drug policies on police/community relations, the safety of law enforcement officers and suspects, police corruption and misconduct, and the financial and human costs associated with current drug policies; (3) to restore the public's respect for law enforcement diminished by enforcing drug prohibition; (4) to reduce the multitude of harms resulting from fighting the war on drugs by ending drug prohibition. Contact at:

LEAP
Web site: www.leap.com

MULTIDISCIPLINARY ASSOCIATION FOR PSYCHEDELIC STUDIES

Multidisciplinary Association for Psychedelic Studies (MAPS) sponsors scientific research designed to develop psychedelics and marijuana into FDA-approved prescription medicines and to educate the public about the risks and benefits of these drugs.

It also sends a quarterly publication to its members, and a large number of government policymakers and academic experts. Contact at:

MAPS
2105 Robinson Avenue
Sarasota, Fl 34232
Telephone: (941) 924-6277
Web site: www.maps.org

RELIGIOUS LEADERS FOR A MORE JUST AND COMPASSIONATE DRUG POLICY

An organization founded by religious leaders who believe that the War on Drugs has failed in its efforts to make the United States free of illicit drugs, and that drug war advocates have contrived laws that are highly unjust, racist in application, a threat to individual freedom, and a danger to the nation's public health. Contact at:

Religious Leaders for a More Just and Compassionate Drug Policy
P.O. Box 282471
Nashville, Tennessee 37228-2471
Telephone: (615) 327-9775
Web site: religiousleadersdrugpolicy.org

EDUCATORS FOR SENSIBLE DRUG POLICY

These educators oppose criminal prohibition of drugs, arrests, prosecution, and imprisonment of otherwise law-abiding citizens for what they do in private. Government prohibition, a proven failure as a drug control strategy, violates the fundamental rights of privacy and personal autonomy guaranteed by the Constitution. "We believe that unless they [drug users] do harm to others, people should not be punished—even if they do harm to themselves" (taken from their web site). Contact at:

Educators for Sensible Drug Policy
Web site: www.teachersagainstprohibition.org

CANADIAN FOUNDATION FOR DRUG POLICY

A nonprofit organization founded in 1993 by several of Canada's leading specialists in drug policy— psychologists, pharmacologists, lawyers, health policy advocates, and public policy researchers—Canadian Foundation for Drug Policy (CFDP) is funded entirely by its members and by contributions from other organizations with an interest in drug policy reform. Contact at:

Canadian Foundation for Drug Policy
70 MacDonald Street
Ottawa, Ontario, Canada K2P 1H6
Telephone: (613) 236-1027
Web site: cfdp.ca

These additional organizations are equally opposed to current national drug-control policies, and can be accessed on their web sites:

Alliance for Cannabis Therapeutics
www.marijuana-as-medicine.org

Americans for Medical Rights
Web site: www.medmjscience.org

Americans for Safe Access
Web site: www.safeaccessnow.org

Cannabis Consumers Campaign
Web site: www.cannabisconsumers.org

Center for Cognitive Liberty and Ethics
Web site: www.cognitiveliberty.org

Change The Climate
Web site: www.changetheclimate.com

Christians for Cannabis
Web site: www.christiansforcannabis.com

Common Sense Justice
Web site: www.commonsensejustice.us

Criminal Justice Policy Foundation
Web site: www.cjpf.org

DanceSafe
Web site: www.dancesafe.org

The Dogwood Center
Web site: www.dogwoodcenter.org

Drug Action Network
Web site: www.drugactionnetwork.com

Drug Reform Coordination Network
Web site: www.drcnet.org

Drug Testing Fails
Web site: www.drugtestingfails.org

Efficacy
Web site: www.efficacy-online.org

Families Against Mandatory Minimums
Web site: www.famm.org

Human Rights and the Drug War
Web site: www.hr95.org

Justice Policy Institute
Web site: www.justicepolicy.org

Marijuana Policy Project
Web site: www.mpp.org

The Media Awareness Project
Web site: www.mapinc.org

Mothers Against Misuse and Abuse
Web site: www.mamas.org

National Drug Strategy Network
Web site: www.ndsn.org

The North American Syringe Exchange Network
Web site: www.nasen.org

Reconsider Forum on Drug Policy
Web site: www.reconsider.org

Students for Sensible Drug Policy
Web site: www.ssdp.org

Veterans for More Effective Drug Strategies
Web site: www.vetsformeds.org

GLOSSARY

A

AA See *Alcoholics Anonymous.*

abstinence The act of refraining from a desired activity, such as drinking or sex.

abstinence violation effect (AVE) The response of feeling shame, guilt, and hopelessness that clients often have after they have lapsed following a period of abstinence.

abuse A maladaptive pattern of substance use or behavior that leads to clinically significant distress or impairment.

acid See *LSD.*

acidhead A street name for a habitual user of LSD.

ACOA Adult child of an addicted person.

acupuncture An ancient method of therapy in which certain points of the body are stimulated by the insertion of needles. Its use in the treatment of drug addiction is a recent application of a very old technique.

acute alcohol withdrawal syndrome Following the abrupt cessation of heavy drinking, body mechanisms compensate for the depressing effects of alcohol with hyperactivity in the nervous system.

addiction A brain and energy disorder that manifests itself in compulsive cravings, loss of control, and self-defeating behaviors that are repeated despite harmful consequences.

addiction assessment A systematic procedure to construct a treatment plan by identifying a patient's strengths and problem areas.

addiction medicine A medical specialty dealing with the treatment of addiction.

addiction severity index A means of rating the severity and scope of an addiction by assessing the patient's medical, legal, and psychological status, as well as family/social relationships and drug use.

addictionologist A clinician specializing in addiction disorders who diagnoses and treats addiction withdrawal and helps in the recovery process.

addictive relationship A single, overwhelming involvement that cuts a person off from other activities in his or her life.

addict offenders Individuals who commit criminal acts to support a substance addiction.

ADHD See *Attention-Deficit Hyperactivity Disorder.*

affect   How an individual's mood appears to others.

affirmations   Statements of recognition about client strengths.

aftercare   The continuing rehabilitation treatment and support provided for a patient following release from an institution.

agonist   A drug that increases the activity of another drug.

agonist substitution   A treatment for substance abuse that replaces the abused drug with one that has similar pharmacological action; for example, nicotine chewing gum for tobacco dependence or methadone for heroin dependence.

AIDS (acquired immune deficiency syndrome)   A set of symptoms, including a massive failure of the immune system, caused by the human immunodeficiency virus (HIV).

alcohol   See *ethanol.*

alcohol clinical index   A versatile instrument used by physicians, nurses, and other health care professionals to identify alcohol problems among patients and clients.

alcohol dependence data schedule   An assessment instrument that distinguishes alcoholics from nonalcoholics.

alcohol dependence scale   A survey to determine the severity of alcohol dependence that considers alcohol withdrawal symptoms, obsessive/compulsive drinking, tolerance, and craving.

alcohol dependence syndrome   A cluster of symptoms secondary to alcohol misuse: withdrawal, compulsion, tolerance, craving, and loss of control over alcohol intake.

alcoholic   One who suffers or has suffered physical, psychological, emotional, social, or occupational harm as the result of excessive or habitual alcohol consumption.

alcoholic family   A family affected by the alcoholism of one or more of its members.

Alcoholics Anonymous (AA)   A worldwide support group formed in 1935 for the purpose of rehabilitating alcoholics; AA originated the twelve-step program.

alcoholism   A disease characterized by the excessive and habitual drinking of alcoholic beverages leading to physical, psychological, and social harm.

allergy   A state of hypersensitivity induced by exposure to a particular antigen resulting in harmful immunologic reactions on subsequent exposures.

altered state   A state of consciousness that differs significantly from normal or baseline.

amnesia   Total or partial loss of memory.

amotivational syndrome   A theorized result of chronic marijuana use: apathy; passivity; lethargy; and inability or unwillingness to concentrate.

amphetamines   A class of stimulants that increase energy and decrease appetite.

anabolic steroids   A class of steroids susceptible to misuse, particularly by athletes to increase muscle mass.

analgesic   A substance that reduces or eliminates pain without causing loss of consciousness or altering sensory perception.

analog   A laboratory-made copy of a drug normally derived from a natural substance. See also *designer drug.*

anesthetic   A drug that causes unconsciousness or a loss of general sensation.

angel dust   A common street name for PCP.

anhedonia   The inability to derive pleasure from situations that usually induce it; a feature of major depressive disorders, some severe personality disorders, and postpsychotic states.

anorexia nervosa   A condition characterized by an intense fear of gaining weight and a distorted body image that leads to unhealthy weight loss from food intake restriction and excessive exercise.

Antabuse   The trademark name for disulfiram, a chemical antagonist used to discourage alcohol ingestion because it produces unpleasant effects such as nausea and extreme flushing when alcohol is consumed.

antagonist   A drug that neutralizes or counteracts the effects of another drug.

antagonist substitution   replacing an abused drug with a prescribed medication that has the same pharmacological effects.

antagonist treatment   The use of pharmaceuticals to block the chemical effects of an abused drug. See also *Antabuse.*

anticonvulsives   Drugs used to prevent seizures.

antidepressants   A family of drugs designed to fight depression. See also *SSRIs* and *tricyclic antidepressants.*

antiepileptic agents   Anticonvulsants taken to reduce the frequency and severity of seizures or as an emergency treatment to stop a prolonged seizure.

antihistamines   Any drug that blocks the action of histamine; used primarily to control the symptoms of allergic conditions.

antihypertensives   Drugs used to lower blood pressure.

antisocial personality disorder   A disorder characterized by a failure to observe social norms and a lifelong history of violating others

anxiety   Sense of general discomfort (typically including apprehension, hypervigilance, and physical symptoms such as muscle tension, fatigue, and sleep disturbance) that does not have a well-defined cause.

anxiety disorders   A set of disorders (panic disorder, generalized anxiety disorder, phobias, and obsessive-compulsive disorders) where fear is the predominant symptom.

anxiolytic   A substance that reduces anxiety such as alcohol, opiates, barbiturates, and the benzodiazepines.

aphrodisiac   Any substance that may increase sexual desire or potency.

aromatherapy   An alternative type of medicine that advocates inhaling or massaging into the skin essential oils from plants for therapeutic purposes.

assertiveness skills   Affirmative and confident behavior that allows one to meet one's needs as an individual.

assessment   An ongoing process through which the counselor collaborates with the client and others to gather and interpret information necessary for planning treatment and evaluating client progress.

assessment tools   Questionnaires and interview schedules that aid systematic evaluation of the strengths and problems of a patient. They may be used to establish the nature or cause of the patient's state, needs of the patient and family, and the best treatment approach.

ATOD   alcohol, tobacco, and other drugs.

Attention-Deficit Hyperactivity Disorder (ADHD)   A group of behavioral disorders involving varying degrees of inattention, impulsiveness, and hyperactivity.

autoimmune condition   The formation of antibodies against an endogenous antigen.

autonomic nervous system   The portion of the nervous system that controls involuntary processes such as heart rate, digestion, and blood pressure.

aversive therapy   A controversial method of treating severely self-injurious behavior in developmentally challenged children. Used in exceptionally life-threatening and nonresponsive cases, this therapy consists of exposing the patient to unpleasant tastes, smells, or electric shock to discourage a set of actions.

axon   The part of the neuron consisting of a single fiber along which an action potential is transmitted to the nerve terminal.

axon terminal   The structure at the end of an axon that produces and releases neurotransmitters into the synapse.

B

BAC   See *blood alcohol concentration*.

bagging   See *huffing*.

barbiturates   A widely used group of drugs made from barbituric acid that produce sedation and anesthesia.

baseline   A measurement, calculation, or location used as a basis of comparison.

Beck depression inventory   An instrument used for the screening and diagnosis of depression and also used extensively to monitor therapeutic progress.

behavior   The specific physical actions and reactions through which an organism interacts with its environment.

behavior addiction   A disorder in which a behavior (e.g., gambling or sexual activity) takes place compulsively, is continued despite significant adverse consequences, and takes up a great deal of the person's mental life.

behavior chain analysis   Assessing how one behavior leads to another that leads to another.

behavior modification therapy   A type of therapy that emphasizes the substitution of desirable responses and behaviors for undesirable ones.

behavioral contract   An agreed-on code of behavior.

benzodiazepines   A large family of drugs including hypnotics, anxiolytics, tranquilizers, anticonvulsants, premedicants, and sedatives.

beta-endorphin   A potent endorphin released by the pituitary gland in response to pain, trauma, exercise, and stress.

bibliotherapy   Reading as a form of supportive psychotherapy. The reading topic may enhance the sharing of information or addressing of emotional issues.

Big Book   The informal title of Alcoholics Anonymous, 3rd edition (AA's "Bible").

binge   An unrestrained indulgence in a substance or behavior.

biomarker   Any chemical in the body with molecular features that make it useful for measuring the progress of a disease or the effects of a treatment.

biopsychosocial model   The view that addiction involves an interplay of biological, intrapersonal, interpersonal, and environmental factors.

bipolar disorder   A cyclic psychosis in which a person alternates between moods of depression and mania.

black market   The illegal trafficking of goods and services.

blackout   1. A temporary loss of consciousness due to decreased blood flow to the brain. 2. Memory loss that occurs during a state of intense intoxication.

blood alcohol concentration   The proportion of a person's blood that consists of alcohol.

blood-brain barrier   Special characteristics of the brain's capillary walls that prevent potentially harmful substances from moving from the bloodstream to the brain or cerebrospinal fluid.

blood doping   The questionable practice of athletes transfusing their own, stored blood to themselves to increase its oxygen-carrying capacity for improved athletic endurance.

borderline personality disorder   A behavioral pattern marked by rapid changes in mood and unstable interpersonal relations, impulsivity, irrationality, and an unstable self-image.

boundary   The demarcation of the level of intimacy in the counselor-client relationship.

Breathalyzer   A device used to determine blood alcohol concentration by measuring the amount of alcohol in a person's exhaled breath.

breath testing   The measurement of the amount of alcohol in the blood by means of a Breathalyzer.

bulimia   An eating disorder that occurs mainly in females, characterized by binge eating followed by self-induced vomiting, laxative, or diuretic abuse, or excessive exercise.

burnout   The condition of having no energy left to care, characterized by physical and emotional exhaustion and increased susceptibility to physical illness and substance abuse.

C

caffeine   A stimulant found naturally in coffee, tea, chocolate, and cocoa.

caffeinism   A toxic condition caused by the chronic ingestion of excessive amounts of caffeine and marked by diarrhea, elevated blood pressure, rapid breathing, heart palpitations, and insomnia.

CAGE questionnaire   A brief, relatively nonconfrontational questionnaire for the detection of alcoholism.

cannabinoid   Drug that possesses the action of smoked marijuana.

cannabinoid receptor   A receptor in the brain that binds THC, the active ingredient in marijuana.

cannabis   See *marijuana.*

carcinogenic   Tending to produce cancer.

cardiovascular system   The heart and blood vessels by which blood is pumped and circulated through the body.

catabolic processes   The metabolic breakdown of complex molecules into simpler ones resulting in a net release of energy.

catastrophizing   Beliefs that the worst possible outcome in a situation will happen.

cell body   The part of a neuron that contains the nucleus and surrounding cytoplasm.

Center for Disease Control and Prevention (CDC)   U.S. government agency that provides facilities and services for the investigation, identification, prevention, and control of disease.

central nervous system l em (CNS)   The brain and spinal cord.

Certification   A professional credential awarded by a private organization, often a freestanding nonprofit organization whose mission is specifically certification or professional association.

chemical   A substance with a distinct molecular composition that is produced by or used in a chemical process.

chemical dependency   A general term to describe a physical or psychological reliance on drugs.

chi energy   The Chinese name for the universal force from Taoist philosophy that binds and pervades all living things.

chipping   The occasional use of a highly addictive substance. For example, using heroin once a month or smoking cigarettes on a very occasional basis.

chronic   Frequent recurrence over a long period.

classical conditioning   The formation of an association between two previously unrelated stimuli.

clinical study   An organized study designed to provide large bodies of clinical data for statistical evaluation.

clonidine   A drug used to treat hypertension, prevent migraines, and diminish opiate withdrawal symptoms.

clothing boundaries   Clothing appropriate to a given relationship. For example, dressing in a seductive manner blurs a health professional's relationship with a client.

cocaine   A highly addictive white crystalline powder used illicitly for euphoric effects. See also *crack*.

codeine   A morphine derivative found in opium, often used in cough remedies.

codependency   A relationship that reinforces and enables an addictive behavior. See also *enabling*.

coexisting (or concurrent) addictions   The presence in one person of two or more addictions.

cofabulation   Explaining nonrecalled behaviors by making up stories that have little relation to reality.

cognitive behavioral therapy   A treatment approach that focuses on changing an individual's thoughts, or cognitive patterns to positively affect his or her behavior and emotional state.

cognitive impairment   A decreased ability to think, concentrate, formulate ideas, reason, and remember.

cognitive triad   The three elements representing the cognitive patterns of people's outlook on life: how they view themselves, the future, and their world experiences.

cold turkey   Sudden cessation of a vice; refers to the "gooseflesh" sensation of withdrawal syndrome.

comorbidity   The presence of additional diseases with reference to an initial index condition that is the subject of study. See also *psychiatric comorbidity.*

compensatory behavior   A conscious or unconscious defense mechanism by which one attempts to make up for real or imagined deficiencies.

competence   The ability to perform in a field or discipline at a level that is consistent with accepted practice and research.

compulsion   An irresistible urge, sometimes performed to relieve anxious thoughts connected with an obsession.

conduct disorder   An adolescent disorder that features deviant and antisocial behavior.

confirmatory drug test   The use of a different analytical process to confirm an initial positive drug screen.

confrontation   1. A face-to-face meeting. 2. The act of forcing or being forced to recognize something, such as an addiction.

conjoint session   A joint counseling session for a couple or family members already receiving counseling independently.

consultation groups   Groups of professionals that gather to discuss cases.

continuing care plan   The equivalent to a treatment plan for aftercare.

continuum of care   A seamless system of health care service: prevention, diagnosis, treatment, and rehabilitation.

contraindication   A declaration that a prescription, procedure, or treatment is unsafe or otherwise inadvisable.

controlled drinking   A method of reducing the risks of alcohol for problem drinkers without abstinence.

coping strategy   A plan that minimizes stress.

cost-effectiveness   The quality of an item or procedure that meets both budget and usefulness requirements.

crack   A cheap and addictive freebase form of cocaine that can be smoked instead of snorted.

crank   Any form of amphetamine drug.

crash   The period following a stimulant binge that results in a prolonged, fitful sleep and accompanying depression. See also *rebound depression.*

craving   A strong yearning or desire, particularly for an addictive substance.

creative visualization   The use of the imagination in setting positive goals.

criminalization of addiction   The concept that drug use by addicts is a crime to be punished, rather than a disease to be treated.

crisis   An acute emotional response to some intense stimulus or demand.

crisis intervention   An active, but temporary, entry into the life of an individual or group during a period of extreme distress to mitigate the impact of the event.

critical incident   The event that triggers the crisis response.

cross-addiction   An addiction to multiple psychoactive drugs.

cross-tolerance   Tolerance to an unfamiliar drug by reason of tolerance developed to another drug with similar mechanisms or effects.

crystal meth   A highly addictive type of amphetamine available in the form of rocks or crystal-like powder.

cue   In conditioning and learning theory, a pattern of stimuli to which an individual has learned to respond.

cue exposure   Therapy to reduce relapse among alcoholics by tempting them with stimuli that induce cravings to drink while preventing them from actually drinking, allowing them to habituate to the cravings.

cybersex   Any type of sexual activity involving the computer, such as downloading pornography, sexual chat rooms, one-on-one real-time sexual exchanges.

D

DARE (Drug Abuse Resistance Education)   A school-based antidrug program taught by police officers.

date rape drug   A tasteless, odorless sedative that can incapacitate an unsuspecting victim and prevent her from resisting sexual assault. Examples include Rohypnol (roofies) and GHB.

DEA   See *Drug Enforcement Administration.*

decomposition   Loss of control or psychotic behavior by a client.

decriminalization   The replacement of jail sentences and criminal records with fines for those found in possession of an illicit drug.

defense mechanism   A largely unconscious strategy to reduce conflict and emotional distress.

delayed grief reaction   A dysfunctional reaction to grief in which a person may not initially experience the pain of loss. However, the pain manifests as chronic depression, preoccupation with body functioning, phobic reactions, and/or acute insomnia.

delusion   A fixed belief maintained despite incontrovertible and obvious evidence from one's own senses and the objective world that the belief is false.

demand reduction strategy   The theory that the best strategy in opposing the drug trade is to focus on reducing the domestic demand for drugs.

dementia   The partial or complete deterioration of mental functioning, often following prolonged and heavy alcohol use.

denial   1. The mechanism by which a person fails to acknowledge some aspect of external reality apparent to others. 2. The failure to admit or realize that one is an addict and causing harm to self or others.

dependence   See *physical dependence* and *psychological dependence.*

depersonalization   Loss of sense of personal identity often with feelings of being detached from or an outside observer of self. See also *altered state.*

depressant   A psychoactive drug that slows the central nervous system, resulting in a tranquilizing effect and the impairment of higher mental function, vision, and movement. See also *barbiturates, sedative,* and *tranquilizer.*

depression   A state of lowered mood, often accompanied by disturbances of sleep, energy, appetite, concentration, interests, and sex drive.

deprivation   The absence of a necessary object or function.

desensitization   A reduced response to a drug due to repeated administrations.

designated driver   A person who agrees not to consume alcohol at a social function in order to drive others home, thereby preventing an occurrence of impaired driving. See also *safe-ride program.*

designer drug   A synthetically manufactured drug. See also *analog*.

detoxification   The process of allowing the body to rid itself of a drug, usually with medical management of withdrawal symptoms.

Diagnostic and Statistical Manual of Mental Disorders **(DSM-IV-TR)**   The most widely used psychiatric classification system for mental disorders.

Dial-a-Ride Program   A nonprofit, community-based transportation system that usually includes wheelchair-accessible vehicles.

diaphragm breathing   Deep and rhythmic breathing, characteristic of relaxation.

disinhibition   The release of socially restrained behaviors, often through the use of psychoactive substances.

disorientation   Mental perplexity with respect to time, place, or person.

dissociation   Disruption in the usually integrated functions of consciousness, memory, identity, or perception.

disulfiram   See *Antabuse*.

diversion   Professionals taking drugs from patients and the workplace for their own use.

dopamine   A neurotransmitter responsible for feelings of pleasure that plays a major role in addictions.

dose-response curve   The often complex relationship between the dose of a drug and the response observed.

double-blind study   An experiment in which neither the subjects nor the administrators are aware of the critical aspects of the experiment, to guard against placebo effects and experimenter bias.

downer   See *depressant*.

drinking pattern   The style in which a person consumes alcohol, aspects include the social setting and variability of drinking.

drug   A chemical substance that alters mood, perception, or consciousness.

drug abuse   The repeated use of a drug despite harmful consequences.

drug abuse screening test   A test that consists of 20 yes-or-no questions about drug use and related problems.

Drug Abuse Warning Network (DAWN)   A surveillance system sponsored by the National Institute on Drug Abuse that records drug-related visits to emergency rooms in the United States.

drug cartels   Networks of drug producers and traffickers.

drug culture   The countercultural movement of the 1960s that made recreational drug use appealing to youth.

Drug Enforcement Administration (DEA)   The U.S. government's lead agency for the enforcement of drug laws.

drug interactions   When two or more drugs are present in the body, they may combine in ways that are good or bad: they may be more effective in treating a problem or they may increase the number or severity of adverse reactions.

drug myopia   A distorted perception of reality caused by a drug such that a person is blinded to what is happening around him or her.

drug paraphernalia   Equipment designed or used for the administration of controlled substances; for example, hash pipes or syringes.

Drug Policy Foundation   A nonprofit organization that advocates harm reduction over prohibition.

drug receptor   Usually a protein, the part of a cell that directly interacts with a chemical.

drug schedule   A five-level classification system used by the U.S. federal government that ranks controlled substances by their potential for abuse and currently accepted medical usage.

drug screening   A clinical laboratory procedure that checks for the presence of certain drugs in a patient's blood. See also *drug test*.

drug slang   Informal street language for describing drugs, varying from neighborhood, city, region, and country. See www.cox-internet.com/dabster/slang.htm#Y for alphabetized examples of slang terms.

drug test   A laboratory examination of biological specimens (urine, hair, or blood) for the presence of psychoactive substances or their metabolic by-products. See also *drug screening*.

drug therapy   The use of chemical substances in the treatment of illness; for example, chemotherapy or pharmacotherapy.

drug trafficking   The possession of an illegal drug with the intent to sell or pass it on to someone else.

dry drunk   Someone who has stopped drinking but still exhibits the same alcoholic behaviors and attitudes. See also *acute alcohol withdrawal syndrome*.

DSM-IV-TR.   Current diagnostic manual of the American Psychiatric Association.

DTs (delirium tremens)   A potentially fatal form of alcohol withdrawal.

dual diagnosis   The presence in a person of both an addictive disorder and a psychiatric disorder. See *psychiatric comorbidity*.

duty to report   The ethical obligation to report harm to others that has already occurred (e.g., the abuse of a child).

duty to warn   The ethical responsibility to report the threat of harm to another person.

dysphoria   A negative or aversive emotional state, often associated with drug withdrawal.

dysynergy   The tendency of one addiction to cause another. See also *cross-addiction* and *gateway drug*.

E

eating disorders   A group of disorders characterized by physiological and psychological disturbances in appetite or food intake. See also *anorexia nervosa* and *bulimia*.

ecstasy   See *MDMA*.

EEG   See *electroencephalogram*.

electroencephalogram   A diagnostic test that measures brain waves using highly sensitive recording equipment attached to the scalp by fine electrodes.

empathy   The understanding of another's emotional state.

empirical   Derived from observation or experiment.

employee assistance programs   Workplace-based programs set up to refer chemically impaired employees for treatment.

enabling   Unwittingly making it easier for clients to use drugs by rescuing them from the consequences of their behavior. See also *institutional enabling.*

endocrine system   The thyroid, adrenal, and pituitary glands, and their hormonal secretions, which are introduced directly into the bloodstream and carried to the parts of the body whose functions they regulate or control.

endogenous   Naturally occurring in the brain or body.

endorphin   A chemical with analgesic properties that occurs naturally in the brain. See also *enkephalin.*

energy channels   In acupuncture tradition, the 14 meridians that act as pathways in the continuous flow of chi energy throughout the body. See also *acupuncture* and *chi energy.*

enkephalin   An endorphin that acts on opiate receptors.

enmeshment   A condition in which two or more people interweave their lives and identities so tightly that it is difficult for any of them to function independently.

Environmental Protection Agency (EPA)   U.S. government department responsible for the protection of human health and the natural environment.

ephedrine   A metabolism-stimulating herb useful in the treatment of the common cold, asthma, and bronchial congestion; as well as weight loss, fat reduction, and muscle maintenance.

epidemiology   The study of the distributions and causes of diseases and disorders in populations.

ethanol   Ethyl alcohol; a grain alcohol with sedative and disinhibiting properties made from the fermentation of sugar, starch, or other carbohydrates.

ether   A type of inhalant.

etiology   The factors associated with the cause of problems or conditions.

euphoria   An exaggerated feeling of physical and mental well-being.

evaluation   A test or systematic assessment, particularly of an outcome as compared to a standard.

existential   Relating to deep philosophical and spiritual questions about meaning and purpose.

exposure   Being presented with a cue that triggers an unhealthy response until it no longer produces that response.

F

fading   Gradually reducing reinforcement over time and ultimately stopping it.

false negative   A test result stating that no drug is present when, in fact, a tested drug or metabolite is present in an amount greater than the threshold or cutoff amount.

false positive   A test result stating that a drug or metabolite is present when, in fact, the drug or metabolite is not present or is in an amount less than the threshold or cutoff value.

family boundaries   The ability of each family member to maintain his or her own sense of self while remaining emotionally connected to the family.

family homeostasis   The balance, customary organization, and functioning continually sought by the family system.

family myth   A well-rehearsed but false notion concerning the family unit.

family ritual A meaningful event involving the entire family and repeated regularly.

family therapy An approach in which all members of the family take part as a group.

Fatal Accident Reporting System A division of the National Highway Traffic Safety Administration that maintains data on traffic fatalities.

FDA See *Food and Drug Administration.*

federal narcotic farms The first treatment centers in the United States for addicts opened in 1929 and operated under the control of the U.S. Public Health Service.

fentanyl An opioid used intravenously as a preoperative anesthetic. It has been prone to abuse by hospital staff for sedation and sleep.

fermentation A metabolic process occurring in many microorganisms that produces energy by breaking down carbohydrates in the absence of oxygen, resulting in either ethanol or lactic acid.

fetal alcohol syndrome/spectrum A condition in children caused by prenatal exposure to alcohol and identified by prenatal and postnatal growth retardation, cranial/facial defects, central nervous system dysfunctions, and organ malformations.

fiduciary The assumption of professional responsibility for the care of another.

fight-or-flight response The physiological reaction when the sympathetic division of the autonomic nervous system is aroused by the sensing of a threat.

flashback The reexperiencing of a past event including illusions, hallucinations, and dissociative episodes.

flooding (or implosion) Total cue exposure all at once.

Food and Drug Administration (FDA) U.S. government agency responsible for setting and enforcing guidelines for the evaluation, licensing, and marketing of food and drugs.

freebase A form of certain drugs that can be very potent. See also *crack* and *ice.*

G

GAF The *DSM's* Axis V Global Assessment of Functioning.

gateway drug An introductory drug that leads to the use of more dangerous drugs.

generic A drug not protected by a trademark.

genetic Pertaining to reproduction, birth, or origin.

glutamate An excitatory neurotransmitter.

grandiosity The pretension of superiority often experienced by those in a manic episode.

grief Sorrow and anxiety due to loss.

group therapy A drug treatment and rehabilitation technique that involves group rather than individual treatment to emphasize that a client's problems are not unique.

guided imagery A self-help technique that focuses the power of the mind on an aspect of the physical body to cause a positive, healing response.

H

habit A recurrent pattern of behavior that is acquired through repetition.

habituation Tolerance to and dependence on something that is psychologically or physically habit-forming, especially alcohol or narcotics.

Haight-Ashbury Free Medical Clinic   A clinic founded in San Francisco in 1967 to meet the medical needs of the waves of hippies who came to the Haight-Ashbury neighborhood during the "Summer of Love."

halcyon   A depressant drug of the benzodiazepine family used to induce sleep.

half-life   The average period of time by which the mass, concentration, or activity of a substance decreases to one-half of its initial value.

halfway house   A sheltered workshop or residence designed to help the adjustment of institutionalized persons, such as mental patients or legal offenders, in the process of release.

hallucination   A visual, auditory, or olfactory perception that is not based in reality.

hallucinogen   Any drug that distorts perceptions and causes hallucinations. See also *psychedelic.*

hallucinogen persisting perception disorder (HPPD)   The spontaneous and sometimes continuous recurrence of the perceptual effects of LSD long after an individual has ingested the drug.

hangover   Headache and nausea as the result of drinking too much alcohol.

harm reduction   Any strategy that aims to reduce substance-related harm to the individual, his family, or society without necessarily stopping drug use.

Harrison Act   The 1914 law that set the stage for criminalizing narcotic addiction in the United States.

hashish   A potent form of cannabis, derived from the resin of the cannabis plant.

Hazelden Foundation   A nonprofit organization that aims to prevent drug abuse and treat dependency through services, research, training, and publications.

hedonic set point   Hypothesized optimal value of the system that regulates the balance between pleasure and discomfort.

hemp   1. The cannabis plant. 2. The coarse, tough fiber made from the cannabis plant. 3. Any drug derived from the cannabis plant. See also *marijuana* and *hashish.*

herbal stimulants   Natural products not regulated by the FDA that contain the stimulants caffeine, ephedrine, and pseudoephedrine.

heroin   Diacetylmorphine, a highly addictive opiate derived from morphine.

heroin maintenance   A program that provides a safe regulated supply of heroin to addicts who fail to respond to traditional treatments. See also *methadone maintenance* and *harm reduction.*

Higher Power   A power greater than oneself; a God of one's own understanding.

HIV (human immunodeficiency virus)   The virus that leads to AIDS.

holistic therapies   Alternative health treatments that work on the premise that mind and body states interconnect.

homeostatic systems   Systems that tend to maintain stability or equilibrium.

hormone   A chemical substance having a specific regulatory effect on the activity of organs.

huffing   To use an inhalant.

hyperactivity   General restlessness or excessive movement.

hypertension   High blood pressure.

hypnotic   A drug that induces sleep.

hypochondria   The persistent conviction that one is ill, often involving symptoms when illness is not present, and persisting despite medical evidence to the contrary.

I

iatrogenic effect   Interventions that produce inadvertent harm or injury to a client, family, or community.

ice   A freebase methamphetamine.

illicit drugs   Unlawful body/mind-altering substances.

imagery   Spontaneous messages from the unconscious to the conscious, much like dreams, that are typically meaningful.

immune system   Organs, cells, and proteins that work to protect the body from harmful microorganisms such as viruses, bacteria, and fungi.

immunoassay   A rapid laboratory technique that can detect extremely small amounts of specific drugs of interest.

impulse control exercise   A treatment for individuals who have difficulty controlling their impulses whereby they are exposed to cravings but restrained from fulfilling them.

incarceration   Confinement; imprisonment.

inebriety   The former term for what today would be called addiction; a person suffering from addiction was known as an inebriate.

informed consent   The process through which potential clients are educated about the risks and benefits of addiction counseling prior to deciding whether to participate in such counseling.

ingestion   The process of taking a substance into the body through the mouth.

inhalants   Volatile solvents that can be inhaled through the nose or huffed by mouth, resulting in short-term psychoactive effects.

inhibitory effect   The blocking of a physical, psychological, or behavioral reaction.

injection   The forcing or driving of fluid under the skin, usually with a needle or syringe.

inpatient treatment   Residential treatment for drug addiction in a hospital or clinic.

insecurity   A feeling of being unprotected and helpless.

insomnia   The inability to fall or stay asleep.

inspiration   The act of drawing air into the lungs.

institutional enabling   Behavior by others in a workplace or other institutional setting that helps addicts avoid the direct or indirect consequences of their own behavior.

intentionality   The state of awareness and planning behind a given act or behavior.

interactional distance   The preferred physical distance used in interpersonal communication; often varies culturally.

interactive addiction disorder   Multiple addictions (e.g., chemical dependence simultaneously with a behavioral addiction such as compulsive gambling) that are intricately involved with one another.

interdiction programs   Border control efforts by the government to keep contraband and other threats from entering the country.

interpersonal skills   The ability to reach others and to relate and maintain a relationship through empathy and listening.

interpersonal therapy   A form of short-term psychotherapy usually consisting of weekly sessions of under an hour, for 3 to 4 months.

intervention   Interceding and confronting a substance abuser with the aim of overcoming his or her denial and inducing the individual to seek treatment.

intoxication   Stimulation, excitement, or stupefaction usually caused by a chemical substance.

intrafamily cohesiveness   The strength of the relationships within the family unit.

intramuscular   Within or into a muscle.

intravenous   Within or into a vein.

intravenous drug user   A drug user who injects substances directly into his or her veins.

involuntary   Not governed by the conscious brain.

J

journaling   The intentional use of reflective writing to further mental, physical, emotional, and spiritual health and wellness.

K

ketamine   A nonbarbiturate anesthetic manufactured as an animal tranquilizer; sometimes used by humans recreationally.

kleptomania   An impulse control disorder that involves stealing objects to relieve tension.

L

LAAM (levoalpha-acetylmethadol)   A longer-acting form of methadone.

lapse   The phase in a relapse cycle where a person has slipped but not returned in earnest to old drug-using behavior.

latency period   1. The interval of time between stimulus and response or exposure and disease. 2. A period of apparent inactivity.

laughing gas   See *nitrous oxide.*

legalization   A regulatory system allowing the production, marketing, sale, and use of a given substance.

legalization debate   The conflict of viewpoints between harm reduction and prohibition policies.

lethal dose   The amount of a substance sufficient to cause death.

leukoplakia   A precancerous condition that is seen as small thickened white patches on mucous membranes.

Librium   Trademark for chlordiazepoxide, a benzodiazepine often used to treat symptoms of alcohol withdrawal.

lifestyle imbalance   The condition that results when a client does not spend time caring for her- or himself in all the important life domains.

longitudinal study   A study composed of repeated observations on the same individual or individuals over an extended period of time.

long-term potentiation   A phenomenon associated with learning and memory wherein repeated stimuli induce a sustained enhancement of synaptic responses.

LSD (lysergic acid diethylamide)   A hallucinogen derived from the ergot fungus.

M

MADD   See *Mothers Against Drunk Driving.*

malnutrition   The state of lacking nutritious food.

mandated   Treatment that authorities require clients to receive.

mania   A state of mood characterized by elation, excitability, and hyperactivity.

manic-depression   See *bipolar disorder.*

marijuana   The flowering tops of the cannabis plant, containing the pyschoactive cannabinoid THC.

Matching Alcoholism Treatments to Client Hetergeneity (MATCH)   A multisite study designed to test whether different types of alcoholics respond differently to specific therapeutic approaches.

maturing out   A natural phenomenon whereby many youthful drug users naturally evolve out of a drug problem as they mature.

MDA (3,4-methylenedioxyamphetamine)   A potentially neurotoxic designer amphetamine with mild hallucinogenic properties that induces feelings of empathy and emotional closeness to others.

MDMA (3,4-methylenedioxymethamphetamine)   A designer amphetamine similar to MDA; it has been advocated as an adjunct to psychotherapy because it heightens feelings of trust and openness.

medicinal marijuana   Marijuana used as a treatment for specific medical conditions. In North America, use and potential use have centered on the treatment of symptoms in severe disease conditions such as AIDS, cancer, multiple sclerosis, epilepsy, and glaucoma.

meditation   A form of contemplation or awareness; a nonjudgmental observation of what arises in one's own mind.

meperidine   A commonly prescribed opioid for postoperative or posttrauma pain.

mescaline   A derivative of the peyote cactus that induces hallucinogenic effects similar to, but milder than, LSD. See also *peyote.*

meta-analytic technique   A statistical procedure for combining data from several studies to analyze the therapeutic effectiveness of specific treatments and to plan future studies.

metabolic disorder   Any problem in the body that interferes with how nutrients are stored or utilized.

metabolism   The process by which energy from the ingestion of food is made available to the organism.

metabolite   The compound remaining after a drug undergoes chemical changes in the body.

methadone   An opioid similar to morphine and heroin, but with less debilitating effects.

methadone maintenance   A program that provides heroin addicts with methadone as a substitute, either for short-term detoxification or long-term maintenance.

methamphetamine   An amphetamine drug with a high potential for abuse. See also *crystal meth* and *ice.*

Michigan Alcohol Screening Test   A screening tool designed to assess the level of a client's involvement with alcohol.

Minnesota Model   A treatment mode based on the philosophy that addiction is a multi-faceted disease requiring multidimensional treatment, but that abstinence is possible. See also *Hazelden Foundation* and *twelve-step programs.*

misogynistic   Strong bias against or hatred toward women.

modeling   A form of social learning based on the imitation of observed behavior.

money laundering   The process by which large amounts of illegally obtained money (from drug trafficking, terrorist activity, or other crime) is given the appearance of having originated from a legitimate source.

mood   A person's emotional state.

morphine   A potent anesthetic and sedative extracted from opium.

mortality   Death.

Mothers Against Drunk Driving (MADD)   A multinational support network of victims and concerned citizens working to stop alcohol-impaired driving.

motivational interviewing   A directive, client-centered counseling style for eliciting behavior change by helping clients explore and resolve ambivalence.

MRI (magnetic resonance imaging)   A diagnostic technique that provides high-quality cross-sectional or three-dimensional images of organs and structures within the body using a massive electromagnet instead of x-rays or other radiation.

Multidisciplinary Association for Psychedelic Studies   A nonprofit research and educational organization that supports the study of the potential medical uses of MDMA, psychedelics, and marijuana.

N

Naltrexone   A long-lasting opiate antagonist used for the treatment of heroin and alcohol addiction.

narcissism   The tendency toward an exaggerated belief in one's superiority and self-importance, paradoxically tied with deep insecurities and admiration-seeking.

narcissistic personality disorder   A type of personality disorder marked by grandiosity, the need for admiration, and a lack of empathy.

narcolepsy   A rare condition in which uncontrollable episodes of sleep occur several times a day.

narcotic   Pain-relieving drug that produces a state of drugged sleep, usually an opioid. See *opioid*.

narcotic farms   Federal prisons in Lexington, Kentucky, and Fort Worth, Texas that offered treatment for narcotic addicts within the federal prison system.

National Council on Alcoholism and Drug Dependence   An organization dedicated to fighting the stigma and the disease of alcoholism and other drug addictions.

National Institute of Alcohol Abuse and Alcoholism   U.S. government division that supports and conducts biomedical and behavioral research on the causes, consequences, treatment, and prevention of alcoholism and alcohol-related problems.

National Institute on Drug Abuse (NIDA)   U.S. government-supported institution that sponsors and formulates policies on issues of drug abuse, drug addiction, and treatment.

National Institutes of Mental Health (NIMH)   One of several agencies of the U.S. government that is a component of the National Institute of Health (NIH) within the Department of Health and Human Services.

National Organization for the Reform of Marijuana Laws (NORML)   A nonprofit lobby group that advocates the decriminalization and legalization of marijuana.

natural high   A feeling of euphoria not resulting from substance use.

natural recovery   The phenomenon whereby many people with drug problems overcome the addiction by themselves.

natural reinforcers   Pleasurable consequences that are the natural result of a behavior.

nausea   A feeling of sickness in the stomach characterized by an urge to vomit.

needle exchange   A program that supplies addicts with fresh clean needles to prevent the spread of disease from needle sharing.

needle sharing   The use of a common needle or syringe between multiple intravenous drug users and the second most common route by which HIV is spread.

negative reinforcer   An undesirable stimulus that encourages the action or behavior and results in its removal.

nervous system   See *central nervous system* and *peripheral nervous system*.

neural adaptation   Habituating a response to a specific stimulus.

neurotransmitters   Molecules released into neural synapses that relay information between neurons. See also *dopamine, glutamate,* and *serotonin*.

neuron   A nervous system cell specialized to receive and transmit information.

neuropathy   irritation or inflammation of a nerve fiber or fibers with symptoms including pain, numbness, and decreased function.

neuropsychological assessment   Assessment of cognitive function and problems.

neurosis   A psychological or personality disorder not attributable to any known neurological dysfunction.

neuroadaptation   the underlying brain changes that can lead to, or be associated with, the development of tolerance and withdrawal.

nicotine   A stimulant, the active drug in tobacco.

nicotine dependence   The physical and/or psychological need to use nicotine-containing products.

NIDA   See *National Institute on Drug Abuse*.

NIMH   See *National Institutes of Mental Health*.

nitrous oxide   A colorless gas used as a mild anesthetic and also recreationally; it can be a nerve toxin at high levels of exposure.

nonprescription drug   A drug that can be purchased from a store without a prescription from a physician. Also called an "over-the-counter drug."

nonresidential treatment   Drug treatment or education occurring in the general community instead of dedicated units such as prisons, hospitals, and detoxification centers.

NORML   See *National Organization for the Reform of Marijuana Laws*.

nutritional disorder   A disorder caused by a deficiency or excess of the elements of nutrition or by the presence of a toxin in the diet. See also *metabolic disorder* and *malnutrition*.

O

obsession   A persistent idea dominating one's thoughts. See also *compulsion*.

operant conditioning   An unconscious form of learning in which behavior is linked to a specific stimulus through reinforcement.

operant strategies   Techniques that use reinforcement or punishment to shape behavior.

opiate   Any drug derived from, or chemically similar to, opium. For example: *morphine, codeine,* and *heroin.*

opioid   Drug that causes the characteristic effects of the opium poppy including analgesia, reward, constipation, and inhibition of respiration.

opiophobia   A health care provider's unfounded fear that patients will become physically dependent on opioids, even when using them properly.

opium   The juice of the unripe seed-capsules of the white Indian poppy, *Papaver somniferum.* Among its active ingredients are morphine and codeine.

Oppositional-defiant disorder   Adolescent disorder featuring defiance toward authority.

out-of-body experience   An altered state of awareness in which one experiences his or her consciousness beyond physical boundaries.

outpatient discharge criteria   Specified requirements to be met before a patient can be appropriately discharged from a facility or program.

outpatient treatment   Nonresidential chemical dependency treatments for individuals who are able to function in the context of their usual living arrangements.

overdose   The consumption of a much larger dose than that habitually used by the individual; it can lead to a serious reaction, including death.

over-the-counter (OTC) drug   See *nonprescription drug.*

P

pain   An unpleasant sensory and emotional experience associated with actual or potential tissue damage.

panic attack   A sudden onset of physiological symptoms such as sweating, trembling, chest pain, and shortness of breath.

panic disorder   An anxiety disorder marked by recurring and unexpected panic attacks.

paradoxical effect   A behavioral response to a drug that differs from a normally evoked response.

paranoia   A psychotic disorder marked by persistent delusions of persecution and suspicion of others' motives as malevolent.

paraphernalia   See *drug paraphernalia.*

parasuicidal   Behavior that involves self-harm without necessarily the intent to die.

parasympathetic nervous system   The subdivision of the autonomic nervous system that operates during relaxed states and conserves energy.

Partnership for a Drug-Free America   An advertising campaign, conducted by a nonprofit coalition of the U.S. communications industries, that encourages kids and teens to reject substance abuse.

passive-aggressive   Usually behind-the-back behavior, such as gossiping, complaining about, or blaming of others.

passive inhalation   See *secondhand smoking.*

patent medicines   Medicines from the early twentieth century that often contained high levels of cocaine, heroin, or alcohol. They were sold directly to the public by traveling peddlers and were available at local stores.

PCP (phencyclidine)   An illegally manufactured hallucinogen originally introduced as an anesthetic.

pep pills   Any of various stimulants in pill or tab form.

peripheral nervous system   The portion of the nervous system outside the brain and spinal cord that handles sensory input and motor output.

personality disorder   An enduring and maladaptive pattern of traits that affects a person's work, family, and social life.

peyote   A cactus found in the southwestern United States and northern Mexico containing the hallucinogen mescaline.

pharmacodynamics   A branch of pharmacology dealing with the reactions between drugs and living systems.

pharmacology   The study of drugs: their sources, appearance, chemistry, actions, and uses.

pharmacotherapy   The treatment of disease, especially mental disorder, with drugs.

phobia   An unrelenting and unreasonable fear disproportionate to the presence or anticipation of a specific object or situation.

Phoenix House   A nonprofit organization founded in 1967 to prevent and treat substance abuse.

physical dependence   The experience of physical withdrawal symptoms caused by abruptly stopping use of a substance. Often confused with addiction, which involves psychological and behavioral characteristics.

placebo   A substance that superficially resembles an active drug but has no pharmacological properties and is administered either as a control in tests or as a psychotherapeutic agent.

polydrug abuse   The simultaneous use of two or more psychoactive substances in quantities and with frequencies that cause the individual significant physiological, psychological, or sociological impairment or distress. See also *cross-addiction*.

positive reinforcer   A desirable stimulus that encourages an action or behavior and results in its occurrence; a reward.

Posttraumatic Stress Disorder (PTSD)   The development of a set of characteristic symptoms after a psychologically traumatizing event.

potency   The effectiveness of a drug in obtaining a particular response.

potentiation   The enhancement of the effect of a drug.

potentiative effect   A special form of synergism that occurs when the administration of one drug results in the magnification of another's potency.

preanesthetic agents   See *sedative, benzodiazepines,* and *fentanyl.*

prenatal alcohol syndrome   See *fetal alcohol syndrome.*

primary prevention   Programs aimed at preventing drug abuse by young people.

prognosis   The prospect of recovery as anticipated from the usual course of the disease.

progressive relaxation   A stress management technique in which individuals tense their muscles to their utmost and then release them gradually.

prohibition   A ban on the manufacture, transportation, sale, and use of a drug.

prophylactic   Preventive measures to stop a problem before it starts.

Prozac   Trademark for fluoxetine, a selective serotonin reuptake inhibitor with low toxicity and without many of the side effects attributed to tricyclic antidepressants.

psilocybin   A hallucinogenic chemical that occurs naturally in certain mushrooms.

psychedelic   A psychoactive drug that produces hallucinatory effects, particularly with vivid colors.

psychiatric comorbidity   The presence of two or more mental disorders, one of which is often substance abuse.

psychoactive   A substance or experience that activates the brain's reward system.

psychoactive drug   Any drug that influences emotions, perceptions, thoughts, motivations, or behaviors.

psychoanalysis   1. A method of investigating the human mind originated by Sigmund Freud. 2. An integrated body of observations and theories on personality development.

psychodrama   An adjunct to psychotherapy in which the patient acts out certain roles or incidents.

psychological dependence   The experience of nonphysical symptoms following the abrupt withdrawal of a substance, characterized by emotional and mental preoccupation with the drug's effects along with a persistent craving.

psychopharmacology   Medical specialty devoted to the study of medications used to treat psychiatric illnesses.

psychosis   A severe mental disorder in which an individual loses contact with reality, involving dramatic disruption of perception, judgment, and thought organization.

psychotherapeutic drugs   A drug prescribed by psychiatrists and other physicians for the management of psychological disorders.

psychotherapy   A spectrum of psychological treatments that aim to change problematic thoughts or feelings.

psychotic patient   An individual being treated for psychosis.

psychotropic medication   Drugs that affect psychological function, behavior, or experience. These include neuroleptics, antipsychotics, antidepressants, stimulants, and anxiolytics.

Q

Quaalude   Trademark for the hypnotic sedative methaqualone, it produces a pattern of pharmacological effects similar to that of certain barbiturates.

quasi-synthetic narcotics   An altered version of a natural drug.

R

Rational-Emotive Behavioral Therapy (REBT)   A psychotherapeutic approach interrelating thought, feeling, and behavior.

rationalization   The act of making excuses to justify behavior that normally would be viewed as unreasonable, illogical, or intolerable.

rebound depression   A more severe second episode of depression following an initial one, often after an abrupt cessation of medication.

recidivism   The relapse of a behavior pattern, often associated with addiction or criminal behavior.

recovery   The development of coping skills and maintenance of a drug-free lifestyle after an addiction.

recovery home   A sober living environment with structured approaches to recovery, counseling, monitoring, and accountability on the part of residents.

recreational user   A person who occasionally uses drugs and does not become addicted.

regulatory boards   Commissions or committees that establish requirements for health care providers and enforce health and safety laws that protect the public from negligent or illegal health care practices.

rehabilitate   To restore to a state of good condition.

reinforcement   The encouragement of a given behavior. See also *positive reinforcer, negative reinforcer,* and *operant conditioning.*

relapse   A return to previous behavior after a period of abstinence.

relapse management   Using relapse prevention methods to control drug use rather than stop it entirely.

relaxation training   Proven strategies that can assist the client to learn to relax such as: progressive muscle relaxation, deep breathing; guided imagery, meditation, and so forth.

remission   The partial or complete abatement of a disorder or disease.

replacement therapy   Substituting, for an addictive substance, a product that will help relieve some of the withdrawal symptoms; for example, a nicotine patch.

residential treatment   A recovery program that provides 24-hour care and support for people who live on the premises of the program for extended periods of time.

reuptake   The process by which neurotransmitters are removed from the synapse and sent back into the axon terminals.

reverse tolerance   The phenomenon in which a smaller dose of a drug comes to have the same effect as the usual dose.

reward   A stimulus that is generally pleasurable or contributes to drive-reduction; one that activates the brain's pleasure center.

reward deficiency syndrome   A genetic predisposition resulting in lowered activity of the pleasure-inducing neurotransmitter dopamine leading to the abuse of drugs, gambling, sex, and so on, as a means of compensation.

risk management   Organizational procedures used to protect clients, staff, and the organization itself.

rites of passage   1. A symbolic ceremony, name change, or physical challenge at puberty. 2. Any ritual of transition.

ritualization   A particular pattern of behavior (rituals) that precedes and accompanies the acting out of addictive behaviors.

S

safe-ride program   Organized transportation for those who plan to drink. See also *designated driver.*

schizophrenia   A type of chronic psychosis characterized by delusions, hallucinations, disorganized thoughts and behavior, and emotional withdrawal.

screen   To test a large number of samples in order to find those having specific desirable properties.

secondary diagnosis   A term applied to a disease or disorder that results from or follows another disease. For example, secondary hypertension may be the result of an underlying primary disorder such as a hormonal problem or kidney disease.

secondary prevention   Programs aimed at stopping further drug abuse by users.

secondhand smoking   The inhalation of exhaled or sidestream smoke.

sedative   A drug with soothing, calming, or tranquilizing effects.

seizure   A sudden convulsion due to involuntary electrical activity in the brain.

self-efficacy   Expectations about one's own capability to perform a behavior.

self-medicate   The belief by some drug users that their drug use helps to reduce symptoms of another problem.

sensitization   Increased drug responsiveness after repeated exposure to a constant dose of a drug.

serotonin   A neurotransmitter involved in the processes of sleep and memory along with other neurological functions.

Severity of Alcohol Dependence Questionnaire (SADQ)   A self-administered test of alcohol dependence composed of five subscales: affective withdrawal, physical withdrawal, withdrawal relief drinking, alcohol consumption, and rapidity of dependence reinstatement.

sex addiction   A pathological preoccupation with sexual behavior.

sexual abuse   Any contact or interaction whereby a vulnerable person (usually a child or adolescent) is used for the sexual stimulation of an older, stronger, or more influential person.

shame   A painful sensation resulting from a consciousness of guilt or impropriety.

shock   A medical emergency in which the organs and tissues of the body are deprived of adequate blood flow, and therefore oxygen; it can result in serious damage or death.

shooting gallery   A place, often an apartment or abandoned building, used by heroin addicts to administer the drug.

side effects   Undesirable physical, emotional, or behavioral effects of medications that may be unrelated to their therapeutic effects.

sidestream smoke   Smoke rising from the ash of the cigarette that can be higher in many carcinogens than the mainstream smoke delivered to the smoker's lungs.

skid row   1. A hangout for alcoholics and vagrants. 2. A term for a convalescent ward in a narcotics hospital.

sleep aid   A general term applied to various drugs that help induce sleep.

slip   A lapse in one's resolve. See also *relapse*.

snorting   Rapid but incomplete inspiration, in which the mouth is kept shut and air drawn in through the nose, to bring a drug into contact with the mucous membranes of the nose and sinus cavities.

snuff   Ground-up moist tobacco usually placed between the bottom lip and gum.

sobriety   The nonuse of drugs.

social drugs   Both legal and illicit drugs that people use at gatherings for their calming, enlightening, and mood-altering effects; for example, alcohol or marijuana used at a party.

social learning theory   A view of learning consistent with conditioning theory that focuses on the role of rewards and punishments. It suggests that drug use is a learned behavior and that it may be changed.

social network intervention   A supplement to medication or therapy that provides someone at risk with regular contact and encouragement from a network of chosen supporters.

social skills training   Techniques for improving communication skills, forming and maintaining interpersonal relationships, resisting peer pressure for substance use, and becoming more assertive.

socialization   The process, beginning at infancy, by which a human being acquires the habits, beliefs, and accumulated knowledge of society through his or her education and training.

somatic nervous system   The portion of the nervous system under voluntary control that operates the skeletal muscles.

speed   The street term for a stimulant, especially methamphetamine.

speedball   The street term for a combined injection of heroin and cocaine.

speed freak   A habitual user of stimulants, especially methamphetamine.

spirituality   An awareness of the relationship between oneself and God and the connectedness between oneself and the universe.

sponsor   A 12-step program mentor or guide.

spontaneous remission   The improvement of ailments without treatment.

SSRIs (selective serotonin reuptake inhibitors)   A class of antidepressants that act by preventing the reuptake of serotonin. Examples include Prozac and Zoloft.

stash   To hoard and hide illegal drugs for safekeeping and future use.

steroids   A group of synthetic, hormone-mimicking compounds including anabolic, cortical, and estrogenic steroids. See also *anabolic steroids*.

stimulant   A psychoactive drug that arouses the central nervous system, increasing energy and alertness.

stimulus control   A strategy to control or limit exposure to a trigger or cue.

sting operation   A law-enforcement operation designed to catch a person in the act of committing a crime.

Students Against Driving Drunk (SADD)   A nonprofit organization that aims to eliminate drunk driving, particularly among young people, by promoting alternatives to drinking and driving through positive peer influence.

sublingual   Under the tongue, a method of drug administration.

substance abuse   Abnormal or aberrant use of drugs.

Substance Abuse Disorder   *DSM-IV-TR* diagnostic category for a person whose substance use has never met the criteria for substance dependence (see substance dependence disorder).

Substance Abuse Proclivity Scale   A diagnostic tool that investigates links between personality and the likelihood of substance abuse.

Substance Abuse Subtle Screening Inventory   A test designed to uncover chemical dependence.

Substance Dependence Disorder   *DSM-IV-TR* diagnostic category for those who exhibit three of the following symptoms: (1) substance taken in larger amounts or over a longer period of time than intended; (2) persistent desire or unsuccessful efforts to cut down; (3) a great deal of time spent in activities necessary to get the substance or recover from its effects; (4) important social, occupational, or recreational activities given up or reduced; (5) continued substance use despite social, psychological, or physical problem; (6) marked tolerance or markedly diminished effect to achieve effect; (7) substance often taken to avoid withdrawal symptoms.

Substance Use Disorder   *DSM-IV-TR* diagnosis based on the following criteria: (1) the individual demonstrates an inability to control his or her use despite cognitive, behavioral, or physiological symptoms and (2) the symptoms have been present for a month.

suicidal ideation   Thoughts of suicide that may or may not be accompanied by a plan.

suicide   The act of killing oneself.

sympathetic nervous system   The subdivision of the autonomic nervous system that operates during heightened states of arousal, releasing energy.

symptomatic relief   The abatement of symptoms.

synapse   The gap between the axon of one neuron and the dendrite of another where neurotransmitters are released.

Syndrome   Pattern of symptoms that occur together and characterize a disorder.

synergism   The simultaneous action of separate agencies to cause a greater total effect than the sum of their individual effects.

synesthesia   A condition, often produced by the use of a hallucinogen, in which one type of stimulation evokes the sensation of another. For example, colors are smelled and sounds are seen.

synthetic narcotics   Narcotics produced entirely within a laboratory, usually in an effort to retain the analgesic properties of morphine without the consequent dangers of tolerance and dependence. See also *meperidine, methadone,* and *fentanyl.*

systematic desensitization   Gradual exposure done in small steps over a period of time.

T

tar   The particulate matter in smoke that is the main cause of lung and throat cancer in smokers.

taxonomy   Systematic classification scheme that organizes concepts according to meaningful or functional categories.

temperance movement   An antialcohol movement that began in the late 1800s.

THC (delta 9-tetrahydrocannabinol)   The main psychoactive molecule in marijuana.

therapeutic alliance   How well client and therapist get along.

Therapeutic Communities of America   Drug-free residential settings that use a hierarchical model with treatment stages that reflect increased levels of personal and social responsibility.

time-out contract   An agreement to recognize and deal with anger before it can become destructive by walking away from an escalating altercation and returning to reconcile after a specific cooling-off period.

tobacco   The nicotine-containing dried leaf of the plant *nicotiana tabacum.*

tolerance   The decreasing effects of a drug on the body, due to repeated ingestion and habituation, resulting in the need to greatly increase amounts of the drug to achieve intoxication.

toxicity   The severity of adverse effects or illnesses produced by a toxin, poison, or drug.

toxicology   The study of the harmful effects of drugs on physiology.

tranquilizer   A drug that calms the central nervous system. Stronger tranquilizers may be used to treat severe anxiety or symptoms of psychotic disorders such as hallucinations, delusions, and confusion.

transdermal   Through skin.

transdermal patch   A type of dressing that releases a drug into the body when in contact with the skin.

trauma   A physical injury or severe emotional shock.

treatment matching   Matching appropriate services to client's needs and worldviews.

treatment plan   A set of determined treatment objectives and the strategies to best attain them.

trial abstinence   An agreed-on period of abstinence as an experiment to try it out.

tricyclic antidepressants   Drugs that treat depression by blocking the reuptake of norepinephrine and serotonin.

trigger   A formerly neutral stimulus that attains the ability to elicit drug cravings due to repeated associations with drug use.

twelve-step program   An approach to counseling, originating in Alcoholics Anonymous, that emphasizes the disease concept, abstinence, and the Twelve Steps.

U

upper   See *stimulant.*

urge surfing   An analogy for coping with an addictive impulse by pinpointing the urge early in its development and then readying one's skills to ride the wave.

urine test   See *drug test.*

V

Valium   Trademark for a depressant drug of the benzodiazepine family that relieves anxiety.

visualization   the consciously chosen, intentional instruction to the unsconscious mind about the will to wellness, to change. See *creative visualization* and *relaxation training.*

volatile drug   See *inhalants.*

voluntary nervous system   See *somatic nervous system.*

W

War on Drugs   The U.S. government's aggressive and expensive effort to crack down on illegal drug use that President Richard Nixon launched in the 1970s.

warning sign   An early indication of an impending event or disease.

withdrawal   A substance-specific physical and cognitive reaction that follows cessation of the regular use of an addictive psychoactive drug.

Women for Sobriety   A nonprofit organization dedicated to helping women overcome alcoholism and other addictions.

workaholic   One who has a compulsive and unrelenting need to work.

World Health Organization (WHO)   The United Nations specialized agency for health, established in 1948, whose stated mission is the attainment by all people of the highest possible level of health.

X

Xanax   A depressant drug of the benzodiazepine family that relieves anxiety.

zero-tolerance laws   Stringent laws that dictate a certain minimum prison sentence for a crime, regardless of a judge's discretion or mitigating circumstances.

REFERENCES

Addiction Technology Transfer Centers National Curriculum Committee. (1998). *Addiction counseling competencies: The knowledge, skills, and attitudes of professional practice* (Treatment Assistance Publication #21; DHHS Publication No. SMA 98-3171). Rockville, MD: Center for Substance Abuse Treatment.

Adler, A. (1929). *The science of living.* New York: Greenberg.

Adler, A. (1958). *What life should mean to you.* New York: Putnam Capricorn.

Alcoholics Anonymous World Services, Inc. (2001). *The Big Book* (4th ed.). New York.

American Psychiatric Association. (2000). *Diagnostic and statistical manual of mental disorders* (4th ed., text rev.). Washington, DC: Author.

American Society of Addiction Medicine. (1991). *Patient placement criteria for the treatment of substance use disorders.* Retrieved April 11, 2004, from http://www.asam.org.

Annis, H. M. (1982). Inventory of drinking situations [Toronto, Ontario: Addiction Research Foundation of Ontario. Assessment]. *British Journal of Addictions, 84,* 1353–1357.

Annis, H. M., & Davis, C. S. (1989). Relapse prevention. In R. K. Hester & W. R. Miller (Eds.), *Handbook of alcoholism treatment approaches: Alternative approaches* (pp. 170–182). New York: Pergamon Press.

Babor, T. F., de la Fuente, J. R., & Saunders, J. (1982). *AUDIT. The alcohol use disorders identification test: Guidelines for use in primary healthcare.* Geneva, Switzerland: World Health Organization.

Bandura, A. (1977). *Social learning theory.* Englewood Cliffs, NJ: Prentice-Hall.

Bandura, A. (1986). *Social foundations of thought and action.* Englewood Cliffs, NJ: Prentice-Hall.

Bardo, M. T. (1998). *Neuropharmacological mechanisms of drug reward: Beyond dopamine in the nucleus accumbens* [Department of Psychology, University of Kentucky, Lexington]. Retrieved April 11, 2004, from http://www.biopsychiatry.com/reward.htm.

Battersby, M. W., Thomas, L., Tolchard, B., & Esterman, A. (2002). The South Oaks Gambling Screen: A review with reference to Australian use. *Journal of Gambling Studies, 18*(3), 257–271.

Beasley, J. D. (2001). Nutritional counseling: How to get the big high. In R. H. Coombs (Ed.), *Addiction recovery tools: A practical handbook* (pp. 291–307). Thousand Oaks, CA: Sage.

Beck, A. (1970). Cognitive therapy: Nature and relation to behavior therapy. *Behavior Therapy, 1,* 184–200.

Beck, A. (1976). *Cognitive therapy and the emotional disorders.* New York: International Universities Press.

Beck, A. T., & Steer, R. A. (1989). *Manual for the Beck's Hopelessness Scale.* San Antonio, TX: Psychological Corporation.

381

Beck, A. T., & Steer, R. A. (1997). Use of the Beck Anxiety and Depression Inventories. *Assessment, 3*(4), 211–219.

Beck, W. H. (1991). *Codependence assessment manual.* Chicago: Administrative Services.

Benson, H., & Stark, M. (1997). *Timeless healing: The power and biology of belief.* New York: Simon & Schuster.

Berkowitz, L. (1993). *Aggression: Its causes, consequences and control.* New York: McGraw-Hill.

Berne, E. (1961). *Transactional analysis in psychotherapy.* New York: Grove Press.

Berne, E. (1972). *What do you say after you say hello?* New York: Grove Press.

Bhat, V. (2001). *Medical malpractice: A comprehensive analysis.* Westport, CT: Auburn House.

Bishop, M. F. (2001). *Managing addictions: Cognitive, emotive, and behavioral techniques.* Northvale, NJ: Aronson.

Blum, K., Cull, J. G., Braverman, E. R., & Comings, D. E. (2000). *Reward deficiency syndrome.* Retrieved January 21, 2004, from http://www.healthyplace.com/Communities/ADD /ask/article/Amer_Sci.html.

Blum, K., & Payne, J. E. (1991). *Alcohol and the addicted brain.* New York: Free Press.

Blume, A. W. (2005). Treating drug problems. In R. H. Coombs & W. A. Howatt (Series eds.), *Book series on treating addictions.* Hoboken, NJ: Wiley.

Blume, A. W., Anderson, B. K., Fader, J. S., & Marlatt, G. A. (2001). Harm reduction programs: Progress rather than perfection. In R. H. Coombs (Ed.), *Addiction recovery tools: A practical resource* (pp. 367–382). Thousand Oaks, CA: Sage.

Boren, J., Onken, L. S., & Carroll, K. M. (2000). *Approaches to drug abuse counseling.* Washington, DC: NIDA, Division of Treatment and Research Development, Behavioral Treatment Development Branch.

Brewington, V., Smith, M., & Lipton, D. (1994). Acupuncture as a detoxification treatment: An analysis of controlled research. *Journal of Substance Abuse Treatment, 11,* 289–307.

Briere, J. (1995). *Trauma symptom inventory: Professional manual.* Odessa, FL: Psychological Assessment Resources.

Brown, R. A. (1980). Conventional education and controlled-drinking education courses with convicted drunk drivers. *Behavior Therapy, 11,* 632–643.

Brown, H. P., & Peterson, J. H. (1991). Assessing spirituality in addiction treatment and follow-up: Development of the Brown-Peterson Recovery Progressive Inventory (B-PRPI). *Alcoholism Treatment Quarterly, 8*(2), 21–50.

Brown, S., Lewis, V., & Liotta, A. (2000). *The family recovery guide: A map for healthy growth.* Oakland, CA: New Harbinger.

Bucholz, K. K., Cadoret, R., Cloninger, C. R., Dinwiddie, S. H., Hesselbrock, V. M., Nurnberger, J. I., Jr., et al. (1994). A new, semi-structured psychiatric interview for use in genetic linkage studies: A report on the reliability of the SSAGA. *Journal of Studies on Alcohol, 55*(2), 149–158.

Budney, A. J., Sigmon, S. C., & Higgins, S. T. (2001). Contingency management using science to motivate change. In R. H. Coombs (Ed.), *Addiction recovery tools: A practical handbook* (pp. 147–172). Thousand Oaks, CA: Sage.

Buelow, G, Hebert, S., & Buelow, S. (1999). *Psychotherapist's resource on psychiatric medications: Issues of treatment and referral.* Belmont, CA: Wadsworth.

Bungy, J. B., Pols, R. G., Mortimer, K. P., Frank, O. R., & Skinner, H. A. (1989). Screening alcohol and drug use in a general practice unit: Comparison of computerized and traditional methods. *Communications Health Studies, 4,* 471–483.

Burns, D. D. (1999). *Feeling good: The new mood therapy.* New York: Avon.

California Association of Alcohol and Drug Counselors. (2001). Retrieved from http://www.caade.org.

Carnes, P. J. (1991) *Don't call it love: Recovering from sexual addiction.* Phoenix, AZ: Gentle Path Press.

Carnes, P. J., Murray, R. E., & Charpentier, L. (2004). Addiction interaction disorder. In R. H. Coombs (Ed.), *Handbook on addictive disorders* (pp. 31–59). Hoboken, NJ: Wiley.

Chamberlain, L. (2004). Understanding and diagnosing compulsive gambling. In R. H. Coombs (Ed.), *Handbook on addictive disorders.* Hoboken, NJ: Wiley.

Chiauzzi, J. (1991). *Preventing relapse in the addictions: A biopscyhosocial approach.* Boston: Allyn & Bacon.

Conklin, C. A., & Tiffany, S. T. (2001). Cue exposure treatment: New thoughts about an old therapy. In R. H. Coombs (Ed.), *Addiction recovery tools: A practical handbook* (pp. 173–190). Thousand Oaks, CA: Sage.

Coombs, R. H. (1997). *Drug-impaired professionals: How physicians, dentists, pharmacists, nurses, attorneys, and airline pilots get into and out of addiction.* Boston: Harvard University Press.

Coombs, R. H. (Ed.). (2001). *Addiction recovery tools: A practical handbook.* Thousand Oaks, CA: Sage.

Coombs, R. H. (Ed.). (2004). *Handbook on addictive disorders: A practical guide to diagnosis and treatment.* Hoboken, NJ: Wiley.

Coombs, R. H. (Ed.). (2005). *Addiction counseling review: Preparing for comprehensive, certification and licensing exams.* Mahwah, NJ: Erlbaum.

Coombs, R. H., Fry, L. J., & Lewis, P. G. (Eds.). (1976). *Socialization in drug abuse.* Cambridge, MA: Schenkman.

Coombs, R. H., & West, L. J. (Eds.). (1991). *Drug testing: Issues and options.* New York: Oxford University Press.

Corey, G. (2000). *Theory and practice of counseling and psychotherapy* (6th ed.). Pacific Grove, CA: Brooks/Cole.

Corey, M. S., & Corey, G. (1998). *Becoming a helper* (3rd ed.). Pacific Grove, CA: Brooks/Cole.

Cormier, B., & Cormier, S. (1998). *Interviewing strategies for helpers fundamental skills and cognitive behavioral interventions.* Pacific Grove, CA: Brooks/Cole.

Correctional Service of Canada, "Relapse Techniques". (n.d.). Retrieved January 25, 2004, from http://www.csc-scc.gc.ca/text/pblct/litrev/treatmod/lit21e_e.shtml.

Corsini, R. J., & Wedding, D. (Eds.). (2001). *Current psychotherapist* (6th ed.). Belmont, CA: Brooks/Cole.

Curry, S. J., & McBride, C. M. (1994). Relapse prevention for smoking cessation: Review and evaluation of concepts and interventions. *Annual Review of Public Health, 15,* 345–366.

Davis, L. J., Hoffmann, N. G., Morse, R. M., & Luehr, J. G. (1992). Substance use disorder diagnostic Schedule (SUDDS): The equivalence and validation of a computer-administered and an interviewer-administered format. *Alcoholism: Clinical and Experimental Research, 16*(2), 250–254.

Deitch, D., Carleton, S., Lowinson, J. H., Ruiz, P., Millman, R. B., & Langrod, J. G. (Eds.). (1997). Education and training of clinical personnel substance abuse: A comprehensive textbook. Baltimore: Williams and Wilkins.

De Leon, G., Melnick, G., Kressel, D., & Jainchill, N. (1994). Circumstances, motivation, readiness, and suitability (the CMRS Scales): Predicting retention in therapeutic community treatment. *American Journal on Drug Alcohol Abuse, 20*(4), 495–515.

Denning, P. (2000). *Practicing harm reduction psychotherapy: An alternative approach to addictions*. New York: Guilford Press.

Denning, P. (2005). Harm reduction programs. In R. H. Coombs (Ed.), *Addiction counseling review: Preparing for comprehensive, certification and licensing exams*. Mahwah, NJ: Erlbaum.

Dennis, M. L., & Rourke, K. M. (1993). *Global appraisal of individual needs*. Research Triangle Park, NC: Research Triangle Institute.

DiClemente, C. C. (1991). Motivational interviewing and the stages of change. In W. R. Miller & S. Rollnick (Eds.), *Motivational interviewing: Preparing people to change addictive behavior* (pp. 191–202). New York: Guilford Press.

DiClemente, C. C., & Carbonari, J. P. (1994). The alcohol abstinence self-efficacy scale. *Journal of Studies of Alcohol, 55*, 141–148.

Domino, G. (2000). *Psychological testing: An introduction*. Upper Saddle River, NJ: Prentice-Hall.

Donovan, D. M., & O'Leary, M. R. (1978). The drinking-related locus of control scale: Reliability, factor structure, and validity. *Journal of Studies on Alcohol, 39*, 759–784.

Dossey, L. (1997). *Prayer is good medicine*. San Francisco: HarperCollins.

Doweiko, H. E. (2002). *Concepts of chemical dependency* (5th ed.). Pacific Grove, CA: Brooks/Cole.

Egan, E. (1994). *The skilled helper: A problem management approach to helping*. Pacific Grove, CA: Brooks/Cole.

Ellis, A. (1962). *Reason and emotions in psychotherapy*. Secaucus, NJ: Citadel.

Ellis, A. (1980). *Growth through thought*. Palo Alto, CA: Science and Behavior Books.

Ellis, A. (1994). *Reason and emotions in psychotherapy* (Rev). Secaucus, NJ: Carol Publishing.

Ellis, A. (1999). *How to make yourself happy and remarkably less disturbable*. Atascadero, CA: Impact.

Erickson, P., Riley, D., Cheung, Y., & O'Hare, P. (Eds.). (1997). *Harm reduction: A new direction for drug policies and programs*. Toronto, Ontario, Canada: University of Toronto Press.

Ewing, J. A. (1984). Detecting alcoholism: The CAGE questionnaire. *Journal of the American Medical Association, 252*, 1905–1907.

Field, L., & Seligman, L. (2005). Psychopathology. In R. H. Coombs (Ed.), *Addiction counseling review: Preparing for comprehensive, certification and licensing exams*. Mahwah, NJ: Erlbaum.

Filstead, W. J., & Mayer, J. E. (1984). Validity of the adolescent alcohol involvement scale: A reply to Riley and Klockars. *Journal of Studies on Alcohol, 45*(2), 188–189.

Finley, J. R., & Lenz, B. S. (1998). *The chemical dependence treatment documentation sourcebook: A comprehensive collection of program management tools, clinical documentation, and psychoeducational materials for substance abuse treatment professionals*. New York: Wiley.

Finley, J. R., & Lenz, B. S. (2003). *Addiction treatment homework planner* (2nd ed.). Hoboken, NJ: Wiley.

Fischer, J., & Corcoran, K. (1994). *Measures for clinical practice: A sourcebook*. (2nd ed.). New York: Free Press.

Flynn, P. M., Hubbard, R. L., & Luckey, J. W. (1995). Individual assessment profile (IAP): Standardizing the assessment of substance abusers. *Journal Substance Abuse Treatment, 12*(3), 213–221.

Foa, E. B., Kozak, M. J., Salkovskis, P. M., Coles, M. E., & Amir, N. (1998). The validation of a new obsessive-compulsive disorder scale. *Psychological Assessment, 10*(3), 206–214.

4 therapy.com. (2004). Retrieved January 4, 2004, from www.4therapy.com.

Frankl, V. (1963). *Man's search for meaning*. New York: Pocket Books.

Freud, S. (1958). Formulation on the two principal of mental functioning. In J. Strachey (Ed. & Trans.), *The standard edition of the complete psychological works of Sigmund Freud* (Vol. 11, pp. 213–227). London: Hogarth Press.

Freud, S. (1961). The infantile genital organization: An interpolation into the theory of sexuality. In J. Strachey (Ed. & Trans.), *The standard edition of the complete psychological works of Sigmund Freud* (Vol. 19, pp. 141–149). London: Hogarth Press.

Friedman, A. S., & Utada, A. (1989). A method for diagnosing and planning the treatment of adolescent drug abusers. *Journal of Drug Education, 19*, 285–312.

Friedman, D. P., & Rusche, S. (1999). *False messengers: How addictive drugs change the brain.* New York: Harwood Academic.

Friedman, H. S., & Schustack, M. W. (2003). *Personality: Classic theories and modern research.* Boston: Allyn & Bacon.

Garner, D. M., Olmsted, M. P., Bohr, Y., & Garfinkel, P. E. (1982). The eating attitudes test: Psychometric features and clinical correlates. *Psychological Medicine, 12*, 871–878.

Glasser, W. (1998). *Choice theory. A new psychology of personal freedom.* New York: Harper-Collins.

Goleman, D. (1995). *Emotional intelligence: Why it can matter more than IQ.* New York: Bantam Books.

Goleman, D. (1998). *Working with emotional intelligence.* New York: Bantam Books.

Goleman, D. (2003). *Destructive emotions: How we can overcome them.* New York: Bantam Books.

Gordis, E. (1993). Alcohol and nutrition. *Alcohol Alert* #22, PH346 from National Institute of Alcohol Abuse and Alcoholism. Retrieved October, 1993 from http://alcoholism .about.com/library/blnaa22.htm.

Gordon, R. (1987). An operational classification of disease prevention. In J. A. Steinberg & M. M. Silverman (Eds.), *Preventing mental disorders* (pp. 20–26). Rockville, MD: U.S. Department of Health and Human Services.

Gorski, T. T. (1989). *Passages through recovery: An action plan for preventing relapse.* Center City, MN: Hazelden.

Gorski, T. T., & Kelley, J. M. (2002). *Counselor's manual for relapse prevention with chemically dependent criminal offender* [Technical Assistance Publication, No. 19. Retrieved January 22, 2004, from http://www.treatment.org/TAPS/TAPS10TOC.html.

Gossop, M., Griffith, P., Powis, B., & Strang, J. (1993). Severity of dependence and HIV risk, II. *AIDS Care, 52*, 159–168.

Guenther, R. M. (1983). The role of nutritional therapy in alcoholism treatment. *International Journal of Biosocial Research, 4*(1), 5–18.

Hare, R. D. (1998). The PCL-R assessment of psychopaths: Some issues and concerns. *Legal and Criminal Psychology, 3*, 101–122.

Harrell, A. V., & Wirtz, P. W. (1989). Screening for adolescent problem drinking: Validation of a multidimensional instrument for case identification. *Psychological Assessment, 1*, 61–63.

Harrell, T. H., & Honaker, L. M. (1991). Cognitive and behavioral dimensions of dysfunction in alcohol and polydrug users. *Journal of Substance Abuse, 5*, 415–426.

Hay, C., & Kinnier, R. (1998). *Homework in counseling.* Retrieved December 2, 2002, from EBSCO Research Data base http://search.epnet.com/direct.asp?an=564230&db=aph.

Heather, N. (1995). *Treatment approaches for alcohol and drug dependence: An introductory guide.* New York: Wiley.

Heather, N., Gold, R., & Rollnick, S. (1991). *Readiness to Change Questionnaire: User's manual* [Technical Report No. 15]. Kensington, Australia: University of New South Wales, National Drug and Alcohol Research Centre.

Heather, N., Rollnick, S., & Bell, A. (1993). Predictive validity of the Readiness to Change Questionnaire. *Addiction, 88*(12) 1667–1677.

Henderson, J. (2005). Professional examinations in alcohol and other drug abuse counseling. In R. H. Coombs (Ed.), *Addiction counseling review: Preparing for comprehensive, certification and licensing exams.* Mahwah, NJ: Erlbaum.

Hodgson, R., Alwyn, T., John, B., Thom, B., & Smith, A. (2002). The FAST alcohol screening. *Alcohol and alcoholism, 37*(1), 61–66.

Hogan, J. A., Gabrielsen, K. R., Luna, N., & Grothaus, D. (2003). *Substance abuse prevention: The intersection of science and practice.* Boston: Allyn & Bacon.

Holden, C. (2001). Behavioral addictions: Do they exist? *Science, 29,* 980–982.

Hollander, E., Buchalter, A. J., & DeCaria, C. M. (2000). Pathological gambling. *Psychiatry Clinics North America, 23,* 629–642.

Hollis, J. W. (1999). *Counselor preparation 1999–2001* (10th ed.). Philadelphia: Brunner-Routledge.

Howatt, W. A. (1995). *Counselling for paraprofessionals: Formulating your eclectic approach.* Kentville, Nova Scotia, Canada: Nova Scotia Community College Press.

Howatt, W. A. (1998). *Journal 51: Defining and achieving new goals.* Kentville, Nova Scotia, Canada: A Way with Words.

Howatt, W. A. (1999). *My personal success coach.* Kentville, Nova Scotia, Canada: A Way with Words.

Howatt, W. A. (2000). *The human services counseling toolbox.* Pacific Grove, CA: Brooks/Cole.

Howatt, W. A. (2001). *Journal 45: A 45-day program to create a new beginning.* Kentville, Nova Scotia, Canada: A Way with Words.

Howatt, W. A. (2002). *Discipline of communication.* Kentville, Nova Scotia, Canada: A Way with Words.

Howatt, W. A. (2003a). *Crisis: Strategies for keeping the workplace safe.* Kentville, Nova Scotia, Canada: A Way with Words.

Howatt, W. A. (2003b). *New beginning: Strategies for dealing with stress.* Kentville, Nova Scotia, Canada: A Way with Words.

Howatt, W. A. (2005). Counseling theories and models (Part 1). In R. H. Coombs (Ed.), *Addiction counseling review: Preparing for comprehensive, certification and licensing exams.* Mahwah, NJ: Erlbaum.

Hunt, W. A., Barnett, L. W., & Branch, L. G. (1971). Relapse rates in addiction programs. *Journal of Clinical Psychology, 27,* 455–456.

Inciardi, J. A., Horowitz, R., & Pottieger, A. E. (1993). *Street kids, street drugs, street crime: An examination of drug use and serious delinquency in Miami.* Belmont, CA: Wadsworth.

Institute of Medicine. (1989). *Prevention and treatment of alcohol problems: Research opportunities.* Washington, DC: National Academy Press.

James, R. K., & Gilliland, B. E. (2001). *Crisis intervention strategies* (4th ed.). Pacific Grove, CA: Brooks/Cole.

Jellinek, E. M. (1960). *The disease concept of alcoholism.* New Haven, CT: College and University Press.

Jung, C. G. (1954a). Civilization in transition. Collected works (Vol. 16). In G. Adler, M. Fordham, & H. Reid (Eds.), *Bollingen series* (Vol. 10). New York: Pantheon Books.

Jung, C. G. (1954b). The practice of psychotherapy. Collected works (Vol. 16). In G. Adler, M. Fordham, & H. Reid (Eds.), *Bollingen series* (Vol. 16). New York: Pantheon Books.

Kaminer, Y., & Bukstein, D. F. (1991). The Teen Addiction Severity Index: Rationale and reliability. *International Journal of Addictions, 26,* 219–226.

Kandel, D. B. (Ed.). (2002). *Stages and pathways of drug involvement: Examining the gateway hypothesis.* Boston: Cambridge University Press.

Kassinove, J. I. (2000). Gambling Attitudes Scales (GAS). In K. Corcoran & J. Fischer (Eds.), *Measures for clinical practice: A sourcebook* (3rd ed., Vol. 2, pp. 306–307). New York: Free Press.

Kazdin, A. E. (1987). Children's depression scale: Validation with psychiatric inpatients. *Journal of Child Psychology, 28*(1), 29–41.

Kendler, K. S., Karkowski, L. M., Neale, M. C., & Prescott, C. A. (2000). Illicit psychoactive substance use, heavy use, abuse, and dependence in a US population-based sample of male twins. *Archives of General Psychiatry, 57*(3), 261–269.

Kern, M., & Lenon, L. (1994). *Take control now!* Available from Life Management Skills, Inc, 9139 W. 24th Street, Los Angeles, CA 90034.

Khantzian, E. J. (1999). *Treating addiction as a human process.* Northvale, NJ: Aronson.

Kurtz, L. F. (2001). Peer support: Key to maintaining recovery. In R. H. Coombs (Ed.), *Addiction recovery tools: A practical handbook* (pp. 257–272). Thousand Oaks, CA: Sage.

Ladouceur, R., Gaboury, A., Dumont, M., & Rochette, P. (1988). Gambling: Relationship between the frequency of wins and irrational thinking. *Journal of Psychology, 122,* 409–414.

Lawson, G. W., Lawson, A. W., & Rivers, P. C. (2000) *Essentials of chemical dependency counseling* (3rd ed.). Rockville, MD: Aspen Press.

Lemanski, M. (2001). *A history of addition and recovery in the United States.* Tucson, AZ: See Sharp Press.

Leshner, A. I. (2001, Spring). Addiction is a brain disease. *Issues in Science and Technology Online.* Retrieved January 21, 2004, from www.nap.cdu/issues/17.3/leshner.htm.

Lesieur, H. R., & Blume, S. B. (1993). Pathological gambling, eating disorders, and the psychoactive substance abuse disorders. *Journal of Addictive Diseases, 12*(3), 89–102.

Leukefeld, C. G., Pickens, R. W., & Schuster, C. R. (1991). Improving drug abuse treatment: Recommendations for research and practice. In R. W. Pickens, C. G. Leukefeld and C. R. Schuster (Eds.), *Improving drug abuse treatment.* National Institute on Drug Abuse Research Monograph Series, DHHS Pub. No (ADM) 91-1754. Washington, DC: US Government Printing Office.

Lewis, B. F., McCusker, J., Hindin, R., Frost, R., & Garfield, F. (1993). Four residential drug treatment programs: Project IMPACT. In J. A. Inciardi, F. M. Tims, & B. W. Fletcher (Eds.), *Innovative approaches in the treatment of drug abuse* (pp. 45–60). Westport, CT: Greenwood Press.

Lewis, J. A. (2005). Assessment, diagnosis and treatment planning. In R. H. Coombs (Ed.), *Addiction counseling review: Preparing for comprehensive, certification and licensing exam.* Mahwah, NJ: Erlbaum.

Lewis, J. A., Dana, R. Q., & Blevins, G. A. (2001). *Substance abuse counseling* (3rd ed.). Pacific Grove, CA: Brooks/Cole.

Marlatt, G. A. (1978). Craving for alcohol, loss of control, and relapse: A cognitive-behavioral analysis. In P. E. Nathan, G. A. Marlatt, & T. Loberg (Eds.), *Alcoholism: New directions in behavioral research and treatment* (pp. 271–314). New York: Plenum Press.

Marlatt, G. A. (1983). The controlled drinking controversy: A commentary. *American Psychologist, 38,* 1097–1110.

Marlatt, G. A., Abrams, D. B., & Lewis, D. C. (2002). *Harm reduction: Pragmatic strategies for managing high-risk behaviors.* New York: Guilford Press.

Marlatt, G. A., & George, W. H. (1984). Relapse prevention: Introduction and overview of the model. *British Journal of Addiction, 79,* 261–273.

Marlatt, G. A., & Gordon, J. R. (1980). Determinants of relapse: Implications of the maintenance of behavior change. In P. O. Davidson & S. M. Davidson (Eds.), *Behavioral medicine: Changing health lifestyles* (pp. 410–452). New York: Brunner/Mazel.

Marlatt, G. A., & Gordon, J. R. (Eds.). (1985). *Relapse prevention.* New York: Guilford Press.

Marlatt, G. A., & Witkiewitz, K. (2002). Harm reduction approaches to alcohol use: Health promotion, prevention, and treatment. *Addict Behavior, 27*(6), 867–886.

Mattick, R. P., Ward, J., & Hall, W. (1998). *Methadone maintenance treatment and other opioid replacement therapies.* New York: Harwood Academic.

Mayer, W. E. (1982). Address to the Third Annual Department of Defense Alcohol and Drug Abuse Conference as cited in Alcoholics Anonymous World Services, *About AA: A Newsletter for Professionals.*

Mayer, J. D., & Salovey, P. (1997). What is emotional intelligence? In P. Salovey & D. Sluyter (Eds.), *Emotional development and emotional intelligence: Implications for educators* (pp. 3–31). New York: Basic Books.

McCown, W. G. (2005). Nonpharmacological addictions. In R. H. Coombs (Ed.), *Family therapy review: Preparing for comprehensive and licensing exams* (pp. 459–481). Mahwah, NJ: Erlbaum.

McCown, W. G., & Chamberlain, L. (2000). *Best possible odds: Contemporary treatment strategies for gambling disorders.* New York: Wiley.

McCrady, B., & Epstein, E. (1999). *Addictions—A comprehensive guidebook.* New York: Oxford University Press.

McLellan, A. T., & Luborsky, L. (1985). New data from the Addiction Severity Index: Reliability and validity in three centers. *Journal of Nervous Mental Disorders, 173,* 412–423.

Meichenbaum, D. (1977). *Cognitive behavior modification: An integrative approach.* New York: Plenum Press.

Metzger D. S., Kushner H., & McLellan, A. T. (1991): *Adolescent problem severity index: Administration manual.* Philadelphia: Biomedical Computer Research Institute.

Michigan Alcohol Screening Test. (n.d.). Retrieved November 30, 2002, from http://www.silcom.com/~sbadp/treatment/mast.htm.

Mieczkowski, T. (2001). Drug testing: A review of drug tests in clinical settings. In R. H. Coombs (Ed.), *Addiction recovery tools: A practical handbook* (pp. 111–126). Thousand Oaks, CA: Sage.

Miller, N. S. (1991). Drug and alcohol addiction as a disease. In N. S. Miller (Ed.), *Comprehensive handbook of drug and alcohol addiction* (pp. 295–309). New York: Marcel Dekker.

Miller, N. S. (2001). Disease orientation: Taking away the shame and blame. In R. H. Coombs (Ed.), *Addiction recovery tools: A practical handbook* (pp. 99–110). Thousand Oaks, CA: Sage.

Miller, N. S., & Gold, M. S. (1990). Multiple addictions: Co-synchronous use of alcohol and drugs. *New York State Journal of Medicine, 90,* 596–600.

Miller, N. S., & Gold, M. S. (1993). A neurochemical basis for alcohol and other drug addiction. *Journal of Psychoactive Drugs, 25,* 121–128.

Miller, W. R., & Marlatt, G. A. (1984). *Manual for the comprehensive drinker profile.* Odessa, FL: Psychological Assessment Resources.

Miller, W. R., & Tonigan, J. S. (1996). Assessing drinkers' motivation for change: The Stages of Change Readiness and Treatment Eagerness Scale (SOCRATES). *Psychology of Addictive Behaviors, 10,* 81–89.

Miller, W. R., Westerberg, V. S., Harris, R. J., & Tonigan, J. S. (1996). What predicts relapse? Prospective testing of antecedent models. *Addiction, 91*(Supplement), S155–S171.

Mills, J. F., Kroner, D. G., & Forth, A. E. (1998). Novaco Anger Scale: Reliability and validity within an adult criminal sample. *Assessment, 5*, 237–248.

Mitchell, J. T. (2005). Managing crises. In R. H. Coombs (Ed.), *Addiction counseling review: Preparing for comprehensive, certification and licensing exams.* Mahwah, NJ: Erlbaum.

Moberg, D. P., & Hahn, L. (1991). The Adolescent Drug Involvement Scale. *Journal of Adolescent Chemical Dependency, 2*(1), 75–88.

Modell, J. G., Glaser, F. B., Mountz, J. M., Cyr, L., & Schmaltz, S. (1992). Obsessive and compulsive characteristics of alcohol abuse and dependence: Quantification by a newly developed questionnaire. *Alcoholism Clinical and Experimental Research, 16*, 266–271.

Monti, P. M. (1989). *Treating alcohol dependence: A coping skills training guide.* New York: Guilford Press.

Morrissey, M. (1998). "Safety issues for counselors who work with violent clients." *Counseling Today Online article.* Retrieved February 19, 2004, from http://www.psychpage.com/learning/library/counseling/counseling_online_danger.html.

NAADAC. (1994). *Treatment and prevention.* Retrieved January 4, 2004, from http://www.naadac.org/documents/display.php?DocumentID=36.

Narcotics Anonymous. (n.d.). Retrieved April 11, 2004, from www.na.org.

National Institute on Alcohol Abuse and Alcoholism. (1993). *Eighth special report to the U.S. Congress on alcohol and health* (NIH Publication No. 94-3699). Washington, DC: National Institutes of Health.

National Institute on Alcohol Abuse and Alcoholism. (n.d.). *Alcohol abstinence self-efficacy scales (AASE).* Retrieved November 22, 2002, from http://www.niaaa.nih.gov/publications/aase.htm.

National Institute on Drug Abuse. (1999a). *Cocaine abuse and addiction* (Publication No. 99-4342). Retrieved February 15, 2004, from http://165.112.78.61/ResearchReports/Cocaine/Cocaine.html.

National Institute on Drug Abuse. (1999b). *Principles of drug addiction treatment.* Retrieved February 15, 2004, from http://www.nida.nih.gov/PODAT/PODATindex.html.

National Institute on Drug Abuse. (2000). *Research report series—prescription drugs: Abuse and addiction.* Retrieved February 15, 2004, from http://www.drugabuse.gov/ResearchReports/Prescription/prescription9.html.

National Institute on Drug Abuse. (n.d.). *Information on common drugs of abuse.* Retrieved February 15, 2004, from http://www.drugabuse.gov/DrugPages.

National Institute on Drugs, Prevention Research. (n.d.). Retrieved January 25, 2004, from http://www.drugabuse.gov/DrugPages/Prevention.html.

Office of Applied Studies. (2003). *Results from the 2002 national survey on drug use and health: National findings* (DHHS Publication No. SMA 03-3836, NHSDA Series H-22). Rockville, MD: Substance Abuse and Mental Health Services Administration.

Parvin, R., & Anderson, G. (1999). What are we worth? Fee decisions of psychologists in private practice. *Women and Therapy, 22*(3), 15–25.

Pavlov, I. P. (1960). *Conditioned reflexes: An investigation of the physiological activity of the cerebral cortex* (G. V. Anrep Trans.). New York: Dover. (Original work published 1927)

Pavot, W., Diener, E., Colvin, R., & Sandvik, E. (1991). Further validation of the Satisfaction with Life Scale: Evidence for the cross-method convergence of well-being measures. *Journal of Personality Assessment, 57*, 149–161.

Peele, S. (1989). *Diseasing of America: Addiction treatment out of control*. Lexington, MA: Lexington Books.

Peele, S. (1975). *Love and addiction*. New York: Taplinger Publishing Co.

Perkinson, R. R., & Jongsma, A. E. (2001). *The addiction treatment planner* (2nd ed.). New York: Wiley.

Perls, F. (1969). *Gestalt therapy verbatim*. New York: Bantam Books.

Perls, F. (1973). *The Gestault approach and eyewitness therapy*. New York: Bantam Books.

Phillips, B. (1999). *Body for life: 12 weeks to mental and physical strength*. New York: HarperCollins.

Popovits, R. M. (2005). Disclosure dilemmas: Legal compliance for counselors. In R. H. Coombs (Ed.), *Addiction counseling review: Preparing for comprehensive, certification and licensing exams*. Mahwah, NJ: Erlbaum.

Powell, D. J., & Brodsky, A. (2004). *Clinical supervision in alcohol and drug abuse counseling*. San Francisco: Jossey-Bass.

Pransky, J. (1991). *Prevention the critical need*. Springfield, MO: Burrell Foundation & Paradigm Press.

Prochaska, J. O. (2003). Enhancing motivation to change. In A. W. Graham & T. K. Schultz (Eds.), *Principles of addiction medicine* (3rd ed.). Chevy Chase, MD: American Society of Addiction Medicine.

Prochaska, J. O., DiClemente, C. C., & Norcross, J. (1992). In search of how people change: Application to addictive behaviors. *American Psychologist, 47*, 1102–1114.

Project MATCH Research Group. (1997). Matching alcoholism treatments to client heterogeneity: Project MATCH post-treatment drinking outcomes. *Journal of Studies on Alcohol, 59*, 7–29.

Record Keeping. (2004). Retrieved January 24, 2004, from http://www.4therapy.com /professional/research/lawandethics/item.php?uniqueid=4614&categoryid=273&.

Reider, N. (2000). Treatment of non-psychiatric alcohol-related disorders: Vitamin deficiencies, zinc deficiency, and anaphylactic reactions. In G. Zernig, A. Saria, M. Kurz, & S. S. O'Malley (Eds.), *Handbook of alcoholism* (pp. 239–241). Boca Raton, FL: CRC Press.

Reynolds, W. M. (1990). Development of a semi structured clinical interview for suicidal behaviors in adolescence. *Journal of Counseling Psychology, 2*, 382–390.

Roberts, A. (Ed.). (2000). *Crisis intervention handbook: Assessment, treatment, and research* (2nd ed.). New York: Oxford University Press.

Robinson, B. (1989). *A guidebook for workaholics, their partners and children, and the clinicians who treat them*. New York: New York University Press.

Rogers, C. (1951). *Client centered therapy*. Boston: Houghton Mifflin.

Rogers, C. (1959). The essence of psychotherapy: A client-centered view. *Annals of Psychotherapy, 1*, 51–57.

Rosengren, D. B., & Wagner, C. C. (2001). Motivational interviewing: Dancing, not wrestling. In R. H. Coombs (Ed.), *Addiction recovery tools: A practical handbook* (pp. 17–34). Thousand Oaks, CA: Sage.

Rotgers, F. (in press). *Treating alcohol problems*. Hoboken, NJ: Wiley.

Rotgers, F., Kern, M., & Hoeltzel, R. (2002). *Responsible drinking: A moderation management approach*. Berkeley, CA: New Harbinger.

Saunders, B., & O'Connor, J. (1996). *Relapse, addiction studies intervention module study manual*. Perth, Australia: Curtin University of Technology.

Schafer, W. (1992). *Stress management for wellness* (2nd ed.). Fort Worth, TX: Harcourt Brace Jovanovich College.

Schmid, J., & Brown, S. (2001). Family treatment: Stage-appropriate psychotherapy for the addicted family. In R. H. Coombs (Ed.), *Addiction recovery tools: A practical handbook* (pp. 273–290). Thousand Oaks, CA: Sage.

Scott, R. L., Kern, M. F., & Coombs, R. H. (2001). Affect-regulation coping-skills training: Managing mood without drugs. In R. H. Coombs (Ed.), *Addiction recovery tools: A practical handbook* (pp. 191–206). Thousand Oaks, CA: Sage.

Selzer, M. L. (1971). The Michigan alcoholism screening test: The quest for a new diagnostic instrument. *American Journal of Psychiatry, 127*(12), 89–94.

Shaffer, H. J., & Albanese, M. (2005). Addiction's defining features. In R. H. Coombs (Ed.), *Addiction counseling review: Preparing for comprehensive, certification and licensing exams*. Mahwah, NJ: Erlbaum.

Shaffer, M. (1982). *Life after stress*. New York: Plenum Press.

Sher, K. J., & Descutner, C. (1986). Reports of parental alcoholism: Reliability across siblings. *Addiction Behavior, 11*, 25–30.

Simoni-Wastila, L., & Strickler, G. (2004). Risk factors associated with problem use of prescription drugs. *American Journal of Public Health, 94*(2), 266–268.

Skinner, B. F. (1971). *Beyond freedom and dignity*. New York: Knopf.

Skinner, H. A. (1984). *Alcohol dependence scale: Users guide*. Toronto, Ontario, Canada: Addiction Research Foundation.

Skinner, H. A., Holt, S., Sheu, W. J., & Israel, Y. (1986). Clinical versus laboratory detection of alcohol abuse: The Alcohol Clinical Index. *British Medical Journal, 292*, 1703–1708.

Smith, D. E., & Seymour, R. B. (2001). Detoxification: Opening the window of opportunity to recovery. In R. H. Coombs (Ed.), *Addiction recovery tools: A practical handbook* (pp. 63–80). Thousand Oaks, CA: Sage.

Smith, M. B., Hoffmann, N. G., & Nederhoed, R. (1992). The development and reliability of the RAATE-CE. *Journal of Substance Abuse, 4*, 355–363.

Smith, M. O., & White, K. P. (2001). Acupuncture: A venerable nonverbal therapy. In R. H. Coombs (Ed.), *Addiction recovery tools: A practical handbook* (pp. 339–366). Thousand Oaks, CA: Sage.

Snarr, C. A., Norris, P. A., & Fahrion, S. L. (2001). Meditation: The path to recovery through inner wisdom. In R. H. Coombs (Ed.), *Addiction recovery tools: A practical handbook* (pp. 307–322). Thousand Oaks, CA: Sage.

Sobell, L. C., Maisto, S. A., Sobell, M. B., & Cooper, A. M. (1979). Reliability of alcohol abusers' self-reports of drinking behavior. *Behavior Research and Therapy, 17*, 157–160.

Sommers-Flanagan, J., & Sommers-Flanagan, R. (2004). *Counseling and psychotherapy theories in context and practice: Skills, strategies, and techniques*. Hoboken, NJ: Wiley.

Southwick, L., & Steele, C. (1987). Restrained drinking: Personality correlates of a control style. *Journal of Drug Issues, 17*(4), 349–358.

Sperry, L., Duffy, D., Tureen, T., & Gillig, S. (2005). Psychopathology. In R. H. Coombs (Ed.), *Family therapy review: Preparing for comprehensive and licensing exams*. Mahwah, NJ: Erlbaum.

Spoth, R., Redmond, C., & Shin, C. (1998). Direct and indirect latent-variable parenting outcomes of two universal family-focused preventive interventions: Extending a public health-oriented research base. *Journal of Consulting and Clinical Psychology, 66*(2), 385–399.

Steele, C. M., & Josephs, R. A. (1990). Alcohol myopia: Its prized and dangerous effects. *American Psychologist, 45*(8), 921–933.

Stewart, S. H., Angelopoulos, M., Baker, J. M., & Boland, F. J. (2000). Relations between dietary restraint and patterns of alcohol use in young adult women. *Psychology of Addictive Behaviors, 14*, 77–82.

Storti, E. A. (1995). *Heart to heart: The honorable approach to motivational intervention.* New York: Carlton.

Storti, E. A. (2001). Motivational intervention: The only failure is the failure to act. In R. H. Coombs (Ed.), *Addiction recovery tools: A practical handbook* (pp. 3–16). Thousand Oaks, CA: Sage.

Storti, E. A., & Keller, J. (1988). *Crisis intervention: Acting against addiction.* New York: Crown.

Stuppaeck, C. H., Barnas, C., Falk, M., Guenther, V., Hummer, M., Pycha, R., et al. (1994). Assessment of the alcohol withdrawal syndrome: Validity and reliability for the translated and modified Clinical Institute Withdrawal Assessment for Alcohol scale (CIWA-A). *Addiction, 89*(10), 1287–1292.

Sweeting, P. D., & Weinberg, J. L. (2000). Gambling: The secret invisible addiction. *Counselor: The Magazine for Addiction Professionals, 1*, 46–50.

Talbott, G. D., & Crosby, L. R. (2001). Recovery contracts: Seven key elements. In R. H. Coombs (Ed.), *Addiction recovery tools: A practical handbook* (pp. 127–146). Thousand Oaks, CA: Sage.

Tarter, R. E., & Laird, S. B. (1992). Validation of the drug use screening inventory. *Journal Psychology of Addictive Behaviors, 6*(4), 233–236.

Thompson, T. G. (n.d.). *22 million in U.S. suffer from substance dependence or abuse* [HIS Secretary, News Release]. Washington, DC: Substance Abuse and Mental Health Services Administration. Retrieved September 5, 2003, from www.hhs.gov/news.

Treating Tobacco Use and Dependence: A Clinical Practice Guideline. (n.d.). National Clearing House. Retrieved April 04, 2004, from http://www.guideline.gov/summary/summary.aspx?doc_id=2360.

Tsuang, M. T., Bar, J. L., Harley, R. M., & Lyons, M. J. (2001). The Harvard Twin Study of Substance Abuse: What we have learned. *Harvard Review Psychiatry, 9*(6), 267–279.

U.S. Department of Health and Human Services, Substance Abuse and Mental Health Services Administration, Office of Applied Studies. (2001). *Summary of findings from the 2000 National Household Survey on Drug Abuse.* Rockville, MD.

Vecchio, R. P. (1991). *Organizational behavior.* Montreal, Quebec, Canada: Dryden Press.

Wallen, J. (1993). *Addiction in human development perspectives on addiction and recovery.* Binghamton, NY: Haworth Press.

Walters, J. (n.d.). *22 million in U.S. suffer from substance dependence or abuse* [HIS Secretary, News Release]. Washington, DC: Substance Abuse and Mental Health Services Administration. Retrieved September 5, 2003, from www.hhs.gov/news.

Washton, A. M. (2001). Group therapy: A clinician's guide to doing what works. In R. H. Coombs (Ed.), *Addiction recovery tools: A practical handbook* (pp. 239–256). Thousand Oaks, CA: Sage.

White, W. (2005). Disclosure dilemmas: Legal compliance for counselors. In R. H. Coombs (Ed.), *Addiction counseling review: Preparing for comprehensive certification and licensing exams.* Mahwah, NJ: Erlbaum.

White, W. (2005). Professional ethics. In R. H. Coombs (Ed.), *Addiction counseling review: Preparing for comprehensive certification and licensing exams.* Mahwah, NJ: Erlbaum.

White, W., & Popovits, R. (2001). *Critical incidents: Ethical issues in the prevention and treatment of addiction.* Bloomington, IL: Lighthouse Institute.

Williams, C. L. (1992). *MMPI-A Content Scales: Assessing psychopathology in adolescents.* Minneapolis: University of Minnesota Press.

Wilson, G. T. (2001). Behavioral therapy. In R. J. Corsini & D. Wedding (Eds.), *Current psychotherapist* (6th ed.). Belmont, CA: Brooks/Cole.

Winters, K. C., Bengston, P., Dorr, D., & Stinchfield, R. (1998). Prevalence and risk factors of problem gambling among college students. *Psychology of Addictive Behaviors, 12,* 127–135.

Wolpe, J. (1982). *The practice of behavioral therapy* (3rd ed.). New York: Pergamon Press.

Wormer, K., & Davis, D. R. (2003). *Addiction treatment: A strengths perspective.* Pacific Grove, CA: Brooks/Cole.

Wubbolding, R. (1988). *Using reality therapy.* New York: Harper & Row.

Wubbolding, R. (1989). Professional issues: Four stages in decision making in suicidal client recovery. *Journal for Reality Therapy, 8*(2), 57–61.

Yalom, I. (1981). *Existential psychotherapy.* New York: Basic Books.

Young, R. M., & Knight, R. G. (1989). The Drinking Expectancy Questionnaire: A revised measure of alcohol related beliefs. *Journal of Psychopathology and Behavioral Assessment, 11,* 99–112.

Zackon, F. (2001). Lifestyle planning and monitoring: Readiness, guidance, and growth. In R. H. Coombs (Ed.), *Addiction recovery tools: A practical handbook* (pp. 207–221). Thousand Oaks, CA: Sage.

Zackon, F., McAuliffe, W., & Chien, J. (1993). *Recovery training and self-help.* Rockville, MD: National Institute on Drug Abuse.

Ziedonis, D. M., & D'Avanzo, K. (1998). Schizophrenia and substance abuse. In H. R. Kranzler & B. J. Rounsaville (Eds.), *Dual diagnosis and treatment* (pp. 427–465). New York: Marcel Dekker.

Ziedonis, D. M., & Krejci, J. (2001). Medications: One tool in the toolbox. In R. H. Coombs (Ed.), *Addiction recovery tools: A practical handbook* (pp. 81–98). Thousand Oaks, CA: Sage.

Zung, B. J. (1980). Factor structure of the Michigan Alcohol Screening Test in a psychotic outpatient population. *Journal of Clinical Psychology, 36,* 1024 1130.

AUTHOR INDEX

SUBJECT INDEX

401